James Thurber

92 Stories

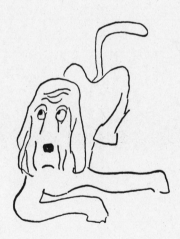

James Thurber

92 Stories

Originally published in separate volumes under the titles:
The Owl in the Attic and Other Perplexities
The Middle-Aged Man on the Flying Trapeze
Let Your Mind Alone! and Other More or Less Inspirational Pieces

with Drawings
by the Author

WINGS BOOKS
NEW YORK • AVENEL, NEW JERSEY

Originally published in separate volumes under the titles:
The Owl in the Attic and Other Perplexities
copyright 1931 by James Thurber
The Middle-Aged Man on the Flying Trapeze
copyright 1935 by James Thurber
Let Your Mind Alone! and Other More or Less Inspirational Pieces
copyright 1935, 1936, 1937 by James Thurber

This 1990 edition is published by Wings Books, distributed by Outlet Book Company, Inc., a Random House Company, 40 Engelhard Avenue, Avenel, New Jersey 07001, by arrangement with Harper & Row, Publishers, Inc.

Printed and bound in the United States of America

Book design by June Marie Bennett

Library of Congress Cataloging-in-Publication Data

Thurber, James, 1894–1961.
  92 stories
  I. Title. II. Title: Ninety-two stories.
PS3539.H94A6 1984   813'.52   84-21751
ISBN: 0-517-45999-X

13   12   11   10   9   8

Contents

The
Owl in
the Attic
and Other Perplexities

For Althea

Contents

Introduction

I SAW Thurber first in the summer of 1919. It was a steaming forenoon, when even the hot streets of Raritonga seemed deserted. The little packet-boat *Numidia* had slipped into the harbor during the night, to discharge copra, and when I saw a skiff being lowered I walked down toward the beach. The skiff had hardly grounded when Thurber stepped ashore, carrying a volume of Henry James and leading a honey bear by a small chain. As it happened, I was not to meet him again until years later, for my schooner left the island that afternoon to coast lazily eastward on the trade wind; but somehow his name kept bobbing up in the port gossip of those seas, and although the news was always fragmentary, the Thurber legend was, I later realized, steadily building in my mind.

There had been some talk in MacDonald's store about the *Numidia*—her doubtful tonnage and her unexplained visit to Penang the previous spring. Where Thurber had come aboard nobody seemed to know. I had drifted all the way to Manila before I again heard his name mentioned, this time in connection with a native ceremony on one of the islands when a young girl named Maia-Lo ("For-you-I-have-no-desire") had woven a special reed mat for the tall dark

5

stranger to occupy alongside her own lovely self. Thurber, only faintly grasping the significance of the gesture, had hung about, trying to talk to the girl's uncle instead of lying down directly on the mat. The delay, so the story went, would have cost him his life if it hadn't been that they found a mechanical match-box trick in his pocket, and the uncle became so intrigued with its mysteries that he forgot the insult.

So the Thurber story ran—always fragmentary, vague. Once he had spent a night in a hotel room in Singapore with another man, trying to untangle a snarled fishing-line. After three hours of pulling the free end of the line through the loop of the snarl, he had abruptly got up and left the hotel. His companion never saw him again. Once, in a sailing-ship in which the cook had been put in irons for knifing a passenger, Thurber had volunteered to prepare breakfast. In the dim light he had made pancake batter out of ordinary stump powder, and had blown up the galley and part of the quarter-deck. It was in this affair that he lost the sight in his left eye, a circumstance that has since greatly influenced his character, because it carried with it the necessity always of sitting on the left side of a person. Once, in Kobe, sick of a fever and believed dying, he had taken the advice of an aunt who wrote him from Columbus, Ohio, directing him to drink tea made from sheep feet. Thurber recovered almost immediately, although the aunt, as I found out later, died.

It is impossible, as well as inadvisable, to sketch his life adequately. I am simply setting down these unconnected incidents, hoping to give some picture of the man, without which (or as Thurber would say "without *whom*") it is difficult to understand the nature of his works. I finally met Thurber in New York, in the spring of 1926. He had come there for a week, to gather up a few soiled clothes which he had left once while passing through on his way to Paris, and had stayed on, taking up his abode in a poorly lighted room on West Thirteenth Street, now the site of a garage. In those days he had very little money and was in constant dread of something falling on his head from buildings—as he still is. I see him now, slinking around the streets, trailing a thin melancholy and leading a terrier bitch. He was a frequent visitor to the downtown restaurants and cafés, and was usually seen at a late breakfast, a morning newspaper on the table, his dog underneath. Sometimes, instead of the dog there was a girl. He began to write in those days, and later to draw. This talent for drawing simple objects with an unsharpened pencil he decided to leave undeveloped, on the advice of friends.

Also in these days he was forming the habits of living and thinking which later were to come out in his writings and drawings. He was early impressed by the seeming impossibility of completing a grammatical sentence. Forced to earn a living by his pen, he actually went through with many sentences that a more scholarly or a more pecunious person would have dropped halfway. It was his early struggle with pronouns and infinitives that we see reflected in his series of articles on modern English usage—a series which here for the first time is collected in book form, but the several chapters of which have worked their way separately into the curricula of many Eastern universities as models of English prose and imperfect communication.

Coincidental with Thurber's grammatical confusion came a renewed interest in and affection for small animals. Peculiarly sensible of a pet's predicament in a house occupied by people, he came to view with a wide sympathy the curious irrelevancies of man and beast, their gropings to come closer to each other, and the wall that divides them. From his boyhood in Columbus, Ohio, when an English bulldog had dominated the Thurber household without actually lending anything to it, he had sensed the dismal as well as the piquant aspects of pethood. Later, when his Scottish terrier gave birth to seven young ones in a two-room apartment in New York City, he enlarged his love for animals and deepened his experience.

In his New York existence, however, more than any other thing he was concerned with the relation between the sexes— that is, as between people rather than animals. Appalled at the grave thrumming of sex itself in the metropolis, he was at once amused and frightened by its manifestations among his friends many of them married. This was the "household" phase of the Thurber ordeal, the phase in which he vainly tried to rationalize the physical equipment of an ordinary apartment occupied by two people, and establish the position of kitchenware in relation to eroticism, children, and dinner engagements. That he was afraid is obvious from the drawings in the book, the bent or "stooped" postures of the males contrasting strongly with the erect and happy stance of the females. Into the real quandary of marriage he read a droll sadness. Above the still cool lake of marriage he saw rising the thin white mist of Man's disparity with Woman. In his drawings one finds not only the simple themes of love and misunderstanding, but also the rarer and tenderer insupport-abilities. He is the one artist that I have ever known, capable of expressing, in a single drawing, physical embarrassment during emotional strain. That is, it is always apparent to Thurber that at the very moment one's heart is caught in an embrace, one's foot may be caught in a piano stool.

Thurber has now served his appprenticeship in life. He has learned to write simple English sentences, he has gone through with the worming of puppies, and he has practically given up trying to find out anything about sex. What he will go on to, no one can say, not knowing the man. At least, safe in these pages, are the records of his sorrows.

E. B. W.

PART ONE
Mr. and
Mrs. Monroe

Tea at Mrs. Armsby's

"MY HUSBAND," said little Mrs. Monroe, "is a collector."

This statement surprised no one more than Mr. Monroe, who was not a collector.

"And what do you collect, Mr. Monroe?" asked Mrs. Armsby, politely.

"Handkerchiefs," said Mrs. Monroe. "He collects hand-kerchiefs."

It was apparent to Mr. Monroe that his wife's remarkable statements were the unfortunate result of their having attended a cocktail party before dropping in, late, at Mrs. Armsby's. The teas which Mrs. Armsby gave on Sundays were the sort at which tea is served. The people who attended them did not attend cocktail parties, which indeed were events almost as alien to their experience as the murders in the Rue Morgue. The Monroes did not like to go to Mrs. Armsby's, but in nearly everyone's life there is a Mrs. Armsby, at whose Sunday teas one feels obliged, at long intervals, to drop in—she was a schoolgirl chum of one's mother, or her husband is an influential man who might help one's own husband to advance. The Monroes were quite young. The others were quite middle-aged and, up to this point, had been discussing the stock market.

"My husband also collects pencils," said Mrs. Monroe. It was warm in the room. The closeness of the air had, as it were, "got to" Mrs. Monroe. One saw this. Fortunately, not more than one—Mr. Monroe himself—saw this, for to the others there was no relationship between the atmosphere and the odd direction the small talk had thus suddenly taken.

"Indeed?" said Mrs. Penwarden.

"My husband has eight hundred and seventy-four thousand pencils," said Mrs. Monroe.

"You collect pencils?" said Mrs. Armsby, with polite interest.

Mr. Monroe was aware that his wife was alluding in a fanciful and distressingly untimely manner to a habit of his, which was to bring home from the office several pencils each day and to leave them on his desk, or failing that, on her dressing table. She frequently spoke to him disapprovingly about such things. For example, he had an unfortunate predilection for leaving towels on her dressing table, too.

"Yes—I—have got a few pencils together—nothing much," said Mr. Monroe, with becoming modesty.

"He has seventy hundred and eighty-nine hundred thousand," said Mrs. Monroe.

"Really?" said Mrs. Penwarden, with evident interest.

"I became interested in pencils in the Sudan," said Mr. Monroe. "The heat is so intense there that it melts the lead in the average Venus or Faber——"

"Or Flaber," said his wife.

"Or Flaber, as the natives call it," continued Mr. Monroe. "The native Sudanese pencil, or vledt, will resist even the most terrific heat—even oxyacetylene. My vledt formed the basis for my collection, which is now of a certain minor importance, perhaps." At this point Mr. Monroe was forced to pause, for his invention had run thin, largely owing to the fact that he knew very little about pencils and nothing at all about the Sudan.

"IT MUST BE INTERESTING TO COLLECT PENCILS," SAID
MR. PENWARDEN.

"It must be interesting to collect pencils," said Mr. Penwarden.

"My husband collects towels, too," said Mrs. Monroe.

"But perhaps my most amusing collection," said Mr. Monroe, "as long as we seem, ha ha, to be discussing my collections . . . is my match folders."

"THOSE LITTLE, AH—MATCHFOLDERS?" ASKED MR. GRIBBING.

"Those little, ah—match folders?" asked Mr. Gribbing.

"Yes. I see them as having a certain value—I mean as forming a record of a trend and as a sort of, well—a sort of chronicle of the present—trend." He had chosen to risk a discussion of match folders rather than towels, but again found it difficult to pretend an easy familiarity with a collection which he did not possess. "I presume, though," said Mr. Monroe, "that match folders are a problem to every woman—if her husband brings as many home as I do." He glanced hopefully from one lady to another and was rewarded by a desultory symposium of viewpoints on paper matches. In this momentary shift of the interest from himself and his wife, he stepped to her side and gripped her shoulder.

"Pull yourself together for the god's sake," said Mr. Monroe.

"I want to lie down," said Mrs. Monroe.

"I'll get your things," said her husband. "Try not to lie down till I get your things."

Hurriedly Mr. Monroe left the room and brought back his wife's coat and handbag.

"My things," said Mrs. Monroe, with bewildering dignity. Her husband deftly assisted her to rise, a process which was more successful than he had dared hope it would be. Their adieux were finally made without anyone falling, or being thrown, Mrs. Monroe abruptly, as is often so happily the case, substituting a charming if rather odd little smile for further statements or observations.

"I should love sometime to see your Sudan pencils," said Mrs. Armsby, at the door.

"You must see them sometime," said Mr. Monroe.

"I had a most enjoyable time," said Mrs. Monroe. It was cooler in the hall. "Goodbye, Mrs. Armsby," she added.

"So glad," said Mrs. Armsby. "Goodbye, dear child." Mr. Monroe opened the door.

"Goodbye, Mrs. Armsby," said Mrs. Monroe, with just a suspicion of tears. "Good——"

"Taxi!" shouted Mr. Monroe, pulling Mrs. Monroe after him, into the street.

The Imperturbable Spirit

MR. MONROE stood fingering some canes in a shop in the Fifties. Canes, it occurred to him, were imperturbable. He liked that adjective, which he had been encountering in a book he was reading on God, ethics, morals, humanism, and so on. The word stood staunch, like a bulwark, rumbled, like a caisson. Mr. Monroe was pleased to find himself dealing in similes.

He finally decided not to buy a cane. Mrs. Monroe was arriving that afternoon on the Leviathan and he would need both hands to wave porters around on the dock. His wife had to be looked after. She was such a child. When imperturbability was at the flood in Mr. Monroe, his wife's nature took on for him a curiously dependent and childlike quality, not at all annoying, considerably endearing, and wholly mythical.

From the cane shop Mr. Monroe wandered to a bookstore. On his imperturbable days it was almost impossible for him to work. He liked to brood and reflect and occasionally to catch glimpses of himself in store windows, slot-machine mirrors, etc., brooding and reflecting. He bought a paperback novel, in the original French, by André Maurois. The gesture—it was purely that for the simple reason that he did not read French—added a vague fillip to his day. Then he walked part way up Fifth Avenue, in the brisk air, and finally hailed a cab.

When he got home he took a bath, put on clean linen and another suit, and sank into a great chair to read some more in the book on God, morals, and so on. In the course of this he looked up three words in a dictionary, "eschatological," "maleficent," and "teleology." He read the definition of the last word twice, frowned, and let it go. Despite the fact that the outlook for mankind was far from bright in the particular chapter he was reading, Mr. Monroe began to feel pretty much the master of his fate. Non-fiction, of a philosophical nature, always affected him that way, regardless of its content.

Mr. Monroe wandered leisurely about the pier, complimenting himself on having remembered to get a customs pass, and on the way his mind kept dealing in interesting ideas. With an imperturbable frown, he watched the big liner nosing in. Did fog at sea imply a malign aspect of the cosmos? If it came and went, without incident, did that

connote luck, or what? Suppose it shielded an iceberg which sank the ship—did that prove the existence of an antic Malice? Mr. Monroe liked the word antic. "Antic," he said, half aloud. He wondered vaguely if he, too, should not write a book about morals, malice, menace, and so on, showing how they could be handled by the imperturbable spirit. . . .

Little Mrs. Monroe, burdened with coats and bundles, rosy, lovely, at length appeared. Mr. Monroe's heart leapt up, but at the same time he set himself as if to receive a service in tennis. He remembered (oh, keenly) as he stepped toward her, how she was wont to regard him as a person likely to "go to pieces" over trifles. Well, she would find him a changed man. He kissed her warmly, but withal in such a strangely masterful manner, that she was at first a little surprised—a tennis player taken aback by a sudden change in the tactics of an old, old opponent. In three minutes of backcourt rallying she figured out that he had been reading something, but she said nothing. She let his lobs go unkilled.

When Mrs. Monroe stood in line at the desk where they assign inspectors, he offered to take her place. "No, no," she whispered. "Just pretend you're not with me. It'll be easier." A slow pallor came upon Mr. Monroe's face.

"Whatta y' got?" he croaked.

"A dozen bottles of Benedictine," she breathed.

"Oh my God!" said Mr. Monroe, dropping, figuratively, his racquet.

An inspector stepped forward and stood waiting.

"So glad," murmured Mrs. Monroe to her husband, collectedly, as to a casual acquaintance. Mr. Monroe fumbled at his hat, and wandered away, tugging at the left sleeve of his coat, a nervous gesture of his. She'd never get away with it. Twelve bottles! Quarts, probably, or magnums —no, it didn't come that way. Well, it came in big, bulky bottles anyway. Let's see, hadn't a new conspiracy law come in? Couldn't they send you to jail now? He could see himself in court, being flayed by a state's attorney. Mr. Monroe had a phobia about law-breaking, even about ordinance-breaking. . . . "Now, gentlemen of the jury . . ." The state's attorney put on his nose glasses, brought out a letter and read it in nasty, slow accents, a horrible, damning letter, which Mr. Monroe had never seen before, but which, fiendishly enough, *was in his own handwriting*. The jury stirred.

"Now wait a minute——" began Mr. Monroe, aloud.

"What *are* you talking about?" demanded his wife.

The courtroom mercifully faded. Mr. Monroe turned and stared at his wife. "Ah—ha, dear!" he said, thickly. "I'm all

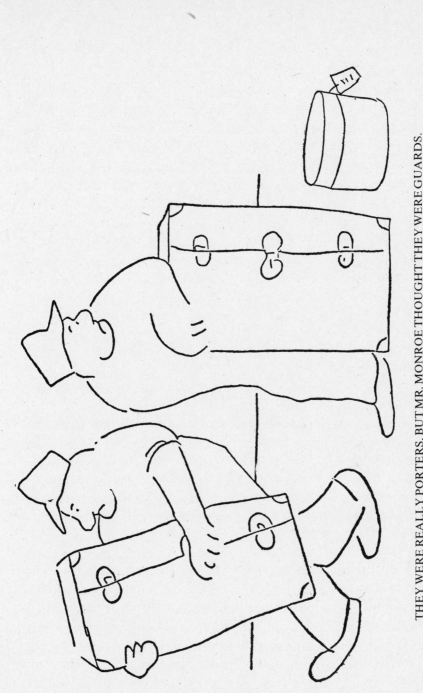

THEY WERE REALLY PORTERS. BUT MR. MONROE THOUGHT THEY WERE GUARDS.

through!" she said, brightly. "Let's go home."

By the time they reached their house, Mr. Monroe was his old self, or rather his new self, again. He had even pretty well persuaded himself that his iron nerve had got the Benedictine through the customs. His strange, masterful manner came back. No sooner had he got into his slippers, however, and reached for his book, than Mrs. Monroe, in the next room, emitted a small squeal. "My hatbox!" she cried. "We left it at the dock!"

"Oh, damn! damn!" said Mr. Monroe. "Well, I'll have to go back after it, that's all. What was in it?"

"Some cute hats I got for almost nothing and—well, that's about all."

"*About* all?"

"Well, three of the bottles."

Mr. Monroe squealed, in turn. "Ah, God," he said, bitterly.

"There's nothing to be afraid of now, silly," his wife said. "They were passed through!"

"I'm not afraid; I'll handle this," murmured her husband.

In a sort of stupor he went out, hailed a cab, and climbed in. Life got you. A scheme of morals? A shield against menace? What good did that do? Impertur—ha! Menace got you—no bigger than a man's hand at first, no bigger than a hatbox. . . . "Now, gentlemen of the jury . . . conspiracy . . . defraud the government . . . seditious . . ."

Mr. Monroe crept whitely through the wide street entrance to the docks. The last stragglers were piling baggage into taxis in the noisy channel beyond. A few suitcases and boxes were still coming down the travelling platform from the dock level above. At the bottom, where they tumbled in a heap, two guards stood to receive them. They were really porters, but Mr. Monroe thought they were guards. They had big jaws. One of them gradually turned into a state's attorney before Mr. Monroe's very eyes! The stricken husband wandered idly over to the other side of the moving platform.

There stood a lonely, sinister hatbox, a trap, a pitfall, Exhibit A. "Now, gentlemen . . ."

"That your box, brother?" asked the state's attorney.

"Oh, no," said Mr. Monroe, "nope." The porter seemed disappointed. Mr. Monroe walked out into the channel where the taxis were. Then he walked back again; out again; and back again. The guards had turned away and were fussing with a trunk. Mr. Monroe trembled. He walked stiffly to the hatbox, picked it up, and walked stiffly through the doorway, out into the street.

"Hey!" cried a loud voice. Mr. Monroe broke into a run. "Taxi!" continued the loud voice. But Mr. Monroe was a hundred yards away. He ran three blocks without stopping, walked half a block, and ran again. He came home by a devious route, rested for a while outside his door, and went in. . . .

That night Mr. Monroe read to his wife from the morals, ethics, and imperturbability book. He read in a deep, impressive voice, and slowly, for there was a lot his wife wouldn't grasp at once.

Mr. Monroe Outwits a Bat

THE MONROES opened their summer place a little late, for carking cares had kept them long in town. The grass was greening and tangled when they arrived, and the house had a woodsy smell. Mr. Monroe took a deep breath. "I'll get a great sleep tonight," he said. He put on some old clothes, pottered around, inspecting doors and windows, whistling. After dinner he went out under the stars and smelled the clear fine air. Abruptly there came to his ears a little scream from inside the house—the scream his wife gave when she dropped a cup or when some other trivial tragedy of the kitchen occurred. Mr. Monroe hurried inside.

"Spider!" cried Mrs. Monroe. "Oh, kill it, kill it!" She always held that a spider, encountered but not slain, turned up in one's bed at night. Mr. Monroe loved to kill spiders for his wife. He whacked this one off a tea towel with a newspaper and scooped it outside the door into the petunia bed. It gave him a feeling of power, and enhanced the sweetness of his little wife's dependence on him. He was still glowing with his triumph, in a small, warm way, when he went to bed.

"Goodnight, dear," he called, deeply. His voice was always a little deeper than usual, after a triumph.

"Goodnight, dear," she called back from her room.

The night was sweet and clear. Nice old creaking sounds ran down the steps and back up again. Some of them sounded like the steps of a person.

"Afraid, dear?" he called out.

"Not with you here," she answered, sleepily. There was a long, pleasant silence. Mr. Monroe began to drowse. A very ominous sound brought him out of it, a distinct flut, a firm, insistent, rhythmic flut.

"Bat!" muttered Mr. Monroe to himself.

At first he took the advent of the bat calmly. It seemed to

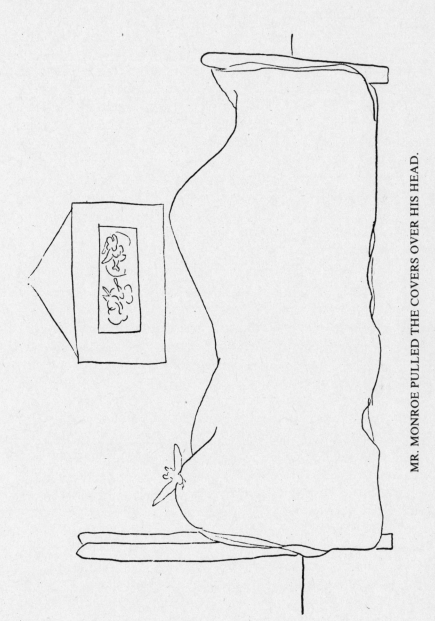

MR. MONROE PULLED THE COVERS OVER HIS HEAD.

be flying high, near the ceiling. He even boldly raised up on his elbows and peered through the dark. As he did so the bat, apparently out of sheer malice, almost clipped the top of his head. Mr. Monroe scrambled under the covers, but instantly recovered his composure and put his head out again—just as the bat, returning in its orbit, skimmed across the bed once more. Mr. Monroe pulled the covers over his head. It was the bat's round.

"Restless, dear?" called his wife, through her open door.

"What?" he said.

"Why, what's the matter?" she asked, slightly alarmed at his muffled tone.

"I'm all right, it's okay," responded Mr. Monroe, from under the covers.

"You sound funny," said his wife. There was a pause.

"Goodnight, dear," called Mr. Monroe, poking his head out to say this, and pulling it in again.

"Goodnight."

He strained his ears to hear through the covers, and found he could. That bat was still flitting above the bed in measured, relentless intervals. The notion came to the warm and stuffy Mr. Monroe that the incessant repetition of a noise at regular intervals might drive a person crazy. He dismissed the thought, or tried to. If the dripping of water on a man's head, slowly, drip, drip, drip—flut, flut, flut . . .

"Damn it," said Mr. Monroe to himself. The bat was apparently just getting into its swing. It was flying faster. The first had just been practice. Mr. Monroe suddenly bethought himself of a great spread of mosquito netting lying in a closet across the room. If he could get that and put it over the bed, he could sleep in peace. He poked his nose out from under a sheet, reached out a hand, and stealthily felt around for a match on a table by the bed—the light switch was yards away. Gradually his head and shoulders emerged. The bat seemed to be waiting for just this move. It zipped past his cheek. He flung himself back under the covers, with a great squeaking of springs.

"John?" called his wife.

"What's the matter now?" he asked querulously.

"What *are* you doing?" she demanded.

"There's a bat in the room, if you want to know," he said. "And it keeps scraping the covers."

"Scraping the covers?"

"Yes, scraping the covers."

"It'll go away," said his wife. "They go away."

"I'll drive it away!" shouted John Monroe, for his wife's tone was that of a mother addressing a child. "How the devil that damn bat ever——" his voice grew dim because he was now pretty far under the bed clothes.

"I can't hear you, dear," said Mrs. Monroe. He popped his head out.

"I say how long is it before they go away?" he asked.

"It'll hang by its feet pretty soon and go to sleep," said his wife, soothingly. "It won't hurt you." This last had a curious effect on Mr. Monroe. Much to his own surprise he sat upright in bed, a little angry. The bat actually got him this time, brushed his hair, with a little "Squeep!"

"Hey!" yelled Mr. Monroe.

"What *is* it, dear?" called his wife. He leaped out of bed, now completely panic-stricken, and ran for his wife's room. He went in and closed the door behind him, and stood there.

"Get in with me, dear," said Mrs. Monroe.

"I'm all right," he retorted, irritably. "I simply want to get something to rout that thing with. I couldn't find anything in my room." He flicked on the lights.

"There's no sense in your getting all worn out fighting a bat," said his wife. "They're terribly quick." There seemed to him to be an amused sparkle in her eyes.

"Well, I'm terribly quick too," grumbled Mr. Monroe, trying to keep from shivering, and he slowly folded a newspaper into a sort of club. With this in his hand he stepped to the door. "I'll shut your door after me," he said, "so the bat won't get in your room." He went out, firmly closing the door behind him. He crept slowly along the hall till he came to his own room. He waited a while and listened. The bat was still going strong. Mr. Monroe lifted the paper club and struck the jamb of the door, from the outside, a terrific blow. "Wham!" went the blow. He hit again. "Wham!"

"Did you get it, dear?" called his wife, her voice coming dimly through her door.

"Okay," cried her husband, "I got it." He waited a long while. Then he slipped, on tiptoe, to a couch in the corridor halfway between his room and his wife's and gently, ever so gently, let himself down upon it. He slept lightly, because he was pretty chilly, until dawn, got up and tiptoed to his room. He peered in. The bat was gone. Mr. Monroe got into bed and went to sleep.

The "Wooing" of Mr. Monroe

LITTLE Mrs. Monroe met the challenge of the very blonde lady with all of her charming directness. She went to Miss Lurell's apartment and said to her, quite simply, "I am Mrs. John Monroe. I have come to tell you some things about John I think you should know." The other woman met her simplicity with icy reticence. "Please understand," pursued Mrs. Monroe, "that I do not wish to interfere. John has told me of the strange beauty of it all. I just wanted to warn you that John is simply terrible with machinery."

"There is no machinery in our association that I can think of," said the lovely Miss Lurell, coldly.

"Oh," said Mrs. Monroe, "there will be. May I smoke?" She lighted a cigarette, her first in months. "Machinery is always bobbing up in John's life. He knows nothing at all about it, but I will say for him that he never runs from it. I might almost say that he attacks it. He attacks machinery."

"I don't believe I understand," said the other, as if to imply that she did not wish to understand. Mrs. Monroe was about to inhale some smoke, thought better of it—she always choked—and smiled amicably.

"Not long ago," she began, "we went for a motor trip to John's university; he hadn't been back there for years. We stayed at a charming place on the campus, called the Union. It was very peaceful. We could see apple trees in blossom, from our window. It was early May——"

"Pray spare yourself memories which can only hurt," murmured the other woman.

"Oh, it was really quite funny." Mrs. Monroe permitted herself what she had intended to be a gay, rippling laugh. "We had been in our room only ten minutes, when John went across the hall to take a shower in a great tiled shower-room for alumni guests. I remember it was twilight, soft and dreamy——" Miss Lurell made a sound as of one who dreads

27

sentimental tears. "Well," continued Mrs. Monroe, "John had forgotten to bring his bathrobe, of course, so he wore his raincoat. He always forgets his bathrobe—and theatre tickets."

"I don't see what you can possibly hope to establish—by all this," interrupted the blonde lady.

"I am telling you such an intimate story, because this was so typical of John," said his wife. "You see he has never really taken a successful shower in his life. He always gets the water to running too cold or too hot. This time it ran too cold. He kept twisting the handle and swearing until a man in the adjoining shower told him to turn it farther to the right. John shot it all the way to the right. Instantly a stream of boiling water flooded the bath. John didn't get scalded, because he had learned not to get fully into a shower: he stands outside and sticks his feet in and then his shoulders. You see, I knew you wouldn't have had any experience of John's showers——"

"You were quite right," said the other, frigidly.

"Well, in a few seconds the whole place was a fog of steam and the heat was frightful. John couldn't reach into the compartment again and turn the handle back, so he began to go 'Woo! Woo!'—like a child. He always goes 'Woo! Woo!' when things go wrong with machinery. Of course he writes beautiful sonnets, which I am sure you appreciate perhaps more deeply than I do, and of course mechanical things are of no importance, but one must know what to do with him in a case like this."

"And what did *you* do?" asked Miss Lurell.

"Well, my dear, first the other man in the boiler-room—as it had now become—climbed up on the wall of his shower and tried to reach over and get at the handle from above, but the intense heat made that impossible. Then he yelled at John to get a window-stick or something with which he could reach down and knock the handle back onto 'Cold.' Of course John was too excited to be of any use himself. Finally,

THE UNIVERSITY ENGINEER HAD TO SHUT OFF THE WATER IN THE
WHOLE INSTITUTION.

in a panic, he rushed across the hall into my room, stark,
raving——"

"Please!" said Miss Lurell.

"Stark, raving naked," continued Mrs. Monroe. "He's so
funny that way, really I just *screamed*. He was still making
that 'Woo! Woo!' noise and I knew instantly he had been
fooling with the works of something. It was just the way he
acted the time he short-circuited all the lights in a theatre
one night between acts—we never found out how he did
that—he got to wandering around and stumbled into a
switch or something, probably thinking it was a water-
cooler."

"Fully dressed, I presume?"

"Oh, it's only when he's driven from a shower or something like that that he hasn't anything on," said Mrs. Monroe, simply. "Well, he began yelling at me to get him a window-stick or something and finally pulled down a curtain rod, curtain and all, and would have rushed back across the hall with it the way he was, but I threw my negligée over him. When he got back the other man had had to leave, for the heat was unbearable. In the end, the university engineer had to shut off the water in the whole institution—all the campus buildings—they phoned him to do that because there was nobody in the Union who knew where the local water-switch was—I mean the one for that building. It was terrible, but that's the way John is—when he fools with machinery, he always disconnects the whole works. Once in a hotel in Nice, he——"

"May I ask," cut in the other woman, "how long you have endured this?"

"Eight years in June," said Mrs. Monroe. "Naturally, I feel that the—next lady—should know what to expect."

"Eight years," murmured Miss Lurell. She rose. Mrs. Monroe rose too.

"*Now* you will know what to do," said Mrs. Monroe. "Don't argue with him when he begins to 'Woo!'—just let him have his own way, but summon somebody instantly."

"I know exactly what to do," said Miss Lurell, with an odd smile. She accompanied little Mrs. Monroe to the door, where she impulsively held out her hand. "Apropos of nothing," drawled the very blonde lady, "may I ask if you play bridge?"

"Oh, very badly," said Mrs. Monroe. "Unless——" she waved a gloved hand at a passing taxi, "unless I hold a perfect grand slam." She smiled back, over her shoulder, and went away.

Mr. Monroe and the Moving Men

MR. MONROE had never really had any experience in moving household goods before he did it, single-handed, on the eighth of August, 1930. The date will always be fixed in his mind that way, formally, formidably. It was rather an unusual time to move, but it couldn't be helped because on the ninth of August wreckers were going to start tearing down the house. Little Mrs. Monroe was away, unavoidably away, terrifyingly away. We have here, then, the makings of a character study—or would have except for the fact that Mr. Monroe didn't really have any character. He had a certain charm, yes; but not character. He evaded difficult situations; he had no talent for firm resolution; he immolated badly; and he wasn't even very good at renunciation, except when he was tired or a little sick. Not, you will see, the man to move household goods into storage when his wife is away.

The packers and movers were to come at two o'clock. Mrs. Monroe could have told her husband that they wouldn't arrive until four-thirty; or he would have known it himself if always before, when they moved, he had not sneaked away from the house. Always before, Mr. Monroe had been just as surprised to find himself in a new place as a mother dog is when she is lifted out from among the shoes in the clothes closet, where she has decided to have her puppies, and put into a lovely airy box with a pink coverlet.

Before she went away, little Mrs. Monroe had led her husband from room to room, pointing out what was to go into storage and what was to be sent to the summer place in Connecticut. It was all quite simple, she told him. Apparently John Monroe hadn't been listening, however, for now, as he walked restlessly from room to room, picking up vases and putting them down again, he found he wasn't sure about anything. He wasn't sure about the china and glassware, for one thing. He stood and stared at them, trying to remember

what it was his wife had said. All that he could recall was that
she had spoken in the slow, precise way in which she always
spoke to him in a crisis, as if he were a little deaf or feeble-
minded. He decided, finally, that the glassware and china
went into storage. Then he decided that they didn't. He tried
to remember whether they already had plates and glasses at
the summer place and realized, of course, that they must
have. They ate there; they lived there. But he also realized
that the ways of women are beyond the simple understanding
of the masculine mind, and that the fact that a wife already
has one set of dishes and glasses is no reason she can't—nay,
mustn't, maybe—have another set. Mr. Monroe sighed, and
went in and turned on the bath water; then he turned it off
again, for there were no towels. By this time it was getting on
toward three o'clock. He took to wandering aimlessly
around, wondering if he should wrap something up, or what.

After a time he came to a halt in front of a large chair—a
large, flowered chair, he would have described it to his wife
over the phone—which, in her tour around the place with
him, little Mrs. Monroe, he felt positive, had said something
very definite about. He wondered what it had been. It now
occurred to him, after deep thought, that his wife must have
spoken only about the things which were to be saved out of
storage—it would have been silly for her to point out the
things that were to go to the warehouse because nine-tenths
of the things were to go to the warehouse. Obviously, then,
reasoned Mr. Monroe—and he was a bit proud of his
brilliance in this matter—obviously she had pointed out only
the things that were to be kept out. Now if he could only
remember which things she had pointed out, he would be
safe. He decided to move away from the flowered chair, to let
it go, for the longer he looked at it the stronger became his
conviction that he had never seen it before in his life. This
took him back to the chinaware and glasses. She must have
said: "And this, John. Remember—all this goes to the
summer place." Certainly. Or maybe she had said: "And

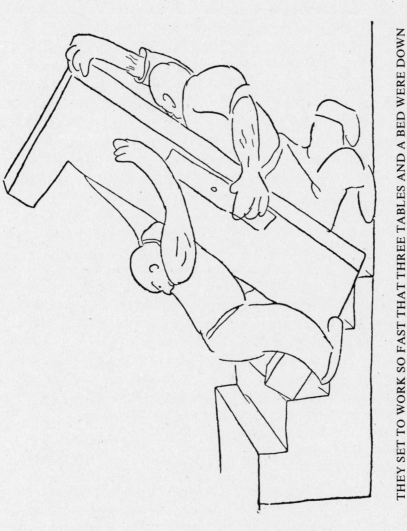

THEY SET TO WORK SO FAST THAT THREE TABLES AND A BED WERE DOWN THE STAIRS BEFORE MR. MONROE COULD SAY ANYTHING.

watch them when they pack this for storage, John; don't let them break anything." Hmm. Mr. Monroe lighted a cigarette and sat down. It was now almost four o'clock. Suppose the moving men didn't come? Well, if they didn't, the wreckers would tear the place down next day, with the furniture in it. Maybe he could prevail on the wreckers, for some enormous sum, to pack and move the stuff out, before they started wrecking. Of course wreckers wouldn't want to do that, but he saw himself dominating them, when they demurred. "See here, my men," he heard himself saying, coldly, "*I'm* in charge here—get that!" He loved himself in that rôle, and was often in it, in his day dreams, which, on this occasion, were abruptly interrupted by the arrival of the packers and movers.

They set to work so fast that three tables and a bed were down the stairs and onto the sidewalk before Mr. Monroe could say anything. Well, he was pretty sure about the great big pieces of furniture, anyway—they must go to storage. Great big pieces of furniture were always stored—that's why storage warehouses were so big. Mr. Monroe began to feel that he was getting a grip on the situation. "What about the china, chief?" one of the men asked him. Mr. Monroe hesitated. "Pack it and let it stand a while," he said, at last. "I want to think about it." From downstairs later he could hear the voices of the men, huge, sweating, rough fellows, joking about him: "This guy wants to think it over—ja get that, Joe?" Mr. Monroe's indecision and evident nervousness began to show up in the movers' attitude toward him. The "chief" and "mister" with which they had first addressed him changed to "buddy" and "pardner" and finally, as Mr. Monroe strove desperately for an air of dignity and authority, to "sonny."

In the end, most of the decisions were made by the men themselves. Joe stood with one of his hairy paws on a small writing desk. "How about this, scout?" he asked. It was a favorite piece of Mrs. Monroe's; John couldn't remember

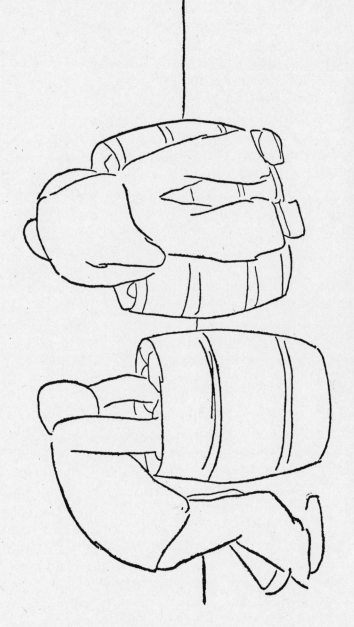

THE PACKERS GOT THE CHINAWARE AND GLASSWARE INTO TWO BARRELS.

whether she had said anything about it; "Okay," said Joe,
and he moved it out. John hadn't said anything. So it went.
Meanwhile two packers had got the chinaware and glasses
into two barrels. "What about it, buddy?" they finally asked
the head of the house. "Well, here's the way it is," he began.
"You see, it's quite a problem. I——" "Better store it,
sonny," said one of the men. "You don't need all this china."
"Does it look like summer china to you?" asked Mr.
Monroe, rather meekly. "Naw, dat's winter china," said a
man named Mike. "Take it away, Bill." Bill took it away, out
to the storage van. Mr. Monroe was now certain that his wife
had wanted it saved out for the summer house. "Oh God,
God," he said to himself, walking around and smoking
rapidly.

By the time the movers reached the kitchen utensils, and
called them to Mr. Monroe's attention, he was becoming
overwhelmed by the idiotic conviction that he was in the
wrong house. What the hell were kitchen utensils doing here?
They were up at the summer place, weren't they? It was only
after an agonizing few moments that he realized they had
rented the summer house furnished. The men, tired of
waiting for directions, picked the kitchenware up and carted
it out to the van. "Okay," murmured Mr. Monroe.

At length, there was nothing left but a few odds and ends,
one of which was a large tin receptacle marked "Flour."
"Can't store this, buddy," one of the men said, showing the
head of the house that the can was two-thirds full of flour,
with a spoon in it. Mr. Monroe took the can, and when none
of the men was looking, shoved the thing into a closet, shut
the door, and sighed. "Everything out of dat closet?" asked
Joe, appearing from somewhere. "Okay," said Mr. Monroe.
"Okay," said Joe. The men went away as quickly as they had
come.

Mr. Monroe sank into a chair, one of the three or four
objects he had saved out for the summer house. He slowly
began to convince himself that all of his decisions—or the

men's, anyway—had been right. After all, they were men experienced in moving. He began to feel pretty good about the whole thing; it was over and done with, thank God. Just then, into the edge of his consciousness, stalked a tall, thin thought. Mrs. Monroe had told him what to do about getting the stuff to the summer house: a certain transfer man, who delivered out of town, was to call; John had been given his name, his address, and his phone number. Mr. Monroe crushed a cigarette in his hand. Then he cried aloud. He couldn't remember the man's name. He couldn't remember anything.

The Monroes Find a Terminal

SHORTLY AFTER nine o'clock little Mrs. Monroe began quietly to put on her things. Mr. Monroe, who was comfortably fixed in a deep chair, under a lamp, looked up apprehensively over his book.

"Where are we going?" he demanded, suspiciously.

"The French poodle gets in from Chicago tonight at nine-thirty," said his wife. "I didn't tell you before because I knew it would spoil your dinner, but it won't be anything, dear. We simply go over and pick up the puppy at the terminal so it won't have to stay all night in the crate. The shipper's letter gives all the directions." She took a letter from her handbag and gave it to her husband. Mr. Monroe, after a profound study, read one sentence aloud, slowly, "Go to the West Terminal on Sixteenth Street and ask for Messenger Car of New York Central train 608, which gets in about nine-thirty."

"It's only a step . . ." began Mrs. Monroe, soothingly. (The Monroes lived, at the time, in the East Sixties.)

"It's just one of those letters that never work out," said John Monroe, wisely. "We'll get way over on Sixteenth Street and we'll see a lot of big, dark, locked buildings lighted by dismal street lamps. I'll ask a man where the West Terminal is and he won't know. You can't go directly to a terminal and get a dog. I've lived long enough to know that."

"You're just trying to be ironical," said his wife. "You always make everything so hard."

"All right, all right," said Mr. Monroe, "but you'll see." He dragged out of his chair, with a hard smile, got his hat and coat, and they went out and hailed a taxi.

"West Terminal," said Mrs. Monroe to the driver.

"What west terminal?" asked the driver. It came out after a long talk in which Mr. Monroe, with a triumphant grin, took no part, that the taxi-man did not know of any west terminal where there might be a dog. Mrs. Monroe ordered him to go to Sixteenth Street and proceed slowly west which, in the end, he did, sharing Mr. Monroe's high skepticism. The street was ill-lighted, noisy with children. The farther west the Monroes went, the bigger, darker, and more firmly locked the buildings were. They passed the M. M. Cohen Co., Paper & Twine, the Ajax Examining and Shrinking Corporation, Ozaman Club No. 2, and a copper riveting works. Nothing looked like a freight terminal. At the corner of Tenth Avenue, Mrs. Monroe commanded the driver to stop near the biggest and darkest building.

"I think this is it," she said, cheerily. Her husband roused himself and peered out.

"National Biscuit Company," he said, and relaxed back into his seat. He began to hum slightly. The driver looked around.

"You might get out and ask somebody," said Mrs. Monroe to her husband. This Mr. Monroe, with strange mutterings, did. He stopped a man, conversed briefly, and returned to the taxi.

"He says a fellow named Joe has an express office on this

street and does piano hauling," said Mr. Monroe, grimly. The chauffeur drove on. Just around the corner in Eleventh Avenue, a hopeful-looking structure loomed up. Mr. Monroe looked out.

"The Economy Wiping Materials Company," he said.

"I can read," said his wife, shortly. After a moment she gave a little cry. "Look, John," she said, "there it is!" She pointed at some freight cars in a small yard across the

avenue. A light glowed in a shack marked "N.Y.C.R.R." They got out of the cab and stumbled across the street. A short, gray, deaf man with silver-rimmed spectacles answered their knock at the door of the shack. He failed from the first to get it quite clear in his mind what was wanted, but he got enough to affirm definitely that there was no poodle in the yards there.

"Where do you think the dog would be?" Mrs. Monroe asked him.

A SHORT, GRAY, DEAF MAN WITH SILVER-RIMMED SPECTACLES.

"Lady," he said, "I don't know," and disappeared. Mrs. Monroe was for going into the yards and knocking on freight cars. "He might bark," she explained. Mr. Monroe led her back to the taxi. "You can't get a dog from a terminal by force," he said, sternly. "We'll go back home and think this thing out. First of all, is it coming freight or express—do you know that?" He had assumed his protective man-of-the-world attitude.

"The express company is shipping it by freight," said his wife, somewhat subdued by the experiences of the evening.

"They don't do that," said Mr. Monroe. "The two things are separate." His tone, however, carried little conviction. "Probably express," he added. "I think it's only furniture that comes freighted."

"I don't suppose," said Mrs. Monroe, "they've given the poor doggy any water."

"The dog has water; we'll get the dog," said her husband, with his best executive air. He held her hand and they drove home in silence.

Back at the apartment, he asked for the phone book, and Mrs. Monroe finally found it on Mr. Monroe's bed. "Now," he said, "look up under New York Central." She did and began to read off, "'General and Exec——'"

"Go on," said Mr. Monroe.

"'Freight stations,'" continued his wife, "'Pier 34 ER ft Rutgers slip, St. Johns Pk Laight & Varick—'"

"Give me the book," said Mr. Monroe, importantly. He took it, flipped over a few pages, frowned, and began to look around nervously.

"Under your chair," said his wife. He reached under his chair and found his tobacco pouch. "Now look under American Railway Express," pursued his wife. Mr. Monroe did this, after filling his pipe.

"Here we are," he said, "'American Railway Express: Tracing department, Claim department, On Hand department'—ah, that's probably it—'438 West 55.' When things are received they are considered on hand and——"

"It couldn't be that," interrupted his wife. "That's where they have dogs for a week or more. Let me have the book." She went over and took it. Carefully and calmly she studied the listings. "Here!" she said. "Terminals: Tenth Avenue and Thirty-third, Lexington and Forty-ninth.' Now Lexington is east and the other west—it must be Tenth Avenue and Thirty-third. I'll call that number."

"No use," said her husband, pityingly. He yawned and

began to remove his shoes. "The shipper couldn't have been that far off—from Sixteenth to Thirty-third Street. If you phone there a guy will answer in a German accent and deny everything. Wait till morning and I'll call up a——" But Mrs. Monroe was already on the phone. Suddenly she was talking, animatedly. "Yes, 608. A little black dog. It is? Oh, you did? Well, that's fine! We'll be right up!" She hung up the receiver. "It's there!" she cried. "The man said he had seen the puppy—the car was just brought in up there. Hurry, let's go right up and get it!"

Mr. Monroe did not hurry. He put his shoes back on slowly, smiling strangely, like a diplomat at a conference.

"You see, my dear," he began, as they started out again, "you have to go at these things carefully and calmly and figure out logically where a dog, shipped from Chicago, would most naturally——" His wife smiled, even more strangely than he had, and kissed him.

"My great big wonderful husband," she said, gently.

Mr. Monroe Holds the Fort

THE COUNTRY house, on this particular wintry afternoon, was most enjoyable. Night was trudging up the hill and the air was sharp. Mr. Monroe had already called attention several times to the stark beauty of the black tree branches limned, as he put it, against the sky. The wood fire had settled down to sleepy glowing in the grate.

"It *is* a little lonely, though," said Mrs. Monroe. (The nearest house was far away.)

"I love it," said her husband, darkly. At moments and in places like this, he enjoyed giving the impression of a strong, silent man wrapped in meditation. He stared, brooding, into the fire. Mrs. Monroe, looking quite tiny and helpless, sat on the floor at his feet and leaned against him. He gave her shoulder two slow, reflective pats.

"I really don't mind staying here when Germaine is here— just we two," said Mrs. Monroe, "but I think I would be terrified if I were alone." Germaine, the maid, a buxom, fearless woman, was in town on shopping leave. The Monroes had thought it would be fun to spend the weekend alone and get their own meals, the way they used to.

"There's nothing in the world to be afraid of," said Mr. Monroe.

"Oh, it gets so terribly black outside, and you hear all kinds of funny noises at night that you don't hear during the day." Mr. Monroe explained to her why that was—expansion (said he) of woodwork in the cold night air, and so on. From there he somehow went into a discussion of firearms, which would have betrayed to practically anyone that his knowledge of guns was limited to a few impressive names like Colt and Luger. They were one of those things he was always going to read up on but never did. He mentioned quietly, however, that he was an excellent shot.

"Mr. Farrington left his pistol here, you know," said Mrs. Monroe, "but I've never touched it—ugh!"

"He did?" cried her husband. "Where is it? I'd like to take a look at it." Mr. Farrington was the man from whom they had taken, on long lease, the Connecticut place.

"It's upstairs in the chest of drawers in the back room," said Mrs. Monroe. Her husband, despite her protests, went up and got it and brought it down. "Please put it away!" said his wife. "Is it loaded? Oh, don't do that! Please!" Mr. Monroe, looking grim and competent, was aiming the thing, turning it over, scowling at it.

"It's loaded all right," he said, "all five barrels."

"Chambers," said his wife.

"Yes," he said. "Let me show you how to use it—after all, you can never tell when you're going to need a gun."

"Oh, I'd never use it—even if one of those convicts that escaped yesterday came right up the stairs and I could shoot him, I'd just stand there. I'd be *paralyzed*!"

"Nonsense!" said Mr. Monroe. "You don't have to shoot a man. Get the drop on him, stand him up with his face against a wall, and phone the police. Look here—" he covered an imaginary figure, backed him against the wall, and sat down at the phone table. "Always keep your eye on him; don't look into the transmitter." Mr. Monroe glared at his man, lifted up the receiver, holding the hook down with his finger, and spoke quietly to the phone. In the midst of this the phone rang. Mr. Monroe started sharply.

"It's for you, dear," he said presently. His wife took the receiver.

How curiously things happen! That is what Mr. Monroe thought, an hour later, as he drove back from the station after taking his wife there to catch the 7:10. Imagine her mother getting one of those fool spells at this time! Imagine expecting a grown daughter to come running every time you felt a little dizzy! Imagine—well, the ways of women were beyond him. He turned into the drive of the country house. Judas, but it was dark! Dark and silent. Mr. Monroe didn't put the machine in the garage. He got out and stood still, listening. Off toward the woods somewhere he heard a thumping noise. Partridge drumming, thought Mr. Monroe. But partridge didn't thump, they whirred—didn't they? Oh, well, they probably thumped at this time of year.

It was good to get inside the house. He built up the fire, and turned on the overhead lights—his wife never allowed them turned on. Then he went into a couple of other rooms and turned on more lights. He wished he had gone in town with her. Of course she'd be back in the morning on the 10:10, and they'd have the rest of that day—Sunday— together. Still . . . he went to the drawer where he had put the revolver and got it out. He fell to wondering whether the thing would work. Long-unused guns often jammed, or exploded. He went out into the kitchen, carrying the pistol. His wife had told him to be sure and get himself a snack. He opened the refrigerator door, looked in, decided he wasn't hungry, and closed it again. He went back to the living-room and began to pace up and down. He decided to put the pistol on the mantel, butt toward him. Then he practiced making quick grabs for it. Presently he sat down in a chair, picked up a *Nation* and began to read, at random: "Two men are intimately connected with the killing of striking workers at Marion, North Carolina. . . ." Where had those convicts his wife mentioned escaped from? Dannemora? Matteawan? How far were those places from this house? Maybe having all the lights on was a bad idea. He got up and turned the upper lights off; and then turned them on again. . . . There was a step outside. Crunch! crunch! . . . Mr. Monroe hurried to the mantel, knocked the gun to the floor, fumbled for it, and stuck it in a hip pocket just as a knock sounded at the door.

"Wha-" began Mr. Monroe, and was surprised to find he couldn't say anything else. The knocking continued. He stepped to the door, stood far to one side, and said, "Yeh?" A cheery voice responded. Reassured, Mr. Monroe opened the door. A motorist wanted to know how to get to the Wilton road. Mr. Monroe told him, speaking quite loudly. Afterwards, lifted up by this human contact, he went back to his reading in the *Nation*: "Around 1:30 A.M. one of the foremen approached young Luther Bryson, 22, one of the victims, and harangued him: "If you strike this time, you ——, we will shoot it out with you.' . . . " Mr. Monroe put the magazine down. He got up and went to the victrola, selected a jazz record, and began to play it. It occurred to him that if there were steps outside, he couldn't hear them. He shut the machine off. The abrupt silence made him stand still, listening. He heard all kinds of noises. One of them came from upstairs—a quick, sliding noise, like a convict slipping into a clothes closet . . . the fellow had a beard and a blue-steel gun . . . a man in the dark had the advantage. Mr. Monroe's mouth began to feel stuffy. "Damn it! This can't go on!" he said aloud, and felt bucked up. Then someone put his heel down sharply on the floor just above. Mr. Monroe tentatively picked up a flashlight, and pulled the pistol from his pocket. The phone rang sharply. "Good God!" said Mr. Monroe, backing against a wall. He slid on to the chair in front of the phone, with the gun in his right hand, and took

BURGLARS FLITTING ABOUT IN THE ATTIC OF A HOUSE IN WHICH THE
MASTER IS HOME ALONE.

up the receiver with his left. When he spoke into the transmitter his eyes kept roving around the room. "H'lo," he said. It was Mrs. Monroe. Her mother was all right. Was he all right? He was fine. What was he doing? Oh, reading. (He kept the gun trained on the foot of the steps leading upstairs.) Well, what would he think if she came back out on that midnight train? Her mother was all right. Would he be too sleepy to wait up and meet her? Hell, no! That was fine! Do that! . . .

Mr. Monroe hung up the receiver with a profound sigh of relief. He looked at his watch. Hm, wouldn't have to leave for the station for nearly two hours. Whistling, he went out to the refrigerator (still carrying the gun) and fetched out the butter and some cold meat. He made a couple of sandwiches (laying the gun on the kitchen table) and took them into the living-room (putting the gun in his pocket). He turned off the overhead lights, sat down, picked up a *Harper's* and began to read. Abruptly, that flitting, clothes-closety sound came from upstairs again. Mr. Monroe finished his sandwiches hurriedly, with the gun on his lap, got up, went from room to room turning off the extra lights, put on his hat and overcoat, locked several doors, went out and got into his car. After all, he could read just as well at the station, and he would be sure of being there on time—might fall asleep otherwise. He started the engine, and whirled out of the drive. He felt for the pistol, which was in his overcoat pocket. He would slip it back into the chest of drawers upstairs later on. Mr. Monroe came to a crossroads and a light. He began to whistle.

The Middle Years

WHEN, as John Monroe was helping the lovely lady on with her coat, she leaned ever so slightly—and unnecessarily—backwards, he was conscious of a quick warm glow. He was even more conscious of a vague perplexity, the reason for which—or one of the reasons, anyway—finally came washing up to him on the stream of memory. This had all happened before, almost precisely as now, but with another girl, and years before. *That* girl, he was painfully reminded, had not meant it. He had afterwards walked feverishly and miserably around in the rain for hours, smoking dozens of cigarettes. He hadn't slept that night.

He was proud of himself that now, going on thirty-six, he took such things more calmly. His heart didn't throb in his throat like a dollar watch. He didn't change color or stammer. He didn't even meet this present lady's eyes at first. He did manage at last, as became a man of the world, to give her a subtle (as he felt) recognition of the dizzy little moment. It was nothing that he said, no extra pressure that he gave her hand. He merely favored her with an intense and wonderful glance (or so he believed it to be), paving the way for a charming sequel without spoiling it all by seeming too youthfully impetuous. Of course if it came to impetuosity, he would show 'em who was impetuous. But, at thirty-five, to make the right effect, one had to go slow. Besides, he was a little tired, the party having lasted infernally late. He was glad that someone else was seeing the lady home this particular night. It was devilishly cold.

He had quite a sneezing spell when he got home, which somehow marred his admiration of himself in a glass. He noted that his hair, graying at the temples, was becoming more attractive every day. He tried a couple of brooding frowns, with his chin resting in his hand, and approved of them. Then he went to bed, resolved to think about the lovely lady quite a while, before falling asleep. He fell asleep in thirty-two seconds.

The next morning he awoke feeling much better than he usually did after being out late. He sprang out of bed quickly—without any of that dizziness which in recent years he had begun to experience if he arose too suddenly. He began whistling as he put a new blade in his razor. It was quite a while before he got at the source of the vague gaiety that lifted him up. Then he remembered the lovely lady, and the incident of the coat. Oddly enough, his spirits dropped

SHE WOULD BE READING, STRETCHED OUT, FILMILY, ON A DIVAN, SOFT, ALLURING.

just a trifle. He was surprised, but they did. His old, or as a matter of actual fact, his fairly recent, sense of perplexity came back. Things got complicated so easily, became weighty. Complications were a damned nuisance. Kept a man up late, kept him figuring. He fought off the sudden apparition of his wife's face, which leaped up to laugh at him, a little mockingly. She was, as luck would have it (he wasn't sure of his own definition of luck here), out of town, and wouldn't be back for a week. Of course, she wouldn't *mind*. He was, after all, old enough not to make a fool of himself. That, in her charmingly humorous way, was all little Mrs.

Monroe had ever required of him in the event of an—ah—of a communion with anyone. Just so he selected a lady that a wife need not be ashamed of. Well, he had. Furthermore, she was probably waiting for him to give her a ring. Well, he would. After breakfast. The laughing face of his wife bobbed up again. He cut himself slightly with a razor, and swore. He couldn't find a clean shirt, and swore again. Damn it, she was *always* out of town!

The knowledge that the lovely lady's husband was in Bermuda had been a part of Mr. Monroe's first fine elation, when he was helping her on with her coat. Since this was the case, he wondered at himself for feeling a definite let-down in his ardor when, in looking up the lady's telephone number at his office, he met her husband's name in the book. The type seemed like a cold, black barrier. He remembered how, in the years behind him, the presence of competition, even of menace, had only spurred him on. In wending his way back among old memories, Mr. Monroe recalled a cold, glittery night of a long-gone December, when he had stood for hours under a girl's window, throwing pebbles up at it until, for the sake of her reputation, she consented to go to the Christmas dance his fraternity was giving, instead of to another fellow's. She had been reported engaged to the other fellow, too. . . . Judas, it had been cold standing under that window! It *must* have been. He rose and closed the window of his office. The day was bitter and gloomy. He decided not to call the lady until after dinner.

A hot bath and a good dinner at a quiet place put Mr. Monroe in pretty fine fettle. He decided to call the lady up at once. When he got back to his apartment, however, he decided, on further reflection, that this would not be very subtle. No, the way to do it was to drop in on her around midnight. She was one of those people who were invariably up, long after midnight. He wondered how they did it, night in and night out. She would be reading, stretched out, filmily, on a divan, soft, alluring. He would make a striking and graceful entrance. To fortify himself for this adventure—the word "ordeal" just grazed his consciousness—he got out a volume of Henry James. He would begin the communion on a mature, a "wonderful" plane. It might become—who knew?—one of those pleasurable, comfortable, and just slightly aching episodes, which mean so much. He was reduced to a momentary confusion, at this point, when it came to him that the lady might have other patterns in mind than those of Henry James. It also crossed his mind that he was lapsing into a basis singularly devoid, somehow, of that impetuosity which, over his cocktail at dinner, he had told himself he had to get into the affair. *Had* to get?—hell, wanted to!

It was just ten o'clock, and he mustn't drop around until midnight, anyway. That would give any other callers a chance to depart. He lighted a cigar and began reading in "The Golden Bowl." The effect of three minutes of this was to make him undeniably drowsy. "Here, here!" he muttered to himself. He got up and dashed some cold water on his face, before going back to his book and cigar. Even so, his lids shortly began to droop again. Mr. Monroe met this situation grimly. He decided to put on his dinner jacket, and he went to the clothes closet and got it out—or parts of it he could find. He had no notion where his studs might be, but he knew that he ought to know. Little Mrs. Monroe's mocking face kept preceding him wherever he went. Finally he got everything together, and laid the array out on a bed. Then he began leisurely to undress. It struck him, as he glimpsed himself in a long glass, that a tall thin man looks like an ass in socks and garters. The thought depressed him terribly.

Instead of changing into his smoking jacket at once, he placed all his clothes over the backs of chairs, put on a pair of pajamas, and lay down on the bed to smoke a cigarette. Cigars were too heavy; they got to you if you needed sleep. He looked at his watch again. It wasn't quite eleven. Mr.

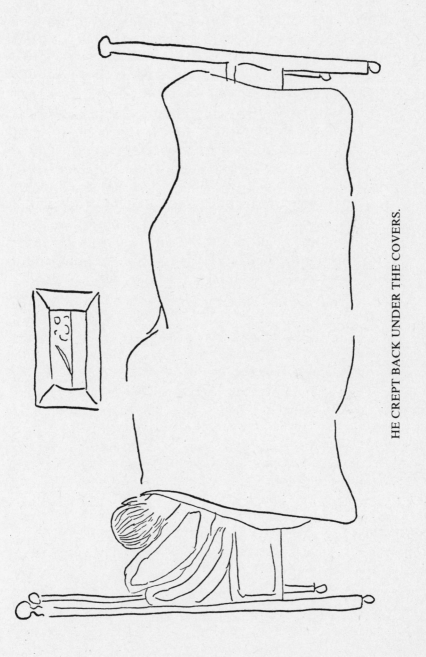

HE CREPT BACK UNDER THE COVERS.

Monroe considered the whole situation again. Perhaps it would be better if he didn't go over until *one*. Then you could be pretty sure any other guests would have departed. Of course he knew that if he waited two hours he would fall asleep. Well, he would set the alarm clock for a quarter to one—give him plenty of time to spring up and get dressed. So he set the clock and crawled beneath the covers.

The loud ringing of the alarm bell woke him, after what seemed only a few minutes. He rose up slowly and shut it off, after which he rested on one elbow for a minute or so. He got, then, with fine resolution, about halfway out of bed, groped for a cigarette, found one, and put it down again without lighting it. Slowly, very slowly, he crept back under the covers, and switched off the light at the head of the bed. He sighed deeply.

PART TWO

The Pet Department

*The idea for the department was suggested by
the daily pet column in the New York Evening Post,
and by several others.*

Q. I enclose a sketch of the way my dog, William, has been lying for two days now. I think there must be something wrong with him. Can you tell me how to get him out of this?

Mrs. L. L. G.

A. I should judge from the drawing that William is in a trance. Trance states, however, are rare with dogs. It may just be ecstasy. If at the end of another twenty-four hours he doesn't seem to be getting anywhere, I should give him up. The position of the ears leads me to believe that he may be enjoying himself in a quiet way, but the tail is somewhat alarming.

Q. Our cat, who is thirty-five, spends all of her time in bed. She follows every move I make, and this is beginning to get to me. She never seems sleepy nor particularly happy. Is there anything I could give her?

Miss L. Mc.

A. There are no medicines which can safely be given to induce felicity in a cat, but you might try lettuce, which is a soporific, for the wakefulness. I would have to see the cat watching you to tell whether anything could be done to divert her attention.

Q. My husband, who is an amateur hypnotizer, keeps trying to get our bloodhound under his control. I contend that this is not doing the dog any good. So far he has not yielded to my husband's influence, but I am afraid that if he once got under, we couldn't get him out of it.

A. A. T.

A. Dogs are usually left cold by all phases of psychology, mental telepathy, and the like. Attempts to hypnotize this particular breed, however, are likely to be fraught with a definite menace. A bloodhound, if stared at fixedly, is liable to gain the impression that it is under suspicion, being followed, and so on. This upsets a bloodhound's life, by completely reversing its whole scheme of behavior.

Q. My wife found this owl in the attic among a lot of ormolu clocks and old crystal chandeliers. We can't tell whether it's stuffed or only dead. It is sitting on a strange and almost indescribable sort of iron dingbat.

MR. MOLLEFF

A. What your wife found is a museum piece—a stuffed cockatoo. It looks to me like a rather botchy example of taxidermy. This is the first stuffed bird I have ever seen with its eyes shut, but whoever had it stuffed probably wanted it stuffed that way. I couldn't say what the thing it is sitting on is supposed to represent. It looks broken.

Q. Our gull cannot get his head down any farther than this, and bumps into things.

H. L. F.

A. You have no ordinary gull to begin with. He looks to me a great deal like a rabbit backing up. If he *is* a gull, it is impossible to keep him in the house. Naturally he will bump into things. Give him his freedom.

Q. My police dog has taken to acting very strange, on account of my father coming home from work every night for the past two years and saying to him, "If you're a police dog, where's your badge?", after which he laughs (my father).

ELLA R.

A. The constant reiteration of any piece of badinage sometimes has the same effect on present-day neurotic dogs that it has on people. It is dangerous and thoughtless to twit a police dog on his powers, authority, and the like. From the way your dog seems to hide behind tables, large vases, and whatever that thing is that looks like a suitcase, I should imagine that your father has carried this thing far enough— perhaps even too far.

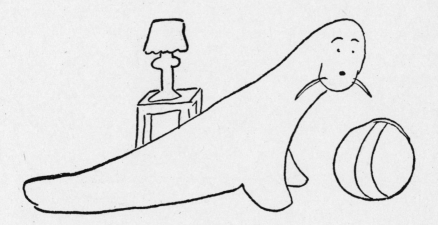

Q. My husband's seal will not juggle, although we have tried everything.

GRACE H.

A. Most seals will not juggle; I think I have never known one that juggled. Seals balance things, and sometimes toss objects (such as the large ball in your sketch) from one to another. This last will be difficult if your husband has but one seal. I'd try him in plain balancing, beginning with a billiard cue or something. It may be, of course, that he is a non-balancing seal.

Q. We have a fish with ears and wonder if it is valuable.

JOE WRIGHT

A. I find no trace in the standard fish books of any fish with ears. Very likely the ears do not belong to the fish, but to some mammal. They look to me like a mammal's ears. It would be pretty hard to say what species of mammal, and almost impossible to determine what particular member of that species. They may merely be hysterical ears, in which case they will go away if you can get the fish's mind on something else.

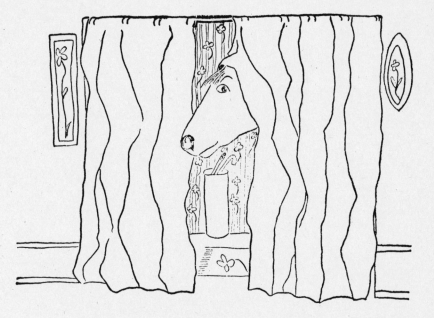

Q. How would you feel if every time you looked up from your work or anything, here was a horse peering at you from behind something? He prowls about the house at all hours of the day and night. Doesn't seem worried about anything, merely wakeful. What should I do to discourage him?

MRS. GRACE VOYNTON

A. The horse is probably sad. Changing the flowered decorations of your home to something less like open meadows might discourage him, but then I doubt whether it is a good idea to discourage a sad horse. In any case speak to him quietly when he turns up from behind things. Leaping at a horse in a house and crying "Roogie, roogie!" or "Whoosh!" would only result in breakage and bedlam. Of course you might finally get used to having him around, if the house is big enough for both of you.

Q. The fact that my dog sits this way so often leads me to
believe that something is preying on his mind. He seems
always to be studying. Would there be any way of finding out
what this is?

ARTHUR

A. Owing to the artificially complex life led by city dogs of
the present day, they tend to lose the simpler systems of
intuition which once guided all breeds, and frequently lapse
into what comes very close to mental perplexity. I myself
have known some very profoundly thoughtful dogs. Usually,
however, their problems are not serious and I should judge
that your dog has merely mislaid something and wonders
where he put it.

Q. We have cats the way most people have mice.

MRS. C. L. FOOTLOOSE

A. I see you have. I can't tell from your communication, however, whether you wish advice or are just boasting.

Q. No one has been able to tell us what kind of dog we have. I am enclosing a sketch of one of his two postures. He only has two. The other one is the same as this except he faces in the opposite direction.

MRS. EUGENIA BLACK

A. I think that what you have is a cast-iron lawn dog. The expressionless eye and the rigid pose are characteristic of metal lawn animals. And that certainly is a cast-iron ear. You could, however, remove all doubt by means of a simple test with a hammer and a cold chisel, or an acetylene torch. If the animal chips, or melts, my diagnosis is correct.

Q. My oldest boy, Ford Maddox Ford Griswold, worked this wooden horse loose from a merry-go-round one night when he and some other young people were cutting up. Could you suggest any use for it in a family of five?

MRS. R. L. S. GRISWOLD

A. I cannot try the patience of my public nor waste my own time dealing with the problems of insensate animals. Already I have gone perhaps too far afield in the case of stuffed birds and cast-iron lawn dogs. Pretty soon I should be giving advice on wire-haired fox terrier weather-vanes.

Q. Mr. Jennings bought this beast when it was a pup in Montreal for a St. Bernard, but I don't think it is. It's grown enormously and is stubborn about letting you have anything, like the bath towel it has its paws on, and the hat, both of which belong to Mr. Jennings. He got it that bowling ball to play with but it doesn't seem to like it. Mr. Jennings is greatly attached to the creature.

MRS. FANNY EDWARDS JENNINGS

A. What you have is a bear. While it isn't my bear, I should recommend that you dispose of it. As these animals grow older they get more and more adamant about letting you have anything, until finally there might not be anything in the house you could call your own—except possibly the bowling ball. Zoos use bears. Mr. Jennings could visit it.

Q. Sometimes my dog does not seem to know me. I think he must be crazy. He will draw away, or show his fangs, when I approach him.

H. M. MORGAN, JR.

A. So would I, and I'm not crazy. If you creep up on your dog the way you indicate in the drawing, I can understand his viewpoint. Put your shirt in and straighten up; you look as if you had never seen a dog before, and that is undoubtedly what bothers the animal. These maladjustments can often be worked out by the use of a little common sense.

Q. After a severe storm we found this old male raven in the study of my father, the Hon. George Morton Bodwell, for many years head of the Latin Department at Tufts, sitting on a bust of Livy which was a gift to him from the class of '92. All that the old bird will say is "Grawk." Can ravens be taught to talk or was Poe merely "romancing"?

MRS. H. BODWELL COLWETHER

A. I am handicapped by an uncertainty as to who says "Grawk," the raven or your father. It just happens that "Arrk" is what ravens say. I have never known a raven that said anything but "Arrk."

Q. I have three Scotch terriers which take things out of closets and down from shelves, etc. My veterinarian advised me to gather together all the wreckage, set them down in the midst of it, and say "ba-ad Scotties!" This, however, merely seems to give them a kind of pleasure. If I spank one, the other two jump me—playfully, but they jump me.

MRS. O. S. PROCTOR

A. To begin with, I question the advisability of having three Scotch terriers. They are bound to get you down. However, it seems to me that you are needlessly complicating your own problem. The Scotties probably think that you are trying to enter into the spirit of their play. Their inability to comprehend what you are trying to get at will in the end make them melancholy, and you and the dogs will begin to drift farther and farther apart. I'd deal with each terrier, and each object, separately, beginning with the telephone, the disconnection of which must inconvenience you sorely.

Q. My husband paid a hundred and seventy-five dollars for this moose to a man in Dorset, Ontario, who said he had trapped it in the woods. Something is wrong with his antlers, for we have to keep twisting them back into place all the time. They're loose.

MRS. OLIPHANT BEATTY

A. You people are living in a fool's paradise. The animal is obviously a horse with a span of antlers strapped onto his head. If you really want a moose, dispose of the horse; if you want to keep the horse, take the antlers off. Their constant pressure on his ears isn't a good idea.

PART THREE

Ladies' and Gentlemen's Guide to Modern English Usage

Inspired by Mr. H. W. Fowler's excellent "Dictionary of Modern English Usage."

Who and Whom

THE NUMBER of people whose use "whom" and "who" wrongly is appalling. The problem is a difficult one and it is complicated by the importance of tone, or taste. Take the common expression, "Whom are you, anyways?" That is of course, strictly speaking, correct—and yet how formal, how stilted! The usage to be preferred in ordinary speech and writing is "Who are you, anyways?" "Whom" should be used in the nominative case only when a note of dignity or austerity is desired. For example, if a writer is dealing with a meeting of, say, the British Cabinet, it would be better to have the Premier greet a new arrival, such as an under-secretary, with a "Whom are you, anyways?" rather than a "Who are you, anyways?"—always granted that the Premier is sincerely unaware of the man's identity. To address a person one knows by a "Whom are you?" is a mark either of incredible lapse of memory or inexcusable arrogance. "How are you?" is a much kindlier salutation.

The Buried Whom, as it is called, forms a special problem. This is where the word occurs deep in a sentence. For a ready example, take the common expression: "He did not know whether he knew her or not because he had not heard whom the other had said she was until too late to see her." The

TO ADDRESS A PERSON ONE KNOWS BY A "WHOM ARE YOU?" IS A
MARK OF INEXCUSABLE ARROGANCE.

simplest way out of this is to abandon the "whom"
altogether and substitute "where" (a reading of the sentence
that way will show how much better it is). Unfortunately, it is
only in rare cases that "where" can be used in place of
"whom." Nothing could be more flagrantly bad, for instance,
than to say "Where are you?" in demanding a person's
identity. The only conceivable answer is "Here I am," which
would give no hint at all as to whom the person was. Thus
the conversation, or piece of writing, would, from being built
upon a false foundation, fall of its own weight.

A common rule for determining whether "who" or

A PROPER GREETING BETWEEN GENTLEMEN OF BREEDING.

"whom" is right is to substitute "she" for "who," and "her" for "whom," and see which sounds the better. Take the sentence, "He met a woman who they said was an actress." Now if "who" is correct then "she" can be used in its place. Let us try it. "He met a woman she they said was an actress." That instantly rings false. It can't be right. Hence the proper usage is "whom."

In certain cases grammatical correctness must often be subordinated to a consideration of taste. For instance, suppose that the same person had met a man whom they said was a street-cleaner. The word "whom" is too austere to use in connection with a lowly worker, like a street-cleaner, and its use in this form is known as False Administration or Pathetic Fallacy.

You might say: "There is, then, no hard and fast rule?" ("was then" would be better, since "then" refers to what is past). You might better say, then (or have said): "There was then (or is now) no hard and fast rule?" Only this, that it is better to use "whom" when in doubt, and even better to re-word the statement, and leave out all the relative pro-nouns, except ad, ante, con, in , inter, ob, post, prae, pro, sub, and super.

Which

THE RELATIVE pronoun "which" can cause more trouble than any other word, if recklessly used. Foolhardy persons sometimes get lost in which-clauses and are never heard of again. My distinguished contemporary, Fowler, cites several tragic cases, of which the following is one: "It was rumoured that Beaconsfield intended opening the Conference with a speech in French, his pronunciation of which language

ELIZA CROSSING THE ICE.

(This conception of the famous incident departs radically from the old and generally accepted notion that Eliza maintained, at all times, a position slightly in advance of the bloodhounds. It also departs radically from other notions.)

leaving everything to be desired . . ." That's as much as Mr. Fowler quotes because, at his age, he was afraid to go any farther. The young man who originally got into that sentence was never found. His fate, however, was not as terrible as that of another adventurer who became involved in a remarkable which-mire. Fowler has followed his devious course as far as he safely could on foot: "Surely what applies to games should also apply to racing, the leaders of which being the very people from whom an example might well be looked for . . ." Not even Henry James could have successfully emerged from a sentence with "which," "whom," and "being" in it. The safest way to avoid such things is to follow in the path of the American author, Ernest Hemingway. In his youth he was trapped in a which-clause one time and barely escaped with his mind. He was going along on solid ground until he got into this: "It was the one thing of which, being very much afraid—for whom has not been warned to fear such things—he . . ." Being a young and powerfully built man, Hemingway was able to fight his way back to where he had started, and begin again. This time he skirted the treacherous morass in this way: "He was afraid of one thing. This was the one thing. He had been warned to fear such things. Everybody has been warned to fear such things." Today Hemingway is alive and well, and many happy writers are following along the trail he blazed.

What most people don't realize is that one "which" leads to another. Trying to cross a paragraph by leaping from "which" to "which" is like Eliza crossing the ice. The danger is in missing a "which" and falling in. A case in point is this: "He went up to a pew which was in the gallery, which brought him under a colored window which he loved and always quieted his spirit."

The writer, worn out, missed the last "which"—the one that should come just before "always" in that sentence. But supposing he had got it in! We would have: "He went up to a pew which was in the gallery, which brought him under a colored window which he loved and which always quieted his spirit." Your inveterate whicher in this way gives the effect of tweeting like a bird or walking with a crutch, and is not welcome in the best company.

It is well to remember that one "which" leads to two and that two "whiches" multiply like rabbits. You should never start out with the idea that you can get by with one "which." Suddenly they are all around you. Take a sentence like this: "It imposes a problem which we either solve, or perish." On a hot night, or after a hard day's work, a man often lets himself get by with a monstrosity like that, but suppose he dictates that sentence bright and early in the morning. It comes to him typed out by his stenographer and he instantly senses that something is the matter with it. He tries to reconstruct the sentence, still clinging to the "which," and gets something like this: "It imposes a problem which we either solve, or which, failing to solve, we must perish on

AMERICAN RABBIT, OR "WHICH."

account of." He goes to the water-cooler, gets a drink, sharpens his pencil, and grimly tries again. "It imposes a problem which we either solve or which we don't solve and . . ." He begins once more: "It imposes a problem which we either solve, or which we do not solve, and from which . . ." The more times he does it the more "whiches" he gets. The way out is simple: "We must either solve this problem, or perish." Never monkey with "which." Nothing except getting tangled up in a typewriter ribbon is worse.

The Split Infinitive

WORD HAS somehow got around that a split infinitive is always wrong. This is of a piece with the sentimental and outworn notion that it is always wrong to strike a lady. Everybody will recall at least one woman of his acquaintance whom, at one time, or another, he has had to punch or slap. I have in mind a charming lady who is overcome by the unaccountable desire, at formal dinners with red and white wines, to climb up on the table and lie down. Her dinner companions used at first to pinch her, under cover of the conversation, but she pinched right back or, what is even less defensible, tickled. They finally learned that they could make her hold her seat only by fetching her a smart downward blow on the head. She would then sit quietly through the rest of the dinner, smiling dreamily and nodding at people, and looking altogether charming.

A man who does not know his own strength could, of course, all too easily overshoot the mark and, instead of producing the delightful languor to which I have alluded, knock his companion completely under the table, an

A CHARMING LADY OVERCOME BY THE UNACCOUNTABLE DESIRE
TO CLIMB UP ON THE TABLE AND LIE DOWN.

awkward situation which should be avoided at all costs
because it would leave two men seated next each other. I
know of one man who, to avert this *faux pas*, used to punch
his dinner companion in the side (she would begin to cry
during the red-wine courses), a blow which can be executed,
as a rule, with less fuss, but which has the disadvantage of
almost always causing the person who is struck to shout. The
hostess, in order to put her guest at her ease, must shout too,
which is almost certain to arouse one of those nervous, high-
strung men, so common at formal dinners, to such a pitch
that he will begin throwing things. There is nothing more
deplorable than the spectacle of a formal dinner party ending
in a brawl. And yet it is surprising how even the most

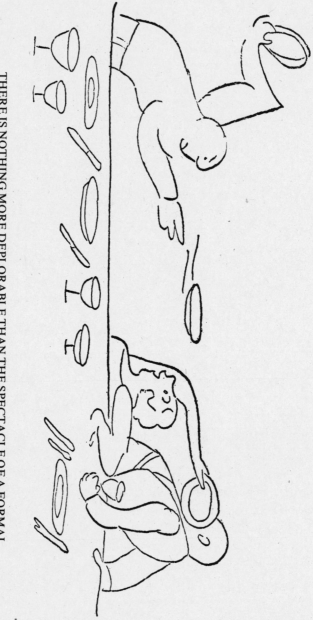

THERE IS NOTHING MORE DEPLORABLE THAN THE SPECTACLE OF A FORMAL
DINNER PARTY ENDING IN A BRAWL.

cultured and charming people can go utterly to pieces when something is unexpectedly thrown at table. They instantly have an overwhelming desire to "join in." Everybody has, at one time or another, experienced the urge to throw a plate of jelly or a half grapefruit, an urge comparable to the inclination that suddenly assails one to leap from high places. Usually this tendency passes as quickly as it comes, but it is astounding how rapidly it can be converted into action once the spell of dignity and well-bred reserve is broken by the sight of, say, a green-glass salad plate flying through the air. It is all but impossible to sit quietly by while someone is throwing salad plates. One is stirred to participation not only by the swift progress of the objects and their crash as they hit something, but also by the cries of "Whammy!" and "Whoop!", with which most men accompany the act of hurling plates. In the end someone is bound to be caught over the eye by a badly aimed plate and rendered unconscious.

My contemporary, Mr. Fowler, in a painstaking analysis of the split infinitive, divides the English-speaking world into five classes as regards this construction: those who don't know and don't care, those who don't know and do care, those who know and approve, those who know and condemn, and those who know and discriminate. (The fact that there was no transition at all between the preceding paragraph and this one does not mean that I did not try, in several different ways, to get back to the split infinitive logically. As in a bridge hand, the absence of a reëntry is not always the fault of the man who is playing the hand, but of the way the cards lie in the dummy. To say more would only make it more difficult that it now is, if possible, to get back to Mr. Fowler.) Mr. Fowler's point is, of course, that there are good split infinitives and bad ones. For instance, he contends that it is better to say "Our object is to further cement trade relations," thus splitting "to cement," than to say "Our object is further to cement trade relations," because the use of "further" before "to cement" might lead the reader to

IT IS ALL BUT IMPOSSIBLE TO SIT QUIETLY WHEN SOMEONE IS THROWING SALAD PLATES.

think it had the weight of "moreover" rather than of "increasingly." My own way out of all this confusion would be simply to say "Our object is to let trade relations ride," that is, give them up, let them go. Some people would regard the abandonment of trade relations, merely for the purpose of avoiding grammatical confusion, as a weak-kneed and unpatriotic action. That, it seems to me, is a matter for each person to decide for himself. A man who, like myself, has no knowledge at all of trade relations, cannot be expected to take the same interest in cementing them as, say, the statesman or the politician. This is no reflection on trade relations.

Only and One

WHERE TO use "only" in a sentence is a moot question, one of the mootest questions in all rhetoric. The purist will say that the expression: "He only died last week," is incorrect, and that it should be: "He died only last week." The purist's contention is that the first sentence, if carried out to a natural conclusion, would give us something like this: "He only died last week, he didn't do anything else, that's all he did." It isn't a natural conclusion, however, because nobody would say that and if anybody did it would be likely to lead to stomping of feet and clapping of hands, because it is one of those singy-songy expressions which set a certain type of person to acting rowdy and becoming unmanageable. It is better just to let the expression go, either one way or the other, because, after all, this particular sentence is of no importance except in cases where one is breaking the news to a mother. In such cases one should begin with: "Mrs.

Gormley, your son has had an accident," or: "Mrs. Gormley, your son is not so good," and then lead up gently to: "He died only last week."

The best way is often to omit "only" and use some other expression. Thus, instead of saying, "He only died last week," one could say: "It was no longer ago than last Thursday that George L. Wodolgoffing became an angel." Moreover, this is more explicit and eliminates the possibility of a misunderstanding as to who died. The greatest care in this regard, by the way, should be taken with the verbs "to die," "to love," "to embezzle," and the like. In this connection, it is well never to use "only" at the beginning of a sentence—"Only one person loves me," for example. This of course makes it necessary to capitalize "Only" and there is the risk of a hurried reader taking it for a proper noun and confusing it with the late Richard Olney, who was Secretary of State under Cleveland.

The indefinite "one" is another source of trouble and is frequently the cause of disagreeable scenes. Such a sentence as "One loves one's friends" is considered by some persons to be stilted and over-formalized, and such persons insist that "One loves his friends" is permissible. It is not permissible, however, because "one" is indefinite and "his" is definite and the combination is rhetorically impossible. This is known as hendiadys and was a common thing in Latin. Rare examples of it still exist and are extremely valuable as antiques, although it is usually unsafe to sit or lie down on one.

The chief objection to a consistent, or "cross-country" use of "one" is that it tends to make a sentence sound like a trombone solo—such as: "One knows one's friends will help one if one is in trouble, or at least one trusts one's friends will help one." Even though this is correct, to the point of being impeccable, there is no excuse for it. The "one" enthusiast should actually take up the trombone and let it go at that.

"One" is, as a matter of fact, too often used for the

personal pronoun. What, for example, could be sillier than to
write a lady like this: "One loves you and one wonders if you
love one." Such a person is going to get nowhere. "I love
you. Do you love me?" is a much simpler and better way to
say it, except, of course, that there is always the danger here
of drifting into a popular ballad of the "Ramona" type.

Some persons use neither the indefinite "one" nor the

GEORGE L. WODOLGOFFING BECOMES AN ANGEL.

definite pronoun, but substitute a pet name and get some
such result as "Mopsy loves Flopsy and wonders if Flopsy
loves Mopsy." This usage frequently gets into the newspapers
and becomes famous, particularly if Flopsy is an ambitious
blonde and Mopsy a wealthy mop-handle manufacturer. The
fault here, however, is not so much with the nouns or
pronouns as with the verb, "to love." Nothing can be done
about the verb "to love."

Whether

. . . A CERTAIN type of person is wont to let "whether" get him down. For one thing, he will wear himself out doubling the alternative. That is, he will write some such clause as "Whether or not the birds will or will not come north this year." Either "or not" or "or will not" should be dropped. If one or the other isn't dropped, an ornithologist can get into all sorts of trouble, such as "Whether or not the nuthatch will or will not hatch, is not known." If the thing goes as far as that, a person should drop ornithology too. A good ornithologist doesn't need "whethers." He should know whether or not the bird will hatch, and say so.

The use of "whether" after "doubt" is another troublesome matter. Yet the rule is simple. When the sentence is affirmative, use "whether"—"I doubt whether he will go." When the sentence is negative, use "that"—"I do not doubt that he will go." Practically nobody remembers this rule, however, and the best thing to do is carry it on a little slip of

THE NUTHATCH.

NOTHING CAN END A COURTSHIP ANY FASTER THAN TO APPEAR
TO BE BOXING.

paper in your pocket and refer to it when needed. In great crises, it is well not to bother with either one. For example, if a gentleman wishes to address a lady as follows, "I no longer doubt whether (that) I love you," the best modern usage is simply to place his arms around her waist. In this case her arms should go around his shoulders. Occasionally a gentleman will put his arms around a lady's shoulders and expect her to put hers around his waist. Since this is contrary to accepted custom, the result often is that both parties reach for the same place, i.e., waist or shoulders, at the same time, and thus appear to be boxing. Nothing can end a courtship any faster than to appear to be boxing. If a gentleman is going to depart from the common practice he should give warning.

The question of when to use "whether or no" instead of "whether or not" will likely never be decided now. Grammarians have avoided the subject since the deplorable experience of Dr. Amos Crawley, M.A., LL.D., who, in his invaluable but, alas, uncompleted monograph, "Clarified Expression," unaccountably got involved, while his wife and servants were away and he was alone in the house, in a construction beginning: "Whether or not 'whether or no' is ever preferable to 'whether or not' depends on whether or not . . ." at which point he was stricken. The best advice is make up your mind and avoid doubt-clauses.

The Subjunctive Mood

THE IMPORTANCE of correct grammar in the home can not be over-estimated. Two young people should make sure that each is rhetorically sound before they get married, because grammatical precision, particularly in mood, is just as important as anything else. Rhetoric and sex, in fact, are so closely related that when one becomes confused they both become confused. Take the subjunctive. Fowler, in his book on modern English usage, says the subjunctive is dying, but adds that there are still a few truly living uses, which he groups under "Alives, Revivals, Survivals and Arrivals." Curiously enough, he leaves out Departures, which it seems to me are just as important as Arrivals. Let us examine the all too common domestic situation where the husband arrives just after another gentleman has departed—or just after he thinks another gentleman has departed (Suppositional Departures lead to just as much bitterness, and even more subjunctives, than Actual Departures).

The wife, in either case, is almost sure to go into the subjunctive—very likely before any accusation is made. Among the most common subjunctives which she will be inclined to use are those of indignation and hauteur, such as "Be that as it may," "Far be it from me," etc. For the moment, she is safe enough in the subjunctive, because her husband has probably gone into it, too, using "Would God I were," "If there be justice," and so on. Wives select the subjunctive usually because it is the best mood in which to

A HUSBAND (LEFT) ENCOUNTERS A LOVER.

spar for time, husbands because it lends itself most easily to ranting and posturing. As long as they both stay in it they are safe. Misunderstandings are almost certain to arise, however, when the husband goes into the indicative, as he is pretty sure to do. He usually does this preparatory to dismissing his suspicions, a step toward which every husband is impelled by his natural egotism. First he will begin with a plain past-tense indicative if-clause—just to show that he knows who the man is—prior to dismissing him.

"If George Spangrell was here," the husband will begin, lighting a cigarette, "I . . ."

"Well, what would you do if he *were*?" demands the wife.

The confusion, which begins at this point, is pretty intricate. The husband has gone into the indicative, but his wife has stayed in the subjunctive and, furthermore, she thinks that he is still there, too. Thus she thinks he intended to say: "If George Spangrell was here [that is, now] I would tell him what I think of him, the low scoundrel." There is no excuse for a wife prematurely imputing such a suspicion or such a rhetorical monstrosity to her husband. What he probably intended to say was merely something like this: "If George Spangrell was here, I wouldn't like it, but of course I know he wasn't, dear." However, misunderstandings now begin to pile up. The husband is instantly made suspicious by her "What would you do if he *were*?" He considers her "were" tantamount to "is." (This quick-tempered construction, of course, makes the "would" in his wife's sentence ridiculous, for, had she meant "is" instead of "were" she would have substituted "will" for "would.") The situation is much too involved now, however, for the husband to make an effort to parse anything. He instantly abandons all grammatical analysis, and begins to look about, peering into the wardrobe, swishing under beds with a cane or umbrella.

His wife now has the advantage of him, not only in mood, but in posture. A woman must naturally view with disdain and contempt any man who is down on all fours unless he had taken that position for the purpose of playing horse with some children—an extenuation which we need not discuss here. To meet her on even terms, the husband should walk, not crawl, from wardrobe to chaise-longue, using the mandatory subjunctive in a firm voice, as follows: "If anyone be in (or under) there, let him come out!" ["Come out" is better here than "emerge" because stronger, but a husband should not fall into the colloquial "Come on out of that!" He may, however, if he so wishes, address the gentleman, whether he be present or not, as "Spangrell" but never "Mr.

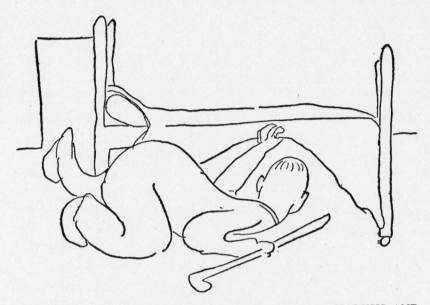

HE INSTANTLY ABANDONS ALL GRAMMATICAL ANALYSIS AND
BEGINS TO SWISH UNDER BEDS.

Spangrell" (Hypocritical Dignification) and certainly never
as "George"—the use of the given name being in extreme
bad taste where no endearment is intended.]

The wife of course will resent all these goings-on, and the
quarrel that results will probably last late into the night.

There are several ways to prevent a situation like this. In
the first place, when a husband says "was" a wife should
instantly respond with "wasn't". Most husbands will take a
"wasn't" at its face value, because it preserves their egotism
and self-respect. On the other hand, "if . . . were" is always
dangerous. Husbands have come to know that a wife's
"if . . . were" usually means that what she is presenting as
purely hypothetical is, in reality, a matter of fact. Thus, if a
wife begins, one evening after an excellent dinner, "Dear,
what would you do, if I were the sort of woman who had,
etc.," her husband knows full well that it is going to turn out
that she is the sort of woman who has. Husbands are

suspicious of all subjunctives. Wives should avoid them. Once a woman has "if . . . were'd" a Mr. Sprangrell, her husband is, nine times out of ten, going to swish under the chaise-longue. Even if he finds no one, the situation becomes extremely awkward, and there is of course always the plaguey hundredth chance that he may discover a strange cane or pair of gloves.

The best of all ways out is for the husband to go instantly into the future indicative and say, with great dignity, "I shall go down to the drugstore." Ordinarily, his wife would reply, "Oh, no you won't," but with all the doubt and suspicion in the air, she will be inclined to humor him and let him have his way. She is certain to, if Spangrell is in the clothes hamper.

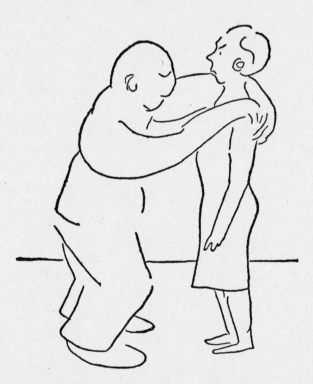

ORDINARILY, HIS WIFE WOULD REPLY, "OH, NO YOU WON'T!"

Exclamation Points and Colons

I SHALL cite, to begin with, a few general "don'ts" for exclamation marks. One general "don't" could well cover the whole thing, for the exclamation mark is never actually necessary, but the shock of giving them all up at once might prove fatal to those unfortunate writers who have become addicts. Yet some excellent books have been written without a single exclamation mark, among them "The Art of Rodin," which is a collection of photographs of the sculptor's statues with a brief foreword by Louis Wenberg, or Weinberg. On the other hand, such eminent stylists and impeccable rhetoricians as Cabell bestrew their novels with exclamation points. Very likely Cabell, who is never really excited about anything, leaves them out, and the linotypers put them in. The whole fabric of English usage, I might say in passing, is complicated by linotypers. They frequently play a game with an author, by mail, similar to chess. The author sends in a manuscript without exclamation marks, the linotyper puts them in, the author takes them out in proof, the linotyper puts them back in, together with a couple of etaoins. That's pretty much inside publishing-house stuff, however, and any further comment on it here—or anywhere else—wouldn't do much good. The "don'ts" with which I am concerned are aimed at the layman, the man and woman letter-writer.

Don't use an exclamation mark in a moment of anger. If you insert one in a fit of temper, lay aside the letter until morning. You will be surprised how silly it will seem then— not only the exclamation mark but the whole letter. That brings us to the colon, or if it doesn't, we'll drag in the colon. It is my contention that a colon could almost always be used in place of an exclamation point. Its use as a symbol of passionate expression is not, I'll grant you, well known, and yet it lends itself to finer shadings of excitement than the exclamation mark, which after all is a hybrid composed, on most typewriters, by striking, successively, the period, the back-spacer, and the apostrophe. This process of synthesis usually takes from six to eight seconds and is very frequently complicated by accidentally striking the upper-case shift-lock key, thus setting the machine so that it writes solely in capitals. In this way a person, after making his exclamation mark, will sometimes go on to write six or eight sentences in capital letters without realizing he is doing it. He then either has to go back over those sentences and draw a diagonal line across each letter—the proofreader's sign for "restore to lower case"—or else, if he lets the capitalized words stand, he must enclose a separate note explaining what happened. All this takes time, and diverts the writer's mind from what he was trying to say. Furthermore, by following his exclamation mark with several lines of capitalized sentences, screaming and bawling across the page, he has made the exclamation mark seem ridiculous and ineffective. The best way to avoid all these complications is to use a pen or pencil. This is, however, the age of the typewriter—even love letters are written on typewriters. Thus it will be helpful to learn that the colon, which is typed by striking only one key, can be employed in the place of the exclamation mark in almost any given sentence where the emotion one wishes to express is of an amatory nature.

Take the sentence "You are wonderful!" That's trite, and it's made triter by the exclamation point, but if one writes it thus: "You are: wonderful," it's certainly not trite and it has a richness that the other hadn't or hasn't—"hadn't" is better, I guess. Nothing so closely resembles the catch in the voice of the lover as that very colon. Instead of shouting the word "wonderful," as the exclamation point does, it forces a choking pause before that word, thus giving an effect of tense, nervous endearment, which is certainly what the writer is after. Of course whether he *should* be after that effect, no matter how the sentence is punctuated, is a separate problem. Sentences of the kind, especially when written by a gentleman

EVEN LOVE LETTERS ARE WRITTEN ON TYPEWRITERS.

to a lady, are never altogether safe. They are almost sure to lead to some further encomium, to some definitely compromising confession. If the gentleman then marries someone else, the lady may sue. Even if he marries someone else and she doesn't sue, he is likely to worry and fret, believing that she will, and the effect on his general health will be about the same as if she did.

I think that Fowler in his "Modern English Usage" does not discriminate as carefully as he should between what is proper and safe in exclamations and what is proper and dangerous. He makes several groupings of proper usages, one of them being "You miserable coward!, You little dear!" Obviously there's a difference in possible ultimate effect here. The former could not very easily lead to a suit for libel, but the latter could easily drift into a suit for breach of promise, and is therefore not safe. Of his other groupings of

EVEN IF HE MARRIES SOMEONE ELSE, AND SHE DOESN'T SUE, HE IS LIKELY
TO WORRY AND FRET, BELIEVING THAT SHE WILL.

recommended usages, I should most assuredly warn any gentleman against writing to any woman any part of the list which Fowler gives as No. 4. This includes: "What a difference it makes!, What I suffered!, How I love you!" If one is going to use a whole group, I'd say take his No. 5, which is, in full: "Not another word!, If only I could!, That it should come to this!, Much care you!, Pop goes the weasel!, A fine friend you have been!" That is not only safe—it leans over backwards. All correspondence would probably be ended after such a letter, and that is always rather more desirable than deplorable.

The Perfect Infinitive

IT IS easy enough to say that a person should live in such a way as to avoid the perfect infinitive after the past conditional, but it is another matter to do it. The observance of the commonest amenities of life constantly leads us into that usage. Let us take a typical case. A gentleman and his wife, calling on friends, find them not at home. The gentleman decides to leave a note of regret couched in a few well-chosen words, and the first thing he knows he is involved in this: "We would have liked to have found you in." Reading it over, the gentleman is assailed by the suspicion that he has too many "haves," and that the whole business has somehow been put too far into the past. His first reaction is to remedy this by dating the note: "9 p.m. Wednesday, Jan. 21, 1931." This at once seems too formal, and with a sigh he starts in again on the sentence itself. That is where he makes a fatal mistake. The simplest way out, as always, is to seek some other method of expressing the thought. In this case the gentleman should simply dash off, "Called. You were out. Sorry," and go home to bed. What he does, however, is to lapse into a profound study of this particular grammatical situation, than which there is no more hazardous mental occupation. His wife should, above all things, not choose this time to nag at him, or hurry him. His condition now calls for the utmost kindness and consideration.

First the victim will change the sentence to: "We would have liked to find you in." Now as a matter of fact, this is correct (barring the use of "would" instead of "should"), but, alas, the gentleman does not realize it. Few people ever do realize it. This is because the present infinitive, "to find," seems to imply success. They therefore fall back on the perfect infinitive, "to have found," because it implies that the thing hoped for did not come to pass. They have fallen back on it so often that, after the ordinary past tenses, its use has come to be counted as idiomatic, even though it is incorrect. After past conditionals, however—such as our gentleman caller has got into—the use of the perfect infinitive is not even idiomatic. It is just dangerous.

The gentleman, with two variants on his hands, takes to mumbling them to himself, first one and then the other— "We would have liked to have found you in," "We would have liked to find you in." After he does this several times, both expressions begin to sound meaningless. They don't make any sense at all, let alone make precise sense. His mental feeling is analogous to the terror that strikes into children's minds when they get to repeating some common word, like "saucer," over and over again, until it sounds idiotic and legendary. At this point it would be infinitely better not to leave any note at all, but the gentleman's education and his strength of mind have been challenged. He takes an envelope out of his pocket and grimly makes a list of all the possible combinations, thus getting: "We would have liked to have found," "We would have liked to find," "We would like to have found," and "We would like to find." A dull pain takes him back of the ears. This is the danger sign, and his wife should have the presence of mind to summon assistance, for he is now out of hand and uncontrollable. What she does, however, is to say, "Here, let me write it." He instantly snarls "I'm no child" or "Get away" or some such thing, and his difficulties are added to by the quarrel which follows. At length he has the bright inspiration of going into the hope clauses and turns out: "We had hoped to have been able to have found." If he has married the right kind of woman, she will hastily scratch a brief word on a calling card, shove it under the door, and drag her husband away. Otherwise he will sink rapidly into a serious mental state, from which it may take him weeks to emerge.

There is a simple rule about past conditionals which will prevent a lapse into that deep contemplation which is so often fatal. After "would have liked," "would have hoped," "would have feared," etc., use the present infinitive. The implication of non-fulfillment is inherent in the governing verb itself, that is, in the "would have liked," etc. You don't have to shade the infinitive to get a nice note of frustration. Let it alone. Dr. Fowler himself says: "Sometimes a writer, dimly aware that 'would have liked to have done' is wrong, is yet so fascinated by the perfect infinitive that he clings to that at all costs." That's what it is—a fascination—like a cobra's for a bird. Avoid the perfect infinitive after the past conditional as you would a cobra.

Adverbal Advice

SOMEONE HAS written in to ask whether to say "I feel bad" or "I feel badly." The question is not so easy as it might seem. Your conscientious grammarian will find out, if he has time, just what is the matter with the person who makes the inquiry, or whether anything is the matter. No one wants to just go ahead and advise a person to say either "I feel bad" or "I feel badly," much less to say both of them, because in so many cases the ailment is purely imaginary. Even if it isn't, solicitude for those who love us and who suffer when we suffer should prevent us from talking about our troubles. Yet that attitude has its drawbacks, because some people cannot suffer in silence, or even imagine they are suffering in silence, without making strange grimaces. This is likely to lead to misunderstandings and unpleasantness. Merely saying nothing, then, is scarcely the best way to avoid the use of "bad" or "badly." On the other hand, the grammarian is reluctant to advise a person who really feels bad, or badly, to say that he feels fine. This might, for one thing, revive that old wall-card about "every day in every way I am getting better and better," an expression the world is well rid of. Physically, it was never really true, and rhetorically it was nothing much.

The thing comes down finally to the necessity for special rules. As a general thing, if the illness or pain really exists, and is acute, it is better to use the shorter word "bad," because it is more easily said and will bring assistance quicker. Furthermore "badly" sounds as if the person who had used it had deliberately chosen a euphemism and therefore couldn't be very sick. In cases of sharp, flashing pains, blind staggers, acute heart attacks, or extreme danger generally, it is wise to abandon all adverbial constructions and resort to exclamations and interjections, such as "help!," "hey!," "hi! hi!," "halloo, there!," and the like.

The use of "I feel bad" and "I feel badly" is rather common in married life, particularly in cases where a husband wishes to stay home from a bridge party. Many husbands also use the expressions merely to gain sympathy or attention, but as a rule they prefer some more ominous statement, such as "I think I am dying, dear," or "I guess it's

IT IS WISE TO RESORT TO EXCLAMATIONS, SUCH AS "HELP!" "HEY!" ETC.

all up with me, Marion." Cold applications or a stiff lecture on the hygiene of eating and drinking will sometimes serve to shut them up.

There is, of course, a special problem presented by the type of person who looks well even when he doesn't feel well, and who is not likely to be believed if he says he doesn't feel well. In such cases, the sufferer should say, "I look well, but I don't feel well." While this usage has the merit of avoiding the troublesome words "bad" and "badly," it also has the disadvantage of being a negative statement. If a person is actually ill, the important thing is to find out not how he doesn't feel, but how he does feel. He should state his symptoms more specifically—"I have a gnawing pain here, that comes and goes," or something of the sort. There is always the danger, of course, that one's listeners will cut in with a long description of how *they* feel; this can usually be avoided by screaming.

THIS CAN USUALLY BE AVOIDED BY SCREAMING.

Another adverbial construction which gives considerable trouble, or will if you let it, is the adverb ending in "-lily." The best thing to do with the adverb in "-lily" is to let it alone. "Lovelily" is an example. You can say "he plays lovelily," but even though the word is perfectly proper, it won't get you anywhere. You might just get by with it at a concert; but try shouting it at a ball game. There isn't one person in ten who will go ahead with a friendship in which the "-lily" adverbs are likely to occur. The possible endings of this sort are numberless: you can even say, and be right, "heavenlily" and "ruffianlily." It is especially advisable to avoid this construction because of its "Thematic Potentiality." Thematic Potentiality is the quality which certain words and phrases have of suggesting a theme song—that is, some such thing as "Heaven Lily O'Mine," "Ruffian Lily, Come Back to Me," "Love Vo-deo-do Lily," and so on. Think of something else.

The
Middle-Aged
Man
on the
Flying
Trapeze

The Gentleman Is Cold

IN THE first chill days of November it was the subject of sharp and rather nasty comment on the part of my friends and colleagues that I went about the draughty streets of town without a hat or overcoat. Once even a stranger who passed me in the street snarled, "Put on your hat and coat!" It seemed to annoy people. They began to insinuate under their breath, and even come right out and say, that I was simply trying to look strange and different in order to attract attention. This accusation was made with increasing bitterness when my hair, which I always forget to have cut, began to get very long. It was obvious, my friends said, that I walked about the city cold and miserable in the hope that people would nudge their companions and say, "There goes Jacob Thurman, the eccentric essayist."

There was, and is, no basis to these charges at all. I have reasons, and good reasons, for not wanting to, for, in fact, not being able to, wear an overcoat. I have just as good reasons about the hat, but I needn't go into them so fully. A week or so ago, however, the smirking remarks and mean innuendoes of my associates forced me one day to put on my overcoat (I couldn't find my hat and I wouldn't buy a new one, because when I try one on and peer in the triplicate

115

mirrors they have in hat shops, I catch unexpected angles of my face which make me look like a slightly ill professor of botany who is also lost). The overcoat, which I bought in 1930, after a brief and losing battle with a sharp-tongued clerk who was taller than I am, does not fit me very well and never did fit me very well. That's one reason I don't like to wear it. Another is that it has no buttons (it didn't have any buttons after the first week) and is extremely difficult to manange in a head wind. In such a wind I used to grab for my hat with both hands, thus letting go the hold I had on my coat to keep it together in front, and the whole thing would belly out all around me. Once, in grabbing for my hat (and missing it, for I was a fraction of a second too late), I knocked my glasses off and was not only caught in a grotesque swirl of overcoat right at the corner of Fifth Avenue and Forty-fourth Street but couldn't see a thing. Several people stopped and watched the struggle without offering to help until finally, when everybody had had his laugh, a woman picked up my glasses and handed them to me. "Here's your glasses," she tittered, grinning at me as if I were a policeman's horse with a sunbonnet. I put the glasses on, gathered the coat together, and walked off with as much dignity as I could, leaving my hat swirling along the street under the wheels of traffic.

It was the twentieth of November this winter that I finally put on my overcoat for the first time. It is a heavy gray one, and looks a little like a dog bed because the strap on the inside of the collar broke and the coat had been lying on the floor of my closet for almost a year. I carried it downstairs from my hotel room to the lobby, and didn't start to put it on until I had reached the revolving doors leading to the street. I had just got one arm into a sleeve when I was suddenly grabbed from behind, a hand shot up under the coat, jerked my undercoat sharply down, and I fell backward, choking, into the arms of the hotel doorman, who had come to my assistance. He is a powerfully built man who brooks no denial of, or interference with, his little attentions and services. He didn't exactly throw me, but I took a pretty bad tossing around.

From the hotel I went, in a badly disturbed state of mind, to my barber's, and I was just reaching into a pocket of the overcoat for my cigarettes and matches when the coat was whisked off me from behind. This was done with great firmness but no skill by the colored porter and bootblack who sneaks up behind people at Joe's barbershop and tears their overcoats off their backs. This porter is not so powerfully built as the doorman at my hotel, but he is sinewy and in excellent condition. Furthermore, he was not wearing an overcoat himself, and the man who *is* wearing an overcoat is at a great disadvantage in a struggle. This porter is also a coat-tugger, belonging to that school of coat-tuggers who reach up under your overcoat after they have helped you on with it and jerk the back of your suit jacket so savagely that the collar of the jacket is pulled away from its proper set around the shoulders and makes you feel loutish and miserable. There is nothing to do about this except give the man a dime.

It wasn't, however, until I went with some fine acquaintances of mine to an excellent restaurant that night that I got into my old familiar plight with the ripped lining of the left sleeve. After dining, the gentlemen in the party were helped on with their coats by one of those slim, silent waiters with the cold and fishy eye of an art critic. He got me adroitly into the right sleeve of my overcoat, and then I stuck my left arm smoothly into the lining of the other sleeve. Running an arm into the ripped lining of an overcoat while people, both acquaintances and strangers, look on and the eye of the struggling waiter gets colder and colder, is one of the most humiliating experiences known to the American male. After it was finally straightened out and I got my arm through the sleeve, I couldn't find any money for a tip; I couldn't even find a dime. I don't like to dwell on that incident.

After leaving the restaurant, we went to a theatre, and there another reason I do not like to wear an overcoat and never will wear an overcoat again reared its terrifying head. In taking off my overcoat to hand it to the unsympathetic hat-check boy, I took off with it the jacket to my dinner clothes and was left standing in the crowded and well-dressed lounge in my shirt-sleeves, with a section of my suspenders plainly visible through the armhole of my waistcoat. So speedily do hat-check boys work that my overcoat and jacket had been whisked to the back of the hat-check room and hung up under a couple of other overcoats before I could do anything about it. The eight or ten seconds that went by before I recovered my dinner jacket were among the worst moments of my life. The only worse experience I can think of was the time my suitcase flopped open on the Madison Avenue car tracks when I was hurrying to make a train at Grand Central.

I tried to pass off the episode of the dinner jacket nonchalantly, but succeeded only in lapsing into that red-faced fixed grin which no truly well-poised man-about-town ever permits himself to lapse into. I reached for my cigarettes, but I found that I had left them in a pocket of my overcoat, so in order to have something to do with my hands—for people were still staring and leering—I gracefully pulled a neatly folded handkerchief from the breast pocket of my dinner jacket, only to discover when I shook it out that it was a clean white silk sock. The last time I had dressed for dinner, I had been unable to find a fresh handkerchief, and after considerable effort had finally folded the sock and tucked it into the pocket of my jacket in such a way that it looked like a handkerchief. Of course, on that occasion I had remembered not to pull the handkerchief out. I had remembered this by grimly repeating it to myself all evening, but that had been several nights before and I had completely

forgotten about the sock.

I would never have brought out all these humiliating revelations had it not been for the fact that even those persons who know me best, for a modest, unassuming man, had really come to believe that I went around town without an overcoat in order to make the same kind of impression that Oscar Wilde made with his sunflower or Sean O'Casey with his brown sweater. I simply want to be mentally at ease, and I have found out after years of experience that I cannot be mentally at ease and at the same time wear an overcoat. Going without an overcoat in bitter weather has, God knows, its special humiliations, but having a kindly old lady come up to me on the street and hand me a dime is nothing compared to the horrors I went through when I wore an overcoat, or tried to wear one.

The Departure of Emma Inch

EMMA INCH looked no different from any other middle-aged, thin woman you might glance at in the subway or deal with across the counter of some small store in a country town, and then forget forever. Her hair was drab and unabundant, her face made no impression on you, her voice I don't remember—it was just a voice. She came to us with a letter of recommendation from some acquaintance who knew that we were going to Martha's Vineyard for the summer and wanted a cook. We took her because there was nobody else, and she seemed all right. She had arrived at our hotel in Forty-fifth Street the day before we were going to leave and we got her a room for the night, because she lived way uptown somewhere. She said she really ought to go back

and give up her room, but I told her I'd fix that.

Emma Inch had a big scuffed brown suitcase with her, and a Boston bull terrier. His name was Feely. Feely was seventeen years old and he grumbled and growled and snuffled all the time, but we needed a cook and we agreed to take Feely along with Emma Inch, if she would take care of him and keep him out of the way. It turned out to be easy to keep Feely out of the way because he would lie grousing anywhere Emma put him until she came and picked him up again. I never saw him walk. Emma had owned him, she said, since he was a pup. He was all she had in the world, she told us, with a mist in her eyes. I felt embarrassed but not touched. I didn't see how anybody could love Feely.

I didn't lose any sleep about Emma Inch and Feely the night of the day they arrived, but my wife did. She told me next morning that she had lain awake a long time thinking about the cook and her dog, because she felt kind of funny about them. She didn't know why. She just had a feeling that they were kind of funny. When we were all ready to leave—it was about three o'clock in the afternoon, for we had kept putting off the packing—I phoned Emma's room, but she didn't answer. It was getting late and we felt nervous—the Fall River boat would sail in about two hours. We couldn't understand why we hadn't heard anything from Emma and Feely. It wasn't until four o'clock that we did. There was a small rap on the door of our bedroom and I opened it and Emma and Feely were there, Feely in her arms, snuffing and snaffling, as if he had been swimming a long way.

My wife told Emma to get her bag packed, we were leaving in a little while. Emma said her bag *was* packed, except for her electric fan, and she couldn't get that in. "You won't need an electric fan at the Vineyard," my wife told her. "It's cool there, even during the day, and it's almost cold at night. Besides, there is no electricity in the cottage we are going to." Emma Inch seemed distressed. She studied my wife's face. "I'll have to think of something else then," she said. "Mebbe

I could let the water run all night." We both sat down and looked at her. Feely's asthmatic noises were the only sounds in the room for a while. "Doesn't that dog ever stop that?" I asked, irritably. "Oh, he's just talking," said Emma. "He talks all the time, but I'll keep him in my room and he won't bother you none." "Doesn't he bother you?" I asked. "He *would* bother me," said Emma, "at night, but I put the electric fan on and keep the light burning. He don't make so much noise when it's light, because he don't snore. The fan kind of keeps me from noticing him. I put a piece of cardboard, like, where the fan hits it and then I don't notice Feely so much. Mebbe I could let the water run in my room all night instead of the fan." I said "Hmmm" and got up and mixed a drink for my wife and me—we had decided not to have one till we got on the boat, but I thought we'd better have one now. My wife didn't tell Emma there would be no running water in her room at the Vineyard.

"We've been worried about you, Emma," I said. "I phoned your room but you didn't answer." "I never answer the phone," said Emma, "because I always get a shock. I wasn't there anyways. I couldn't sleep in that room. I went back to Mrs. McCoy's on Seventy-eighth Street." I lowered my glass. "You went back to Seventy-eighth Street last *night?*" I demanded. "Yes, sir," she said. "I had to tell Mrs. McCoy I was going away and wouldn't be there any more for a while—Mrs. McCoy's the landlady. Anyways, I never sleep in a hotel." She looked around the room. "They burn down," she told us.

It came out that Emma Inch had not only gone back to Seventy-eighth Street the night before but had walked all the way, carrying Feely. It had taken her an hour or two, because Feely didn't like to be carried very far at a time, so she had had to stop every block or so and put him down on the sidewalk for a while. It had taken her just as long to walk back to our hotel, too; Feely, it seems, never got up before afternoon—that's why she was so late. She was sorry. My wife and I finished our drinks, looking at each other, and at Feely.

Emma Inch didn't like the idea of riding to Pier 14 in a taxi, but after ten minutes of cajoling and pleading she finally got in. "Make it go slow," she said. We had enough time, so I asked the driver to take it easy. Emma kept getting to her feet and I kept pulling her back onto the seat. "I never been in an automobile before," she said. "It goes awful fast." Now and then she gave a little squeal of fright. The driver turned his head and grinned. "You're O.K. wit' me, lady," he said. Feely growled at him. Emma waited until he had turned away again, and then she leaned over to my wife and whispered. "They all take cocaine," she said. Feely began to make a new sound—a kind of high, agonized yelp. "He's singing," said Emma. She gave a strange little giggle, but the expression of her face didn't change. "I wish you had put the Scotch where we could get at it," said my wife.

If Emma Inch had been afraid of the taxicab, she was terrified by the *Priscilla* of the Fall River Line. "I don't think I can go," said Emma. "I don't think I could get on a boat. I didn't know they were so big." She stood rooted to the pier, clasping Feely. She must have squeezed him too hard, for he screamed—he screamed like a woman. We all jumped. "It's his ears," said Emma. "His ears hurt." We finally got her on the boat, and once aboard, in the salon, her terror abated somewhat. Then the three parting blasts of the boat whistle rocked lower Manhattan. Emma Inch leaped to her feet and began to run, letting go of her suitcase (which she had refused to give up to a porter) but holding onto Feely. I caught her just as she reached the gangplank. The ship was on its way when I let go of her arm.

It was a long time before I could get Emma to go to her stateroom, but she went at last. It was an inside stateroom, and she didn't seem to mind it. I think she was surprised to find that it was like a room, and had a bed and a chair and a washbowl. She put Feely down on the floor. "I think you'll have to do something about the dog," I said. "I think they put them somewhere and you get them when you get off." "No, they don't," said Emma. I guess, in this case, they didn't. I don't know. I shut the door on Emma Inch and Feely, and went away. My wife was drinking straight Scotch when I got to our stateroom.

The next morning, cold and early, we got Emma and Feely off the *Priscilla* at Fall River and over to New Bedford in a taxi and onto the little boat for Martha's Vineyard. Each move was as difficult as getting a combative drunken man out of the night club in which he fancies he has been insulted. Emma sat in a chair on the Vineyard boat, as far away from sight of the water as she could get, and closed her eyes and held onto Feely. She had thrown a coat over Feely, not only to keep him warm but to prevent any of the ship's officers from taking him away from her. I went in from the deck at intervals to see how she was. She was all right, or at least all right for her, until five minutes before the boat reached the dock at Woods Hole, the only stop between New Bedford and the Vineyard. Then Feely got sick. Or at any rate Emma said he was sick. He didn't seem to me any different from what he always was—his breathing was just as abnormal and irregular. But Emma said he was sick. There were tears in her eyes. "He's a very sick dog, Mr. Thurman," she said. "I'll have to take him home." I knew by the way she said "home" what she meant. She meant Seventy-eighth Street.

The boat tied up at Woods Hole and was motionless and we could hear the racket of the deckhands on the dock loading freight. "I'll get off here," said Emma, firmly, or with more firmness, anyway, than she had shown yet. I explained to her that we would be home in half an hour, that everything would be fine then, everything would be wonderful. I said Feely would be a new dog. I told her people sent sick dogs to Martha's Vineyard to be cured. But it was no good. "I'll have to take him off here," said Emma. "I always have to take him home when he is sick." I talked to her eloquently about the loveliness of Martha's Vineyard and the nice houses and the nice people and the wonderful accommodations for dogs. But I knew it was useless. I could tell by looking at her. She was going to get off the boat at Woods Hole.

"You really can't do this," I said, grimly, shaking her arm. Feely snarled weakly. "You haven't any money and you don't know where you are. You're a long way from New York. Nobody ever got from Woods Hole to New York alone." She didn't seem to hear me. She began walking toward the stairs leading to the gangplank, crooning to Feely. "You'll have to go all the way back on boats," I said, "or else take a train, and you haven't any money. If you are going to be so stupid and leave us now, I can't give you any money." "I don't want any money, Mr. Thurman," she said. "I haven't earned any money." I walked along in irritable silence for a moment; then I gave her some money. I made her take it. We got to the gangplank. Feely snaffled and gurgled. I saw now that his eyes were a little red and moist. I know it would do no good to summon my wife—not when Feely's health was at stake. "How do you expect to get home from here?" I almost shouted at Emma Inch as she moved down the gangplank. "You're way out on the end of Massachusetts." She stopped and turned around. "We'll walk," she said. "We like to walk, Feely and me." I just stood still and watched her go.

When I went up on deck, the boat was clearing for the Vineyard. "How's everything?" asked my wife. I waved a hand in the direction of the dock. Emma Inch was standing there, her suitcase at her feet, her dog under one arm, waving goodbye to us with her free hand. I had never seen her smile before, but she was smiling now.

There's an Owl in My Room

I SAW Gertrude Stein on the screen of a newsreel theatre one afternoon and I heard her read that famous passage of hers about pigeons on the grass, alas (the sorrow is, as you know, Miss Stein's). After reading about the pigeons on the grass alas, Miss Stein said, "This is a simple description of a landscape I have seen many times." I don't really believe that this is true. Pigeons on the grass alas may be a simple description of Miss Stein's own consciousness, but it is not a simple description of a plot of grass on which pigeons have alighted, are alighting, or are going to alight. A truly simple description of the pigeons alighting on the grass of the Luxembourg Gardens (which, I believe, is where the pigeons alighted) would say of the pigeons alighting there only that they were pigeons alighting. Pigeons that alight anywhere are neither sad pigeons nor gay pigeons, they are simply pigeons.

It is neither just nor accurate to connect the word alas with pigeons. Pigeons are definitely not alas. They have nothing to do with alas and they have nothing to do with hooray (not even when you tie red, white, and blue ribbons on them and let them loose at band concerts); they have nothing to do with mercy me or isn't that fine, either. White rabbits, yes, and Scotch terriers, and bluejays, and even hippopotamuses, but not pigeons. I happen to have studied pigeons very closely and carefully, and I have studied the effect, or rather the lack of effect, of pigeons very carefully. A number of pigeons alight from time to time on the sill of my hotel window when I am eating breakfast and staring out the window. They never alas me, they never make me feel alas; they never make me feel anything.

Nobody and no animal and no other bird can play a scene so far down as a pigeon can. For instance, when a pigeon on my window ledge becomes aware of me sitting there in a chair in my blue polka-dot dressing-gown, worrying, he pokes his head far out from his shoulders and peers sideways at me, for all the world (Miss Stein might surmise) like a timid man peering around the corner of a building trying to ascertain whether he is being followed by some hoofed fiend or only by the echo of his own footsteps. And yet it is *not* for all the world like a timid man peering around the corner of a building trying to ascertain whether he is being followed by a hoofed fiend or only by the echo of his own footsteps, at all. And that is because there is no emotion in the pigeon and no power to arouse emotion. A pigeon looking is just a pigeon looking. When it comes to emotion, a fish, compared to a pigeon, is practically beside himself.

A pigeon peering at me doesn't make me sad or glad or apprehensive or hopeful. With a horse or a cow or a dog it would be different. It would be especially different with a dog. Some dogs peer at me as if I had just gone completely crazy or as if they had just gone completely crazy. I can go so far as to say that most dogs peer at me that way. This creates in the consciousness of both me and the dog a feeling of alarm or downright terror and legitimately permits me to work into a description of the landscape, in which the dog and myself are figures, a note of emotion. Thus I should not have minded if Miss Stein had written: dogs on the grass, look out, dogs on the grass, look out, look out, dogs on the grass, look out Alice. That would be a simple description of dogs on the grass. But when any writer pretends that a pigeon makes him sad, or makes him anything else, I must instantly protest that this is a highly specialized fantastic impression created in an individual consciousness and that therefore it cannot fairly be presented as a simple description of what actually was to be seen.

People who do not understand pigeons—and pigeons can be understood only when you understand that there is nothing to understand about them—should not go around describing pigeons or the effect of pigeons. Pigeons come closer to a zero of impingement than any other birds. Hens embarrass me the way my old Aunt Hattie used to when I was twelve and she still insisted I wasn't big enough to bathe myself; owls disturb me; if I am with an eagle I always pretend that I am not with an eagle; and so on down to swallows at twilight who scare the hell out of me. But pigeons have absolutely no effect on me. They have absolutely no effect on anybody. They couldn't even startle a child. That is why they are selected from among all birds to be let loose, with colored ribbons attached to them, at band concerts, library dedications, and christenings of new dirigibles. If any

body let loose a lot of owls on such an occasion there would be rioting and catcalls and whistling and fainting spells and throwing of chairs and the Lord only knows what else.

From where I am sitting now I can look out the window and see a pigeon being a pigeon on the roof of the Harvard Club. No other thing can be less what it is not than a pigeon can, and Miss Stein, of all people, should understand that simple fact. Behind the pigeon I am looking at, a blank wall of tired gray bricks is stolidly trying to sleep off oblivion; underneath the pigeon the cloistered windows of the Harvard Club are staring in horrified bewilderment at something they have seen across the street. The pigeon is just there on the roof being a pigeon, having been, and being, a pigeon and, what is more, always going to be, too. Nothing could be simpler than that. If you read that sentence aloud you will instantly see what I mean. It is a simple description of a pigeon on a roof. It is only with an effort that I am conscious of the pigeon, but I am acutely aware of a great sulky red iron pipe that is creeping up the side of the building intent on sneaking up on a slightly tipsy chimney which is shouting its head off.

There is nothing a pigeon can do or be that would make me feel sorry for it or for myself or for the people in the world, just as there is nothing I could do or be that would make a pigeon feel sorry for itself. Even if I plucked his feathers out it would not make him feel sorry for himself and it would not make me feel sorry for myself or for him. But try plucking the quills out of a porcupine or even plucking the fur out of a jackrabbit. There is nothing a pigeon could be, or can be, rather, which could get into my consciousness like a fumbling hand in a bureau drawer and disarrange my mind or pull anything out of it. I bar nothing at all. You could dress up a pigeon in a tiny suit of evening clothes and put a tiny silk hat on his head and a tiny gold-headed cane under his wing and send him walking into my room at night. It would make no impression on me. I would not shout, "Good god amighty, the birds are in charge!" But you could send an owl into my room, dressed only in the feathers it was born with, and no monkey business, and I would pull the covers over my head and scream.

No other thing in the world falls so far short of being able to do what it cannot do as a pigeon does. Of being *unable* to do what it *can* do, too, as far as that goes.

The Topaz Cufflinks Mystery

WHEN THE motorcycle cop came roaring up, unexpectedly, out of Never-Never Land (the way motorcycle cops do), the man was on his hands and knees in the long grass beside the road, barking like a dog. The woman was driving slowly along in a car that stopped about eighty feet away; its headlights shone on the man: middle-aged, bewildered, sedentary. He got to his feet.

"What's goin' on here?" asked the cop. The woman giggled. "Cock-eyed," thought the cop. He did not glance at her.

"I guess it's gone," said the man. "I—ah—could not find it."

"What was it?"

"What I lost?" The man squinted, unhappily. "Some— some cufflinks; topazes set in gold." He hesitated: the cop didn't seem to believe him. "They were the color of a fine Moselle," said the man. He put on a pair of spectacles which he had been holding in his hand. The woman giggled.

"Hunt things better with ya glasses off?" asked the cop. He pulled his motorcycle to the side of the road to let a car pass. "Better pull over off the concrete, lady," he said. She drove the car off the roadway.

"I'm nearsighted," said the man. "I can hunt things at a distance with my glasses on, but I do better with them off if I am close to something." The cop kicked his heavy boots through the grass where the man had been crouching.

"He was barking," ventured the lady in the car, "so that I could see where he was." The cop pulled his machine up on its standard; he and the man walked over to the automobile.

"What I don't get," said the officer, "is how you lose ya cufflinks a hunderd feet in front of where ya car is; a person usually stops his car *past* the place he loses somethin', not a hunderd feet before he gits *to* the place."

131

The lady laughed again; her husband got slowly into the car, as if he were afraid the officer would stop him any moment. The officer studied them.

"Been to a party?" he asked. It was after midnight.

"We're not drunk, if that's what you mean," said the woman, smiling. The cop tapped his fingers on the door of the car.

"You people didn't lose no topazes," he said.

"Is it against the law for a man to be down on all fours beside a road, barking in a perfectly civil manner?" demanded the lady.

"No, ma'am," said the cop. He made no move to get on his motorcycle, however, and go on about his business. There was just the quiet chugging of the cycle engine and the auto engine, for a time.

"I'll tell you how it was, Officer," said the man, in a crisp, new tone. "We were settling a bet. O. K.?"

"O. K.," said the cop. "Who win?" There was another pulsing silence.

"The lady bet," said her husband, with dignity, as though he were explaining some important phase of industry to a newly hired clerk, "the lady bet that my eyes would shine like a cat's do at night, if she came upon me suddenly close to the ground alongside the road. We had passed a cat, whose eyes gleamed. We had passed several persons, whose eyes did *not* gleam——"

"Simply because they were above the light and not under it," said the lady. "A man's eyes would gleam like a cat's if people were ordinarily caught by headlights at the same angle as cats are." The cop walked over to where he had left his motorcycle, picked it up, kicked the standard out, and wheeled it back.

"A cat's eyes," he said, "are different than yours and mine. Dogs, cats, skunks, it's all the same. They can see in a dark room."

"Not in a *totally* dark room," said the lady.

"Yes, they can," said the cop.

"No, they can't; not if there is no light at all in the room, not if it's absolutely *black*," said the lady. "The question came up the other night; there was a professor there and he said there must be at least a ray of light, no matter how faint."

"That may be," said the cop, after a solemn pause, pulling at his gloves. "But people's eyes don't shine—I go along these roads every night an' pass hunderds of cats and hunderds of people."

"The people are never close to the ground," said the lady.

"*I* was close to the ground," said her husband.

"Look at it this way," said the cop. "I've seen wildcats in *trees* at night and *their* eyes shine."

"There you are!" said the lady's husband. "That proves it."

"I don't see how," said the lady. There was another silence.

"Because a wildcat in a tree's eyes are higher than the level of a man's," said her husband. The cop may possibly have followed this, the lady obviously did not; neither one said anything. The cop got on his machine, raced his engine, seemed to be thinking about something, and throttled down. He turned to the man.

"Took ya glasses off so the headlights wouldn't make ya glasses shine, huh?" he asked.

"That's right," said the man. The cop waved his hand, triumphantly, and roared away. "Smart guy," said the man to his wife, irritably.

"I still don't see where the wildcat proves anything," said his wife. He drove off slowly.

"Look," he said. "You claim that the whole thing depends on how *low* a *cat's* eyes are; I——"

"I didn't say that; I said it all depends on how *high* a *man's* eyes . . ."

Casuals of the Keys

IF YOU know the more remote little islands off the Florida coast, you may have met—although I greatly doubt it—Captain Darke. Darrell Darke. His haunted key is, for this reason and that, the most inaccessible of them all. I came upon it quite by chance and doubt that I could find it again. I saw him first that moment when my shining little launch, so impudently summer-resortish, pushed its nose against the lonely pier on which he stood. Tall, dark, melancholy, his white shirt open at the throat, he reminded me instantly of that other solitary wanderer among forgotten islands, the doomed Lord Jim.

I stepped off the boat and he came toward me with a lean brown hand out-thrust. "I'm Darke," he said, simply, "Darrell Darke." I shook hands with him. He seemed pleased to encounter someone from the outside world. I found out later that no white man had set foot on his remote little key for several years.

He took me to a little thatched hut and waved me to a bamboo chair. It was a pleasant place, with a bed of dried palm leaves, a few withered books, some fishing equipment, and a bright rifle. Darke produced from somewhere a bottle with a greenish heavy liquid in it, and two glasses. "Opono," he said, apologetically. "Made from the sap of the opono tree. Horrible stuff, but kicky." I asked him if he would care for a touch of Bacardi, of which I had a quart on the launch, and he said he would. I went down and got it. . . .

"A newspaperman, eh?" said Darke, with interest, as I filled up the glasses for the third time. "You must meet a lot of interesting people." I really felt that I had met a lot of interesting people and, under slight coaxing, began to tell about them: Gene Tunney, Eddie Rickenbacker, the Grand Duchess Marie, William Gibbs McAdoo. Darke listened to

135

my stories with quick attention, thirsty as he was for news of the colorful civilization which, he told me, he had put behind him twenty years before.

"You must," I said at last, to be polite, "have met some interesting people yourself."

"No," he said. "All of a stripe, until you came along. Last chap that put in here, for example, was a little fellow name of Mark Menafee who turned up one day some three years ago in an outboard motor. He was only a trainer of fugitives from justice." Darke reached for the glass I had filled again.

"I never heard of anyone being that," I said. "What did he do?"

"He coached fugitives from justice," said Darke. "Seems Menafee could spot one instantly. Take the case of Burt Fredericks he told me about. Fredericks was a bank defaulter from Connecticut. Menafee spotted him on a Havana boat— knew him from his pictures in the papers. 'Hello, Burt,' says Menafee, casually. Fredericks whirled around. Then he caught himself and stared blankly at Menafee. 'My name is Charles Brandon,' he says. Menafee won his confidence and for a fee and his expenses engaged to coach Fredericks not to be caught off his guard and answer to the name of Burt. He'd shadow Fredericks from city to city, contriving to come upon him unexpectedly in dining-rooms, men's lounges, bars, and crowded hotel lobbies. 'Why Burt!' Menafee would say, gaily, or 'It's old Fredericks!' like someone meeting an old friend after years. Fredericks got so he never let on—unless he was addressed as Charlie or Brandon. Far as I know he was never caught. Menafee made enough to keep going, coaching fugitives, but it was a dullish kind of job." Darke fell silent. I sat watching him.

"Did you ever meet any other uninteresting people?" I asked.

"There was Harrison Cammery," said Darke, after a moment. "He put in here one night in a storm, dressed in full evening clothes. Came from New York—I don't know how.

There never was a sign of a boat or anything to show how he got here. He was always that way while he was here, dully incomprehensible. He had the most uninteresting of manias, which is monomania. He was a goldfish-holder." Darke stopped and seemed inclined to let the story end there.

"What do you mean, a goldfish-holder?" I demanded.

"Cammery had been a professional billiard-player," said Darke. "He told me that the strain of developing absolutely nerveless hands finally told on him. He had trained so that he could balance five BB shot on the back of each of his fingers indefinitely. One night, at a party where the host had a bowl of goldfish, the guests got to trying to catch them with one grab of their hand. Nobody could do it until Cammery tried. He caught up one of the fish and held it lightly in his closed hand. He told me that the wettish fluttering of that fish against the palm of his hand became a thing he couldn't forget. He got to snatching up goldfish and holding them, wherever he went. At length he had to have a bowl of them beside the table when he played his billiard matches, and would hold one between innings the way tennis-players take a mouthful of water. The effect finally was to destroy his muscular precision, so he took to the islands. One day he was gone from here—I don't know how. I was glad enough. A singularly one-track and boring fellow."

"Who else has put in here?" I asked, filling them up again.

"Early in 1913," said Darke, after a pause in which he seemed to make an effort to recall what he was after, "early in 1913 an old fellow with a white beard—must have been seventy-five or eighty—walked into this hut one day. He was dripping wet. Said he swam over from the mainland and he probably did. It's fifty miles. Lots of boats can be had for the taking along the main coast, but this fellow was apparently too stupid to take one. He was as dull about everything as about that. Used to recite short stories word for word—said he wrote them himself. He was a writer like you, but he didn't seem to have met any interesting people. Talked only about himself, where he'd come from, what he'd done. I didn't pay any attention to him. I was glad when, one night, he disappeared. His name was . . ." Darke put his head back and stared at the roof of his hut, striving to remember. "Oh, yes," he said. "His name was Bierce. Ambrose Bierce."

"You say that was in 1913, early in 1913?" I asked, excitedly.

"Yes, I'm sure of it," said Darke, "because it was the same year C-18769 showed up here."

"Who was C-18769?" I asked.

"It was a carrier pigeon," said Darke. "Flew in here one night tuckered by the trip from the mainland, and flopped down on that bed with its beak open, panting hard. It was red-eyed and dishevelled. I noticed it had something sizable strapped under its belly and I saw its registration number, on a silver band fastened to its leg: C-18769. When it got rested up it hung around here for quite a while. I didn't pay much attention to it. In those days I used to get the New York papers about once a month off a supply boat that used to put in at an island ten miles from here. I'd row over. One day I saw a notice in one of the papers about this bird. Some concern or other, for a publicity stunt, had arranged to have this bird carry a thousand dollars in hundred-dollar bills from the concern's offices to the place where the bird homed, some five hundred miles away. The bird never got there. The papers had all kinds of theories: the bird had been shot and robbed, it had fallen in the water and drowned, or it had got lost."

"The last was right," I said. "It must have got lost."

"Lost, hell," said Darke. "After I read the stories I caught it up one day, suddenly, and examined the packet strapped to it. It only had four hundred and sixty-five dollars left."

I felt a little weak. Finally, in a small voice, I asked: "Did you turn it over to the authorities?"

"Certainly not," said Darrell Darke. "A man or a bird's life is his own to lead, down here. I simply figured this pigeon for a fool, and let him go. What could he do, after the money was gone? Nothing." Darke rolled and lighted a cigarette and smoked a while, silently. "That's the kind of beings you meet with down here," he said. "Stupid, dullish, lacking in common sense, fiddling along aimlessly. Menafee, Cammery, Bierce, C-18769—all the same. It gets monotonous. Tell me more about this Grand Duchess Marie. She must be a most interesting person."

A Preface to Dogs

AS SOON as a wife presents her husband with a child, her capacity for worry becomes acuter: she hears more burglars, she smells more things burning, she begins to wonder, at the theatre or the dance, whether her husband left his service revolver in the nursery. This goes on for years and years. As the child grows older, the mother's original major fear—that the child was exchanged for some other infant at the hospital—gives way to even more magnificent doubts and suspicions: she suspects that the child is not bright, she doubts that it will be happy, she is sure that it will become mixed up with the wrong sort of people.

This insistence of parents on dedicating their lives to their children is carried on year after year in the face of all that dogs have done, and are doing, to prove how much happier the parent-child relationship can become, if managed without sentiment, worry, or dedication. Of course, the theory that dogs have a saner family life than humans is an old one, and it was in order to ascertain whether the notion is pure legend or whether it is based on observable fact that I have for four years made a careful study of the family life of dogs. My conclusions entirely support the theory that dogs have a saner family life than people.

In the first place, the husband leaves on a woodchuck-hunting expedition just as soon as he can, which is very soon, and never comes back. He doesn't write, makes no provision for the care or maintenance of his family, and is not liable to prosecution because he doesn't. The wife doesn't care where he is, never wonders if he is thinking about her, and although she may start at the slightest footstep, doesn't do so because she is hoping against hope that it is he. No lady dog has ever been known to set her friends against her husband, or put detectives on his trail.

This same lack of sentimentality is carried out in the mother dog's relationship to her young. For six weeks—but only six weeks—she looks after them religiously, feeds them (they come clothed), washes their ears, fights off cats, old women, and wasps that come nosing around, makes the bed, and rescues the puppies when they crawl under the floor boards of the barn or get lost in an old boot. She does all these things, however, without fuss, without that loud and elaborate show of solicitude and alarm which a woman displays in rendering some exaggerated service to her child.

At the end of six weeks, the mother dog ceases to lie awake at night harking for ominous sounds; the next morning she snarls at the puppies after breakfast, and routs them all out of the house. "This is forever," she informs them, succinctly. "I have my own life to live, automobiles to chase, grocery boys' shoes to snap at, rabbits to pursue. I can't be washing and feeding a lot of big six-weeks-old dogs any longer. That phase is definitely over." The family life is thus terminated, and the mother dismisses the children from her mind—frequently as many as eleven at one time—as easily as she did her husband. She is now free to devote herself to her career and to the novel and astonishing things of life.

In the case of one family of dogs that I observed, the mother, a large black dog with long ears and a keen zest for living, tempered only by an immoderate fear of toads and turtles, kicked ten puppies out of the house at the end of six weeks to the day—it was a Monday. Fortunately for my observations, the puppies had no place to go, since they hadn't made any plans, and so they just hung around the barn, now and again trying to patch things up with their mother. She refused, however, to entertain any proposition leading to a resumption of home life, pointing out firmly that she was, by inclination, a chaser of bicycles and a hearth-fire watcher, both of which activities would be insupportably cluttered up by the presence of ten helpers. The bicycle-chasing field was overcrowded, anyway, she explained, and the hearth-fire-watching field even more so. "We could chase parades together," suggested one of the dogs, but she refused to be touched, snarled, and drove him off.

It is only for a few weeks that the cast-off puppies make overtures to their mother in regard to the reëstablishment of a home. At the end of that time, by some natural miracle that I am unable clearly to understand, the puppies suddenly one day don't recognize their mother any more, and she doesn't recognize them. It is as if they had never met, and is a fine idea, giving both parties a clean break and a chance for a fresh start. Once, some months after this particular family had broken up and the pups had been sold, one of them, named Liza, was brought back to "the old nest" for a visit. The mother dog of course didn't recognize the puppy and promptly bit her in the hip. They had to be separated, each grumbling something about you never know what kind of dogs you're going to meet. Here was no silly, affecting reunion, no sentimental tears, no bitter intimations of neglect, or forgetfulness, or desertion.

If a pup is not sold or given away, but is brought up in the same household with its mother, the two will fight bitterly, sometimes twenty or thirty times a day, for maybe a month. This is very trying to whoever owns the dogs, particularly if they are sentimentalists who grieve because mother and child don't know each other. The condition finally clears up: the two dogs grow to tolerate each other and, beyond growling a little under their breath about how it takes all kinds of dogs to make up a world, get along fairly well together when their paths cross. I know of one mother dog and her half-grown daughter who sometimes spend the whole day together hunting woodchucks, although they don't speak. Their association is not sentimental, but practical, and is based on the fact that it is safer to hunt woodchucks in pairs than alone. These two dogs start out together in the morning, without a word, and come back together in the evening, when they part, without saying good night, whether they have had any luck or not. Avoidance of farewells, which are always stuffy and sometimes painful, is another thing in which it seems to me dogs have better sense than people.

Well, one day the daughter, a dog about ten months old,

seemed, by some prank of nature which again I am unable clearly to understand, for a moment or two, to recognize her mother, after all those months of oblivion. The two had just started out after a fat woodchuck who lives in the orchard. Something got wrong with the daughter's ear—a long, floppy ear. "Mother," she said, "I wish you'd look at my ear." Instantly the other dog bristled and growled. "I'm not your mother," she said, "I'm a woodchuck-hunter." The daughter grinned. "Well," she said, just to show that there were no hard feelings, "that's not my ear, it's a motorman's glove."

Guessing Game

An article was found after your departure in the room which you occupied. Kindly let us know if you have missed such an article, and if so, send us a description and instructions as to what disposition you wish made of same. For lack of space, all Lost and Found articles must be disposed of within two months.

LOST AND FOUND DEPARTMENT
HOTEL LEXINGTON
Lexington Ave. & 48th St., New York
Per R. E. Daley.

DEAR MR. DALEY:
THIS WHOLE thing is going to be much more complicated than you think. I have waited almost two weeks before answering your postcard notification because I have been unable to figure out what article I left behind. I'm sorry now I didn't just forget the whole business. As a matter of fact, I did try to forget it, but it keeps bobbing

up in my mind. I have got into an alphabetical rut about it; at night I lie awake naming articles to myself: bathrobe, bay rum, book, bicycle, belt, baby, etc. Dr. Prill, my analyst, has advised me to come right out and meet you on the subject.

So far, I have been able to eliminate, for certain, only two articles. I never remember to take pajamas or a hairbrush with me, so it couldn't be pajamas or a hairbrush you found. This does not get us very far. I have, however, ransacked the house and I find that a number of things are missing, but I don't remember which of them, if any, I had with me at the Lexington that night: the vest to my blue suit, my life-insurance policy, my Scotch terrier Jeannie, the jack out of the automobile tool case, the bottle-opener that is supposed to be kept in the kitchen drawer, the glass top to the percolator, a box of aspirin, a letter from my father giving my brother William's new address in Seattle, a roll of films (exposed) for a 2A Kodak, my briefcase (missing since 1927), etc. The article you have on hand might be any of these (with the exception of the briefcase). It would have been entirely possible for me, in the state of mind I was in that Friday, to have gone about all day with the automobile jack in my hand.

The thing that worries me most is the possibility that what I left in my room was something the absence of which I have not yet discovered and may never discover, unless you give me some hint. Is it animal, vegetable, or mineral? Is it as big as I am? Twice as big? Smaller than a man's hand? Does it have a screw-on top? Does it make any kind of regular ticking noise when in operation? Is it worth, new, as much as a hundred dollars? A thousand dollars? Fifty cents? It isn't a bottle of toothache drops, is it? Or a used razor blade? Because I left them behind on purpose. These questions, it seems to me, are eminently fair. I'm not asking you some others I could think of, such as: Does it go with the pants and coat of a blue suit? Can it bark? Can it lift the wheel of an automobile off the ground? Can it open a bottle? Does it relieve pain? Is it a letter from somebody? Does anybody get any money out of it when I am dead, providing I keep the payments up?

I think you should let me know whether you are willing to answer yes or no to my first set of questions, as in all games of this sort. Because if you are just going to stand there with a silly look on your face and shake your head and keep repeating "Can't guess what it i-yis, can't guess what it i-yis!", to hell with it. I don't care if it's a diamond ring.

I take it for granted, of course, that I really did leave an article in the room I occupied. If I didn't, and this thing turns out to be merely a guessing game in which the answer is Robert E. Lee's horse, or something, you'll never be able to answer your phone for a whole year without running the chance of it's being me, reserving dozens of rooms in a disguised voice and under various assumed names, reporting a fire on the twenty-third floor, notifying you that your bank balance is overdrawn, pretending, in a husky guttural, that you are the next man the gang is going to put on the spot for the shooting of Joe the Boss over in Brooklyn.

Of course, I'm a little sore about the thing the way it is. If you had been a guest at my house and had gone away leaving your watch or your keyring behind, would I send you a penny postcard asking you to guess what you had left behind? I would now, yes; but I mean before this all happened. Supposing everybody did business that way. Supposing your rich and doting uncle wired you: "I'm arriving Grand Central some time next month. Meet me." Or, worse yet, supposing that instead of issuing a summons naming a definite crime or misdemeanor, the courts sent out a postcard reading: "I know what's going to happen to you-oo!" We'd all be nervous wrecks.

The only thing I see to do right now is comply with your request for a description of the article I left in that

room. It is a large and cumbersome iron object, usually kept in a kitchen drawer, entitling my wife, upon my death, to a certain payment of money; it barks when in operation and, unless used when the coffee reaches the boiling point, will allow the liquid to spill out on the stove; it is signed by my father's name, is sensitive to light, relieves neuralgic pains, and is dark blue in color.

I have, of course, the same suspicion that you seem to have; namely, that maybe the object wasn't left behind by me but by somebody else who occupied the room before I did or who occupied it at the same time I did, without either one of us knowing the other was there. And I'll tell you why. The night that I was at your hotel, the room clerk took a message out of my box when he reached for my key. The message was for a Mr. Donovan. I looked at it and said it didn't belong to me. "You haven't a Mr. Donovan with you?" he asked. I said no, but he didn't seem to be convinced. Perhaps whatever was left behind in my room was left behind by Mr. Donovan. I have an idea that, after all, Mr. Donovan and I may have occupied the same room, since his mail was in my box; perhaps he always arrived just after I had left the room and got out each time just before I came back. It's that kind of city.

I'm glad, anyway, that I have two months before the article is returned to the insurance company or sent to the pound, or whatever. It gives me time to think.

Everything Is Wild

IN THE first place it was a cold and rainy night and the Cortrights lived eighteen miles away, in Bronxville. "Eighteen hundred miles," Mr. Brush put it, bitterly. He got the car out of the Gramercy Lane garage, snarling savagely at the garage man, an amiable and loquacious fellow who spoke with an accent and who kept talking about winter oil and summer oil, and grinning, and repeating himself. As they drove out, Mrs. Brush told her husband that he didn't have to be so mean, the man hadn't done anything to him. "He kept yelling about oil, didn't he?" demanded Mr. Brush. "I know about oil. Nobody has to tell me about oil." Mrs. Brush kept her voice abnormally low, the way she always did when he was on the verge of a tantrum. "He wasn't yelling," she said. "He'll probably ruin the car some night, the way you acted."

The drive to Bronxville was as bad as Mr. Brush expected it would be. He got lost, and couldn't find Bronxville. When he did find Bronxville, he couldn't find the Woodmere Apartments. "You'll have to ask somebody where it is," said Mrs. Brush. He didn't want to ask anybody anything, but he stopped in front of a bright little barbershop, got out, and went inside. The barber he encountered turned out to be a garrulous foreigner. Sure, he knew where eez these Woodmare Apartamen. "Down is street has a concrete breech," he said. "It go under but no up to the first raid light. Quick, like this, before turn!" The barber made swift darting angles in the air with his hand. He also turned completely around. "So not down these light, hah?" he finished up. Mr. Brush snarled at him and went outside.

"Well?" asked Mrs. Brush. She knew by his silence that he hadn't found out anything. "*I'll* go in and ask next time," she said. Mr. Brush drove on. "The guy didn't know what he was talking about," he said. "He's crazy." Finally, after many twists and turns, most of them wrong, they drove up in front of the Woodmere. "Hell of an apartment building," said Mr. Brush. Mrs. Brush didn't answer him.

The dinner, fortunately, was quite nice. Mr. Brush had expected, indeed he had predicted, that there would be a lot of awful people, but the Brushes were the only guests. The

Cortrights were charming, there wasn't a radio, and nobody talked about business or baseball. Also there was, after dinner, Mr. Brush's favorite liqueur, and he was just settling comfortably into a soft chair, glass in hand, when the doorbell rang. A man and a woman were brought into the room and introduced—a Mr. and Mrs. Spreef, as Brush got it. The name turned out to be Spear. Mr. Brush didn't like them. They were quite nice, but he never liked anybody he hadn't met before.

After a flurry of trivial talk, during which Spear told a story about a fellow who had been courting a girl for fifteen years, at which everybody laughed but Brush, who grinned fixedly, the hostess wanted to know if people would like to play poker. There were pleased murmurs, a grunt from Brush, and in a twinkling a card table was pulled out from behind something and set up. Mrs. Cortright brightly explained that one leg of the table was broken, but she thought it would hold up all right. Mr. Brush didn't actually say that he thought it wouldn't, but he looked as if he did.

Mr. Spear won the deal. "This is dealer's choice, Harry," his hostess told him. "Change on each deal." Harry squealed. "O. K." he said. "How about a little old Duck-in-the-Pond?" The ladies giggled with pleasure. "Whazzat?" grumbled Brush. He hated any silly variation of the fine old game of poker. He instantly dropped out of the hand and sat staring at Mr. Spear. Mr. Spear, it came to him, looked like Chevalier. Mr. Brush hated Chevalier.

The next deal fell to Brush and he immediately named straight poker as his game. Mrs. Spear said she was crazy about Duck-in-the-Pond and why didn't they just keep on playing that? "Straight poker," said Mr. Brush, gruffly. "Oh," said Mrs. Spear, her smile vanishing. Mr. Brush won the straight-poker hand with three of a kind.

Mrs. Spear was the next dealer. "Seven-card stud," she said, "with the twos and threes wild." The women all gave little excited screams. Mrs. Cortright said she was crazy about seven-card stud with something wild. Mrs. Spear said she was, too. Mr. Brush said yah. Mrs. Spear won the hand with four kings—that is, two kings, a deuce, and a trey. Mr. Cortright, the next dealer, announced that they would now play Poison Ivy. This was a nuisance Mr. Brush had never heard of. It proved to be a variation of poker in which each player gets four cards, and five others are placed face down on the table to be turned up one at a time. The lowest card,

when all are turned up, becomes the wild card. Mr. Brush rolled his cigar from one corner of his mouth to the other, and narrowed his eyes. He scowled at Chevalier, because Chevalier kept repeating that Poison Ivy was the nuts. Brush folded up his hand and sat stiffly in his chair, rolling his cigar and grunting. Four aces won that hand, and in doing so had to beat four other aces (there were two fours in the hand on the table, and they were low).

So the game went wildly on, with much exclaiming and

giggling, until it came Mr. Brush's time to deal again. He sat up very straight in his chair and glared around the table. "We'll play Soap-in-Your-Eye this time," he said, grimly. Mrs. Spear screeched. "Oh, I don't know that!" she cried. Brush rolled his cigar at her. "Out West they call it Kick-in-the-Pants," he said. Mrs. Brush suggested that they better play Duck-in-the-Pond again, or Poison Ivy. "Soap-in-Your-Eye," said Brush, without looking at her. "How does it go?" asked Cortright.

"The red queens, the fours, fives, sixes, and eights are wild," said Mr. Brush. "I'll show you." He dealt one card to each person. Then he dealt another one around, face up this time. "Ah," he exclaimed, "Mrs. Spear draws a red queen on the second round, so it becomes forfeit. It can be reinstated, however, if on the next round she gets a black four. I'll show you." Mr. Brush was adroit with cards and he contrived it so that Mrs. Spear did get a black four on the next round. "Ho," said Brush, "that makes it interesting. Having foured your queen, you can now choose a card, any card, from the deck." He held up the deck and she selected a card. "Now if you don't want that card," continued Brush, "you can say 'Back' or 'Right' or 'Left,' depending on whether you want to put it back in the deck or pass it to the person at your right or the person at your left. If you decide to keep it, you say 'Hold.' The game, by the way, is sometimes called Hold Back or Right and Left. Get it?"

"I don't think so," said Mrs. Spear. She looked vaguely at the card she had drawn. "Hold, I guess," she said.

"Good," said Brush. "Now everybody else draws a card." Everybody did, Mrs. Brush trying to catch her husband's eye, but failing. "Now," said Brush, "we each have four cards, two of which everybody has seen, and two of which they haven't. Mrs. Spreef, however, has a Hold. That is, having black-foured her red queen, she is privileged to call a jack a queen or a trey a four or any other card just one point under a wild card, a wild card. See?" Nobody, apparently, saw.

"Why don't we just play Poison Ivy again?" asked Mrs. Brush. "Or a round of straight poker?"

"I want to try this," said Brush. "I'm crazy about it." He dealt two more cards around, face down. "We all have six cards now," he went on, "but you can't look at the last two—even after the game is over. All you can look at is the four cards in your hand and this one." He put a card face down in the middle of the table. "That card is called Splinter-Under-Your-Thumb and is also wild, whatever it is," he explained. "All right, bet." Everybody was silent for several seconds, and then they all checked to him. Brush bet five chips. Mrs. Spear, encouraged in a dim way by the fact that she had black-foured her red queen, thus reinstating it after forfeit, stayed, and so did Mrs. Cortright (who always stayed), but the others dropped out. The two ladies put in five chips each, and called Mr. Brush. He turned up the card in the middle of the table—the queen of diamonds. "Hah!" said Brush. "Well, I got a royal flush in spades!" He laid down the four of diamonds, the eight of hearts, and a pair of sixes. "I don't see how you have," said Mrs. Spear, dubiously. "Sure," said Brush. "The queen of diamonds is a wild card, so I call it the ace of spades. All my other cards are wild, so I call them king, queen, jack, ten of spades." The women laid their hands down and looked at Brush. "Well, you both got royal flushes, too," he said, "but mine is spades and is high. You called me, and that gave me the right to name my suit. I win." He took in the chips.

The Brushes said good night and left shortly after that. They went out to the elevator in silence, and in silence they went out to the car, and in silence they drove off. Mr. Brush at last began to chortle. "Darn good game, Soap-in-Your-Eye," he said. Mrs. Brush stared at him, evilly, for a full minute. "You terrible person," she said. Mr. Brush broke into loud and hearty laughter. He ho-hoed all the way down the Grand Concourse. He had had a swell time after all.

The State of Bontana

I AM sure that it must have been Dudley Pierce who introduced Oral Categories into our little group. A curious light comes into his eyes when people gather together in a comfortable room and begin to talk. Dudley can hardly wait for a lull in the conversation; very often, indeed, he makes a lull in the conversation: "How about some Oral Categories?" he will shout, much to the annoyance of whoever is saying to whomever else, "What! You don't know André Simon's 'The Art of Good Living'? But one cannot——"

Oral Categories, as you may know, goes like this. Whoever is It takes a letter, say M, and the others wait, more or less breathlessly, for him to name a category. Suppose he has taken M and says, "A make of automobile!" Then the first person who names an automobile beginning with M—Marmon, for example—wins a point. The first player to win five points is It and he, in turn, selects another letter and names more categories, and so it goes until people get tired of it, or bored, or, as has been happening more and more often in our circle, annoyed, hurt, or downright angry.

The game has, as a matter of fact, thrown a clear white light for me upon some of my friends who, until it was instituted among us, were simply the pleasant, conventional figures that most of our friends are—those friends, I mean, whom we rarely become intimate with but nevertheless think we know quite well by mingling with them, year in and year out, at parties. They have taken on color and character for me, dropped their masks, spoken in unfamiliar tones, stood out sharply in strange and new postures.

There is, for instance, Viola Drake. The fact that she was married, about a year ago, to Holman Drake brought her into our group. Until Categories came along we had all supposed that her silences draped, charmingly enough, an almost total lack of interest in anything except Holman.

Certainly no one had been able to draw her out on any subject (I see now that no one tried the right ones). She became, quite suddenly, articulate and varied in this peculiar game. I recall the night that the letter A and the category Bird came up. "Avocet," said Viola in her low, cool voice before anyone else spoke (most of us shout out our answers excitedly). There was a rustle and a muttering. Then: "What kind of a bird is that?" demanded Myra Hertzman, shrilly. "I never heard of a whatever-it-is." Myra's voice always has the pitch and fever of a person describing a train wreck. None of the rest of us, I think, had heard of an avocet either. "It's a water bird with long legs and a long curved bill," said Viola. Somebody looked it up in a dictionary and there, of course, it was.

Michael Lindsey announced, in the admiring pause that followed, that we had all missed Auk. "Yes," said Kaley Geren, "and Albatross." Then somebody else observed that there didn't seem to be any other birds than those three whose names began with A. "Not many, certainly," said Viola. I asked her if she knew any more. "Well," she said, "there are the Ash-throated Flycatcher and the Arkansas Kingbird, if you would allow them. They're very real," she said to Myra, smiling. We were impressed; there was a murmur of approbation. When Viola a moment later said "Arachne" and won the next category also, I began to realize for the first time that this lady had been beaten into her silences by our continuous gabble about liquor and books and economics.

But if our little game has brought Viola into flower, so to speak, it has definitely made enemies of Michael Lindsey and Kaley Geren, who, up until Categories, had maintained a polite friendship despite their fundamental differences of opinion about Chianti, John Dos Passos, and Marxism. It began the night that Lindsey had the letter B and named as a category "a kind of camel." Nobody answered for many minutes. Lindsey smiled his superior smile. "Give up?" he asked. "Wait a second," said Geren. "I know it as well as you do." "*Big* camel!" squealed Myra Hertzman, giggling. Myra always has her joke, her series of jokes, about every letter and category that are named. "How about a camel named Bert?" she added. Geren, who was trying to think, frowned at her. "Give up?" said Lindsey, again. "No, no," said Geren. "Wait a second." Lindsey's smile became definitely smug. Geren, I feel sure, actually knew the word, but he had groped his way into a morass of B's. The psychological pitfalls and illusions of the game are many. The answer in this particular case—Bactrian, of course, though none of us could think of it—was on the end of Geren's tongue, on the edge of his mind, but so were a lot of other words beginning with B, including Big Camel and Bert Camel. In the end, bewitched by alliterations, Geren abruptly shouted out "Bucephalus!" thinking, for a wild moment, that he had got his hands on the word he was seeking for. Lindsey laughed. "Bucephalus was the war horse of Alexander the Great, Kaley," he said, patronizingly. "Of course it was," said Kaley. "I know that. I know that as well as you know it, but—" "But you just couldn't think of it, could you, dear?" asked his wife, innocently. She was, I think, merely trying to avert what she discerned as approaching trouble between the two, but Kaley took it to mean that she thought he didn't know what Bucephalus was. He understands the nuances of her inflections better than I do, but I think he was wrong. "Certainly I know it!" snapped Kaley. "Everybody knows it!" "I don't know it!" screamed Myra. "Anyway, nobody's got the answer to the big bad camel yet!" That brought Geren back to that. He had to give up, still insisting he knew but couldn't think. "Bactrian," said Lindsey smoothly. Geren sniffed and made a gesture. Lindsey lighted a cigarette. That was the beginning of a growing formality between them and, as far as I know, a widening chasm between the Gerens themselves, for I could foresee a cold, tense argument in their car on the way home:

"Just exactly why you see fit to hold me up to ridicule before that fellow Lindsey is, of course, your own . . ."

Nobody (unless it is Garrison) has been made more miserable by our favorite game than John Almond. Almond has as fine a mind and as wide a general knowledge as any man I know, but he invariably becomes mind-tied when Oral Categories is started. If you took R and then said "Name a flower" he would be unable, for some strange reason, to think of Rose. He just sits there, staring at the floor, a heavy, angry look on his face. I daresay the machinery of his mentality is too complex for him to turn out instantly an obvious and meagre little word. But he is sensitive and easily annoyed. The game has got to him. He worries about it, hates it, but comes back to it the way an unlucky player comes back to the roulette table. Grace Almond, confident of his potential superiority, has taken to railing at him merrily during the games. "Poor Johnny didn't do very well at his lessons in school," she will say. That always gives Lindsey—and Myra Hertzman—a laugh (Myra would get a laugh out of any sudden announcement, even that someone had dropped dead). Almond pretends to take the joking in all good humor, but recently it has been apparent to me that he forces his smile. I think that on their way home from the last party the Almonds must have "had it out," because John did not win one point that night and Grace blithely called attention to it at the door and patted his cheek and said, "Poor Johnny didn't do so well at his lessons in school." She doesn't hit on many little quips and when she does she holds onto them. I think this one had the effect on John of a half-finished mug of ale that has stood all night and I imagine that he said so and I imagine that she slept in the guest-room, crying.

It was Garrison, however, who took the worst beating at our last party. He doesn't come to our parties often, has never enjoyed the game, and rarely gets into it, preferring to sit in a corner and read a book or (as I have often noticed) look at Louise Grayson with furtive eyes. He did get into the game this last night, however. Lillian Garrison, jumpy, small, with a rasping voice, fairly tugged him into it: "Now you're *not* going to *sit* there and *read* all evening!" He came into it the way Jeffries came into the ring with Jack Johnson, if you happen to remember.

Garrison is, or was, one of the ablest executives in town, a quiet, fiftyish, forceful man who loves the last firm dignified word and is bred to a posture of dominance. In the very first category his "Pierce-Arrow" trailed in a bad third behind his own wife's "Packard" and Lindsey's "Peerless" and he felt, I could see, a little silly, for he had barked out his futile answer in a voice of peremptory command. It was a bad start and for several categories thereafter he maintained a haughty silence. Lindsey eventually won and became It again—for the third or fourth time—whereupon Kaley Geren got up and muttered something about he guessed he'd mix another drink.

Lindsey took the letter B. "Name a state in the Union!" he snapped. "Boston!" shouted someone, excitedly, and then flushed as the others hooted. Of course there was then a long silence, for there is no state beginning with B. "Bassachusetts!" squealed Myra Hertzman. "Bidaho! Butah! Bontana!"

"All right," said Lindsey, finally. "There is no state with B. All right, I'll take—*a kind of bird!*"

"Beagle!" roared Garrison instantly, very erect, red in the face, a bit pontifical. He had been beautifully tricked by Myra's Bidaho, Butah, etc., into putting a B in front of Eagle. Everybody, of course, shouted with laughter. It was a long time dying down. Myra Hertzman laughed till she cried. Garrison laughed, too, but in a strange, choked, artificial way, as if he were being sick in an airplane. He crossed his legs and flung one arm over the back of his chair and glared at Myra as if he would have liked to choke her slowly and pleasurably to death. He didn't look at Louise Grayson. "Bb-beagle," chortled Myra, with tears streaming. "He said Beagle!" Dudley Pierce quietly won that round, in the confusion, with Barnswallow.

"All right, all right!" said Lindsey. "Here comes another. Here comes another. Ready? *A kind of dog!*"

"Beagle," said Viola Drake instantly, in her cool, even voice. Nobody else, I am sure, would have thought of saying it: we had all been tricked again as far as naming that particular breed of dog went, all except the inimitable Viola—and Kaley Geren, who was out in the kitchen moodily mixing drinks. Garrison apparently took Viola's answer as the further rubbing in of an insult. His face became heavily flushed again. Presently he observed that it was infernally late. I imagine that on the way home he suddenly "began on" Mrs. Garrison. "*Beagle!* Bah! Bird-dog, Baffin Bay hound, Bulldog, Boxer!" He probably shouted at her, pounding the steering wheel with one gloved hand. "The hell

with all those shallow-pated people! The hell with all of
them, especially that simpering, giggling, empty-headed——
—–——— of a Hertzman woman!"

It is, I am sure, a bad game; a bad game for friends, unless
they are the very best of friends. It is much better to play
some nice, comfortable card game—say Red Dog.

Mr. Pendly and the Poindexter

MR. PENDLY hadn't driven the family car for five years,
since, to be exact, the night of the twenty-third of October,
1930, when he mistook a pond for a new concrete road and
turned off onto it. He didn't really drive into the pond, only
hovered at the marge, for Mrs. Pendly shut off the ignition
and jerked the emergency brake. Mr. Pendly was only forty-
two, but his eyes weren't what they had been. After that
night, Mrs. Pendly always drove the car. She even drove it
during the daytime, for although Mr. Pendly could see in the
daytime, his nerve was gone. He was obsessed with the fear
that he wouldn't see the traffic lights, or would get them
mixed up with lights on storefronts, or would jam on his
brakes when postmen blew their whistles. You can't drive
toward a body of water thinking it's made of concrete
without having your grip on yourself permanently loosened.

Mr. Pendly was not particularly unhappy about the actual
fact of not driving a car any more. He had never liked to
drive much. It galled him slightly that his wife could see
better than he could and it gave him a feeling of inferiority to
sit mildly beside her while she solved the considerable
problems of city traffic. He used to dream at night of
descending, in an autogiro, on some garden party she was

attending: he would come down in a fine landing, leap out, shout "Hahya, Bee!," sweep her into the machine, and zoom away. He used to think of things like that while he was riding with her.

One day Mrs. Pendly said she thought they ought to trade in the old car for another one. What she had in mind was a second-hand Poindexter—she was tired of small cars. You could, she said, get perfectly marvellous bargains in 1932 and 1933 Poindexters. Mr. Pendly said he supposed you could. He didn't know anything about Poindexters, and very little about any automobile. He knew how to make them go and how to stop them, and how to back up. Mrs. Pendly was not good at backing up. When she turned her head and looked behind her, her mind and hands ceased to coördinate. It rather pleased Mr. Pendly that his wife was not good at backing up. Still, outside of that, she knew more about cars than he ever would. The thought depressed him.

Mrs. Pendly went to the Poindexter Sales Company, up near Columbus Circle, one day, spent an hour looking around the various floors with a salesman named Huss, and located finally what she described to her husband that evening as a perfectly lovely bargain. True, it was a '31 model, but a late '31 model and not an early '31 model. Mr. Pendly said he didn't think there ever were two models in one year, but she said Mr. Huss told her there were, that everybody knew there were, and that you could tell by the radiator cap.

She took Mr. Pendly up to the Poindexter place the next afternoon to see the car. They had to wait a long time for Mr. Huss. Mr. Pendly got restless. All the shining Poindexter 16's in the main showroom seemed to him as big as hook-and-ladders and as terrifying. He worried because he knew Mr. Huss would expect him to ask acute technical questions about the car, to complain of this and that. Mr. Huss, finding out that Mr. Pendly didn't know anything at all about automobiles, would sniff in surprise and disdain. A husband whose wife drove the car!

Mr. Huss turned out to be a large, vital man. Mr. Pendly was vital enough, but not as large as Mr. Huss. Their meeting was not much fun for either one. As they got into an elevator to go to the sixth floor, where the lovely bargain was, Mr. Huss kept referring to it as a nice job. The sixth floor was filled with second-hand cars and with mechanics, pounding and buffing and tinkering. Mr. Pendly had the same feeling in the presence of mechanics that, as a child, he had had during church sermons: he felt that he was at the mercy of malignant powers beyond his understanding.

When they stood in front of the Poindexter that Mrs. Pendly had picked out, Huss said to Mr. Pendly: "Whatta you think of that for a piece of merchandise?" Mr. Pendly touched a front fender with his fingers. The salesman waited for him to say something, but he didn't say anything. The only part of a car that Mr. Pendly could think of at the moment was the fan belt. He felt it would be silly to ask to see the fan belt. Maybe Poindexters didn't have fan belts. Mr. Pendly frowned, opened the back door, and shut it. He noticed the monogram of the previous owner on the door. "That monogram," said Mr. Pendly, "would have to come off." Since it seemed that this was all Mr. Pendly had to say, his wife and Mr. Huss ignored him and got into an intricate talk about grinding valves, relining brakes, putting in a new battery. Mr. Pendly felt the way he used to in school when he hadn't prepared his homework. He waited for an opening to cut in on the conversation and thought he saw one when Mrs. Pendly said that she didn't like the car not having a vacuum pump. Mr. Pendly jumped to the conclusion that a vacuum pump was something you could buy and put under the back seat, like a fire-extinguisher. "We could pick up a vacuum pump in any accessory shop," he said. Both his wife and Mr. Huss gave him a surprised look and then went on to the question of the rear tires.

Mr. Pendly wandered sadly over to where a mechanic was lying under a big car. As he got there, the mechanic crawled out from under, jumped up, and brushed against Mr. Pendly. "Look out, Bud," said the mechanic, who was chewing tobacco. Bud walked back to where his wife and Mr. Huss were. He had suddenly thought of the word "transmission," and had some idea of asking Mr. Huss about that. It occurred to him, however, that maybe free-wheeling had done away with transmission and that he would just be showing his ignorance. Mr. Huss was trying to get the luggage compartment at the back of the Poindexter open, because Mrs. Pendly said she had to see how large it was. The key wouldn't work. Mr. Huss shouted for somebody named Mac, and presently the chewing mechanic walked over. He couldn't open the compartment either, and went away. Mrs. Pendly and the salesman walked off to look at the compartment on a similar car, and Mr. Pendly set to work. In a few minutes he found out what was the matter. You had to press down on the cover and then turn the key! He had the back open when his wife and Huss returned. They didn't pay any attention to it. They were talking about mileage.

"I got the back open," said Mr. Pendly, finally.

"This was a chauffeur-driven car," said Mr. Huss. "And it was handled like a watch. There's another hundred thousand miles in it."

"The front seat would have to be lowered," said Mrs. Pendly, "I couldn't be stuck way up in the air like that."

"We'll take care of that," said Huss. "That'll be easy."

"You want to see into the back now?" asked Mr. Pendly.

"And you'd be sure to have the brakes tested?" Mrs. Pendly said to Huss.

"Those brakes will be A-1 when the job leaves this room," said Huss. "We never turn out a piece of merchandise here that isn't A-1."

Mr. Pendly shut the baggage compartment. Then he opened it again. He did this a couple more times.

"Come on, Bert," his wife said.

On the way home—Mrs. Pendly had decided to think the bargain over, although Huss said somebody else would snap it up if she didn't snap it up—Mr. Pendly sat beside his wife in their old car and thought. She prattled along about the Poindexter but he didn't really hear, although now and then he grunted some answer in a monotone. He was imagining that, as he sauntered over to Mac, Mac got out from under the big car he was working on and said: "Well, it's got me licked." Mr. Pendly smiled. "Yeah?" he said, slowly removing his coat and vest. He handed them to Mac. Then he crawled under the car, looked the works over coldly, tinkered delicately and expertly with a couple of rods and a piston, tightened a winch gasket, blew softly into a valve, and crawled out again. He put on his coat and vest. "Try her now," he said, indifferently, to Mac. Mac tried her. She worked beautifully. The big mechanic turned slowly to Mr. Pendly and held out an oily hand. "Brother," said Mac, "I hand it to you. Where did you ev——?"

"What's the matter; are you in a trance or what?" asked Mrs. Pendly, pulling her husband's sleeve. He gave her a cold, superior look.

"Never mind about me," he said.

The Indian Sign

"MR. PINWITHER is doing wonders with the new Cora Allyn letter," Mrs. Bentley told her husband. He winced slightly. Three letters about the old lady hadn't been enough; somebody had had to turn up another one.

"That's fine," said Mr. Bentley, taking off his overcoat

and hanging it up in the hall closet.

"It's all about their moving to New Milford—in 1667," said Mrs. Bentley. "There's nothing new in it, he says, about the Indians." She seemed disappointed.

"That's fine," said Mr. Bentley again. His wife, on the verge of a new eagerness, apparently didn't hear.

"*And*," she said, "Cora learned a new word today!" *This* Cora, Mr. Bentley knew, was of course his little daughter. He really meant his "That's fine" this time. Still, he winced again. He had wanted to name his daughter Rosemary, after a dream. But his wife and all the stern and silly pride of the Allyns had been behind "Cora." Since a certain day almost three hundred years ago the first female born into every ramification of the Allyn family had been named Cora: "After old Cora Cora herself," as Henry Bentley said at the Comics' Club the night his daughter was born.

The original Cora Allyn, his little girl's great-great-great-great-great-grandmother, had slain nineteen Pequot Indians single-handed in an incredible and dimly authenticated struggle near New London, Connecticut, in 1643, or 1644. The Allyns could never be positive of the year, for the letters bearing upon the incident were almost three centuries old, yellow and brittle and written crisscross, the thrifty and illegible Colonial method of saving postage charges. Two were undated and the date of the other was faded and tricky, like all of the writing in the three priceless heirlooms of the Allyn family. The letters purported to have been written by one Loyal Holgate, supposedly a young divine, and—Bentley had examined them carefully, or as carefully as anyone who was not an Allyn was allowed to—there apparently *were* passages in them about one Cora Allyn's having slain nineteen Indians. Some of the most eminent antiquarians in the country, including Mr. Pinwither, had pored over the letters. They had all but one brought out of the vague, faint scrawlings virtually the same story of the early New England lady's heroic deed. The saturnine Murray Kraull had, it is true, doubted that the word "nineteen" was really "nineteen" and even that "Pequots" was "Pequots." He had, indeed, gone so far as to suggest that the phrase might be "no male peacocks," for which heresy he had practically been hustled out of Mrs. Bentley's mother's house. The other experts had all conformed, however, to the letter—and the number—of the legend. In Henry Bentley's mind, as in Mr. Kraull's, there would always remain a doubt.

Mr. Bentley, quietly and in secret, had long been elaborating on his doubt. So far as he had been able to find out, there was no record of a Cora Allyn who had slain nineteen Indians. There had been a rather famous incident in which a band of Pequots killed a Mrs. Anne Williamson, a Massachusetts woman who had settled near Stamford, but that was all. Once, to make a dinner topic, he had tossed out timidly to his wife that he had come upon an old history of the state at his office and so far had found in it no reference to any woman who had killed nineteen Indians. Mrs. Bentley's quick, indignant look had caused him to mumble the rest of his suspicions into his shirt-front. It was the closest he ever came to expressing openly his feeling in the matter.

"The new letter," said Mrs. Bentley, as they walked into the living-room, "tells some more about Rockbottom Thraillkill, the minister who established the third church in what is now New Milford. It was called Appasottowams then, or something like that. It is all in Mr. Pinwither's report."

"That's close enough," said Mr. Bentley. He strove to change the subject. "What did my little girl say today?" he asked.

"Cora? She said 'telephone.'"

"That's fine," said Mr. Bentley. It was terrible the way he allowed the name Cora to affect him. There were literally hundreds of Coras among his wife's connections. They kept recurring, like leaf blight, among the spreading branches of the Allyn family. And scarcely a day went by but what someone alluded to the first, great Cora. He encountered her glib ghost at all family gatherings, on all holidays, and before, during, and after every family ceremony, such as marriage, birth, christening, divorce, and death.

Mrs. Bentley talked about the small excitements of her day during dinner. Her husband affected to listen, and now and then gave a sympathetic grunt, but he was quietly contemplating that early American heroine who was so damnably intertwined with his life. Supposing that the story about her *were* true? Why be so insistently conscious and so eternally proud of an ancestor who killed nineteen Indians? Her openmouthed, wild-eyed gestures during the unmatronly ordeal, the awkwardness of her stance, the disarray of her apparel, must have been disturbingly unattractive. The vision of his little daughter's forebear, who up to her great hour had undoubtedly depended rather charmingly upon a sturdy pioneer husband, suddenly learning that she was more than a match for nineteen males affected Henry Bentley dismally; it saddened him to be continually carried back along the rocky, well-forgotten roads of American life to the prophetic figure of Cora Allyn, standing there against the sky, with her matchlock or her hunting knife or her axe handle, so outrageously and significantly triumphant.

Henry had often tried to get a picture of the famous Cora's husband, old Coppice Allyn. There was little mention of him in the frail letters of almost three centuries ago. Old Coppice was rarely mentioned by the Allyns, either; he remained staunch but indistinct, like a figure in the background of a wood-cut. He had cleared away trees, he had built a house, he had dug a well, he had had a touch of brain fever—things like that: no vivid, red, immortal gestures. What must he have thought that April evening (not "April" but "apple," Kraull had made it out) when he came home from the fields to find a new gleam in his wife's eyes and nineteen new corpses under her feet? He must have felt some vague, alarming resentment; he must have realized, however dimly,

that this was the beginning of a new weave in the fabric of life in the Colonies. Poor old Coppice!

"I want to show you," said Mrs. Bentley after dinner, "Mr. Pinwither's report. Of course it's just a preliminary. Mother sent it over."

"That's fine," said Mr. Bentley. He watched his wife go out of the room and tried to be glad that she, at least, was not a Cora; her oldest sister held that honor. That was something. Mr. Bentley seized the chance, now that he was alone, to reflect upon his latest clandestine delving into the history of the Connecticut Indians. The Pequots, he had discovered in a book that very afternoon, had been woefully incompetent fighters. Some early militarist had written of them that, fighting as they did, they "couldn't have killed seven people in seven years." They shot their arrows high into the air: anybody could see them coming and step out of the way. The Colonial militiamen used to pick up the flinted sticks, break them in two, and laugh at their helpless foes. Even when the shafts did get home, they almost never killed; a neckcloth would turn them aside or even, as in the case of one soldier, a piece of cheese carried in one's pocket. Poor, pathetic, stupid old Pequots! Brave they had undeniably been, but dumb. Mr. Bentley had suddenly a rather kindly feeling for the Pequots. And he had, at the same time, a new, belittling vision of that grand old lady, the first Cora: he saw her leisurely firing through a chink in the wall of her house, taking all afternoon to knock off nineteen Indians who had no chance against her, who stood on the edge of a clearing firing arrows wistfully into the sky until one of the white woman's blunderbuss slugs—a tenpenny nail or a harness buckle—struck them down. If only they had rushed her! If only one of them had been smart enough to light the end of an arrow and stick it burning in the roof of the Allyn house! They would have finished her off fast enough if they had ever got her outside! Mr. Bentley's heart beat faster and his eyes blinked brightly.

"What is it?" asked Mrs. Bentley, coming back into the room. Her husband looked so eager and pleased, sitting there.

"I was just thinking," he said.

Mr. Pinwither's preliminary report on the new letter was long and dull. Mr. Bentley tried to look interested: he knew better than to appear indifferent to any holy relic connected with the Great Cora.

"Cora's had such a day!" said Mrs. Bentley, as they were preparing for bed. "She went to sleep playing with those toy soldiers and Indians her Uncle Bert gave her." Mr. Bentley had one of his vivid pictures of Uncle Bert. "Um," he said, and went downstairs to get his aspirin box out of his coat.

Before he went to bed, Mr. Bentley stopped in the nursery to have a good-night look at his little sleeping daughter. She lay sweetly with her hands curled above her head. Mr. Bentley regarded the little girl with sad eyes. The line of her forehead and the curve of her chin were (or so the Allyns hysterically claimed) the unmistakable sign of the Great Cora, the proof of the child's proud heritage, the latest blaze along the trail. He stood above her, thinking, a long time.

When Mr. Bentley went back to the bedroom, it was pitch-dark; his wife had turned out the light. He tiptoed in. He heard her slow, deep breathing. She was sound asleep.

"Henry?" she called suddenly out of the blackness. Surprised, he did not answer.

"Henry!" she said. There was uneasiness and drowsy bewilderment in her voice.

To Henry Bentley, standing there in the darkness, there came a quick, wild urge. He tried to restrain it, and then, abruptly, he gave way to it, with a profound sense of release. Patting the fingers of his right hand rapidly against his open lips, he gave, at the top of his voice, the Pequot war whoop: "Ah-wah-wah-wah-wah!"

The Private Life of Mr. Bidwell

FROM WHERE she was sitting, Mrs. Bidwell could not see her husband, but she had a curious feeling of tension: she knew he was up to something.

"What are you doing, George?" she demanded, her eyes still on her book.

"Mm?"

"What's the matter with you?"

"Pahhhhh-h-h," said Mr. Bidwell, in a long, pleasurable exhale. "I was holding my breath."

Mrs. Bidwell twisted creakingly in her chair and looked at him; he was sitting behind her in his favorite place under the parchment lamp with the street scene of old New York on it. "I was just holding my breath," he said again.

"Well, please don't do it," said Mrs. Bidwell, and went back to her book. There was silence for five minutes.

"George!" said Mrs. Bidwell.

"Bwaaaaaa," said Mr. Bidwell. "What?"

"Will you please *stop* that?" she said. "It makes me nervous."

"I don't see how that bothers you," he said. "Can't I breathe?"

"You can breathe without holding your breath like a goop," said Mrs. Bidwell. "Goop" was a word that she was fond of using; she rather lazily applied it to everything. It annoyed Mr. Bidwell.

"Deep breathing," said Mr. Bidwell, in the impatient tone he used when explaining anything to his wife, "is good exercise. You ought to take more exercise."

"Well, please don't do it around me," said Mrs. Bidwell, turning again to the pages of Mr. Galsworthy.

At the Cowans' party, a week later, the room was full of chattering people when Mrs. Bidwell, who was talking to Lida Carroll, suddenly turned around as if she had been summoned. In a chair in a far corner of the room, Mr. Bidwell was holding his breath. His chest was expanded, his chin drawn in; there was a strange stare in his eyes, and his face was slightly empurpled. Mrs. Bidwell moved into the line of his vision and gave him a sharp, penetrating look. He deflated slowly and looked away.

Later, in the car, after they had driven in silence a mile or more on the way home, Mrs. Bidwell said, "It seems to me you might at least have the kindness not to hold your breath

in other people's houses."

"I wasn't hurting anybody," said Mr. Bidwell.

"You looked silly!" said his wife. "You looked perfectly crazy!" She was driving and she began to speed up, as she always did when excited or angry. "What do you suppose people thought—you sitting there all swelled up, with your eyes popping out?"

"I wasn't all swelled up," he said angrily.

"You looked like a goop," she said. The car slowed down, sighed, and came to a complete, despondent stop.

"We're out of gas," said Mrs. Bidwell. It was bitterly cold and nastily sleeting. Mr. Bidwell took a long, deep breath.

The breathing situation in the Bidwell family reached a critical point when Mr. Bidwell began to inhale in his sleep, slowly, and exhale with a protracted, growling "woooooooo." Mrs. Bidwell, ordinarily a sound sleeper (except on nights when she was sure burglars were getting in), would wake up and reach over and shake her husband. "George!" she would say.

"Hawwwwww," Mr. Bidwell would say, thickly. "Wahs maa nah, hm?"

After he had turned over and gone back to sleep, Mrs. Bidwell would lie awake, thinking.

One morning at breakfast she said, "George, I'm not going to put up with this another day. If you can't stop blowing up like a grampus, I'm going to leave you." There was a slight, quick lift in Mr. Bidwell's heart, but he tried to look surprised and hurt.

"All right," he said. "Let's not talk about it."

Mrs. Bidwell buttered another piece of toast. She described to him the way he sounded in his sleep. He read the paper.

With considerable effort, Mr. Bidwell kept from inflating his chest for about a week, but one night at the McNally's he hit on the idea of seeing how many seconds he could hold his breath. He was rather bored by the McNally's party, anyway. He began timing himself with his wrist-watch in a remote corner of the living-room. Mrs. Bidwell, who was in the kitchen talking children and clothes with Bea McNally, left her abruptly and slipped back into the living-room. She stood quietly behind her husband's chair. He knew she was there, and tried to let out his breath imperceptibly.

"I see you," she said, in a low, cold tone. Mr. Bidwell jumped up.

"Why don't you let me alone?" he demanded.

"Will you please lower your voice?" she said, smiling so that if anyone were looking he wouldn't think the Bidwells were arguing.

"I'm getting pretty damned tired of this," said Bidwell in a low voice.

"You've ruined my evening!" she whispered.

"You've ruined mine, too!" he whispered back. They knifed each other, from head to stomach, with their eyes.

"Sitting here like a goop, holding your breath," said Mrs. Bidwell. "People will think you are an idiot." She laughed, turning to greet a lady who was approaching them.

Mr. Bidwell sat in his office the next afternoon, a black, moist afternoon, tapping a pencil on his desk, and scowling. "All right, then, get out, get out!" he muttered. "What do I care?" He was visualizing the scene when Mrs. Bidwell would walk out on him. After going through it several times, he returned to his work, feeling vaguely contented. He made up his mind to breathe any way he wanted to, no matter what she did. And, having come to this decision, he oddly enough, and quite without effort, lost interest in holding his breath.

Everything went rather smoothly at the Bidwells' for a month or so. Mr. Bidwell didn't do anything to annoy his wife beyond leaving his razor on her dressing-table and forgetting to turn out the hall light when he went to bed. Then there came the night of the Bentons' party.

Mr. Bidwell, bored as usual, was sitting in a far corner of the room, breathing normally. His wife was talking animatedly with Beth Williamson about negligees. Suddenly her voice slowed and an uneasy look came into her eyes: George was up to something. She turned around and sought him out. To anyone but Mrs. Bidwell he must have seemed like any husband sitting in a chair. But his wife's lips set tightly. She walked casually over to him.

"What are you doing?" she demanded.

"Hm?" he said, looking at her vacantly.

"What are you *doing*?" she demanded, again. He gave her a harsh, venomous look, which she returned.

"I'm multiplying numbers in my head," he said, slowly and evenly, "if you must know." In the prolonged, probing examination that they silently, without moving any muscles save those of their eyes, gave each other, it became solidly, frozenly apparent to both of them that the end of their endurance had arrived. The curious bond that held them together snapped—rather more easily than either had supposed was possible. That night, while undressing for bed, Mr. Bidwell calmly multiplied numbers in his head. Mrs. Bidwell stared coldly at him for a few moments, holding a stocking in her hand; she didn't bother to berate him. He paid no attention to her. The thing was simply over.

George Bidwell lives alone now (his wife remarried). He never goes to parties any more, and his old circle of friends rarely sees him. The last time that any of them did see him, he was walking along a country road with the halting, uncertain gait of a blind man: he was trying to see how many steps he could take without opening his eyes.

The Curb in the Sky

WHEN CHARLIE Deshler announced that he was going to marry Dorothy, someone said he would lose his mind posthaste. "No," said a wit who knew them both, "post hoc." Dorothy had begun, when she was quite young, to finish sentences for people. Sometimes she finished them wrongly, which annoyed the person who was speaking, and sometimes she finished them correctly, which annoyed the speaker even more.

"When William Howard Taft was—" some guest in Dorothy's family's home would begin.

"President!" Dorothy would pipe up. The speaker may have meant to say "President" or he may have meant to say "young," or "Chief Justice of the Supreme Court of the United States." In any case, he would shortly put on his hat and go home. Like most parents, Dorothy's parents did not seem to be conscious that her mannerism was a nuisance. Very likely they thought that it was cute, or even bright. It is even probable that when Dorothy's mother first said "Come, Dorothy, eat your—" and Dorothy said "Spinach, dear," the former telephoned Dorothy's father at the office and told him about it, and he told everybody he met that day about it—and the next day and the day after.

When Dorothy grew up she became quite pretty and so even more of a menace. Gentlemen became attracted to her and then attached to her. Emotionally she stirred them, but mentally she soon began to wear them down. Even in her late teens she began correcting their English. "Not 'was,' Arthur," she would say, "'were.' 'Were prepared.' See?" Most of her admirers tolerated this habit because of their interest in her lovely person, but as time went on and her interest in them remained more instructive than sentimental, they slowly drifted away to less captious, if dumber, girls.

Charlie Deshler, however, was an impetuous man, of the sweep-them-off-their-feet persuasion, and he became engaged to Dorothy so quickly and married her in so short a time that, being deaf to the warnings of friends, whose concern he regarded as mere jealousy, he really didn't know anything about Dorothy except that she was pretty and bright-eyed and (to him) desirable.

Dorothy as a wife came, of course, into her great flowering: she took to correcting Charlie's stories. He had travelled widely and experienced greatly and was a truly excellent *raconteur*. Dorothy was, during their courtship, genuinely interested in him and in his stories, and since she had never shared any of the adventures he told about, she could not know when he made mistakes in time or in place or in identities. Beyond suggesting a change here and there in the number of a verb, she more or less let him alone. Charlie spoke rather good English, anyway—he knew when to say "were" and when to say "was" after "if"—and this was another reason he didn't find Dorothy out.

I didn't call on them for quite a while after they were married, because I liked Charlie and I knew I would feel low if I saw him coming out of the anesthetic of her charms and beginning to feel the first pains of reality. When I did finally call, conditions were, of course, all that I had feared. Charlie began to tell, at dinner, about a motor trip the two had made to this town and that—I never found out for sure what towns, because Dorothy denied almost everything that Charlie said. "The next day," he would say, "we got an early start and drove two hundred miles to Fairview—" "Well," Dorothy would say, "I wouldn't call it *early*. It wasn't as early as the first day we set out, when we got up about *seven*. And we only drove a hundred and eighty miles, because I remember looking at that mileage thing when we started."

"Anyway, when we got to Fairview—" Charlie would go on. But Dorothy would stop him. "Was it Fairview that day, darling?" she would ask. Dorothy often interrupted Charlie by asking him if he were right, instead of telling him that he was wrong, but it amounted to the same thing, for if he would reply: "Yes, I'm sure it was Fairview," she would say: "But it *wasn't*, darling," and then go on with the story herself. (She called everybody that she differed from "darling.")

Once or twice, when I called on them or they called on me, Dorothy would let Charlie get almost to the climax of some interesting account of a happening and then, like a tackler from behind, throw him just as he was about to cross the goal-line. There is nothing in life more shocking to the nerves and to the mind than this. Some husbands will sit back amiably—almost it seems, proudly—when their wives interrupt, and let them get on with the story, but these are beaten husbands. Charlie did not become beaten. But his wife's tackles knocked the wind out of him, and he began to realize that he would have to do something. What he did was rather

ingenious. At the end of the second year of their marriage, when you visited the Deshlers, Charlie would begin some outlandish story about a dream he had had, knowing that Dorothy could not correct him on his own dreams. They became the only life he had that was his own.

"I thought I was running an airplane," he would say, "made out of telephone wires and pieces of old leather. I was trying to make it fly to the moon, taking off from my bedroom. About halfway up to the moon, however, a man who looked like Santa Claus, only he was dressed in the uniform of a customs officer, waved at me to stop—he was in a plane made of telephone wires, too. So I pulled over to a cloud. 'Here,' he said to me, 'you can't go to the moon, if you are the man who invented these wedding cookies.' Then he showed me a cookie made in the shape of a man and woman being married—little images of a man and a woman and a minister, made of dough and fastened firmly to a round, crisp cookie base." So he would go on.

Any psychiatrist will tell you that at the end of the way Charlie was going lies madness in the form of monomania. You can't live in a fantastic dream world, night in and night out and then day in and day out, and remain sane. The substance began to die slowly out of Charlie's life, and he began to live entirely in shadow. And since monomania of this sort is likely to lead in the end to the reiteration of one particular story, Charlie's invention began to grow thin and he eventually took to telling, over and over again, the first dream he had ever described—the story of his curious flight toward the moon in an airplane made of telephone wires. It was extremely painful. It saddened us all.

After a month or two, Charlie finally had to be sent to an asylum. I was out of town when they took him away, but Joe Fultz, who went with him, wrote me about it. "He seemed to like it up here right away," Joe wrote. "He's calmer and his eyes look better." (Charlie had developed a wild, hunted look.) "Of course," concluded Joe, "he's finally got away from that woman."

It was a couple of weeks later that I drove up to the asylum to see Charlie. He was lying on a cot on a big screened-in porch, looking wan and thin. Dorothy was sitting on a chair beside his bed, bright-eyed and eager. I was somehow surprised to see her there, having figured that Charlie had, at least, won sanctuary from his wife. He looked quite mad. He began at once to tell me the story of his trip to the moon. He got to the part where the man who looked like Santa Claus waved at him to stop. "He was in a plane made of telephone wires, too," said Charlie. "So I pulled over to a curb——"

"No. You pulled over to a *cloud*," said Dorothy. "There aren't any curbs in the *sky*. There *couldn't* be. You pulled over to a cloud."

Charlie sighed and turned slightly in his bed and looked at me. Dorothy looked at me, too, with her pretty smile.

"He always gets that story wrong," she said.

Mr. Preble Gets Rid of His Wife

MR. PREBLE was a plump middle-aged lawyer in Scarsdale. He used to kid with his stenographer about running away with him. "Let's run away together," he would say, during a pause in dictation. "All righty," she would say.

One rainy Monday afternoon, Mr. Preble was more serious about it than usual.

"Let's run away together," said Mr. Preble.

"All righty," said his stenographer. Mr. Preble jingled the keys in his pocket and looked out the window.

"My wife would be glad to get rid of me," he said.

"Would she give you a divorce?" asked the stenographer.

"I don't suppose so," he said. The stenographer laughed.

"You'd have to get rid of your wife," she said.

Mr. Preble was unusually silent at dinner that night. About half an hour after coffee, he spoke without looking up from his paper.

"Let's go down in the cellar," Mr. Preble said to his wife.

"What for?" she said, not looking up from her book.

"Oh, I don't know," he said. "We never go down in the cellar any more. The way we used to."

"We never did go down in the cellar that I remember," said Mrs. Preble. "I could rest easy the balance of my life if I never went down in the cellar." Mr. Preble was silent for several minutes.

"Supposing I said it meant a whole lot to me," began Mr. Preble.

"What's come over you?" his wife demanded. "It's cold down there and there is absolutely nothing to do."

"We could pick up pieces of coal," said Mr. Preble. "We might get up some kind of a game with pieces of coal."

"I don't want to," said his wife. "Anyway, I'm reading."

"Listen," said Mr. Preble, rising and walking up and down. "Why won't you come down in the cellar? You can read down there, as far as that goes."

"There isn't a good enough light down there," she said, "and anyway, I'm not going to go down in the cellar. You may as well make up your mind to that."

"Gee whiz!" said Mr. Preble, kicking at the edge of a rug. "Other people's wives go down in the cellar. Why is it you never want to do anything? I come home worn out from the office and you won't even go down in the cellar with me. God knows it isn't very far—it isn't as if I was asking you to go to the movies or some place."

"I don't want to *go!*" shouted Mrs. Preble. Mr. Preble sat down on the edge of a davenport.

"All right, all *right*," he said. He picked up the newspaper again. "I wish you'd let me tell you more about it. It's—kind of a surprise."

"Will you quit harping on that subject?" asked Mrs. Preble.

"Listen," said Mr. Preble, leaping to his feet. "I might as well tell you the truth instead of beating around the bush. I want to get rid of you so I can marry my stenographer. Is there anything especially wrong about that? People do it every day. Love is something you can't control——"

"We've been all over that," said Mrs. Preble. "I'm not going to go all over that again."

"I just wanted you to know how things are," said Mr. Preble. "But you have to take everything so literally. Good Lord, do you suppose I really wanted to go down in the cellar and make up some silly game with pieces of coal?"

"I never believed that for a minute," said Mrs. Preble. "I knew all along you wanted to get me down there and bury me."

"You can say that now—after I told you," said Mr. Preble. "But it would never have occurred to you if I hadn't."

"You didn't tell me; I got it out of you," said Mrs. Preble. "Anyway, I'm always two steps ahead of what you're thinking."

"You're never within a mile of what I'm thinking," said Mr. Preble.

"Is that so? I knew you wanted to bury me the minute you set foot in this house tonight." Mrs. Preble held him with a glare.

"Now that's just plain damn exaggeration," said Mr. Preble, considerably annoyed. "You knew nothing of the sort. As a matter of fact, I never thought of it till just a few minutes ago."

"It was in the back of your mind," said Mrs. Preble. "I suppose this filing woman put you up to it."

"You needn't get sarcastic," said Mr. Preble. "I have plenty of people to file without having her file. She doesn't know anything about this. She isn't in on it. I was going to tell her you had gone to visit some friends and fell over a cliff. She wants me to get a divorce."

"That's a laugh," said Mrs. Preble. "*That's* a laugh. You may bury me, but you'll never get a divorce."

"She knows that! I told her that," said Mr. Preble. "I mean—I told her I'd never get a divorce."

"Oh, you probably told her about burying me, too," said Mrs. Preble.

"That's not true," said Mr. Preble, with dignity. "That's between you and me. I was never going to tell a soul."

"You'd blab it to the whole world; don't tell me," said Mrs. Preble. "I know you." Mr. Preble puffed at his cigar.

"I wish you were buried now and it was all over with," he said.

"Don't you suppose you would get caught, you crazy thing?" she said. "They always get caught. Why don't you go to bed? You're just getting yourself all worked up over nothing."

"I'm not going to bed," said Mr. Preble "I'm going to bury you in the cellar. I've got my mind made up to it. I don't know how I could make it any plainer."

"Listen," cried Mrs. Preble, throwing her book down, "will you be satisfied and shut up if I go down in the cellar? Can I have a little peace if I go down in the cellar? Will you let me alone then?"

"Yes," said Mr. Preble. "But you spoil it by taking that attitude."

"Sure, sure, I always spoil everything. I stop reading right in the middle of a chapter. I'll never know how the story comes out—but that's nothing to you."

"Did I make you start reading the book?" asked Mr. Preble. He opened the cellar door. "Here, you go first."

"Brrr," said Mrs. Preble, starting down the steps. "It's *cold* down here! You *would* think of this, at this time of year! Any other husband would have buried his wife in the summer."

"You can't arrange those things just whenever you want to," said Mr. Preble. "I didn't fall in love with this girl till late fall."

"Anybody else would have fallen in love with her long before that. She's been around for years. Why is it you always let other men get in ahead of you? Mercy, but it's dirty down here! What have you got there?"

"I was going to hit you over the head with this shovel," said Mr. Preble.

"You were, huh?" said Mrs. Preble. "Well, get that out of your mind. Do you want to leave a great big clue right here in the middle of everything where the first detective that comes snooping around will find it? Go out in the street and find some piece of iron or something—something that doesn't belong to you."

"Oh, all right," said Mr. Preble. "But there won't be any piece of iron in the street. Women always expect to pick up a piece of iron anywhere."

"If you look in the right place you'll find it," said Mrs. Preble. "And don't be gone long. Don't you dare stop in at the cigarstore. I'm not going to stand down here in this cold cellar all night and freeze."

"All right," said Mr. Preble. "I'll hurry."

"And shut that *door* behind you!" she screamed after him. "Where were you born—in a barn?"

A Portrait of Aunt Ida

MY MOTHER'S Aunt Ida Clemmens died the other day out West. She was ninety-one years old. I remember her clearly, although I haven't thought about her in a long time and never saw her after I was twenty. I remember how dearly she loved catastrophes, especially those of a national or international importance. The sinking of the *Titanic* was perhaps the most important tragedy of the years in which I knew her. She never saw in such things, as her older sisters, Emma and Clara, did, the vengeance of a Deity outraged by Man's lust for speed and gaiety; she looked for the causes deep down in the dark heart of the corporate interests. You could never make her believe that the *Titanic* hit an iceberg. Whoever *heard* of such a thing! It was simply a flimsy prevarication devised to cover up the real cause. The real cause she could not, or would not, make plain, but somewhere in its black core was a monstrous secret of treachery and corrupt goings-on—men were like that. She came later on to doubt the courage of the brave gentlemen on the sinking ship who at the last waved goodbye smilingly and smoked cigarettes. It was her growing conviction that most of them had to be shot by the ship's officers in order to prevent them from crowding into the lifeboats ahead of the older and less attractive women passengers. Eminence and wealth in men Aunt Ida persistently attributed to deceit, trickery, and impiety. I think the only famous person she ever trusted in her time was President McKinley.

The disappearance of Judge Crater, the Hall-Mills murder, the Starr Faithfull case, and similar mysteries must have made Aunt Ida's last years happy. She loved the unsolvable and the unsolved. Mysteries that were never cleared up were brought about, in her opinion, by the workings of some strange force in the world which we do not thoroughly understand and which God does not intend that we ever shall understand. An invisible power, a power akin to electricity and radio (both of which she must have regarded as somehow or other blasphemous), but never to be isolated or channelled. Out of this power came murder, disappearances, and supernatural phenomena. All persons connected in any way whatever with celebrated cases were tainted in Aunt Ida's sight—and that went for prosecuting attorneys, too (always "tricky" men). But she would, I'm sure, rather have had a look at Willie Stevens than at President Roosevelt, at Jafsie than at the King of England, just as she would rather have gone through the old Wendel house than the White House.

*   *   *

Surgical operations and post-mortems were among Aunt Ida's special interests, although she did not believe that any operation was ever necessary and she was convinced that post-mortems were conducted to cover up something rather than to find something out. It was her conviction that doctors were in the habit of trying to obfuscate or distort the true facts about illness and death. She believed that many of her friends and relatives had been laid away without the real causes of their deaths being entered on the "city books." She was fond of telling a long and involved story about the death of one of her first cousins, a married woman who had passed away at twenty-five. Aunt Ida for thirty years contended that there was something "behind it." She believed that a certain physician, a gentleman of the highest reputation, would some day "tell the truth about Ruth," perhaps on his deathbed. When he died (without confessing, of course), she said after reading the account in the newspaper that she had dreamed of him a few nights before. It seemed that he had called to her and wanted to tell her something but couldn't.

Aunt Ida believed that she was terribly psychic. She had warnings, premonitions, and "feelings." They were invariably intimations of approaching misfortune, sickness, or death. She never had a premonition that everything was going to be all right. It was always that Grace So-and-So was not going to marry the man she was engaged to, or that Mr. Hollowell, who was down in South America on business, would never return, or that old Mrs. Hutchins would not last out the year (she missed on old Mrs. Hutchins for twenty-two years but finally made it). Most all of Aunt Ida's forewarnings of financial ruin and marital tragedy came in the daytime while she was marketing or sitting hulling peas; most all of her intimations of death appeared to her in dreams. Dreams of Ohio women of Aunt Ida's generation were never Freudian; they were purely prophetic. They dealt with black hearses and white hearses rolling soundlessly along through the night, and with coffins being carried out of houses, and with tombstones bearing names and dates, and with tall, faceless women in black veils and gloves. Most of Aunt Ida's dreams foretold the fate of women, for what happened to women was of much greater importance to Aunt Ida than what happened to men. Men usually "brought things on themselves"; women, on the other hand, were usually the victims of dark and devious goings-on of a more or less supernatural nature.

Birth was, in some ways, as dark a matter to Aunt Ida as death. She felt that most babies, no matter what you said or anybody else said, were "not wanted." She believed that the children of famous people, brilliant people, and of first, second, or third cousins would be idiotic. If a child died young, she laid it to the child's parentage, no matter what the immediate cause of death might have been. "There is something in that family," Aunt Ida used to say, in her best funeral voice. This something was a vague, ominous thing, both far off and close at hand, misty and ready to spring, compounded of nobody could guess exactly what. One of Aunt Ida's favorite predictions was "They'll never raise that baby, you mark my words." The fact that they usually did never shook her confidence in her "feelings." If she was right once in twenty times, it proved that she knew what she was talking about. In foretelling the sex of unborn children, she was right about half the time.

Life after death was a source of speculation, worry, and exhilaration to Aunt Ida. She firmly believed that people could "come back" and she could tell you of many a house that was haunted (barrels of apples rolled down the attic steps of one of them, I remember, but it was never clear why they did). Aunt Ida put no faith in mediums or séances. The dead preferred to come back to the houses where they had lived and to go stalking through the rooms and down the halls. I think Aunt Ida always thought of them as coming back in the flesh, fully clothed, for she always spoke of them as "the dead," never as ghosts. The reason they came back was that they had left something unsaid or undone that must be corrected. Although a descendant of staunch orthodox Methodists, some of them ministers, Aunt Ida in her later years dabbled a little in various religions, superstitions, and even cults. She found astrology, New Thought, and the theory of reincarnation comforting. The people who are bowed down in this life, she grew to believe, will have another chance.

Aunt Ida was confident that the world was going to be destroyed almost any day. When Halley's comet appeared in 1910, she expected to read in the papers every time she picked them up the news that Paris had gone up in flames and that New York City had slid into the ocean. Those two cities, being horrible dens of vice, were bound to go first; the smaller towns would be destroyed in a more leisurely fashion with some respectable and dignified ending for the pious and the kindly people.

Two of Aunt Ida's favorite expressions were "I never heard of such a thing" and "If I never get up from this chair. . . ." She told all stories of death, misfortune, grief, corruption, and disaster with vehemence and exaggeration. She was hampered in narration by her inability to think of names, particularly simple names, such as Joe, Earl, Ned, Harry, Louise, Ruth, Bert. Somebody usually had to prompt her with the name of the third cousin, or whomever, that she was trying to think of, but she was unerring in her ability to remember difficult names the rest of us had long forgotten. "He used to work in the old Schirtzberger & Wallenheim saddle store in Naughton Street," she would say. "What *was* his name?" It would turn out that his name was Frank Butler.

Up to the end, they tell me, Aunt Ida could read without her glasses, and none of the commoner frailties of senility affected her. She had no persecution complex, no lapses of memory, no trailing off into the past, no unfounded bitternesses—unless you could call her violent hatred of cigarettes unfounded bitterness, and I don't think it was, because she actually knew stories of young men and even young women who had become paralyzed to the point of losing the use of both legs through smoking cigarettes. She tended to her begonias and wrote out a check for the rent the day she took to her bed for the last time. It irked her not to be up and about, and she accused the doctor the family brought in of not knowing his business. There was marketing to do, and friends to call on, and work to get through with. When friends and relatives began calling on her, she was annoyed. Making out that she was really sick! Old Mrs. Kurtz, who is seventy-two, visited her on the last day, and when she left, Aunt Ida looked after her pityingly. "Poor Cora," she said, "she's failin', ain't she?"

The Luck of Jad Peters

AUNT EMMA Peters, at eighty-three—the year she died—still kept in her unused front parlor, on the table with Jad Peters's collection of lucky souvenirs, a large rough fragment of rock weighing perhaps twenty pounds. The rock stood in the centre of a curious array of odds and ends: a piece of tent canvas, a chip of pine wood, a yellowed telegram, some old newspaper clippings, the cork from a bottle, a bill from a surgeon. Aunt Emma never talked about the strange collection except once, during her last days, when somebody asked her if she wouldn't feel better if the rock were thrown away. "Let it stay where Lisbeth put it," she said. All that I know about the souvenirs I have got from other members of

the family. A few of them didn't think it was "decent" that
the rock should have been part of the collection, but Aunt
Lisbeth, Emma's sister, had insisted that it should be. In fact,
it was Aunt Lisbeth Banks who hired a man to lug it to the
house and put it on the table with the rest of the things. "It's
as much God's doing as that other clutter-trap," she would
say. And she would rock back and forth in her rocking chair
with a grim look. "You can't taunt the Lord," she would
add. She was a very religious woman. I used to see her now
and again at funerals, tall, gaunt, grim, but I never talked to
her if I could help it. She liked funerals and she liked to look
at corpses, and that made me afraid of her.

Just back of the souvenir table at Aunt Emma's, on the
wall, hung a heavy-framed, full-length photograph of Aunt
Emma's husband, Jad Peters. It showed him wearing a hat
and overcoat and carrying a suitcase. When I was a little boy
in the early nineteen-hundreds and was taken to Aunt
Emma's house near Sugar Grove, Ohio, I used to wonder
about that photograph (I didn't wonder about the rock and
the other objects, because they weren't put there till much
later). It seemed so funny for anyone to be photographed in a
hat and overcoat and carrying a suitcase, and even funnier to
have the photograph enlarged to almost life size and put
inside so elaborate a frame. When we children would sneak
into the front parlor to look at the picture, Aunt Emma
would hurry us out again. When we asked her about the
picture, she would say, "Never you mind." But when I grew
up, I learned the story of the big photograph and of how Jad
Peters came to be known as Lucky Jad. As a matter of fact, it
was Jad who began calling himself that; once when he ran for
a county office (and lost) he had "Lucky Jad Peters" printed
on his campaign cards. Nobody else took the name up except
in a scoffing way.

It seems that back in 1888, when Jad Peters was about
thirty-five, he had a pretty good business of some kind or

other which caused him to travel around quite a lot. One week he went to New York with the intention of going on to Newport, later, by ship. Something turned up back home, however, and one of his employees sent him a telegram reading "Don't go to Newport. Urgent you return here." Jad's story was that he was on the ship, ready to sail, when the telegram was delivered; it had been sent to his hotel, he said, a few minutes after he had checked out, and an obliging clerk had hustled the messenger boy on down to the dock. That was Jad's story. Most people believed, when they heard the story, that Jad had got the wire at his hotel, probably hours before the ship sailed, for he was a great one at adorning a tale. At any rate, whether or not he rushed off the ship just before the gangplank was hauled up, it sailed without him and some eight or nine hours out of the harbor sank in a storm with the loss of everybody on board. That's why he had the photograph taken and enlarged: it showed him just as he was when he got off the ship, he said. And that is how he came to start his collection of lucky souvenirs. For a few years he kept the telegram, and newspaper clippings of the ship disaster, tucked away in the family Bible, but one day he got them out and put them on the parlor table under a big glass bell.

From 1888 up until 1920, when Jad died, nothing much happened to him. He is remembered in his later years as a garrulous, boring old fellow whose business slowly went to pieces because of his lack of industry and who finally settled down on a small farm near Sugar Grove and barely scraped out an existence. He took to drinking in his sixties, and from then on made Aunt Emma's life miserable. I don't know how she managed to keep up the payments on his life-insurance policy, but some way or other she did. Some of her relatives said among themselves that it would be a blessing if Jad died in one of his frequent fits of nausea. It was pretty well known that Aunt Emma had never liked him very much—she married him because he asked her to twice a week for seven years and because there had been nobody else she cared about; she stayed married to him on account of their children and because her people always stayed married. She grew, in spite of Jad, to be a quiet, kindly old lady as the years went on, although her mouth would take on a strained, tight look when Jad showed up at dinner time from wherever he had been during the day—usually from down at Prentice's store in the village, where he liked to sit around telling about the time he just barely got off the doomed boat in New York harbor in '88 and adding tales, more or less fantastic, of more recent close escapes he had had. There was his appendicitis operation, for one thing: he had come out of the ether, he would say, just when they had given him up. Dr. Benham, who had performed the operation, was annoyed when he heard this, and once met Jad in the street and asked him to quit repeating the preposterous story, but Jad added the doctor's bill to his collection of talismans, anyway. And there was the time when he had got up in the night to take a swig of stomach bitters for a bad case of heartburn and had got hold of the carbolic-acid bottle by mistake. Something told him, he would say, to take a look at the bottle before he uncorked it, so he carried it to a lamp, lighted the lamp, and he'd be gol-dam if it wasn't carbolic acid! It was then that he added the cork to his collection.

Old Jad got so that he could figure out lucky escapes for himself in almost every disaster and calamity that happened in and around Sugar Grove. Once, for example, a tent blew down during a wind storm at the Fairfield County Fair, killing two people and injuring a dozen others. Jad hadn't gone to the fair that year for the first time in nine or ten years. Something told him, he would say, to stay away from the fair that year. The fact that he always went to the fair, when he did go, on a Thursday and that the tent blew down on a Saturday didn't make any difference to Jad. He hadn't been there and the tent blew down and two people were killed. After the accident, he went to the fair grounds and cut a piece of canvas from the tent and put it on the parlor table next to the cork from the carbolic-acid bottle. Lucky Jad Peters!

I think Aunt Emma got so that she didn't hear Jad when he was talking, except on evenings when neighbors dropped in, and then she would have to take hold of the conversation and steer it away from any opening that might give Jad a chance to tell of some close escape he had had. But he always got his licks in. He would bide his time, creaking back and forth in his chair, clicking his teeth, and not listening much to the talk about crops and begonias and the latest reports on the Spencers' feeble-minded child, and then, when there was a long pause, he would clear his throat and say that that reminded him of the time he had had a mind to go down to Pullen's lumber yard to fetch home a couple of two-by-fours to shore up the chicken house. Well, sir, he had pottered around the house a little while and was about to set out for Pullen's when something told him not to go a step. And it was that very day that a pile of lumber in the lumber yard let go and crushed Grant Pullen's leg so's it had to be amputated. Well, sir, he would say—but Aunt Emma would cut in on him at this point. "Everybody's heard that old chestnut," she would say, with a forced little laugh, fanning herself in quick strokes with an old palm-leaf fan. Jad would go sullen and rock back and forth in his chair, clicking his teeth. He wouldn't get up when the guests rose to go—which they always did at this juncture. The memento of his close escape from the Pullen lumber-yard disaster was, of course, the chip of pine wood.

I think I have accounted for all of Jad's souvenirs that I remember except the big rough fragment of rock. The story of the rock is a strange one. In August, 1920, county engineers were widening the channel of the Hocking River just outside of Sugar Grove and had occasion to do considerable blasting out of river-bed rock. I have never heard Clem Warden tell the story himself, but it has been told to me by people who have. It seems that Clem was walking along the main street of Sugar Grove at about a quarter to four when he saw Jad coming along toward him. Clem was an old crony of Jad's—one of the few men of his own generation who could tolerate Jad—and the two stopped on the sidewalk and talked. Clem figured later that they had talked for about five minutes, and then either he or Jad said something about getting on, so they separated, Jad going on toward Prentice's store, slowly, on account of his rheumatic left hip, and Clem going in the other direction. Clem had taken about a dozen steps when suddenly he heard Jad call to him. "Say, Clem!" Jad said. Clem stopped and turned around, and here was Jad walking back toward him. Jad had taken about six steps when suddenly he was flung up against the front of Matheny's harness store "like a sack o' salt," as Clem put it. By the time Clem could reach him, he was gone. He never knew what hit him, Clem said, and for quite a few minutes nobody else knew what hit him, either. Then somebody in the crowd that gathered found the big muddy rock lying in the road by the gutter. A particularly big shot of dynamite, set off in the river bed, had hurtled the fragment through the air with terrific force. It had come flying over the four-story Jackson Building like a cannon ball and had struck Jad Peters squarely in the chest.

I suppose old Jad hadn't been in his grave two days before the boys at Prentice's quit shaking their heads solemnly over the accident and began making funny remarks about it. Cal Gregg's was the funniest. "Well, sir," said Cal, "I don't suppose none of us will ever know what it was now, but somethin' must of told Jad to turn around."

I Went to Sullivant

I WAS reminded the other morning—by what, I don't remember and it doesn't matter—of a crisp September morning last year when I went to the Grand Central to see a little boy of ten get excitedly on a special coach that was to take him to a boys' school somewhere north of Boston. He had never been away to school before. The coach was squirming with youngsters; you could tell, after a while, the novitiates, shining and tremulous and a little awed, from the more aloof boys, who had been away to school before, but they were all very much alike at first glance. There was for me (in case you thought I was leading up to that) no sharp feeling of old lost years in the tense atmosphere of that coach, because I never went away to a private school when I was a little boy. I went to Sullivant School in Columbus. I thought about it as I walked back to my hotel.

Sullivant was an ordinary public school, and yet it was not like any other I have ever known of. In seeking an adjective to describe the Sullivant School of my years—1900 to 1908—I can only think of "tough." Sullivant School was tough. The boys of Sullivant came mostly from the region around Central Market, a poorish district with many colored families and many white families of the laboring class. The school district also included a number of homes of the upper classes because, at the turn of the century, one or two old residential streets still lingered near the shouting and rumbling of the market, reluctant to surrender their fine old houses to the encroaching rabble of commerce, and become (as, alas, they now have) mere vulgar business streets.

I remember always, first of all, the Sullivant baseball team. Most grammar-school baseball teams are made up of boys in the seventh and eighth grades, or they were in my day, but with Sullivant it was different. Several of its best players were in the fourth grade, known to the teachers of the school as

the Terrible Fourth. In that grade you first encountered
fractions and long division, and many pupils lodged there for
years, like logs in a brook. Some of the more able baseball-
players had been in the fourth grade for seven or eight years.
Then, too, there were a number of boys, most of them
colored (about half of the pupils at Sullivant were colored),
who had not been in the class past the normal time but were
nevertheless deep in their teens. They had avoided starting to
school—by eluding the truant officer—until they were ready
to go into long pants, but he always got them in the end. One
or two of these fourth-graders were seventeen or eighteen
years old, but the dean of the squad was a tall, husky young
man of twenty-two who was in the fifth grade (the teachers of
the third and fourth had got tired of having him around as
the years rolled along and had pushed him on). His name was
Dana Waney and he had a mustache. Don't ask me why his
parents allowed him to stay in school so long. There were
many mysteries at Sullivant that were never cleared up. All I
know is why he kept on in school and didn't go to work: he
liked playing on the baseball team, and he had a pretty easy
time in class, because the teachers had given up asking him
any questions at all years before. The story was that he had
answered but one question in the seventeen years he had been
going to classes at Sullivant and that was "What is one use of
the comma?" "The commy," said Dana, embarrassedly
unsnarling his long legs from beneath a desk much too low
for him, "is used to shoot marbles with." ("Commies" was
our word for those cheap, ten-for-a-cent marbles, in case it
wasn't yours.)

The Sullivant School baseball team of 1905 defeated
several high-school teams in the city and claimed the high-
school championship of the state, to which title it had, of
course, no technical right. I believe the boys could have
proved their moral right to the championship, however, if
they had been allowed to go out of town and play all the
teams they challenged, such as the powerful Dayton and

Toledo nines, but their road season was called off after a terrific fight that occurred during a game in Mt. Sterling, or Piqua, or Zenia—I can't remember which. Our first baseman— Dana Waney—crowned the umpire with a bat during an altercation over a called strike and the fight was on. It took place in the fourth inning, so of course the game was never finished (the battle continued on down into the business section of the town and raged for hours, with much destruction of property), but since Sullivant was ahead at the time 17 to 0 there could have been no doubt as to the outcome. Nobody was killed. All of us boys were sure our team could have beaten Ohio State University that year, but they wouldn't play us; they were scared.

Waney was by no means the biggest or toughest guy on the grammar-school team; he was merely the oldest, being about a year the senior of Floyd, the colored centre-fielder, who could jump five feet straight into the air without taking a running start. Nobody knew—not even the Board of Education, which once tried to find out—whether Floyd was Floyd's first name or his last name. He apparently only had one. He didn't have any parents, and nobody, including himself, seemed to know where he lived. When teachers insisted that he must have another name to go with Floyd, he would grow sullen and ominous and they would cease questioning him, because he was a dangerous scholar in a schoolroom brawl, as Mr. Harrigan, the janitor, found out one morning when he was called in by a screaming teacher (all our teachers were women) to get Floyd under control after she had tried to whip him and he had begun to take the room apart, beginning with the desks. Floyd broke into small pieces the switch she had used on him (some said he also ate it; I don't know, because I was home sick at the time with mumps or something). Harrigan was a burly, iron-muscled janitor, a man come from a long line of coal-shovellers, but he was no match for Floyd, who had, to be sure, the considerable advantage of being more aroused than Mr.

Harrigan when their fight started. Floyd had him down and was sitting on his chest in no time, and Harrigan had to promise to be good and to say "Dat's what Ah get" ten times before Floyd would let him up.

I don't suppose I would ever have got through Sullivant School alive if it hadn't been for Floyd. For some reason he appointed himself my protector, and I needed one. If Floyd was known to be on your side, nobody in the school would dare be "after" you and chase you home. I was one of the ten or fifteen male pupils in Sullivant School who always, or almost always, knew their lessons, and I believe Floyd admired the mental prowess of a youngster who knew how many continents there were and whether or not the sun was inhabited. Also, one time when it came my turn to read to the class—we used to take turns reading American history aloud—I came across the word "Duquesne" and knew how to pronounce it. That charmed Floyd, who had been slouched in his seat idly following the printed page of his worn and pencilled textbook. "How you know dat was Dukane, boy?" he asked after class. "I don't know," I said. "I just knew it." He looked at me with round eyes. "Boy, dat's sump'n," he said. After that, word got around that Floyd would beat the tar out of anybody that messed around me. I wore glasses from the time I was eight and I knew my lessons, and both of those things were considered pretty terrible at Sullivant. Floyd had one idiosyncrasy. In the early nineteen-hundreds, long warm furry gloves that came almost to your elbows were popular with boys, and Floyd had one of the biggest pairs in school. He wore them the year around.

Dick Peterson, another colored boy, was an even greater figure on the baseball team and in the school than Floyd was. He had a way in the classroom of blurting out a long deep rolling "beee—eee—ahhhh!" for no reason at all. Once he licked three boys his own size single-handed, really single-handed, for he fought with his right hand and held a mandolin in his left hand all the time. It came out uninjured.

Dick and Floyd never met in mortal combat, so nobody ever knew which one could "beat," and the scholars were about evenly divided in their opinions. Many a fight started among them after school when that argument came up. I think school never let out at Sullivant without at least one fight starting up, and sometimes there were as many as five or six raging between the corner of Oak and Sixth Streets and the corner of Rich and Fourth Streets, four blocks away. Now and again virtually the whole school turned out to fight the Catholic boys of the Holy Cross Academy in Fifth Street near Town, for no reason at all—in winter with snowballs and iceballs, in other seasons with fists, brickbats, and clubs. Dick Peterson was always in the van, yelling, singing, beeee-ahing, whirling all the way around when he swung with his right or (if he hadn't brought his mandolin) his left and missed. He made himself the pitcher on the baseball team because he was the captain. He was the captain because everybody was afraid to challenge his self-election, except Floyd. Floyd was too lazy to pitch and he didn't care who was captain, because he didn't fully comprehend what that meant. On one occasion, when Earl Battec, a steam-fitter's son, had shut out Mound Street School for six innings without a hit, Dick took him out of the pitcher's box and went in himself. He was hit hard and the other team scored, but it didn't make much difference, because the margin of Sullivant's victory was so great. The team didn't lose a game for five years to another grammar school. When Dick Peterson was in the sixth grade, he got into a saloon brawl and was killed.

When I go back to Columbus I always walk past Sullivant School. I have never happened to get there when classes were letting out, so I don't know what the pupils are like now. I am sure there are no more Dick Petersons and no more Floyds, unless Floyd is still going to school there. The play yard is still entirely bare of grass and covered with gravel, and the sycamores still line the curb between the schoolhouse fence and the Oak Street car line. A street-car line running past a schoolhouse is a dangerous thing as a rule, but I remember no one being injured while I was attending Sullivant. I do remember, however, one person who came very near being injured. He was a motorman on the Oak Street line, and once when his car stopped at the corner of Sixth to let off passengers, he yelled at Chutey Davidson, who played third base on the ball team, and was a member of the Terrible Fourth, to get out of the way. Chutey was a white boy, fourteen years old, but huge for his age, and he was standing on the tracks, taking a chew of tobacco. "Come ahn down offa that car an' I'll knock your block off!" said Chutey, in what I can only describe as a Sullivant tone of voice. The motorman waited until Chutey moved slowly off the tracks; then he went on about his business. I think it was lucky for him that he did. There were boys in those days.

The Civil War Phone-Number Association

MR. RUDY Vallée, in an interview (or maybe it was in an article), has said that sometimes when he goes backstage he is saddened at the sight of the members of his band sitting around reading detective stories. "They should try to improve their memories," said Mr. Vallée, "by associating telephone numbers, for instance, with the date of the Civil War."

This remarkable statement can be picked to pieces by any skillful Civil War telephone-number associator. In the first place, the use of the phrase "for instance" in the position we find it implies that Mr. Vallée thinks it is a good idea to sit

around associating *various* things with the date of the Civil
War ("telephone numbers, for instance"). Such a practice
would confound even Salo Finkelstein, the lightning calcu-
lator. If a person has put in the afternoon associating his
bank balance, his automobile license plates, and the total
amount of his debts with the date of the Civil War, he is not
going to be able to call up a phone number when he wants to;
he is going to call up the money he has in the bank or the
number on the back of his car. In the second place, it is futile
to sit around, backstage or anywhere else, merely associating
telephone numbers with the date of the Civil War and not
calling anybody up. The purpose of the War of the Rebellion
system of remembering phone numbers is not to keep them
in the forefront of the mind, whence they can be brought up
and recited to oneself as if they were limericks, but to tuck
them away in the back of the mind, whence they can be called
forth when needed and used for the practical purpose of
getting in touch with somebody.

And in the third place, I must, as one of the oldest surviving veterans of the Civil War Telephone-Number Association, take firm exception to the expression "the date of the Civil War." The Civil War was full of dates, many of them—such as September 19, the date of the Battle of Chickamauga—as important and helpful as the war years themselves. Mr. Vallée's "date" would seem to indicate that he goes simply by 1861, the year the war began, or 1865, the year it ended. These would be useful in fixing in one's mind only about half a dozen numbers, such as Bryant 9-1861, Wickersham 2-1865, maybe Watkins 9-1961 (if you remember to subtract a hundred years), and possibly Gramercy 7-5681. This last is, of course, 1865 backward and seems simple; but in a phone booth, without a pencil, one could call up practically everybody in the south-central part of town without getting the right party, unless one were very good at visualizing four digits backward.

If I were Mr. Vallée and knew only one date for the Civil War, I should certainly give up the whole system of association and write the numbers I wanted to remember in a small book and carry it about with me. Even I, who know dozens of Civil War dates, including the hour of day that Stonewall Jackson was shot, sometimes wish I had gone in for the "jotting down" system. Using that method, if you get mad at somebody, you can cross out his number in the little notebook and be quit of it, whereas if you have it filed away in your mind alongside of Pickett's charge, it is there ineradicably. I still know the phone number of a girl who gave me the go-by in 1920, and now and then, as the years roll away, it flicks around the back of my head annoyingly, like a deer fly, upsetting my day. The phone number of the American Embassy in Paris, for which I no longer have any possible use, often keeps me awake at night: Passy 12 . 50. Particularly on trains: Passy douze cinquante, Passy douze cinquante, chant the iron wheels on the rails.

*   *   *

It was eight years ago that I began to go in for associating telephone numbers with troop movements, in a big way. At that time, which was before the fifth digit got into Manhattan phone numbers and made my life and Mr. Vallée's even harder than they had been, my telephone number was Algonquin 9618. For some reason, that was hard for me. The Civil War fell down, in this case, almost completely, for although there was '61 in the middle to remember it by, the 9 and 8 didn't seem to mean much. It was then that I began to toy with other wars, the war with Spain naturally (and unfortunately) suggesting itself because of 98. As a result, I would phone 9861 and then 6198 and in the end go completely to pieces and try all the permutations until I had run the entire gamut of numbers in the Algonquin exchange, from 1689, the lowest, to 9861, the highest. For an old war associator to quit fiddling his life away in a phone booth and look up his number in the directory would be, of course, an unthinkable defeat that would leave its mark. The way I finally got Algonquin 9618 fixed in my mind, where it still stands as staunchly and as uselessly as an iron hitching post in a concrete walk, was to bring in the World War. I saw that by subtracting 4 from the last two digits—18—and adding it to the first two—96—I could make an even 100 of the first two. This made 14 out of the last two. I now had 10014 as a key number. This was useless unless I could plant in my memory some story, some war anecdote, which would break 10014 down into the proper arrangement of digits. The story I invented was this: that I had ended the war—that is, made '18 out of '14—by sending overseas a male quartet from my company of 100 men (I figured myself as captain of a company with the full regulation Civil War strength of 100 men). This gave me, logically and smoothly, 9618.

My invention of the war anecdote was the beginning of an elaborate system of remembering telephone numbers in which sometimes as many as seven wars were involved, together with the movement of not only male quartets but bowling teams, football squads, rowing crews, and the like. For instance, to remember one number, I figured myself as an officer in the war with Mexico (a certain Lieutenant Chelsea) who sent a baseball nine to the aid of Napoleon at the Battle of Waterloo. The key number was 4615; the correct reading 3724. I simply sent my 9 from '46 to '15, you see.

The danger of this kind of preoccupation lies in the likelihood of confusing fact with fancy, shadow with substance, one's imaginary character with one's actual character. My reactions and reflexes in the workaday world began to be prompted now and then by the nature of my responsibilities as an officer in wars that ended long ago. I would sometimes, in the office, bark commands at my superiors. Things finally got so bad that for more than two years I never phoned anybody. In this way I managed to slough off from my overburdened subconscious something in the neighborhood of a hundred and eighty numbers. Along with these vanished a lot of wearisome maneuvers, such as the activities of a golfing foursome in the Seminole Indian War, and the extraordinary advent of three basketball teams at the Battle of Saratoga. Now I am back to a fairly normal basis, with the phone numbers of only about ninety-five people thundering in the indexes of my mind. Of these people, I am in actual contact with perhaps thirty. The others have moved away, or have broken up housekeeping, or have cut me off, or are dead. Their silly phone numbers, however, linger still, often in the night marching wearily along the border of a dream, on their way back from Moscow, General Pierre Gustave Toutant Beauregard riding ahead, the American Davis Cup team of 1919 bringing up the rear. Hooting and mocking, laughing and crying, they pass in review, all the old, lost numbers.

I wish I were a member of Rudy Vallée's band, peacefully reading a detective story.

Back to the Grades

WHEN I read in the newspapers that young James Cox Brady, who is a director in fifty corporations, had started shovelling coal in the boiler-room of one of them in order to learn the business, I was reminded of the time that I went back to grammar school. I rëentered the fifth grade, because it was in the fifth grade that I had first begun to lose my way; and also because the desks in the lower grades were too small for me—I couldn't get my knees under them. I feel that there is more to be learned by going back to the fifth grade than by shovelling coal in a boiler-room. All you can learn in the latter case is how to shovel coal into a boiler, which can't be much of a help to a director of a corporation. Young Mr. Brady may, of course, have had some idea of studying the psychology of his fellow-workers, but he is bound to be disappointed in that, because all boiler-workers are Slavs and all they ever say is "Strook 'em." Let us imagine Mr. Brady trying to get at the psychology of one of his shovel-mates, a Slav named Wieneszciewcz. "How do you like this life?" says Mr. Brady, between shovels. "Strook 'em," says Mr. Wieneszciewcz. "What do you do for relaxation and entertainment—after work hours, I mean?" asks Mr. Brady. "Strook 'em," says Mr. Wieneszciewcz. In a little under an hour, a director of a corporation is going to learn all there is to know about shovelling coal and what his fellow-workers are thinking. Going back to the fifth grade is a richer experience.

I was thirty-four going on thirty-five when I returned to grammar school. My failure to grasp sentence-parsing, fractions, decimals, long division, and, especially, "problems," had after a quarter of a century begun to show up in my life and work. Although a family man of property, I discovered that I didn't understand taxation, gas-meter readings, endowment or straight-pay insurance policies, compound or simple interest, time-tables, bank balances, and electric-light bills. Nor could I get much meaning out of the books and articles which were being written all the time on economics and politics. Long stretches of Walter Lippmann meant nothing to me. One evening after we had returned from a contract-bridge game, my wife said to me, earnestly: "You ought to go back to the fifth grade." I suggested just as earnestly that she, too, should start over again, beginning with the first grade (she is younger than I am), but we finally compromised on my going back to the fifth grade.

I went to live with my parents when I returned to the grammar grades. The first morning of school, I couldn't find my hat. "If you'd hang up your hat, you'd know where it was," my mother said. "Let him find it himself; don't you hunt for it," said my father. I finally found it in the dog house with my baseball glove. Miss Malloy (the same teacher

I had had in the fifth grade in 1905) made me stay after school for being tardy. She didn't remember me at first, but she finally did. "My, you have shot up like a weed!" she said. I was somewhat embarrassed. "You have shot up like a weed, too," I said.

Since I was used to staying up until one and two o'clock in the morning, I never got to sleep at ten and was usually late for school. I had to stay after class and write, a hundred times, the lines beginning: "Lost, somewhere between sunrise and sunset, two golden hours." "Don't cramp your fingers; get a free and easy wrist motion," Miss Malloy said. "Aw," I said, and grinned. She told me to wipe the smile off my face. I wouldn't, and she made me learn "To a Water Fowl" by heart.

Long division came a trifle easier to me at thirty-four than it had when I was ten, but I was so bad at problems that I had to stay after class and clean the blackboard-erasers. It was fun leaning out the window and slapping them against the wall of the building; the chalk spurted like smoke from a gun and got into your nose, and the erasers left little white rectangles on the bricks. Afterward I drew a picture of Miss Malloy on the blackboard and went home.

Miss Malloy would stay after class and help me with my problems in arithmetic. I had brought her some applejack one morning and she would sip the applejack while I struggled with the problems. "I'll ask my father to help me with the problems," I said one afternoon when, at the end of an hour, I hadn't got anywhere and neither had Miss Malloy—except with the applejack. Miss Malloy didn't say anything. She looked at me. "Fines' fatha ev' had," she said. "Fines' probblums ev' solve, too." She began to cry and I went home.

I started Father off on a problem about if twenty men can excavate two hundred and thirty cubic yards of earth in five and a half hours, how many cubic yards of earth can five men excavate in an hour and a quarter? Father had first failed to make anything of that problem about the time that the Wright brothers got their improbable airship off the ground at Kitty Hawk, but he started in on it again with considerable assurance. His first answer came out in hours instead of yards; his next answer was 1,987,000 cubic yards, which he had arrived at by changing the hours into seconds; and he finally wound up by discovering what a fifth of a man could excavate in three months. "Men don't work on an hour-and-a-quarter schedule in practical experience," said Father, at last. Mother said that that wasn't the idea. "Then what *is* the idea?" shouted Father. The argument that followed aroused Grandfather, who for several years now had been laboring under the delusion that time had turned backward and that Father was courting Mother again. "Lovers' quarrels!" he cackled from the head of the stairs, and went cackling back to bed. He thought McKinley was President. I often wonder who he thought I was.

The next morning I told Mother I was too sick to go to school. "Where are you sick?" she said. I told her I had terrible pains in my stomach. "Be a big middle-aged soldier and get up!" she coaxed. "I don't want to be a big middle-aged soldier," I whined. She made me take some awful medicine. At breakfast, Father said he was going to take me out of school, that he and myself and Grandfather were simply losing ground all the time. He said he had dreamed about Christy Mathewson and the San Francisco earthquake and a lot of other things of twenty-five years ago. Grandfather said that Hayes had stolen the election from Tilden and to mark his words there would be hell to pay. Father told me I could go to school that day, for the last time, and get my books. "I don't propose to go through the fifth grade again at my age!" said Father, vehemently. Grandfather was furious. "You git your chores done and hike on to school or I'll whup your hide off!" he shouted at Father. We had to change the subject.

I didn't really drop out of school that day; I was thrown out. A little girl named Virginia Morrison, who sat at a desk across the aisle from me, had all the answers to the problems right. She was always laughing at me and sticking her tongue out at me from behind her geography. I finally pulled her hair, and she yelled. Miss Malloy came down the aisle and hit me across the hand with a ruler. I took the ruler away from her, sat on top of my desk, turned her over my knee, and spanked her.

My analyst (who is also losing ground steadily) told me later that it was a happy thing that I had been able to go back to school and spank my teacher. He said that noticeably good results would begin to show up in my life. They haven't, though.

Hell Only Breaks Loose Once
(Written After Reading James M. Cain's
"The Postman Always Rings Twice")

I

THEY KICKED me out of college when I was about twenty-seven. I went up to see the Dean and tried to hand him a couple of laughs but it was no good. He said he couldn't put me back in college but I could hang around the office and sweep out and wash windows. I figured I better be rambling and I said I had a couple of other offers. He told me to sit down and think it over so I sat down.

Then she came in the room. She was tall and thin and had

a white frowning forehead and soft eyes. She wasn't much to look at but she was something to think about. As far as she and I were concerned he wasn't in the room. She leaned over the chair where I was sitting and bit me in the ear. I let her have it right under the heart. It was a good one. It was plenty. She hit the floor like a two-year-old.

"What fell?" asked the Dean, peering over his glasses. I told him nothing fell.

II

After a while I said I guessed I'd hang around and go to work for him. "Do what?" he asked. He had forgot all about me, but I hung around. I liked him and he liked me but neither one of us cared what happened to the other.

When the Dean went out to lunch I walked into a rear office and she was there. I began to tremble all over like a hooch dancer. She was fussing with some papers but I could see she wasn't really doing anything. I walked close to her. It was like dying and going to Heaven. She was a little like my mother and a little like the time I got my hip busted in a football scrimmage. I reached over and let her have one on the chin and she went down like a tray of dishes. I knew then I would be beating her up the rest of my life. It made me feel like it was April and I was a kid again and had got up on a warm morning and it was all misty outdoors and the birds were singing.

III

"Hi, Dean," I said to him when he got back from lunch. "What is it?" he asked. I could tell he thought he had never

seen me before. I told him what it was. "Excellent," he said, looking surprised. He still didn't know what it was. She came out of the back room and he asked her what she wanted. He never remembered seeing anybody.

I took her out to lunch. It was sweet in the lunchroom and I kicked her under the table and broke her ankle. It was still broken when I carried her back to the Dean's office.

"Who do you wish to see?" he asked, looking over his glasses at us. I wanted to grind his glasses into his skull. She said we both worked there. He said that was excellent, but he wasn't looking for work. I told him to think it over and she and I went into the back room. I let her have one over the eye but it was a glancing blow and didn't knock her out. She cracked down on me with a paperweight and I went out like a light but I took her with me. She broke her head in the fall. We were unconscious for about an hour. A couple of guys were bending over us when we came to. They said they were from a place named Lang's, a cleaning establishment. The Dean had got the idea we were a bear rug and was going to send us out to be dry-cleaned. He was pretty dumb but I liked him.

IV

"What do you want to work for that guy for?"

"I'm his secretary."

"What do you want to work for him for?"

"I said I'm his secretary."

"Keep talking."

"I have to work for him. He's my husband." I felt pretty sick then.

"That's tough. You oughtn't to be married to him. He doesn't know what it's all about."

"He lectures in his sleep."

"That must be swell."

"I don't want to be his wife. I want to be yours."

"You are mine."

"Let me have it again," she said. I gave her a short left jab on the button. She was dizzy for days.

V

The Dean was too absent-minded to notice she was bruised all the time. It made me sick seeing him sitting at his desk trying to remember what it was all about. One day he began dictating a letter to me but I didn't pay any attention. I went on dusting a chair. Pretty soon he went out to lunch and I went in the back room. She was there and I began to shiver like a tuning fork. I stroked her hair. I had never done that before. It was like going to sleep.

"There is one out for us," she told me.

"Okay," I said.

VI

He was sitting at his desk trying to figure out who he was when I hit him over the conk with an auto crank. I thought he would fold up like a leather belt, but he didn't. It didn't faze him. "Somebody's at the door," he said. I was shaking a little but I went to the door and opened it. There wasn't anybody there. I stood to one side so he could look out of the door into the hall. It was empty. "I thought I heard somebody knock," he said. It made me cold.

VII

We fixed him finally. I got him up on top of the university water tower one night to see the aurora borealis. There wasn't any aurora borealis but he was too dumb to notice that. It was swell up there on the tower. It smelled pretty. It smelled of jasmine. I felt like the first time I ever kissed a girl.

I rigged up one of those double flights of steps like tap-dancers dance up and down on and told him to get up on top of it.

"I don't want to get up on top of that," he said.

"You want to see the aurora borealis, don't you?"

"Most certainly."

"Then get up on top of that."

He got up on top of it and I climbed up after him. The thing was rickety but he didn't notice.

"What are we doing up here?" he asked me.

"Look at the aurora," I said, pointing at the sky. He looked and while we were standing there she came up on top of the steps with us. He didn't pay any attention to her. I swayed from side to side and started the thing teetering. I beat her up a little and then I beat him up a little. He looked like he had been spanked by an old aunt. The thing was swinging bad now, from one side to the other. I knew it was going over.

VIII

We all fell six flights. He was dead when they picked him up. She was dead too. I was near to her, but she was a long way off. I was dying, they told me. So I dictated this to a guy from the D.A.'s office, and here it is. And that's all, except I hope it's pretty in Heaven and smells like when the lilacs first come out on May nights in the Parc Monceau in Paris.

The Man Who Was Wetly

*(After Reading an Anthology of
British Short Stories)*

A HALF-DOZEN of us were discussing that curious thing
called life and the singular interrelationship between penalty
and reward one night in the fireplace of the Cathay Cyclists'
Club. "It seems rather warm in here, you know," said
Empringham, who had, I knew, been wounded four times at
Vimy Ridge. We moved out of the fireplace into the club
room. It became a little cooler. Masters brought in another
large tray of gooseberry wine and spiced walnuts, and for a
time we were silent.

"Sitting in that fireplace," mused Empringham, finally,
"reminded me of a curious adventure I had one night in New
York City."

Lord Burleigh laughed. "I had supposed," he said, "that
there were no singular adventures to be had in New York
City. How about it, Buell?" This last was addressed to me, as
being the only American present.

"Oh," I said, "we don't, of course, have your mysterious
fog which shrouds London in a—ah——"

"Mysterious fog," put in little Bailey.

"Precisely," mused Empringham. "But I assure you there
is mystery also to be found in clear streets. Shall I tell you my
story?"

"No," said the Earl of Leaves, a bald, choleric man, who
got up and abruptly left the room.

"Curious chap, Leaves," mused young Priestley. "I
remember one night in the Sudan. A curious rain had come
up and cooled that furnace of a jungle, in which you could
hear Snider rifles squibbing wetly. Several of us subalterns
were sitting around in our fatigue uniforms, when out of the
jungle——"

"Jungle!" cried Empringham, slapping his leg. "The jungle is a state of mind. Your rain, my dear fellow, was a state of mind, too. Would it surprise you if I said that New York is also a jungle, also a state of mind?"

No one spoke for a minute.

"Let's see, where was I?" began young Priestley, again. "Oh, yes. It had rained, as I say, and the Sniders were squibbing——"

"Wetly," I prompted him, for Priestley had been wounded at Nantes and sometimes remembered rather slowly.

"Dear old Wetly!" cried Empringham. "What a chap he was! I last saw him in Port Said. God, how he had changed! At first I didn't know him. I was pricing some sherids at a native sampan in the marketplace when a fellow seized my shoulder—there in that hustings, that shambles! I supposed, of course, the man was a beggar and I threw off his arm a bit gruffly. 'Have on with you,' I said. 'Cheero, Empringham,' he said, and I saw that it was Wetly."

"That, of course," chimed in Leaves, who had returned to the room because he hadn't been able to find anything to do in any of the other rooms, "that is a decision which, at some time or other, in the lives of all of us, a man must make for himself, all alone—without the help of God or man. Lord, what solitude can encompass a man in the midst of a teeming city!" He held up a curious object for us to look at. It did not seem, at first glance, extraordinary, being only a singular china figurine of a Napoleonic cavalryman standing beside his horse.

"Who is it?" asked Dunleavy, sourly. "Wetly?" We all fell silent, for it was unusual indeed when Kerry Dunleavy said anything. This was, in point of fact, the first thing he had said since 1908 when, fresh from Indian service, with the insignia of a subaltern on his shoulders, a pretty wife whom he had married God knows where, and the livid scar of a Sikh tamarinth across one cheek, he walked into the Cyclists' Club, took his old familiar chair, the leather one by the window, and called for a Scotch and soda.

"Damme," mused Dunleavy, "it was amazing, I tell you. There hadn't been a sound, except the drip, drip of rain falling from the huge leaves of the pelango trees, which the natives thatch their huts with. I was running over the company accounts at a little table, doing the best I could by the light of a beastly kerosene lamp and smoking that vile native tobacco to fend off the mosquitoes and flet-flet flies, when the door opened and a man wearing the uniform of Her Majesty's Death's Head Hussars staggered into the room. He was ghastly pale and, I could see at a glance, badly wounded at Ypres. Without a word he walked in an uncertain line over to the table and snatched up the champagne glass out of which I had been drinking that fiendish native pongo-pongo, or gluelike liqueur. He stood there wavering, then proposed a toast and——"

"Shattered the glass in his hand!" cried young Priestley.

"Good God!" cried Empringham, pushing back his chair

and rising to his feet. We all stared at him.

"Take it easy, old chap," I said, for I liked Empringham and knew that his old wounds still bothered him.

"I say, what is the matter?" cried young Priestley, who was, as we all knew, too young to know what was the matter.

"Did he give this toast when he shattered that glass?" demanded Empringham, in an odd, strained voice, white as a sheet. "Did he say, when he broke that glass: 'The Queen, God bless her'?" There was a singular, strained silence. We all looked at Dunleavy.

"That," said Dunleavy in a low, tense voice, "that is what he said." Empringham fixed us all in turn with a curious, wide-eyed stare. Outside the rain beat against the windows. Empringham's chair toppled to the floor with a clatter as loud as that of a brass shield falling.

"Gentlemen," said Empringham, "that toast has not been drunk for more than one hundred and fifty years."

"Good God!" cried young Priestley.

"Good God!" muttered little Bailey.

"Good God!" I mused, softly. Old Masters moved over and took up the tray, its wine and walnuts untouched. He was about to turn away when, as if on second thought, he removed the walnut bowl and set it before us.

"Nuts, gentlemen," said Masters, and withdrew.

If Grant Had Been Drinking at Appomattox

(Scribner's Magazine published a series of three articles: "If Booth Had Missed Lincoln," "If Lee Had Not Won The Battle of Gettysburg," and "If Napoleon Had Escaped to America." This is the fourth.)

THE MORNING of the ninth of April, 1865, dawned beautifully. General Meade was up with the first streaks of crimson in the eastern sky. General Hooker and General Burnside were up, and had breakfasted, by a quarter after eight. The day continued beautiful. It drew on toward eleven o'clock. General Ulysses S. Grant was still not up. He was asleep in his famous old navy hammock, swung high above the floor of his headquarters' bedroom. Headquarters was distressingly disarranged: papers were strewn on the floor; confidential notes from spies scurried here and there in the breeze from an open window; the dregs of an overturned bottle of wine flowed pinkly across an important military map.

Corporal Shultz, of the Sixty-fifth Ohio Volunteer Infantry, aide to General Grant, came into the outer room, looked around him, and sighed. He entered the bedroom and shook the General's hammock roughly. General Ulysses S. Grant opened one eye.

"Pardon, sir," said Corporal Shultz, "but this is the day of surrender. You ought to be up, sir."

"Don't swing me," said Grant, sharply, for his aide was making the hammock sway gently. "I feel terrible," he added, and he turned over and closed his eye again.

"General Lee will be here any minute now," said the Corporal firmly, swinging the hammock again.

"Will you cut that out?" roared Grant. "D'ya want to make me sick, or what?" Shultz clicked his heels and saluted. "What's he coming here for?" asked the General.

"This is the day of surrender, sir," said Shultz. Grant grunted bitterly.

"Three hundred and fifty generals in the Northern armies," said Grant, "and he has to come to *me* about this. What time is it?"

"You're the Commander-in-Chief, that's why," said Corporal Shultz. "It's eleven twenty-five, sir."

"Don't be crazy," said Grant. "Lincoln is the Commander-in-Chief. Nobody in the history of the world ever surrendered before lunch. Doesn't he know that an army surrenders on its stomach?" He pulled a blanket up over his head and settled himself again.

"The generals of the Confederacy will be here any minute now," said the Corporal. "You really ought to be up, sir."

Grant stretched his arms above his head and yawned.

"All right, all right," he said. He rose to a sitting position and stared about the room. "This place looks awful," he growled.

"You must have had quite a time of it last night, sir," ventured Shultz.

"Yeh," said General Grant, looking around for his clothes. "I was wrassling some general. Some general with a beard."

Shultz helped the commander of the Northern armies in the field to find his clothes.

"Where's my other sock?" demanded Grant. Shultz began to look around for it. The General walked uncertainly to a table and poured a drink from a bottle.

"I don't think it wise to drink, sir," said Shultz.

"Nev' mind about me," said Grant, helping himself to a second, "I can take it or let it alone. Didn' ya ever hear the story about the fella went to Lincoln to complain about me drinking too much?" 'So-and-So says Grant drinks too much,' this fella said. 'So-and-So is a fool,' said Lincoln. So this fella went to What's-His-Name and told him what Lincoln said and he came roarin' to Lincoln about it. 'Did you tell So-and-So I was a fool?' he said. 'No,' said Lincoln, 'I thought he knew it.'" The General smiled, reminiscently, and had another drink. "*That's* how I stand with Lincoln," he said, proudly.

The soft thudding sound of horses' hooves came through the open window. Shultz hurriedly walked over and looked out.

"Hoof steps," said Grant, with a curious chortle.

"It is General Lee and his staff," said Shultz.

"Show him in," said the General, taking another drink. "And see what the boys in the back room will have."

Shultz walked smartly over to the door, opened it, saluted, and stood aside. General Lee, dignified against the blue of the April sky, magnificent in his dress uniform, stood for a moment framed in the doorway. He walked in, followed by his staff. They bowed, and stood silent. General Grant stared

at them. He only had one boot on and his jacket was unbuttoned.

"I know who you are," said Grant. "You're Robert Browning, the poet."

"This is General Robert E. Lee," said one of his staff, coldly.

"Oh," said Grant. "I thought he was Robert Browning. He certainly looks like Robert Browning. There was a poet for you, Lee: Browning. Did ja ever read 'How They Brought the Good News from Ghent to Aix'? 'Up Derek, to saddle, up Derek, away; up Dunder, up Blitzen, up Prancer, up Dancer, up Bouncer, up Vixen, up——'"

"Shall we proceed at once to the matter in hand?" asked General Lee, his eyes disdainfully taking in the disordered room.

"Some of the boys was wrassling here last night," explained Grant. "I threw Sherman, or some general a whole lot like Sherman. It was pretty dark." He handed a bottle of Scotch to the commanding officer of the Southern armies, who stood holding it, in amazement and discomfiture. "Get a glass, somebody," said Grant, looking straight at General Longstreet. "Didn't I meet you at Cold Harbor?" he asked. General Longstreet did not answer.

"I should like to have this over with as soon as possible," said Lee. Grant looked vaguely at Shultz, who walked up close to him, frowning.

"The surrender, sir, the surrender," said Corporal Shultz in a whisper.

"Oh sure, sure," said Grant. He took another drink. "All right," he said. "Here we go." Slowly, sadly, he unbuckled his sword. Then he handed it to the astonished Lee. "There you are, General," said Grant. "We dam' near licked you. If I'd been feeling better we *would* of licked you."

One More April

(An Effort to Start Another Novel about the Galsworthy Characters, Taking Them Up Where He Left Off)

ON THE second day after the sailing of the transatlantic liner *Picardy* for America, in April, 1935, three English people who were unknown to each other came into the main dining saloon from wholly different staterooms and began to play piquet together. This breach of form affected them all in precisely the same way: each one sat perhaps seven feet from the card table so that, even with arms extended at full length, it was impossible to bring the cards near enough to the playing surface to lay them upon it. One of these three was a young woman of about twenty-two, one a darkish man of perhaps forty-three, and one a man of between ninety-five and a hundred.

The younger man spoke suddenly.

The effect of his breach of form on the others was diverse: the olderish man leaned forward as if to examine the table legs, with a sort of weathered skepticism; the young woman turned a surprised look upon the speaker.

"Didn't I meet you at my wedding?" she queried. "I am Fleur Desert, the second daughter of Dinny Mont, who married Wilfred Desert; the first daughter was Celia. There are two brothers, Michael and Michael." The younger man's mouth lost its disdainful look.

"I am your sister's brother-in-law, Cherrill Desert."

The older man spoke unexpectedly.

"Forsyte Desert's nephew, eh? Old Derek Mont's cousin. What's become of young Cherrill Desert? Still wandering sallowly about the East, I'll wager, writing verse."

Desert smiled and shook his head.

"I am Cherrill Desert," he said. The older man looked surprised.

"And probably died there," he grunted.

Fleur Desert thought: "He can't have been home for many years."

"Cherrill Desert married Dinny Mont's second daughter, Fleur," she said. "They have two children, Dinny and Fleur." A slight color stained her cheeks. The disdainful look which had been about to return to the young man's lips did not.

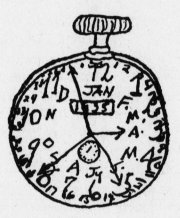

"I remember you perfectly," he said. "You are Wilfred Desert's daughter."

"Old Derek Mont's cousin's wife," said the older man, with a sort of skeptical weatheredness. "Forsyte Desert's niece-in-law."

The other two looked at him with frank surprise.

"I am Uncle Adrian," said the older man. "Or his brother, Mark. I cannot always remember which. However, if I'm Mark, he's going to be confoundedly seasick." He glared about the saloon, which was filled with surprised card tables. "I like the way these tables stand up," he said. The ship rocked a bit. "Mark never had a stomach for the ocean." He chuckled unexpectedly.

Fleur thought: "He's Adrian. Uncle Lawrence always said Adrian Mont knew tables."

The older man gave up his study of the card tables.

"Rather leggish. But they hold up." He took out a surprised old watch which chimed the days and months and years. It struck April fifth, 1935.

"My goodness! Aunt Sheila's birthday!" cried Fleur. "And I've forgotten to send her a radiogram!"

The older man smiled and spoke abruptly.

"I was at Somebody Mont's, or her mother's," he said, "the day all these birthday parties started. Ronald Ferse was there, and a small Chinese boy, and Aunt Alison and her youngest, little Anne, and Uncle Hilary and Tony. Monty Muskham, too—who became Musky Montham. The war turned him around. And Uncle Lawrence, my father's brother. And the Dingo children, Celia and Moriston." He frowned. "All scattered now. All scattered then, as far as that goes."

The disdainful look returned to the younger man's lips.

"Ronald Ferse is in coal and feed, Hilary and Tony's daughter, Jean, went in for one-old-cat behind Government House in Rangoon. I don't know what became of the Chinese boy. Uncle Lawrence is translating the Foreign Office records into Russian for the Soviet—confounded officialism! The Dingo children married each other and broke old Forsyte Dingo's heart."

"Forsyte Dingo was in love with Celia Dingo, wasn't he?" queried the more weathered of the two men. The dark look deepened on the face of the more disdainful of the two men.

"Forsyte Dingo was her father," he said. "And her father-in-law, too—after she married her brother."

The old man chuckled unexpectedly.

"Like to see old Forsyte again," he said. "The two of us could play four-handed bridge." He looked at Dinny Mont's daughter, for whose mother he had gone away to the East.

He wondered who she was. It didn't make much difference. All these women, he understood, were the same woman; he was two men, like old Forsyte Dingo, and outnumbered them all. Perhaps it was what kept him going—that and his nice eye for tables—providing he was Adrian. Mark Mont was never a man for tables. The old man twiddled the setting arrangement of his watch, turning it back to 1894, and suddenly discovered that, except for his shoes and socks, his legs were quite bare. Through some surprising and unexpected oversight he had forgotten to put on his trousers. This breach of form had an immediate effect on the others. Wilfrid Desert's son-in-law arose and so did Dinny Mont's daughter. The older man's face was masked in a sort of shrewd suspicion.

"I for one," he said, "shall never leave this spot." The young man laughed and turned his dark eyes on Fleur.

"Will you have lunch with me tomorrow?" he queried.

"I will. Where?"

"Right here on the ship. It'll be easier. We're two days out, you know." They crossed the saloon together.

Fleur thought: "He's as quick as ever. He sees through things."

The older man sat where he was—where, indeed, he intended always to sit unless they came and carried him away, or brought him the rest of his clothes. "England, England!" he murmured. It disturbed him that Adrian Mont, the solid one of the two Mont brothers, should lose his pants. Suddenly he began to feel sickish.

With a faint smile of relief, he thought: "I'm Mark!"

How to See a Bad Play

ONE OF my friends, who is a critic of the drama, invited me to accompany him last season to all the plays which he suspected were not going to be good enough or interesting enough to take his girl to. His suspicions were right in each instance, and there were dozens of instances. I don't know why I kept accepting his invitations to first nights of dubious promise, but I did. Perhaps it was sheer fascination. I know a man, an inveterate smoker of five-cent cigars, who once refused my offer of a Corona: he said he just couldn't go the things. Bad plays can get that kind of hold on you; anyway, they did on me. (I'm not going to go to *any* plays this season; I'm going to ski, and play lotto.)

I still brood about some of the situations, characters, tactics, and strategies I ran into last season in the more awful plays. I thank whatever gods may be that very few lines of dialogue, however, come back at night to roost above my chamber door. As a matter of fact, the only line that haunts me is one from "Reprise," during the first scene of the first act of which a desperate young man is prevented from jumping off the balustrade of a penthouse (all plays set in penthouses are terrible) by another young man. The desperate young man then has three or four shots of what he describes as "excellent brandy" and the other man asks him if he still wants to jump. "No," says the desperate young man. "Your brandy has taken my courage." That marked the first time in the history of the world when three or four slugs of excellent brandy took a desperate man's courage. I find myself thinking about it.

It was in this very same play, "Reprise" (or was it "Yesterday's Orchids"?), that the double-wing-back formation and triple lateral pass reached a new height. I have drawn a little diagram (Fig. 1) to illustrate what I mean. There was really no business in the play, only a great deal of talk, and the director must have found out early—probably during the first rehearsal—that the way the play was written the characters were just going to sit in chairs or on chaise longues and talk to each other, so he got them to moving around. After all, there has to be action of some kind in every play. Fig. 1 shows one of the more intricate moves that were made, as accurately as I can remember it now (I may have left out a couple of shifts, but it's close enough). Character A, to begin with, is standing at the right (A 1) of the handsome chair, centre rear, and Character B is sitting (B 1) on the chaise longue. A moves over (A 2) and sits on the foot of the chaise longue, whereupon B gets up and moves to position

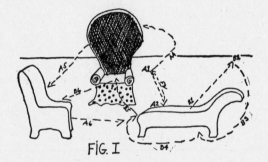

FIG. I

B 2 and then around the chaise longue (B 3) to the same place he had been sitting, as A reverses his field (A 3), circles around the big chair (A 4), and goes to the little chair (A 5). B now moves to the foot of the chaise longue (B 4), and then goes over and sits in the big chair (B 5). As he does so, A moves over and sits on the foot of the chaise longue again (A 6), then B crosses to the little chair (B 6), thus completing a full circle, with variations. All this time a lot of dialogue was going on, dealing with some brand-new angle on sex, but I was so engrossed in following the maze of crisscrosses that I didn't take in any of it, and hence, as far as sex knowledge goes, I am just where I was before I went to the play. There were a great many other involved crossings and recrossings, and what are known on the gridiron as Statue of Liberty plays, in this drama, but the one I have presented here was my favorite.

Another formation that interested me in several of the plays I studied was what I call the back-to-back emotional scene (Fig. 2). The two characters depicted here are, strange as it may seem, "talking it out." In some plays in which this formation occurred they were declaring their love for each other; in others she was telling him that she was in love with someone else, or he was telling her that he had to go to South America because he was in love with her sister or because he thought she was in love with his brother, or his father-in-law, or something of the sort. I have witnessed a number of

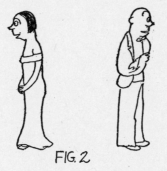

FIG. 2

emotional scenes in real life, but I have just happened to miss any in which the parties involved moved past each other and faced things out back to back. Apparently I don't get around as much as playwrights do.

Fig. 3 illustrates another position that was frequently to be seen on our stage last season: the woman, standing, comforting the man, sitting. In this curious entanglement, so different from anything that has ever happened to me, the position of the arms is always just as I have shown it in the picture and the woman's head is always lifted, as if she were studying a cobweb in a far corner of the ceiling. Sometimes she closes her eyes, wherupon the man opens his. When they break away, it is quite simple to go into the back-to-back formation. Some years ago, along about the time of "Merton of the Movies," the comforting scene was done in quite a different manner: the woman sat on the chair, and the man got down on his knees and put his head in her lap. But times have changed.

In Fig. 4, we take up the character who bobbed up (and down) oftenest in last year's bad plays (she bobbed up and down in some of the better plays, too, but mostly in the bad plays); namely, the elderly lady who is a good sport, a hard drinker, and an authority on sex. There was one such lady in the forgettable "Yesterday's Reprise" (or was it "Orchids"?). She could get away with half a quart of brandy between dinner time and bedtime (3 A.M.), and when she went to bed

FIG. 3

finally she took the bottle with her—"I'm going to put a nipple on this thing and go to bed," she announced as she made her exit. This type of old lady was also given to a stream of epigrams, such as: "At twenty, one is in love with love; at thirty, love is in love with one; at forty, one is in love with two; at fifty, one does not care what two are in love with one; and at sixty," etc., etc. It doesn't have to make a great deal of sense; the sophisticates in the audience always laugh, and one or two who have been through a lot applaud.

There were a lot of other trick moves, positions, and characters in last year's plays, but I have neither the time nor the inclination to remind you of all of them. In winding up the season, I might mention two postures that were very prevalent. It was customary, in the theatre of 1934-35, for juveniles to sit down backward, or wrong-side-out, in straight chairs—that is, facing the back of the chair with their arms crossed on the top of it and their chins on their arms. This position indicated nonchalance and restless energy. Of course, it has been resorted to for years (and years), but last season was the biggest season for it that I can recall; almost no man under forty-five sat down with his back to the chair back. Another popular position—for juveniles and ingénues—was sitting on the extreme edge of a davenport or chaise longue. It seems that nowadays a young couple in love never

FIG. 4

relax and lean back against anything; they must sit (and it is one of the few face-to-face postures in the modern theatre) on the very edge of whatever they are sitting on, their legs thrust backward, their bodies inclined sharply forward, their eyes sparkling, and their words coming very fast. From this position, as from the standing-sitting position (Fig. 3), it is easy to stand up, work the double-crossing maneuver, and go into the back-to-back emotional scene. Apparently young people no longer meet on their feet, face to face, and engage in the obsolete practice of putting their arms around each other. As I say, times have changed. Or maybe it's only the theatre that has changed.

How to Listen to a Play

PRACTICALLY ALL the people I know who write plays want to read them to me. Furthermore, they do read them to me. I don't know why they select me to read plays to, because I am a very bad listener indeed, one of the worst listeners in the United States. I am always waiting for people to stop talking, or reading plays, so that I can talk, or read plays. Unfortunately, I have no plays to read to people (although I am always planning to write some) and, at forty, I do not talk as fast as I used to, or get into it as quickly, so that people with plays under their arms, or in their hip pockets, or even just vaguely outlined in their minds, get the jump on me. It is in the lobby of a hotel which I shall call the Cherokee that I am most often trapped by play readers. I frequently wander into the lobby looking for my hat or overcoat, which I am in the habit of forgetting and leaving there. Play readers seem to know this, for they are generally lurking near where I have left my hat or coat, waiting to pounce. They pounce very fast. "Listen!" a play reader will say, confronting me without even a hello or a how-are-you. "The action takes place in a roadside hot-dog stand, with the usual what's-its-names and so-and-sos scattered here and there, a gasoline pump down right, and a cabin or two on the backdrop. Ella is this girl in charge of the stand; she is pretty, charming, and intelligent but can't get away from the stand to go to school or anything on account of her paralyzed mother, who is paralyzed but sinister, and very strong—she's the menace, see, but she doesn't come on until later. Ella is arranging the salt and mustard and what's-this on the counter when Harry comes on. Ella: 'Hello, Harry.' Harry: 'Hello, Ella.' You can see they are in love——"

"Who can?" I used to ask, bitterly, or "How can you?", but I gave that up because interruptions other than "That's fine," "Swell," and the like are lost on people who read plays to you. What I usually do now is find a comfortable chair, lean back, close my eyes, put an index finger alongside one cheek, and, frowning slightly, pretend to be engrossed. It used to be difficult to do this for more than one act without dozing, but now I can do it for all three, saying "That's fine" or "Swell" at intervals, although I haven't actually taken in a word. A semi-doze, which even now I occasionally lapse into, is worse than complete sleep, because one finds oneself, in a semi-doze, now and then answering questions in the script. For instance, this question occurred in the second act of a play a woman was reading to me recently: "How've you been, Jim?" "Fine," I answered, coming out of my doze without quite knowing where I was. "How've *you* been?" That was a terrible moment for both of us, but I got out of it some way.

Some play readers buy you drinks while you listen, but you can't count on it, and it really isn't a good idea to drink during the reading of a three-act play, because it takes about an hour and a half to read a three-act play and you can get pretty cock-eyed in an hour and a half, especially if you are keeping your mind a blank. Many a time I have walked unsteadily out of the Cherokee at three-thirty in the afteroon, drunk as a lord, with nothing left to do but go to my apartment and go to sleep. As a rule, on these occasions I wake up about ten-thirty P.M., having accomplished nothing and with the whole heavy dull night ahead of me. Play readers don't care about that. They are selfish people.

I can think of no plays, no matter how fine, from "Macbeth" to "What Price Glory?", that I would like to have read to me. I like to see them played or to read them myself, but I have never liked having *anything* read to me (the italics have been mine since I was a little boy). But no playwright will turn his play over to you (or at least he won't to me) so that it can be read alone and at your convenience. Playwrights like to read their plays aloud, because they think you will miss the full rich flavor of certain scenes if they don't. They do not seem to realize that a woman reading a man's part, or a man reading a woman's part, is not only dull but ineffective; but I do, I realize it.

Seven or eight years ago, when I first started in listening to plays, I would actually absorb the sense of the first few scenes before my mind began to wander and my eyes to rove. It really is advisable to comprehend a little of what has been read to you, because the moment is bound to come when the man or woman actually finishes the thing and stops reading. Then he or she is going to say, "Well, what do you think of the character of Rose?" The only thing to say to this is "I think the character of Rose is fine. You've got her down beautifully"; then you can go back quickly to the first scene of the first act (the one you listened to) and dwell on that. No playwright wants to dwell very long with you on the first scene of his first act (they are always crazy about their second and third acts), but if you are adroit enough, you can always work back to that first scene no matter what the playwright wants to have your opinion on. "That," you can say of the second or third act, "is perfect as it stands, perfect. I wouldn't change a line. Nor would I in that magnificent first scene where Ella and Harry discover they are in love." Etc., etc.

It is useless to rely on some friend, wandering around the lobby, to extricate you from your predicament. I've tried that and it only caused more anguish. Once, when a playwright was slowly nearing his second-act curtain (where Harry and Ella rediscover that they are in love, or discover that they are not in love, or are in love with someone else, as the play may be), I slyly signalled a friend to come to my rescue. He walked over to where the playwright and I were sitting. "Good Lord!" I cried, jumping to my feet and facing the newcomer. "I completely forgot about you! We're late now, aren't we? We'll have to hurry!" He stared at me. "Late for what? Hurry where?" he asked. I had a frightful time getting out of that.

If the play reader is bad, the plot outliner is even worse, because you don't have to meet the eyes of the reader, he being intent on his manuscript, but you can't get away from the eyes of the outliner He usually begins something like this: "There's this girl, see, and the guy, and her paralyzed mother, who she suspects knows where she has hidden the franchise and naturally doesn't want Ella to leave the room because he'll get it. She knows that Ella is in love with Ella—I mean Harry, the fellow, see?—but the old girl sees through him even if she doesn't, only she can't talk, she can't speak, see, and let the girl know, let Ella know her suspicions." Even if you listen with intense concentration, you can't follow the plot of a plot outliner. It gets more and more involved as it goes along and is bound to be filled with such terms as "upstage" and "downstage," which I always get mixed up so that I don't know where I am, or where Ella is or the old lady.

I am trying to be kind and considerate to everybody, out of repentance for the life I have led, but some day a play reader or a plot outliner is going to push me too far and I am going to get up in the middle of the first scene and scream. I am going to scream until the manager comes. I am going to scream until the ambulance and the police and the photographers come. I don't care how much people may talk.

The Funniest Man You Ever Saw

EVERYBODY SEEMED surprised that I had never met Jack Klohman.

"Judas, I didn't know there was anybody who didn't know

Jack Klohman," said Mr. Potter, who was big and heavy, of body and mind. "He's funnier'n hell." Mr. Potter laughed and slapped his knee. "He's the funniest man you ever saw."

"He certainly is funny," said somebody else.

"He's marvellous," drawled a woman I didn't like. Looking around the group I discovered I didn't like any of them much, except Joe Mayer. This was undoubtedly unfair, for Joe was the only one I knew very well. The others had come over to the table where we were sitting. Somebody had mentioned Jack Klohman and everybody had begun to laugh.

"Do you know him, Joe?" I asked.

"I know him," said Joe, without laughing.

"Judas," went on Potter, "I'll never forget one night at Jap Rudolph's. Klohman was marvellous that night. This was a couple years ago, when Ed Wynn was here in a new show—let's see, what the devil was it? Not 'The Crazy Fool.'"

"'The Perfect Fool,'" said somebody else.

"Yes. But it wasn't that," said Potter. "What the dickens was it? Well, never mind; anyway there was a scene in it where——"

"Was it 'Simple Simon'?" asked the blonde girl who was with Creel.

"No. It was a couple years before that," said Potter.

"Oh, I know," said the blonde girl. "It was—now wait—it was 'The Manhatters'!"

"Ed Wynn wasn't in that," said Creel. "Wynn wasn't in that show."

"Well, it doesn't make much difference," said Potter. "Anyway, in this scene he has a line where——"

"'Manhattan Mary'!" cried Griswold.

"That's it!" said Potter, slapping his knee. "Well, in this scene he comes on with a rope, kind of a lariat——"

"Halter," said Griswold. "It was a halter."

"Yes, that's right," said Potter. "Anyway, he comes on

with this halter——"

"Who comes on?" asked Joe Mayer. "Klohman?"

"No, no," said Potter. "Wynn comes on with the halter and walks up to the footlights and some guy asks him what he's got the rope for, what he's doing with the halter. 'Well,' says Wynn, 'I've either lost a horse or found a piece of rope——'"

"I think he said: 'I've either found a piece of rope or lost a horse,'" said Griswold. "Losing the horse coming last is funnier."

"Well, anyway," said Potter, "Jack Klohman used to elaborate on the idea and this night at Jap Rudolph's I thought we'd all pass away."

"I nearly did," said Joe Mayer.

"What did this Klohman do?" I asked finally, cutting in on the general laughter.

"Well," said Potter, "he'd go out into the kitchen, see, and come in with a Uneeda biscuit and he'd say: 'Look, I've either lost a biscuit box or found a cracker'—that's the right order, Gris—'I've either lost a biscuit box or lost'—I mean found—'a cracker.'"

"I guess you're right," said Griswold.

"It sounds right," said Joe Mayer.

"Then he'd do the same thing with everything he picked up, no matter what," said Potter. "Finally he went out of the room and was gone half an hour or so and then he comes down the stairs and holds up this faucet and says: 'I've either lost a bathtub or found a faucet.' He'd unscrewed a faucet from the bathtub and comes downstairs with this faucet—see what I mean? Laugh? I thought I'd pass away."

Everybody who had been at Jap Rudolph's that night roared with laughter.

"But that wasn't anything," said Potter. "Wait'll you hear. Along about two in the morning he slips out again, see?—all the way out of the house this time. Well, I'll be doggoned if that guy didn't come back carrying part of an honest-to-God chancel rail! He did! I'm telling you! Son-of-a-gun had actually got into a church somehow and wrenched part of this chancel rail loose and there he was standing in the door and he says: 'I've either lost a church or found a chancel rail.' It was rich. It was the richest thing I ever saw. Helen Rudolph had gone to bed, I remember—she wasn't very well—but we got her up and he did it again. It was rich."

"Sounds like a swell guy to have around," I said.

"You'd darn near pass away," said Potter.

"You really would," said Joe Mayer.

"He's got a new gag now," said one of the women. "He's got a new gag that's as funny as the dickens. He keeps taking things out of his pockets or off of a table or something and says that he's just invented them. He always takes something that's been invented for *years*, say like a lead pencil or something, and goes into this long story about how he thought it up one night. I remember he did it with about twenty different things one night at Jap's——"

"Jap Rudolph's?" I asked.

"Yes," said the woman. "He likes to drop in on them, so you can usually find him there, so we usually drop in on them too. Well, this night he took out a package of those Life Savers and handed us each one of the mints and——"

"Oh, yes, I remember that!" said Potter, slapping his knee and guffawing.

"Gave us each one of these mints," went on the woman, "and asked us what we thought of them—asked us whether we thought they'd go or not. 'It's a little thing I thought up one day,' he said. Then he'd go on with a long rigmarole about how he happened to think of the idea, and——"

"And then he'd take a pencil out of his pocket," cut in Potter, "and ask you what you thought of the eraser on the end of it. 'Just a little gadget I thought up the other night,' he'd say. Then he says he'll show you what it's for, so he makes everybody take a piece of paper and he says: 'Now everybody make some pencil marks on the paper; any kind—

I won't look,' so then he goes into another room and says to
let him know when you're ready. So we all make marks on
the pieces of paper and somebody goes and gets him out of
the other room——"

"They always go and get him out of the other room," Joe
Mayer said to me.

"Sure," said Potter. "So he comes out with his sleeves
rolled up, like a magician, and——"

"But the *funniest* thing he does," began the woman whom
Potter had interrupted.

"And he gathers up the papers and erases the marks with
the eraser and he says: 'Oh, it's just a novelty; I'm not going
to try to market it.' Laugh? I thought I'd pass away. Of
course you really ought to see him do it; the way he does it is
a big part of it—solemn and all; he's always solemn, always
acts solemn about it."

"The *funniest* thing he does," began the interrupted
woman again, loudly, "is fake card tricks. He——"

"Oh, yes!" cried Potter, roaring and slapping his knee.
"He does these fake card tricks. He——" Here the recollection
of the funny man's antics proved too much for Potter and he
laughed until he cried. It was several minutes before he could
control himself. "He'll take a pack of cards," he finally
began again. "He'll take a pack of cards——" Once more the
image of Klohman taking a pack of cards was too much for
the narrator and he went off into further gales of laughter.
"He'll take this pack of cards," Potter eventually said once
more, wiping his eyes, "and ask you to take any card and you
take one and then he says: 'Put it anywhere in the deck' and
you do and then he makes a lot of passes and so on——"

"Like a magician," said Joe Mayer.

"Yes," said Potter. "And then he draws out the wrong
card, or maybe he *looks* at your card first and then goes
through the whole deck till he finds it and shows it to you
or——"

"Sometimes he just lays the pack down and acts as if he'd never started any trick," said Griswold.

"Does he do imitations?" I asked. Joe Mayer kicked my shins under the table.

"Does he do *imitations*?" bellowed Potter. "Wait'll I tell you——"

The Black Magic of Barney Haller

IT WAS one of those hot days on which the earth is uninhabitable; even as early as ten o'clock in the morning, even on the hill where I live under the dark maples. The long porch was hot and the wicker chair I sat in complained hotly. My coffee was beginning to wear off and with it the momentary illusion it gives that things are Right and life is Good. There were sultry mutterings of thunder. I had a quick feeling that if I looked up from my book I would see Barney Haller. I looked up, and there he was, coming along the road, lightning playing about his shoulders, thunder following him like a dog.

Barney is (or was) my hired man. He is strong and amiable, sweaty and dependable, slowly and heavily competent. But he is also eerie: he trafficks with the devil. His ears twitch when he talks, but it isn't so much that as the things he says. Once in late June, when all of a moment sabres began to flash brightly in the heavens and bowling balls rumbled, I took refuge in the barn. I always have a feeling that I am going to be struck by lightning and either riven like an old apple tree or left with a foot that aches in rainy weather and a habit of fainting. Those things happen. Barney came in, not to escape the storm to which he is, or pretends to be, indifferent, but to put the scythe away. Suddenly he said the first of those things that made me, when I was with him, faintly creepy. He pointed at the house. "Once I see dis boat come down de rock," he said. It is phenomena like that of which I stand in constant dread: boats coming down rocks, people being teleported, statues dripping blood, old regrets and dreams in the form of Luna moths fluttering against the windows at midnight.

Of course I finally figured out what Barney meant—or what I comforted myself with believing he meant: something about a bolt coming down the lightning rod on the house; a commonplace, an utterly natural thing. I should have dismissed it, but it had its effect on me. Here was a stolid man, smelling of hay and leather, who talked like somebody out of Charles Fort's books, or like a traveller back from Oz. And all the time the lightning was zigging and zagging around him.

On this hot morning when I saw Barney coming along with his faithful storm trudging behind him, I went back frowningly to my copy of "Swann's Way." I hoped that Barney, seeing me absorbed in a book, would pass by without saying anything. I read: ". . . I myself seemed actually to have become the subject of my book: a church, a quartet, the rivalry between Francis I and Charles V . . ." I could feel Barney standing looking at me, but I didn't look at him.

"Dis morning bime by," said Barney, "I go hunt grotches in de voods."

"That's fine," I said, and turned a page and pretended to be engrossed in what I was reading. Barney walked on; he had wanted to talk some more, but he walked on. After a paragraph or two, his words began to come between me and the words in the book. "Bime by I go hunt grotches in de voods." If you are susceptible to such things, it is not difficult to visualize grotches. They fluttered into my mind: ugly little creatures, about the size of whippoorwills, only covered with

blood and honey and the scrapings of church bells. Grotches
. . . Who and what, I wondered, really was this thing in the
form of a hired man that kept anointing me ominously, in
passing, with abracadabra?

Barney didn't go toward the woods at once; he weeded the
corn, he picked apple boughs up off the lawn, he knocked a
yellow jacket's nest down out of a plum tree. It was raining
now, but he didn't seem to notice it. He kept looking at me
out of the corner of his eye, and I kept looking at him out of
the corner of my eye. "Vot dime is it, blease?" he called to me
finally. I put down my book and sauntered out to him.
"When you go for those grotches," I said, firmly, "I'll go
with you." I was sure he wouldn't want me to go. I was right;
he protested that he could get the grotches himself. "I'll go
with you," I said, stubbornly. We stood looking at each
other. And then, abruptly, just to give *him* something to
ponder over, I quoted:

> "I'm going out to clean the pasture spring;
> I'll only stop to rake the leaves away
> (And wait to watch the water clear, I may):
> I shan't be gone long.—You come too."

It wasn't, I realized, very good abracadabra, but it served:
Barney looked at me in a puzzled way. "Yes," he said,
vaguely.

"It's five minutes of twelve," I said, remembering he had
asked.

"Den we go," he said, and we trudged through the rain
over to the orchard fence and climbed that, and opened a
gate and went out into the meadow that slopes up to the
woods. I had a prefiguring of Barney, at some proper spot in
the woods, prancing around like a goat, casting off his false
nature, shedding his hired man's garments, dropping his
Teutonic accent, repeating diabolical phrases, conjuring up
grotches.

There was a great slash of lightning and a long bumping of

thunder as we reached the edge of the woods.

I turned and fled. Glancing over my shoulder, I saw Barney standing and staring after me. . . .

It turned out (on the face of it) to be as simple as the boat that came down the rock. Grotches were "crotches": crotched saplings which he cut down to use as supports under the peach boughs, because in bearing time they became so heavy with fruit that there was danger of the branches snapping off. I saw Barney later, putting the crotches in place. We didn't have much to say to each other. I can see now that he was beginning to suspect me too.

About six o'clock next evening, I was alone in the house and sleeping upstairs. Barney rapped on the door of the front porch. I knew it was Barney because he called to me. I woke up slowly. It was dark for six o'clock. I heard rumblings and saw flickerings. Barney was standing at the front door with his storm at heel! I had the conviction that it wasn't storming anywhere except around my house. There couldn't, without the intervention of the devil or one of his agents, be so many lightning storms in one neighborhood.

I had been dreaming of Proust and the church at Combray and *madeleines* dipped in tea, and the rivalry between Francis I and Charles V. My head whirled and I didn't get up. Barney kept on rapping. He called out again. There was a flash, followed by a sharp splitting sound. I leaped up. This time, I thought, he is here to get me. I had a notion that he was standing at the door barefooted, with a wreath of grape leaves around his head, and a wild animal's skin slung over his shoulder. I didn't want to go down, but I did.

He was as usual, solid, amiable, dressed like a hired man. I went out on the porch and looked at the improbable storm, now on in all its fury. "This is getting pretty bad," I said, meaningly. Barney looked at the rain placidly. "Well," I said, irritably, "what's up?" Barney turned his little squinty blue eyes on me.

"We go to the garrick now and become warbs," he said.

"The hell we do!" I thought to myself, quickly. I was uneasy—I was, you might even say, terrified—but I determined not to show it. If he began to chant incantations or to make obscene signs or if he attempted to sling me over his shoulder, I resolved to plunge right out into the storm, lightning and all, and run to the nearest house. I didn't know what they would think at the nearest house when I burst in upon them, or what I would tell them. But I didn't intend to accompany this amiable-looking fiend to any garrick and become a warb. I tried to persuade myself that there was some simple explanation, that warbs would turn out to be as innocuous as boats on rocks and grotches in the woods, but the conviction gripped me (in the growling of the thunder) that here at last was the Moment when Barney Haller, or whoever he was, had chosen to get me. I walked toward the steps that lead to the lawn, and turned and faced him, grimly.

"Listen!" I barked, suddenly. "Did you know that even when it isn't brillig I can produce slithy toves? Did you happen to know that the mome rath never lived that could outgrabe me? Yeah and furthermore I can become anything I want to; even if I were a warb, I wouldn't have to keep on being one if I didn't want to. I can become a playing card at will, too; once I was the jack of clubs, only I forgot to take my glasses off and some guy recognized me. I . . ."

Barney was backing slowly away, toward the petunia box at one end of the porch. His little blue eyes were wide. He saw that I had him. "I think I go now," he said. And he walked out into the rain. The rain followed him down the road.

I have a new hired man now. Barney never came back to work for me after that day. Of course I figured out finally what he meant about the garrick and the warbs: he had simply got horribly mixed up in trying to tell me that he was going up to the garret and clear out the wasps, of which I have thousands. The new hired man is afraid of them. Barney could have scooped them up in his hands and thrown them out a window without getting stung. I am sure he trafficked with the devil. But I am sorry I let him go.

The Remarkable Case of Mr. Bruhl

SAMUEL O. BRUHL was just an ordinary-looking citizen, like you and me, except for a curious, shoe-shaped scar on his left cheek, which he got when he fell against a wagon-tongue in his youth. He had a good job as treasurer for a syrup-and-fondant concern, a large, devout wife, two tractable daughters, and a nice home in Brooklyn. He worked from nine to five, took in a show occasionally, played a bad, complacent game of golf, and was usually in bed by eleven o'clock. The Bruhls had a dog named Bert, a small circle of friends, and an old sedan. They had made a comfortable, if unexciting, adjustment to life.

There was no reason in the world why Samuel Bruhl shouldn't have lived along quietly until he died of some commonplace malady. He was a man designed by Nature for an uneventful life, an inexpensive but respectable funeral, and a modest stone marker. All this you would have predicted had you observed his colorless comings and goings, his mild manner, the small stature of his dreams. He was, in brief, the sort of average citizen that observers of Judd Gray thought Judd Gray was. And precisely as that mild little family man was abruptly hurled into an incongruous tragedy, so was Samuel Bruhl suddenly picked out of the hundreds of men just like him and marked for an extravagant and unpredictable end. Oddly enough it was the shoe-shaped scar on his left cheek which brought to his heels a Nemesis he had never dreamed of. A blemish on his heart, a tic in his soul would have been different; one would have blamed Bruhl for whatever anguish an emotional or spiritual flaw laid him open to, but it is ironical indeed when the Furies ride down a man who has been guilty of nothing worse than an accident in his childhood.

Samuel O. Bruhl looked very much like George ("Shoe-scar") Clinigan. Clinigan had that same singular shoe-shaped scar on his left cheek. There was also a general resemblance in height, weight, and complexion. A careful study would have revealed very soon that Clinigan's eyes were shifty and Bruhl's eyes were clear, and that the syrup-and-fondant company's treasurer had a more pleasant mouth and a higher forehead than the gangster and racketeer, but at a glance the similarity was remarkable.

Had Clinigan not become notorious, this prank of Nature would never have been detected, but Clinigan did become notorious and dozens of persons observed that he looked like Bruhl. They saw Clinigan's picture in the papers the day he was shot, and the day after, and the day after that. Presently someone in the syrup-and-fondant concern mentioned to someone else that Clinigan looked like Mr. Bruhl, remarkably like Mr. Bruhl. Soon everybody in the place had commented on it, among themselves, and to Mr. Bruhl.

Mr. Bruhl rather laughed it off at first, but one day when Clinigan had been in the hospital a week, a cop peered closely at Mr. Bruhl when he was on his way home from work. After that, the little treasurer noticed a number of other strangers staring at him with mingled surprise and alarm. One small, dark man hastily thrust a hand into his coat pocket and paled slightly.

Mr. Bruhl began to worry. He began to imagine things. "I hope this fellow Clinigan doesn't pull through," he said one morning at breakfast. "He's a bad actor. He's better off dead."

"Oh, he'll pull through," said Mrs. Bruhl, who had been

reading the morning paper. "It says here he'll pull through. But it says they'll shoot him again. It says they're sure to shoot him again."

The morning after the night that Clinigan left the hospital, secretly, by a side door, and disappeared into the town, Bruhl decided not to go to work. "I don't feel so good today," he said to his wife. "Would you call up the office and tell them I'm sick?"

"You don't look well," said his wife. "You really don't look well. Get down, Bert," she added, for the dog had jumped upon her lap and whined. The animal knew that something was wrong.

That evening Bruhl, who had mooned about the house all day, read in the papers that Clinigan had vanished, but was believed to be somewhere in the city. His various rackets required his presence, at least until he made enough money to skip out with; he had left the hospital penniless. Rival gangsters, the papers said, were sure to seek him out, to hunt him down, to give it to him again. "Give him what again?" asked Mrs. Bruhl when she read this. "Let's talk about something else," said her husband.

It was little Joey, the officeboy at the syrup-and-fondant company, who first discovered that Mr. Bruhl was afraid. Joey, who went about with tennis shoes on, entered the treasurer's office suddenly—flung open the door and started to say something. "Good God!" cried Mr. Bruhl, rising from his chair. "Why, what's the matter, Mr. Bruhl?" asked Joey. Other little things happened. The switchboard girl phoned Mr. Bruhl's desk one afternoon and said there was a man waiting to see him, a Mr. Globe. "What's he look like?" asked Bruhl, who didn't know anybody named Globe. "He's small and dark," said the girl. "A small, dark man?" said Bruhl. "Tell him I'm out. Tell him I've gone to California." The personnel, comparing notes, decided at length that the treasurer was afraid of being mistaken for Shoescar and put on the spot. They said nothing to Mr. Bruhl about this,

because they were forbidden to by Ollie Breithofter, a fattish clerk who was a tireless and inventive practical joker and who had an idea.

As the hunt went on for Clinigan and he still wasn't found and killed, Mr. Bruhl lost weight and grew extremely fidgety. He began to figure out new ways of getting to work, one requiring the use of two different ferry lines; he ate his lunch in, he wouldn't answer bells, he cried out when anyone dropped anything, and he ran into stores or banks when cruising taxi-drivers shouted at him. One morning, in setting the house to rights, Mrs. Bruhl found a revolver under his pillow. "I found a revolver under your pillow," she told him that night. "Burglars are bad in this neighborhood," he said. "You oughtn't to have a revolver," she said. They argued

about it, he irritably, she uneasily, until time for bed. As
Bruhl was undressing, after locking and bolting all the doors,
the telephone rang. "It's for you, Sam," said Mrs. Bruhl. Her
husband went slowly to the phone, passing Bert on the way.
"I wish I was you," he said to the dog, and took up the
receiver. "Get this, Shoescar," said a husky voice. "We
trailed you where you are, see? You're cooked." The receiver
at the other end was hung up. Bruhl shouted. His wife came
running. "What is it, Sam, what is it?" she cried. Bruhl, pale,
sick-looking, had fallen into a chair. "They got me," he
moaned. "They got me." Slowly, deviously, Minnie Bruhl
got it out of her husband that he had been mistaken for
Clinigan and that he was cooked. Mrs. Bruhl was not very
quick mentally, but she had a certain intuition and this
intuition told her, as she trembled there in her nightgown
above her broken husband, that this was the work of Ollie
Breithofter. She instantly phoned Ollie Breithofter's wife
and, before she hung up, had got the truth out of Mrs.
Breithofter. It was Ollie who had called.

The treasurer of the Maskonsett Syrup & Fondant
Company, Inc., was so relieved to know that the gangs
weren't after him that he admitted frankly at the office next
day that Ollie had fooled him for a minute. Mr. Bruhl even
joined in the laughter and wisecracking, which went on all
day. After that, for almost a week, the mild little man had
comparative peace of mind. The papers said very little about
Clinigan now. He had completely disappeared. Gang warfare
had died down for the time being.

One Sunday morning Mr. Bruhl went for an automobile
ride with his wife and daughters. They had driven about a
mile through Brooklyn streets when, glancing in the mirror
above his head, Mr. Bruhl observed a blue sedan just behind
him. He turned off into the next side street, and the sedan
turned off too. Bruhl made another turn, and the sedan

followed him. "Where are you going, dear?" asked Mrs. Bruhl. Mr. Bruhl didn't answer her, he speeded up, he drove terrifically fast, he turned corners so wildly that the rear wheels swung around. A traffic cop shrilled at him. The younger daughter screamed. Bruhl drove right on, weaving in and out. Mrs. Bruhl began to berate him wildly. "Have you lost your mind, Sam?" she shouted. Mr. Bruhl looked behind him. The sedan was no longer to be seen. He slowed up. "Let's go home," he said. "I've had enough of this."

A month went by without incident (thanks largely to Mrs. Breithofter) and Samuel Bruhl began to be himself again. On the day that he was practically normal once more, Sluggy Pensiotta, alias Killer Lewis, alis Stranger Koetschke, was shot. Sluggy was the leader of the gang that had sworn to get Shoescar Clinigan. The papers instantly took up the gang-war story where they had left off. Pictures of Clinigan were published again. The slaying of Pensiotta, said the papers, meant but one thing: it meant that Shoescar Clinigan was cooked. Mr. Bruhl, reading this, went gradually to pieces once more.

After another week of skulking about, starting at every noise, and once almost fainting when an automobile back-fired near him, Samuel Bruhl began to take on a remarkable new appearance. He talked out of the corner of his mouth, his eyes grew shifty. He looked more and more like Shoescar Clinigan. He snarled at his wife. Once he called her "Babe," and he had never called her anything but Minnie. He kissed her in a strange, new way, acting rough, almost brutal. At the office he was mean and overbearing. He used peculiar language. One night when the Bruhls had friends in for bridge—old Mr. Creegan and his wife—Bruhl suddenly appeared from upstairs with a pair of scarlet pajamas on, smoking a cigarette, and gripping his revolver. After a few loud and incoherent remarks of a boastful nature, he let fly at a clock on the mantel, and hit it squarely in the middle. Mrs.

Bruhl screamed. Mr. Creegan fainted. Bert, who was in the kitchen, howled. "What's the matta you?" snarled Bruhl. "Ya bunch of softies."

Quite by accident, Mrs. Bruhl discovered, hidden away in a closet, eight to ten books on gangs and gangsters, which Bruhl had put there. They included "Al Capone," "You Can't Win," "10,000 Public Enemies" and a lot of others; and they were all well thumbed. Mrs. Bruhl realized that it was high time something was done, and she determined to have a doctor for her husband. For two or three days Bruhl had not gone to work. He lay around in his bedroom, in his red pajamas, smoking cigarettes. The office phoned once or twice. When Mrs. Bruhl urged him to get up and dress and go to work, he laughed and patted her roughly on the head. "It's a knockover, kid," he said. "We'll be sitting pretty. To hell with it."

The doctor who finally came and slipped into Bruhl's bedroom was very grave when he emerged. "This is a psychosis," he said, "a definite psychosis. Your husband is living in a world of fantasy. He has built up a curious defence mechanism against something or other." The doctor suggested that a psychiatrist be called in, but after he had gone Mrs. Bruhl decided to take her husband out of town on a trip. The Maskonsett Syrup & Fondant Company, Inc., was very fine about it. Mr. Scully said of course. "Sam is very valuable to us, Mrs. Bruhl," said Mr. Scully, "and we all hope he'll be all right." Just the same he had Mr. Bruhl's accounts examined, when Mrs. Bruhl had gone.

Oddly enough, Samuel Bruhl was amenable to the idea of going away. "I need a rest," he said. "You're right. Let's get the hell out of here." He seemed normal up to the time they set out for the Grand Central and then he insisted on leaving from the 125th Street station. Mrs. Bruhl took exception to this, as being ridiculous, whereupon her doting husband snarled at her. "God, what a dumb moll *I* picked," he said to

Minnie Bruhl, and he added bitterly that if the heat was put to him it would be his own babe who was to blame. "And what do you think of *that*?" he said, pushing her to the floor of the cab.

They went to a little inn in the mountains. It wasn't a very nice place, but the rooms were clean and the meals were good. There was no form of entertainment, except a Tom Thumb golf course and an uneven tennis court, but Mr. Bruhl didn't mind. He said it was too cold outdoors, anyway. He stayed indoors, reading and smoking. In the evening he played the mechanical piano in the dining-room. He liked to play "More Than You Know" over and over again. One night, about nine o'clock, he was putting in his seventh or eighth nickel when four men walked into the dining-room. They were silent men, wearing overcoats, and carrying what appeared to be cases for musical instruments. They took out various kinds of guns from their cases, quickly, expertly, and walked over toward Bruhl, keeping step. He turned just in time to see them line up four abreast and aim at him. Nobody else was in the room. There was a cumulative roar and a series of flashes. Mr. Bruhl fell and the men walked out in single file, rapidly, nobody having said a word.

Mrs. Bruhl, state police, and the hotel manager tried to get the wounded man to talk. Chief Witznitz of the nearest town's police force tried it. It was no good. Bruhl only snarled and told them to go away and let him alone. Finally, Commissioner O'Donnell of the New York City Police Department arrived at the hospital. He asked Bruhl what the men looked like. "I don't know what they looked like," snarled Bruhl, "and if I did know I wouldn't tell you." He was silent a moment, then: "Cop!" he added, bitterly. The Commissioner sighed and turned away. "They're all like that," he said to the others in the room. "They never talk." Hearing this, Mr. Bruhl smiled, a pleased smile, and closed his eyes.

Something to Say

Hugh Kingsmill and I stimulated each other to such a pitch that after the first meeting he had a brain storm and I lay sleepless all night and in the morning was on the brink of a nervous breakdown.—William Gerhardi's "Memoirs of a Polyglot."

ELLIOT VEREKER was always coming into and going out of my life. He was the only man who ever continuously stimulated me to the brink of a nervous breakdown. I met him first at a party in Amawalk, New York, on the Fourth of July, 1927. He arrived about noon in an old-fashioned horse cab, accompanied by a lady in black velvet whom he introduced as "my niece, Olga Nethersole." She was, it turned out, neither his niece nor Olga Nethersole. Vereker was a writer; he was gaunt and emaciated from sitting up all night talking; he wore an admiral's hat which he had stolen from an admiral. Usually he carried with him an old Gladstone bag filled with burned-out electric-light bulbs which it was his pleasure to throw, unexpectedly, against the sides of houses and the walls of rooms. He loved the popping sound they made and the tinkling sprinkle of fine glass that followed. He had an inordinate fondness for echoes. "Halloooo!" he would bawl, wherever he was, in a terrific booming voice that could have conjured up an echo on a prairie. At the most inopportune and inappropriate moments he would snap out frank four-letter words, such as when he was talking to a little child or the sister of a vicar. He had no reverence and no solicitude. He would litter up your house, burn bedspreads and carpets with lighted cigarette stubs, and as likely as not depart with your girl and three or four of your most prized books and neckties. He was enamored of breaking phonograph records and phonographs; he liked to tear sheets and pillowcases in two; he would unscrew the doorknobs from your doors so that if you were in you

258

couldn't get out and if you were out you couldn't get in. His was the true artistic fire, the rare gesture of genius. When I first met him, he was working on a novel entitled "Sue You Have Seen." He had worked it out, for some obscure reason, from the familiar expression "See you soon." He never finished it, nor did he ever finish, or indeed get very far with, any writing, but he was nevertheless, we all felt, one of the great original minds of our generation. That he had "something to say" was obvious in everything he did.

Vereker could converse brilliantly on literary subjects: Proust, Goethe, Voltaire, Whitman. Basically he felt for them a certain respect, but sometimes, and always when he was drunk, he would belittle their powers and their achievements in strong and pungent language. Proust, I later discovered, he had never read, but he made him seem more clear to me, and less important, than anybody else ever has. Vereker always liked to have an electric fan going while he talked and he would stick a folded newspaper into the fan so that the revolving blades scuttered against it, making a noise like the rattle of machine-gun fire. This exhilarated him and exhilarated me, too, but I suppose that it exhilarated him more than it did me. He seemed, at any rate, to get something out of it that I missed. He would raise his voice so that I could hear him above the racket. Sometimes, even then, I couldn't make out what he was saying. "What?" I would shout. "You heard me!" he would yell, his good humor disappearing in an instant.

I had, of course, not heard him at all. There was no reasoning with him, no convincing him. I can still hear the musketry of those fans in my ears. They have done, I think, something to me. But for Vereker, and his great promise, one could endure a great deal. He would talk about the interests implicated in life, the coincidence of desire and realization, the symbols behind art and reality. He was fond of quoting Santayana when he was sober.

"Santayana," he would say when he was drinking, "has

weight; he's a ton of feathers." Then he would laugh
roaringly; if he was at Tony's, he would flounder out into the
kitchen, insulting some movie critic on the way, and repeat
his line to whoever was there, and come roaring back.

Vereker had a way of flinging himself at a sofa, kicking
one end out of it; or he would drop into a fragile chair like a
tired bird dog and something would crack. He never seemed
to notice. You would invite him to dinner, or, what happened
oftener, he would drop in for dinner uninvited, and while you
were shaking up a cocktail in the kitchen he would disappear.
He might go upstairs to wrench the bathtub away from the
wall ("Breaking lead pipe is one of the truly enchanting
adventures in life," he said once), or he might simply leave
for good in one of those inexplicable huffs of his which were
a sign of his peculiar genius. He was likely, of course, to
come back around two in the morning bringing some awful

woman with him, stirring up the fire, talking all night long, knocking things off tables, singing, or counting. I have known him to lie back on a sofa, his eyes closed, and count up to as high as twenty-four thousand by ones, in a bitter, snarling voice. It was his protest against the regularization of a mechanized age. "Achievement," he used to say, "is the fool's gold of idiots." He never believed in doing anything or in having anything done, either for the benefit of mankind or for individuals. He would have written, but for his philosophical indolence, very great novels indeed. We all knew that, and we treated him with a deference for which, now that he is gone, we are sincerely glad.

Once Vereker invited me to a house which a lady had turned over to him when she went to Paris for a divorce. (She expected to marry Vereker afterward but he would not marry her, nor would he move out of her house until she took legal action. "American women," Vereker would say, "are like American colleges: they have dull, half-dead faculties.") When I arrived at the house, Vereker chose to pretend that he did not remember me. It was rather difficult to carry the situation off, for he was in one of his black moods. It was then that he should have written, but never did; instead he would gabble brilliantly about other authors. "Goethe," he would say, "was a wax figure stuffed with hay. When you say that Proust was sick, you have said everything. Shakespeare was a dolt. If there had been no Voltaire, it would not have been necessary to create one." Etc. I had been invited for the weekend and I intended to stay; none of us ever left Vereker alone when we came upon him in one of his moods. He frequently threatened suicide and six or seven times attempted it but, in every case, there was someone on hand to prevent him. Once, I remember, he got me out of bed late at night at my own apartment. "I'm going through with it this time," he said, and darted into the bathroom. He was fumbling around for some poison in the medicine chest, which fortunately contained none, when I ran in and pleaded with him. "You have so many things yet to do," I said to him. "Yes," he said, "and so many people yet to insult." He talked brilliantly all night long, and drank up a bottle of cognac that I had got to send to my father.

I had gone to the bathroom for a shower, the time he invited me to his lady's house, when he stalked into the room. "Get out of that tub, you common housebreaker," he said, "or I shall summon the police!" I laughed, of course, and went on bathing. I was rubbing myself with a towel when the police arrived—he had sent for them! Vereker would have made an excellent actor; he convinced the police that he had never seen me before in his life. I was arrested, taken away, and locked up for the night. A few days later I got a note from Vereker. "I shall never ask you to my house again," he wrote, "after the way I acted last Saturday." His repentances, while whimsical, were always as complete as the erratic charades which called them forth. He was unpredictable and, at times, difficult, but he was always stimulating. Sometimes he keyed you up to a point beyond which, you felt, you could not go.

Vereker had a close escape from death once which I shall never forget. A famous American industrialist had invited a number of American writers and some visiting English men of letters out to his Long Island place. We were to make the trip in a huge bus that had been chartered for the purpose. Vereker came along and insisted, when we reached Long Island, on driving the bus. It was an icy night and he would put on the brakes at a curve, causing the heavy vehicle to skid ponderously. Several times we surged perilously near to a ditch and once the bus snapped off a big tree like a match. I remember that H. G. Bennett was along, and Arnold Wells, the three Sitwells, and four or five Waughs. One of them finally shut off the ignition and another struck Vereker over the head with a crank. His friends were furious. When the car stopped, we carried him outside and put him down on the hard, cold ground. Marvin Deane, the critic, held Vereker's head, which was bleeding profusely, in his lap, looked up at the busload of writers, and said: "You might have killed him! And he is a greater genius than any of you!" It was superb. Then the amazing Vereker opened his eyes. "That goes for me, too," he said, and closed them again.

We hurried him to a hospital, where, in two days, he was on his feet again; he left the hospital without a word to anybody, and we all chipped in to pay the bill. Vereker had some money at the time which his mother had given him but, as he said, he needed it. "I am glad he is up and out," I said to the nurse who had taken care of him. "So am I," she said. Vereker affected everybody the same way.

Some time after this we all decided to make up a fund and send Vereker to Europe to write. His entire output, I had discovered, consisted of only twenty or thirty pages, most of them bearing the round stain of liquor glasses; one page was the beginning of a play done more or less in the style of Gertrude Stein. It seemed to me as brilliant as anything of its kind.

We got together about fifteen hundred dollars and I was delegated to approach Vereker, as tactfully as possible. We knew that it was folly for him to go on the way he was, dissipating his talent; for weeks he had been in one of his blackest moods: he would call on people, drink up their rye, wrench light-brackets off the walls, hurl scintillating gibes at his friends and at the accepted literary masters of all time, through whose superficiality Vereker saw more clearly, I think, than anybody else I have ever known. He would end up by bursting into tears. "Here, but for the gracelessness of God," he would shout, "stands the greatest writer in the history of the world!" We felt that, despite Vereker's drunken exaggeration, there was more than a grain of truth in what he said: certainly nobody else we ever met had, so utterly, the fire of genius that blazed in Vereker, if outward manifestations meant anything.

He would never try for a Guggenheim fellowship. "Guggenheim follow-sheep!" he would snarl. "Fall in line, all of you little men! Don't talk to me about Good-in-time fellowships!" He would go on that way, sparklingly, for an hour, his tirade finally culminating in one of those remarkable fits of temper in which he could rip up any apartment at all, no matter whose, in less than fifteen minutes.

Vereker, much to my surprise and gratification, took the fifteen hundred dollars without making a scene. I had suspected that he might denounce us all, that he might go into one of his brilliant philippics against Money, that he might even threaten again to take his life, for it had been several months since he had attempted suicide. But no; he snarled a bit, it is true, but he accepted the money. "I'm cheap at twice the price," he said.

It was the most money Vereker had ever had in his life and of course we should have known better than to let him have it all at once. The night of the day I gave it to him he cut a wide swath in the cheaper West Side night clubs and in Harlem, spent three hundred dollars, insulted several women, and figured in fist fights with a policeman, two taxi-drivers, and two husbands, all of whom won. We instantly decided to arrange his passage on a ship that was sailing for Cherbourg three nights later. Somehow or other we kept him out of trouble until the night of the sailing, when we gave a going-away party for him at Marvin Deane's house. Everybody was there: Gene Tunney, Sir Hubert Wilkins, Count von Luckner, Edward Bernays, and the literary and artistic crowd generally. Vereker got frightfully drunk. He denounced everybody at the party and also Hugh Walpole, Joseph Conrad, Crane, Henry James, Hardy, and Meredith. He dwelt on the subject of "Jude the Obscure." "Jude the Obscure," he would shout, "Jude the Obscene, June the Obscude, Obs the June Moon."

He combined with his penetrating critical evaluations and his rare creative powers a certain unique fantasy not unlike that of Lewis Carroll. I once told him so. "Not unlike your goddam grandmother!" he screamed. He was sensitive; he hated to be praised to his face; and then of course he held the works of Carroll in a certain disesteem.

Thus the party went on. Everybody was speechless, spellbound, listening to Elliot Vereker. You could not miss his force. He was always the one person in a room. When it got to be eleven o'clock, I felt that we had better round up Vereker and start for the docks, for the boat sailed at midnight. He was nowhere to be found. We were alarmed. We searched every room, looked under beds, and into closets, but he was gone. Some of us ran downstairs and out into the street, asking cab-drivers and passersby if they had seen him, a gaunt, tall, wild man with his hair in his eyes. Nobody had. It was almost eleven-thirty when somebody thought to look on the roof, to which there was access by a ladder through a trapdoor. Vereker was there. He lay sprawled on his face, the back of his head crushed in by a blow from some heavy instrument, probably a bottle. He was quite dead. "The world's loss," murmured Deane, as he looked down at the pitiful dust so lately the most burning genius we had ever been privileged to know, "is Hell's gain."

I think we all felt that way.

Snapshot of a Dog

I RAN across a dim photograph of him the other day, going through some old things. He's been dead twenty-five years. His name was Rex (my two brothers and I named him when we were in our early teens) and he was a bull terrier. "An American bull terrier," we used to say, proudly; none of your English bulls. He had one brindle eye that sometimes made him look like a clown and sometimes reminded you of a politician with derby hat and cigar. The rest of him was white except for a brindle saddle that always seemed to be slipping off and a brindle stocking on a hind leg. Nevertheless, there was a nobility about him. He was big and muscular and beautifully made. He never lost his dignity even when trying to accomplish the extravagant tasks my brothers and myself used to set for him. One of these was the bringing of a ten-foot wooden rail into the yard through the back gate. We would throw it out into the alley and tell him to go get it. Rex was as powerful as a wrestler, and there were not many things that he couldn't manage somehow to get hold of with his great jaws and lift or drag to wherever he wanted to put them, or wherever we wanted them put. He would catch the rail at the balance and lift it clear of the ground and trot with great confidence toward the gate. Of course, since the gate was only four feet wide or so, he couldn't bring the rail in broadside. He found that out when he got a few terrific jolts, but he wouldn't give up. He finally figured out how to do it, by dragging the rail, holding onto one end, growling. He got a great, wagging satisfaction out of his work. We used to bet kids who had never seen Rex in action that he could catch a baseball thrown as high as they could throw it. He almost never let us down. Rex could hold a baseball with ease in his mouth, in one cheek, as if it were a chew of tobacco.

He was a tremendous fighter, but he never started fights. I don't believe he liked to get into them, despite the fact that he came from a line of fighters. He never went for another dog's throat but for one of its ears (that teaches a dog a lesson), and he would get his grip, close his eyes, and hold on. He could hold on for hours. His longest fight lasted from dusk until almost pitch-dark, one Sunday. It was fought in East Main Street in Columbus with a large, snarly nondescript that belonged to a big colored man. When Rex finally got his ear grip, the brief whirlwind of snarling turned to screeching It was frightening to listen to and to watch. The Negro boldly picked the dogs up somehow and began swinging them around his head, and finally let them fly like a hammer in a hammer throw, but although they landed ten feet away with a great plump, Rex still held on.

The two dogs eventually worked their way to the middle of the car tracks, and after a while two or three streetcars were held up by the fight. A motorman tried to pry Rex's jaws open with a switch rod; somebody lighted a fire and made a torch of a stick and held that to Rex's tail, but he paid no attention. In the end, all the residents and storekeepers in the neighborhood were on hand, shouting this, suggesting that. Rex's joy of battle, when battle was joined, was almost tranquil. He had a kind of pleasant expression during fights, not a vicious one, his eyes closed in what would have seemed to be sleep had it not been for the turmoil of the struggle. The Oak Street Fire Department finally had to be sent for—I don't know why nobody thought of it sooner. Five or six pieces of apparatus arrived, followed by a battalion chief. A hose was attached and a powerful stream of water was turned on the dogs. Rex held on for several moments more while the torrent buffeted him about like a log in a freshet. He was a hundred yards away from where the fight started when he finally let go.

The story of that Homeric fight got all around town, and some of our relatives looked upon the incident as a blot on the family name. They insisted that we get rid of Rex, but we were very happy with him, and nobody could have made us give him up. We would have left town with him first, along any road there was to go. It would have been different, perhaps, if he had ever started fights, or looked for trouble. But he had a gentle disposition. He never bit a person in the ten strenuous years that he lived, nor ever growled at anyone except prowlers. He killed cats, that is true, but quickly and neatly and without especial malice, the way men kill certain animals. It was the only thing he did that we could never cure him of doing. He never killed, or even chased, a squirrel. I don't know why. He had his own philosophy about such things. He never ran barking after wagons or automobiles. He didn't seem to see the idea in pursuing something you couldn't catch, or something you couldn't do anything with, even if you did catch it. A wagon was one of the things he couldn't tug along with his mighty jaws, and he knew it. Wagons, therefore, were not a part of his world.

Swimming was his favorite recreation. The first time he ever saw a body of water (Alum Creek), he trotted nervously along the steep bank for a while, fell to barking wildly, and finally plunged in from a height of eight feet or more. I shall always remember that shining, virgin dive. Then he swam upstream and back just for the pleasure of it, like a man. It was fun to see him battle upstream against a stiff current, struggling and growling every foot of the way. He had as much fun in the water as any person I have known. You didn't have to throw a stick in the water to get him to go in. Of course, he would bring back a stick to you if you did throw one in. He would even have brought back a piano if you had thrown one in.

That reminds me of the night, way after midnight, when he went a-roving in the light of the moon and brought back a small chest of drawers that he found somewhere—how far from the house nobody ever knew; since it was Rex, it could easily have been half a mile. There were no drawers in the chest when he got it home, and it wasn't a good one—he hadn't taken it out of anybody's house; it was just an old cheap piece that somebody had abandoned on a trash heap. Still, it was something he wanted, probably because it presented a nice problem in transportation. It tested his mettle. We first knew about his achievement when, deep in the night, we heard him trying to get the chest up onto the porch. It sounded as if two or three people were trying to tear the house down. We came downstairs and turned on the porch light. Rex was on the top step trying to pull the thing up, but it had caught somehow and he was just holding his own. I suppose he would have held his own till dawn if we hadn't helped him. The next day we carted the chest miles away and threw it out. If we had thrown it out in a nearby alley, he would have brought it home again, as a small token of his integrity in such matters. After all, he had been taught to carry heavy wooden objects about, and he was proud of his prowess.

I am glad Rex never saw a trained police dog jump. He was just an amateur jumper himself, but the most daring and tenacious I have ever seen. He would take on any fence we pointed out to him. Six feet was easy for him, and he could do eight by making a tremendous leap and hauling himself over finally by his paws, grunting and straining; but he lived and died without knowing that twelve- and sixteen-foot walls were too much for him. Frequently, after letting him try to go over one for a while, we would have to carry him home. He would never have given up trying.

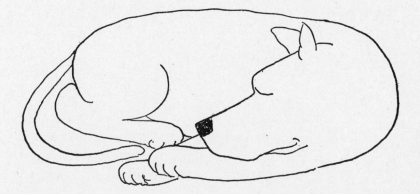

There was in his world no such thing as the impossible. Even death couldn't beat him down. He died, it is true, but only, as one of his admirers said, after "straight-arming the death angel" for more than an hour. Late one afternoon he wandered home, too slowly and too uncertainly to be the Rex that had trotted briskly homeward up our avenue for ten years. I think we all knew when he came through the gate that he was dying. He had apparently taken a terrible beating, probably from the owner of some dog that he had got into a fight with. His head and body were scarred. His heavy collar with the teeth marks of many a battle on it was awry; some of the big brass studs in it were sprung loose from the leather. He licked at our hands and, staggering, fell, but got up again. We could see that he was looking for someone. One of his three masters was not home. He did not get home for an hour. During that hour the bull terrier fought against death as he had fought against the cold, strong current of Alum Creek, as he had fought to climb twelve-foot walls. When the person he was waiting for did come through the gate, whistling, ceasing to whistle, Rex walked a few wabbly paces toward him, touched his hand with his muzzle, and fell down again. This time he didn't get up.

The Evening's at Seven

HE HADN'T lighted the upper light in his office all afternoon and now he turned out the desk lamp. It was a quarter of seven in the evening and it was dark and raining. He could hear the rattle of taxicabs and trucks and the sound of horns. Very far off a siren screamed its frenzied scream and he thought: it's a little like an anguish dying with the years.

When it gets to Third Avenue, or Ninety-fifth Street, he thought, I won't hear it any more.

I'll be home, he said to himself, as he got up slowly and slowly put on his hat and overcoat (the overcoat was damp), by seven o'clock, if I take a taxicab, I'll say hello, my dear, and the two yellow lamps will be lighted and my papers will be on my desk, and I'll say I guess I'll lie down a few minutes before dinner, and she will say all right and ask two or three small questions about the day and I'll answer them.

When he got outside of his office, in the street, it was dark and raining and he lighted a cigarette. A young man went by whistling loudly. Two girls went by talking gaily, as if it were not raining, as if this were not a time for silence and for remembering. He called to a taxicab and it stopped and he got in, and sat there, on the edge of the seat, and the driver finally said where to? He gave a number he was thinking about.

She was surprised to see him and, he believed, pleased. It was very nice to be in her apartment again. He faced her, quickly, and it seemed to him as if he were facing somebody in a tennis game. She would want to know (but wouldn't ask) why he was, so suddenly, there, and he couldn't say: I gave a number to a taxi-driver and it was your number. He couldn't say that; and besides, it wasn't that simple.

It was dark in the room and still raining outside. He lighted a cigarette (not wanting one) and looked at her. He watched her lovely gestures as of old and she said he looked tired and he said he wasn't tired and he asked her what she had been doing and she said oh, nothing much. He talked, sitting awkwardly on the edge of a chair, and she talked, lying gracefully on a chaise-longue, about people they had known and hadn't cared about. He was mainly conscious of the rain outside and of the soft darkness in the room and of other rains and other darknesses. He got up and walked around the room looking at pictures but not seeing what they were, and

realizing that some old familiar things gleamed darkly, and
he came abruptly face to face with something he had given
her, a trivial and comic thing, and it didn't seem trivial or
comic now, but very large and important and embarrassing,
and he turned away from it and asked after somebody else he
didn't care about. Oh, she said, and this and that and so and
such (words he wasn't listening to). Yes, he said, absently, I
suppose so. Very much, he said (in answer to something else),
very much. Oh, she said, laughing at him, not *that* much! He
didn't have any idea what they were talking about.

She asked him for a cigarette and he walked over and gave
her one, not touching her fingers but very conscious of her
fingers. He was remembering a twilight when it had been
raining and dark, and he thought of April and kissing and
laughter. He noticed a clock on the mantel and it was ten
after seven. She said you never used to believe in clocks. He
laughed and looked at her for a time and said I have to be at
the hotel by seven-thirty, or I don't get anything to eat; it's
that sort of hotel. Oh, she said.

He walked to a table and picked up a figurine and set it
down again with extreme care, looking out of the corner of
his eye at the trivial and comic and gigantic present he had
given her. He wondered if he would kiss her and when he
would kiss her and if she wanted to be kissed and if she were
thinking of it, but she asked him what he would have to eat
tonight at his hotel. He said clam chowder. Thursday, he
said, they always have clam chowder. Is that the way you
know it's Thursday, she said, or is that the way you know it's
clam chowder?

He picked up the figurine and put it down again, so that he
could look (without her seeing him look) at the clock. It was
eighteen minutes after seven and he had the mingled
thoughts clocks gave him. You mustn't, she said, miss your
meal. (She remembered he hated the word meal.) He turned
around quickly and went over quickly and sat beside her and

took hold of one of her fingers and she looked at the finger and not at him and he looked at the finger and not at her, both of them as if it were a new and rather remarkable thing.

He got up suddenly and picked up his hat and coat and as suddenly put them down again and took two rapid determined steps toward her, and her eyes seemed a little wider. A bell rang. Oh that, she said, will be Clarice. And they relaxed. He looked a question and she said: my sister; and he said oh, of course. In a minute it was Clarice like a small explosion in the dark and rainy day talking rapidly of this and that: my dear he and this awful and then of all people so nothing loth and I said and he said, if you can imagine that! He picked up his hat and coat and Clarice said hello to him and he said hello and looked at the clock and it was almost twenty-five after seven.

She went to the door with him looking lovely, and it was lovely and dark and raining outside and he laughed and she laughed and she was going to say something but he went out into the rain and waved back at her (not wanting to wave back at her) and she closed the door and was gone. He lighted a cigarette and let his hand get wet in the rain and the cigarette get wet and rain dripped from his hat. A taxicab drove up and the driver spoke to him and he said: what? and: oh, sure. And now he was going home.

He was home by seven-thirty, almost exactly, and he said good evening to old Mrs. Spencer (who had the sick husband), and good evening to old Mrs. Holmes (who had the sick Pomeranian), and he nodded and smiled and presently he was sitting at his table and the waitress spoke to him. She said: the Mrs. will be down, won't she? and he said yes, she will. And the waitress said clam chowder tonight, and consommé: you always take the clam chowder, ain't I right? No, he said, I'll have the consommé.

Smashup

WHEN TOMMY Trinway was fifteen years old, he knocked a lamp off the family surrey trying to drive it, behind the old family mare, Maud, into Bitzer's livery stable in Columbus. Maud, nearing bed and board, had trotted up suddenly, jerking one rein from young Trinway's hands, and as a result she had veered to the left and a lamp had been knocked off the carriage as it entered the stable. That happened a long time ago—it was in 1909—but it had had a lasting effect on Tommy. He was not allowed to drive Maud after that— Maud, who was fat-bellied and gentle and sixteen—but his younger brother Ned could drive her, and that had had an effect on Tommy, too. He took to reading books instead of going out and playing games with the fellows. His mother worried about him.

When the Trinways bought a Rambler, Tommy's old accident with the carriage rose out of his past to plague him. He was nineteen then, but everybody said he was too nervous to drive the Rambler. Tommy didn't insist. He was afraid to drive the Rambler. He would dream at night of driving it, sometimes with his cap on backward, at sixty miles an hour, like Barney Oldfield; but mostly he would dream of driving it into the sides of buildings and off the tops of buildings. Once in a while, at breakfast, Tommy would reach the verge of announcing that he was going to learn to drive the auto—you were somebody in those days if your family had a Rambler and you drove it—but his big moment would always pass, his courage would wear off, and he never asserted himself. He became a studious young man, a young man of thought and not of action. Once he had played tennis with some ability, and more promise, and he had been a fair dancer, too, but he seldom played tennis any more—when he did, Ned beat him—and he never went to dances. His mother still worried about him, but nodboy else did. He was looked upon as a sedentary young man, a natural born student.

Tommy became slightly bald in his twenties and he took to wearing glasses, but he was not unattractive. At least, he was not unattractive to Betty Carter. She fell in love with him. She felt that there was something deep, if not profound, behind Tommy's moody silences, and the way he wrinkled his brow, and his slow, uncertain smile. She got him to go to dances again once in a while, and she told him she liked the way he danced. She decided that he had a future. Tommy brightened somewhat under Betty's admiration. When he was twenty-eight, she married him.

Tommy Trinway did not want to drive the car his wife picked out for him to buy. But he bought it and he learned to drive it. He would practice in the early morning in a park at the edge of town (never with Betty, though; he didn't want her to see him groping and fumbling). He got so he could drive well enough, but he never liked it. He was always uneasy in traffic. Drivers of cars behind him would sound their klaxons irritably, and sometimes shout at him as they roared past on his left. Now and then, seeing in his mirror a big car rushing up behind, he would signal it on, slow down, and pull over to the side of the road. Betty used to laugh at him for that and call him silly. Pleasantly enough—at first. She drove very fast herself, with keen concentration, quick reflexes, and evident enjoyment. Tommy would find himself studying her, when she was driving. There was an assured set to her mouth and a certain glint in her eyes. It dismayed him slightly.

Betty finally took over the driving of the car entirely. Tommy began to get in the seat beside the driver's seat after the day in Broad Street when he absently put the gears in reverse and banged into a Pierce-Arrow parked behind him. He sat puzzled and helpless until Betty said firmly, "Let me get at the wheel." He moved over and let her get at the wheel. After that, Betty drove wherever they went. The more she drove, the faster she drove. She was always whirling out of line to pass cars ahead. Tommy lived in dread of a head-on collision, and sometimes Betty would become conscious of his tenseness. "Don't be so silly," she would say to him. "You're jumpy as a cat." When the gibe was new, he would laugh, and say something funny, maybe, and sometimes, after a moment, she would pat him on the shoulder. But it got so that he didn't answer her, and she kept both hands on the wheel.

Betty sprained her left wrist—the first accident she had had in their ten years of married life—the summer they spent at West Dennis, on the Cape. "You're going to *have* to drive now," she told Tommy. "Sure," he said. "Sure. I'll drive." But he was silent at mealtimes and he looked miserable. He kept thinking of the day when he had gone out to the garage in Betty's absence and tried to back the car out and drive it around a little. She had gone somewhere in the Laytons' car to play tennis. Tommy had been thirty-nine years old that day, and something about being thirty-nine had made him determined to go out and drive the car. He started the engine after some trouble (he forgot for a while to switch on the ignition) and practiced shifting gears. He found himself trembling just doing that, and when he accidentally pressed his wrist on the klaxon button and it screamed at him, he jumped and took his foot off the clutch, and the car leaped forward and shook him up a bit before the engine choked and died. He hadn't told Betty about the incident. Once she would merely have laughed about it; but she wouldn't now, he thought.

In the days before they were to start to New York, Tommy would take the car out on the roads early in the morning, before there was much traffic. He managed fairly well, but his coordination was slow, and once or twice he put the brake on hard without letting his clutch out and killed the engine. That would give him a sense of helplessness and panic, and he would sit for a long time without starting the engine again, remembering the time he had knocked the lamp off the surrey. He had hated Bitzer, he reflected, recalling the livery-stable man perfectly—a stumpy, bow-legged man with a beard. Tommy had not told the family about that accident when he went home. They had found out about it the next morning from Bitzer. Tommy had been afraid to tell the family, just as he had been afraid to tell Betty about trying to back the car out of the garage.

One morning when he was out practicing driving, he came to a wide, straight concrete road, and pretty soon, to his own surprise, he had the car up to fifty miles an hour, and then fifty-five, and then sixty. He kept it at sixty for a little while, and as he roared along he suddenly began to chant loudly, for some crazy reason, "Little Bet-ty Bit-zer, little Bet-ty Bit-zer!" Then he slowed down as abruptly as he had started up, and stopped chanting. He felt pretty good when he drove back to the house and got breakfast. "The coffee is too strong," said Betty. "The coffee is swell," he told her. She widened her eyes. "Well!" she said. "Old cocksure!" Their laughter was a little strained, like the laughter of two people who have just met.

*   *   *

The day that he started to drive the car to New York, with his wife beside him, Tommy Trinway felt vaguely that his future with her lay before him on the roads, obscure and ominous. He drove steadily, a little stiffly, and not fast. Other cars complained briefly, and roared past. Once in a while, when Tommy wavered, Betty would start up and make as if to grab the wheel, but she didn't. "Well!" she would begin, impatiently, and stop. They went along most of the time in silence. When, after many hours of driving and more stops than Betty thought were necessary, Tommy came out of the quiet of the Hutchinson River Parkway into the clangor and tangle of Fordham and felt the menace of the Bronx ahead of him, he almost drove to one side and stopped, but he didn't; he kept on, slowly. He was tired and worn. He had driven a long way, over good roads and over narrow, twisting roads. His shoulders ached from leaning tensely forward. The Bronx loomed up before him, like an ether nightmare he had had as a boy. Only there had been, that time, finally oblivion, and here now were unending shouts and banging, and the roaring of elevated trains overhead, and a snarl of broad, ugly streets curving off in every direction, and big, sweaty women pushing baby carriages, and scowling men in shirt sleeves jabbering, and trucks rumbling and pounding by, and taxis rushing around him, and lights turning red and green under their iron hoods, and policemen making formidable gestures with their huge hands.

He got through it somehow. Once a cop blew a series of quick, petulant blasts on his whistle and Betty snapped, "Speed it up! You're blocking people!" and he had speeded up, narrowly missing the front fender of a laundry truck, whose driver shouted some profanity at him. "I wish I could take that wheel," Betty said. Tommy's heart was beating painfully in his throat and he didn't answer. Betty had to tell him which turns to make all the way. Once she cried, "Good God, watch the *lights*!" He finally reached the entrance to

Central Park at 110th Street. As they drove through the
Park, she settled back and sighed. "Well, we're going to
make it alive, I guess," she said. "Yeah," said Tommy,
tightly. "For heaven's sake, relax a little," she told him. "I'm
all right," said Tommy, with an effort at sharpness that
failed. He wasn't all right.

It was at Sixth Avenue and Forty-seventh Street that doom
shot out in front of his car. The doom of an angular woman
of sixty, the doom of Tommy and Betty. It happened in a
flash. The woman had reached the line of "L" pillars nearer
the east curb and was hovering there uncertainly, waiting to
cross to the west curb. A taxi going north whisked by her and
she saw that no other car was close behind it. She darted into
the path of Tommy's car, coming the other way. He had a
quick, hot sense of horror, buildings and people writhed
around him, the brakes of cars screamed. Then all the noises
of the city stopped. Everything stopped. "Nice piece of
drivin', mister," a voice was saying, and Tommy looked up
at a policeman standing beside the door of his car. The
policeman walked toward the back of the car, and Tommy
opened the door and leaned out and followed him with his
eyes. A man was supporting the angular old woman. She was
grinning idiotically. "I guess she's all right," the man told the
policeman. "I seen it. He didn't hit her. He just grazed her."
"You're lucky, lady," said the policeman. "You can thank
your stars that fella can drive like that. You wanta stay on
the sidewalk when you see that red light. This street ain't no
playgrounds." Cars began to sound their klaxons and a
streetcar bell clanged. The cop motioned to Tommy to back
up. Tommy saw then, for the first time, that he had whirled
his car sharply to the right and had come to a stop only a few
inches from an "L" pillar. "We just barely grazed her," said
Betty. "The crazy fool." Tommy started to back up. "Take
the emergency brake off," said Betty. Tommy frowned and
let the brake forward. He backed up and straightened out

and went on. "Close call, buddy," said a grinning taxi-driver, passing him.

"I guess I rate a drink," said Tommy, as they went into the lobby of their hotel. He had turned the car over to the doorman with a proud sigh. Something heavy had dropped away from him. "I guess we both rate a drink," said Betty. They sat down in big chairs in a corner and ordered Scotch and soda. Tommy stretched his legs languidly. "Well," he said, "nobody got killed." "No, thank God," said Betty. "But somebody *would* have if I hadn't jerked on the hand brake. You never think of the hand brake. You'd have hit that pillar sure, and killed both of us." Tommy looked at her coldly. "Oh, *yeah?*" he said. She raised her eyebrows in surprise and indignation at his tone; the match she was about to hold to her cigarette went out. "What's the matter with you?" she asked. The waiter brought their drinks, put them down, and went away. "Nothing is the matter with me," said Tommy. "I'm fine." She stared at her husband over the cigarette and, striking another match, still stared. He stared back at her. He tossed off his Scotch with a new, quick gesture, set the glass down, got up, and lounged over to the desk. "We'll want two single rooms tonight, Mr. Brent," he said to the man at the desk. Mr. Brent looked over his glasses in some surprise as Tommy signed the register and then walked jauntily out the revolving doors into the street, whistling.

The Man on the Train

I INSTANTLY felt as if I had stumbled into a wrong apartment in which someone was dressing And yet I had merely glanced across the aisle of a train at a man I had never seen before, who looked back at me. I had the quick, unreasonable feeling that there must be something I could do for him. It was almost as if he had spoken. And yet I met his gaze for only a moment or two and then we both turned away. It happened a long time ago—four or five years—and it is as meaningless to my life as an old forgotten telephone number; but there it is, as sharp as any memory I have of a friend. It comes up before me, clear, irrelevant, and uncalled for, at unexpected hours.

I had never seen the man before and I would not recognize him if I saw him again. I couldn't tell you the color of the suit he wore, or how large he was, or even whether he had a hat on. All that is gone, like the roads and rains and houses that whisk past you when you are riding on a train; the man as a person is as lost to me as the lonely figures that wave at you from fields when your train goes by. But I remember his eyes as well as I remember anything.

There is something lugubrious about the expression of a man with a toothache. I think I could always pick out such a sufferer instantly: a man with a toothache looks, crazily enough, as if he were trying not to laugh. But this was not a look of physical pain. I felt, for some odd reason, as if the cause for it were on the tip of my mind; as if, by some little extra effort, I could divine the dark experience, whatever it was.

I remember it was a fine afternoon in April or May. I had walked to the Grand Central and bought some brightly covered magazines, and I had slumped down comfortably in a rear coach, and a dozen women without faces came into the coach, and a dozen men who were merely suits of clothes. I was only vaguely conscious of them, as movement and murmuring; but I became acutely aware of him. He had made no sign of any kind, I had not yet seen him, but I was aware of him as one becomes aware on entering a room that one's name has just been spoken there.

I looked up finally, under a kind of compulsion, and saw

him. He was not looking at me. He was sitting tensely on the
edge of the seat across the aisle, one hand lying limply on his
knee, the other clutching tightly the back of the seat in front
of him. The train hadn't yet begun to move out of the
darkness and closeness of the Grand Central cavern. I had
the feeling that the man wanted to jump up and get off the
train, run off; but he just sat there, one hand clutching the
seat-back, the other lying limply on his knee. He turned his
head and looked at me. I didn't look at him again all during
the ride.

The people on the coach thinned out at every stop, moving
heavily, without energy, through the aisle; seeming sodden
and damp although it was a bright dry afternoon. One man
sitting in front of me, with his head lolling back, snored
raspingly. I tried to read, but couldn't. I was too conscious of
the man across the aisle, still sitting, I was certain, as he had
been before the train started—as if he were about to get up
and protest against something, some incredible thing that
was about to come to pass. But he didn't get up; I don't
believe he ever relaxed, or made any movement at all, except
when the conductor stopped to take up his ticket. I thought
the conductor spoke to him, a sentence or two, but I didn't
hear the man answer. The conductor went slowly on.

It was a bright sunny trip and I became drowsy after South
Norwalk, but I couldn't sleep; the man stuck too keenly in
my consciousness. I don't know just where he got off, but
after a time I felt that he was no longer there. The tension
and uncomfortableness went out of me. I had closed my eyes,
but I opened them and began to leaf through a magazine.
When I glanced furtively across the aisle, I saw that he had
gone. There was only the snoring man, deeper in dream now,
and a woman's hat peeking over the back of a seat far in
front of me. I began to feel a little foolish about my
awareness of the man who had gone. I had probably
exaggerated the whole thing: made catastrophe out of
predicament.

The train whistled for my station. I think I would have dismissed the man from my mind if the conductor had not come back through the coach, saying something in a disinterested drone about not forgetting your parcels. I was standing up, gathering my magazines together, trying to decide which ones to leave, when he stopped beside me. He was one of those gray-haired, placid conductors who seem beyond excitement, impervious to concern of any kind. I don't know why he felt impelled to speak to me, but apparently he did. It is a little startling when a conductor begins talking to you about something unconnected with tickets, or towns, or time. "Ja notice that fella was sittin' opposite you?" he asked me. He indicated the seat the man had sat in. "Poor fella just lost his little girl," he said.

The Greatest Man in the World

LOOKING BACK on it now, from the vantage point of 1940, one can only marvel that it hadn't happened long before it did. The United States of America had been, ever since Kitty Hawk, blindly constructing the elaborate petard by which, sooner or later, it must be hoist. It was inevitable that some day there would come roaring out of the skies a national hero of insufficient intelligence, background, and character successfully to endure the mounting orgies of glory prepared for aviators who stayed up a long time or flew a great distance. Both Lindbergh and Byrd, fortunately for national decorum and international amity, had been gentlemen; so had our other famous aviators. They wore their laurels gracefully, withstood the awful weather of publicity, married excellent women, usually of fine family, and quietly retired to private

life and the enjoyment of their varying fortunes. No
untoward incidents, on a worldwide scale, marred the
perfection of their conduct on the perilous heights of fame.
The exception to the rule was, however, bound to occur and
it did, in July, 1937, when Jack ("Pal") Smurch, erstwhile
mechanic's helper in a small garage in Westfield, Iowa, flew a
second-hand, single-motored Bresthaven Dragon-Fly III
monoplane all the way around the world, without stopping.

Never before in the history of aviation had such a flight as
Smurch's ever been dreamed of. No one had even taken
seriously the weird floating auxiliary gas tanks, invention of
the mad New Hampshire professor of astronomy, Dr.
Charles Lewis Gresham, upon which Smurch placed full
reliance. When the garage worker, a slightly built, surly,
unprepossessing young man of twenty-two, appeared at
Roosevelt Field early in July, 1937, slowly chewing a great
quid of scrap tobacco, and announced "Nobody ain't seen
no flyin' yet," the newspapers touched briefly and satirically
upon his projected twenty-five-thousand-mile flight. Aëro-
nautical and automotive experts dismissed the idea curtly,
implying that it was a hoax, a publicity stunt. The rusty,
battered, second-hand plane wouldn't go. The Gresham
auxiliary tanks wouldn't work. It was simply a cheap joke.

Smurch, however, after calling on a girl in Brooklyn who
worked in the flap-folding department of a large paper-box
factory, a girl whom he later described as his "sweet
patootie," climbed nonchalantly into his ridiculous plane at
dawn of the memorable seventh of July, 1937, spit a curve of
tobacco juice into the still air, and took off, carrying with
him only a gallon of bootleg gin and six pounds of salami.

When the garage boy thundered out over the ocean the
papers were forced to record, in all seriousness, that a mad,
unknown young man—his name was variously misspelled—
had actually set out upon a preposterous attempt to span the

world in a rickety, one-engined contraption, trusting to the long-distance refuelling device of a crazy schoolmaster. When, nine days later, without having stopped once, the tiny plane appeared above San Francisco Bay, headed for New York, spluttering and choking, to be sure, but still magnificently and miraculously aloft, the headlines, which long since had crowded everything else off the front page—even the shooting of the Governor of Illinois by the Vileti gang— swelled to unprecedented size, and the news stories began to run to twenty-five and thirty columns. It was noticeable, however, that the accounts of the epoch-making flight touched rather lightly upon the aviator himself. This was not because facts about the hero as a man were too meagre, but because they were too complete.

Reporters, who had been rushed out to Iowa when Smurch's plane was first sighted over the little French coast town of Serly-le-Mer, to dig up the story of the great man's life, had promptly discovered that the story of his life could not be printed. His mother, a sullen short-order cook in a shack restaurant on the edge of a tourists' camping ground near Westfield, met all inquiries as to her son with an angry "Ah, the hell with him; I hope he drowns." His father appeared to be in jail somewhere for stealing spotlights and laprobes from tourists' automobiles; his young brother, a weak-minded lad, had but recently escaped from the Preston, Iowa, Reformatory and was already wanted in several Western towns for the theft of money-order blanks from post offices. These alarming discoveries were still piling up at the very time that Pal Smurch, the greatest hero of the twentieth century, blear-eyed, dead for sleep, half-starved, was piloting his crazy junk-heap high above the region in which the lamentable story of his private life was being unearthed, headed for New York and a greater glory than any man of his time had ever known.

The necessity for printing some account in the papers of the young man's career and personality had led to a remarkable predicament. It was of course impossible to reveal the facts, for a tremendous popular feeling in favor of the young hero had sprung up, like a grass fire, when he was halfway across Europe on his flight around the globe. He was, therefore, described as a modest chap, taciturn, blond, popular with his friends, popular with girls. The only available snapshot of Smurch, taken at the wheel of a phony automobile in a cheap photo studio at an amusement park, was touched up so that the little vulgarian looked quite handsome. His twisted leer was smoothed into a pleasant smile. The truth was, in this way, kept from the youth's ecstatic compatriots; they did not dream that the Smurch family was despised and feared by its neighbors in the obscure Iowa town, nor that the hero himself, because of numerous unsavory exploits, had come to be regarded in Westfield as a nuisance and a menace. He had, the reporters discovered, once knifed the principal of his high school—not mortally, to be sure, but he had knifed him; and on another occasion, surprised in the act of stealing an altarcloth from a church, he had bashed the sacristan over the head with a pot of Easter lilies; for each of these offences he had served a sentence in the reformatory.

Inwardly, the authorities, both in New York and in Washington, prayed than an understanding Providence might, however awful such a thing seemed, bring disaster to the rusty, battered plane and its illustrious pilot, whose unheard-of flight had aroused the civilized world to hosannas of hysterical praise. The authorities were convinced that the character of the renowned aviator was such that the limelight of adulation was bound to reveal him, to all the world, as a congenital hooligan mentally and morally unequipped to cope with his own prodigious fame. "I trust," said the Secretary of State, at one of many secret Cabinet meetings called to consider the national dilemma, "I trust that his mother's prayer will be answered," by which he referred to Mrs. Emma Smurch's wish that her son might be drowned. It

was, however, too late for that—Smurch had leaped the Atlantic and then the Pacific as if they were millponds. At three minutes after two o'clock on the afternoon of July 17, 1937, the garage boy brought his idiotic plane into Roosevelt Field for a perfect three-point landing.

It had, of course, been out of the question to arrange a modest little reception for the greatest flier in the history of the world. He was received at Roosevelt Field with such elaborate and pretentious ceremonies as rocked the world. Fortunately, however, the worn and spent hero promptly swooned, had to be removed bodily from his plane, and was spirited from the field, without having opened his mouth once. Thus he did not jeopardize the dignity of this first reception, a reception illumined by the presence of the Secretaries of War and the Navy, Mayor Michael J. Moriarity of New York, the Premier of Canada, Governors

Fanniman, Groves, McFeely, and Critchfield, and a brilliant array of European diplomats. Smurch did not, in fact, come to in time to take part in the gigantic hullabaloo arranged at City Hall for the next day. He was rushed to a secluded nursing home and confined in bed. It was nine days before he was able to get up, or to be more exact, before he was permitted to get up. Meanwhile the greatest minds in the country, in solemn assembly, had arranged a secret conference of city, state, and government officials, which Smurch was to attend for the purpose of being instructed in the ethics and behavior of heroism.

On the day that the little mechanic was finally allowed to get up and dress and, for the first time in two weeks, took a great chew of tobacco, he was permitted to receive the newspapermen—this by way of testing him out. Smurch did not wait for questions. "Youse guys," he said—and the *Times* man winced—"youse guys can tell the cock-eyed world dat I put it over on Lindbergh, see? Yeh—an' made an ass o' them two frogs." The "two frogs" was a reference to a pair of gallant French fliers who, in attempting a flight only halfway round the world, had, two weeks before, unhappily been lost at sea. The *Times* man was bold enough, at this point, to sketch out for Smurch the accepted formula for interviews in cases of this kind; he explained that there should be no arrogant statements belittling the achievements of other heroes, particularly heroes of foreign nations. "Ah, the hell with that," said Smurch. "I did it, see? I did it, an' I'm talkin' about it." And he did talk about it.

None of this extraordinary interview was, of course, printed. On the contrary, the newspapers, already under the disciplined direction of a secret directorate created for the occasion and composed of statesmen and editors, gave out to a panting and restless world that "Jacky," as he had been arbitrarily nicknamed, would consent to say only that he was very happy and that anyone could have done what he did. "My achievement has been, I fear, slightly exaggerated," the

Times man's article had him protest, with a modest smile.
These newspaper stories were kept from the hero, a
restriction which did not serve to abate the rising malevolence
of his temper. The situation was, indeed, extremely grave, for
Pal Smurch was, as he kept insisting, "rarin' to go." He
could not much longer be kept from a nation clamorous to
lionize him. It was the most desperate crisis the United States
of America had faced since the sinking of the *Lusitania*.

On the afternoon of the twenty-seventh of July, Smurch
was spirited away to a conference-room in which were
gathered mayors, governors, government officials, behaviorist
psychologists, and editors. He gave them each a limp, moist
paw and a brief unlovely grin. "Hah ya?" he said. When
Smurch was seated, the Mayor of New York arose and, with
obvious pessimism, attempted to explain what he must say
and how he must act when presented to the world, ending his
talk with a high tribute to the hero's courage and integrity.
The Mayor was followed by Governor Fanniman of New
York, who, after a touching declaration of faith, introduced
Cameron Spottiswood, Second Secretary of the American
Embassy in Paris, the gentleman selected to coach Smurch in
the amenities of public ceremonies. Sitting in a chair, with a
soiled yellow tie in his hand and his shirt open at the throat,
unshaved, smoking a rolled cigarette, Jack Smurch listened
with a leer on his lips. "I get ya, I get ya," he cut in, nastily.
"Ya want me to ack like a softy, huh? Ya want me to act like
that—— baby-face Lindbergh, huh? Well, nuts to that,
see?" Everyone took in his breath sharply; it was a sigh and a
hiss. "Mr. Lindbergh," began a United States Senator,
purple with rage, "and Mr. Byrd—" Smurch, who was
paring his nails with a jackknife, cut in again. "Byrd!" he
exclaimed. "Aw fa God's sake, *dat* big—" Somebody shut
off his blasphemies with a sharp word. A newcomer had
entered the room. Everyone stood up, except Smurch, who,
still busy with his nails, did not even glance up. "Mr.

Smurch," said someone, sternly, "the President of the United States!" It had been thought that the presence of the Chief Executive might have a chastening effect upon the young hero, and the former had been, thanks to the remarkable coöperation of the press, secretly brought to the obscure conference-room.

A great, painful silence fell. Smurch looked up, waved a hand at the President. "How ya comin'?" he asked, and began rolling a fresh cigarette. The silence deepened. Someone coughed in a strained way. "Geez, it's hot, ain't it?" said Smurch. He loosened two more shirt buttons, revealing a hairy chest and the tattooed word "Sadie" enclosed in a stencilled heart. The great and important men in the room, faced by the most serious crisis in recent American history, exchanged worried frowns. Nobody seemed to know how to proceed. "Come awn, come awn," said Smurch. "Let's get the hell out of here! When do I start cuttin' in on de parties, huh? And what's they goin' to be *in* it?" He rubbed a thumb and forefinger together meaningly. "Money!" exclaimed a state senator, shocked, pale. "Yeh, money," said Pal, flipping his cigarette out of a window. "An' big money." He began rolling a fresh cigarette. "Big money," he repeated, frowning over the rice paper. He tilted back in his chair, and leered at each gentleman, separately, the leer of an animal that knows its power, the leer of a leopard loose in a bird-and-dog shop. "Aw fa God's sake, let's get some place where it's cooler," he said. "I been cooped up plenty for three weeks!"

Smurch stood up and walked over to an open window, where he stood staring down into the street, nine floors below. The faint shouting of newsboys floated up to him. He made out his name. "Hot dog!" he cried, grinning, ecstatic. He leaned out over the sill. "You tell 'em, babies!" he shouted down. "Hot diggity dog!" In the tense little knot of men standing behind him, a quick, mad impulse flared up. An unspoken word of appeal, of command, seemed to ring through the room. Yet it was deadly silent. Charles K. L. Brand, secretary to the Mayor of New York City, happened to be standing nearest Smurch; he looked inquiringly at the President of the United States. The President, pale, grim, nodded shortly. Brand, a tall, powerfully built man, once a tackle at Rutgers, stepped forward, seized the greatest man in the world by his left shoulder and the seat of his pants, and pushed him out the window.

"My God, he's fallen out the window!" cried a quick-witted editor.

"Get me out of here!" cried the President. Several men sprang to his side and he was hurriedly escorted out of a door toward a side-entrance of the building. The editor of the Associated Press took charge, being used to such things. Crisply he ordered certain men to leave, others to stay; quickly he outlined a story which all the papers were to agree on, sent two men to the street to handle that end of the tragedy, commanded a Senator to sob and two Congressmen to go to pieces nervously. In a word, he skillfully set the stage for the gigantic task that was to follow, the task of breaking to a grief-stricken world the sad story of the untimely, accidental death of its most illustrious and spectacular figure.

The funeral was, as you know, the most elaborate, the finest, the solemnest, and the saddest ever held in the United States of America. The monument in Arlington Cemetery, with its clean white shaft of marble and the simple device of a tiny plane carved on its base, is a place for pilgrims, in deep reverence, to visit. The nations of the world paid lofty tributes to little Jacky Smurch, America's greatest hero. At a given hour there were two minutes of silence throughout the nation. Even the inhabitants of the small, bewildered town of Westfield, Iowa, observed this touching ceremony; agents of the Department of Justice saw to that. One of them was especially assigned to stand grimly in the doorway of a little shack restaurant on the edge of the tourists' camping ground just outside the town. There, under his stern scrutiny, Mrs.

Emma Smurch bowed her head above two hamburger steaks sizzling on her grill—bowed her head and turned away, so that the Secret Service man could not see the twisted, strangely familiar, leer on her lips.

One Is a Wanderer

THE WALK up Fifth Avenue through the slush of the sidewalks and the dankness of the air had tired him. The dark was coming quickly down, the dark of a February Sunday evening, and that vaguely perturbed him. He didn't want to go "home," though, and get out of it. It would be gloomy and close in his hotel room, and his soiled shirts would be piled on the floor of the closet where he had been flinging them for weeks, where he had been flinging them for months, and his papers would be disarranged on the tops of the tables and on the desk, and his pipes would be lying around, the pipes he had smoked determinedly for a while only to give them up, as he always did, to go back to cigarettes. He turned into the street leading to his hotel, walking slowly, trying to decide what to do with the night. He had had too many nights alone. Once he had enjoyed being alone. Now it was hard to be alone. He couldn't read any more, or write, at night. Books he tossed aside after nervously flipping through them; the writing he tried to do turned into spirals and circles and squares and empty faces.

I'll just stop in, he thought, and see if there are any messages; I'll see if there have been any phone calls. He hadn't been back to the hotel, after all, for—let's see—for almost five hours; just wandering around. There might be some messages. I'll just stop in, he thought, and see; and maybe I'll have one brandy. I don't want to sit there in the lobby again and drink brandy; I don't want to do that.

He didn't go through the revolving doors of the hotel, though. He went on past the hotel and over to Broadway. A man asked him for some money. A shabbily dressed woman walked by, muttering. She had what he called the New York Mouth, a grim, set mouth, a strained, querulous mouth, a mouth that told of suffering and discontent. He looked in the window of a cane-and-umbrella shop and in the window of a cheap restaurant, a window holding artificial pie and cake, a cup of cold coffee, a plate of artificial vegetables. He got into the shoving and pushing and halting and slow flowing of Broadway. A big cop with a red face was striking his hands together and kidding with a couple of girls whom he had kept from crossing the street against a red light. A thin man in a thin overcoat watched them out of thin, emotionless eyes.

It was a momentary diversion to stand in front of the book counter in the drugstore at Forty-fifth Street and Broadway and look at the books, cheap editions of ancient favorites, movie editions of fairly recent best-sellers. He picked up some of the books and opened them and put them down again, but there was nothing he wanted to read. He walked over to the soda counter and sat down and asked for hot chocolate. It warmed him up a little and he thought about going to the movie at the Paramount; it was a movie with action and guns and airplanes, and Myrna Loy, the kind of movie that didn't bother you. He walked down to the theatre and stood there a minute, but he didn't buy a ticket. After all, he had been to one movie that day. He thought about going to the office. It would be quiet there, nobody would be there; maybe he could get some work done; maybe he could answer some of the letters he had been putting off for so long.

It was too gloomy, it was too lonely. He looked around the office for a while, sat down at his typewriter, tapped out the alphabet on a sheet of paper, took a paper-clip, straightened it, cleaned the "e" and the "o" on the typewriter, and put the cover over it. He never remembered to put the cover over the typewriter when he left in the evening. I never, as a matter of fact, remember anything, he thought. It is because I keep trying not to; I keep trying not to remember anything. It is an empty and cowardly thing, not to remember. It might lead you anywhere; no, it might stop you, it might stop you from getting anywhere. Out of remembrance comes everything; out of remembrance comes a great deal, anyway. You can't do anything if you don't let yourself remember things. He began to whistle a song because he found himself about to remember things, and he knew what things they would be, things that would bring a grimace to his mouth and to his eyes, disturbing fragments of old sentences, old scenes and gestures, hours, and rooms, and tones of voice, and the sound of a voice crying. All voices cry differently; there are no two voices in the whole world that cry alike; they're like footsteps and fingerprints and the faces of friends . . .

He became conscious of the song he was whistling. He got up from the chair in front of his covered typewriter, turned out the light, and walked out of the room to the elevator, and there he began to sing the last part of the song, waiting for the elevator. "Make my bed and light the light, for I'll be home late tonight, blackbird, bye bye." He walked over to his hotel through the slush and the damp gloom and sat down in a chair in the lobby, without taking off his overcoat. He didn't want to sit there long.

"Good evening, sir," said the waiter who looked after the guests in the lobby. "How are you?"

"I'm fine, thank you," he said. "I'm fine. I'll have a brandy, with water on the side."

He had several brandies. Nobody came into the lobby that he knew. People were gone to all kinds of places Sunday night. He hadn't looked at his letter box back of the clerk's desk when he came in, to see if there were any messages there. That was a kind of game he played, or something. He never looked for messages until after he had had a brandy. He'd look now after he had another brandy. He had another brandy and looked. "Nothing," said the clerk at the desk, looking too.

He went back to his chair in the lobby and began to think about calling up people. He thought of the Graysons. He saw the Graysons, not as they would be, sitting in their apartment, close together and warmly, but as he and Lydia had seen them in another place and another year. The four had shared a bright vacation once. He remembered various attitudes and angles and lights and colors of that vacation. There is something about four people, two couples, that like each other and get along; that have a swell time; that grow in intimacy and understanding. One's life is made up of twos, and of fours. The Graysons understood the nice little arrangements of living, the twos and fours. Two is company, four is a party, three is a crowd. One is a wanderer.

No, not the Graysons. Somebody would be there on Sunday night, some couple, some two; somebody he knew, somebody they had known. That is the way life is arranged. One arranges one's life—no, two arrange their life—in terms of twos, and fours, and sixes. Marriage does not make two people one, it makes two people two. It's sweeter that way, and simpler. All this, he thought, summoning the waiter, is probably very silly and sentimental. I must look out that I don't get to that state of tipsiness where all silly and lugubrious things seem brilliant divinations of mine, sound and original ideas and theories. What I must remember is that such things are sentimental and tiresome and grow out of not working enough and out of too much brandy. That's what I must remember. It is no good remembering that it takes four to make a party, two to make a house.

People living alone, after all, have made a great many things. Let's see, what have people living alone made? Not love, of course, but a great many other things: money, for example, and black marks on white paper. "Make this one a double brandy," he told the waiter. Let's see, who that I *know* has made something alone, who that I know *of* has made something alone? Robert Browning? No, not Robert Browning. Odd, that Robert Browning would be the first person he thought of. "And had you only heard me play one tune, or viewed me from a window, not so soon with you would such things fade as with the rest." He had written that line of Browning's in a book once for Lydia, or Lydia had written it in a book for him; or they had both written it in a book for each other. "Not so soon with you would such things fade as with the rest." Maybe he didn't have it exactly right; it was hard to remember now, after so long a time. It didn't matter. "Not so soon with you would such things fade as with the rest." The fact is that all things do fade; with twos, and with fours; all bright things, all attitudes and angles and lights and colors, all growing in intimacy and understanding.

I think maybe I'll call the Bradleys, he thought, getting up out of his chair. And don't, he said to himself, standing still a moment, don't tell me you're not cockeyed now, because you are cockeyed now, just as you said you wouldn't be when you got up this morning and had orange juice and coffee and determined to get some work done, a whole lot of work done; just as you said you wouldn't be but you knew you would be, all right. You knew you would be, all right.

The Bradleys, he thought, as he walked slowly around the lobby, avoiding the phone booths, glancing at the headlines of the papers on the newsstand, the Bradleys have that four-square thing, that two-square thing—that two-square thing, God damn them! Somebody described it once in a short story that he had read: an intimacy that you could feel, that you could almost take hold of, when you went into such a house, when you went into where such people were, a warming thing, a nice thing to be in, like being in warm sea water; a little embarrassing, too, yes, damned embarrassing, too. He would only take a damp blanket into that warmth. That's what I'd take into that warmth, he told himself, a damp blanket. They know it, too. Here comes old Kirk again with his damp blanket. It isn't because I'm so damned unhappy—I'm not so damned unhappy—it's because they're so damned happy, damn them. Why don't they know that? Why don't they do something about it? What right have they got to flaunt it at me, for God's sake? . . . Look here now, he told himself, you're getting too cockeyed now; you're getting into one of those states, you're getting into one of those states that Marianne keeps telling you about, one of those states when people don't like to have you around . . . Marianne, he thought. He went back to his chair, ordered another brandy, and thought about Marianne.

She doesn't know how I start my days, he thought, she only knows how I end them. She doesn't even know how I started my life. She only knows me when night gets me. If I could only be the person she wants me to be, why, then I would be fine, I would be the person she wants me to be. Like ordering a new dress from a shop, a new dress that nobody ever wore, a new dress that nobody's ever going to wear but you. I wouldn't get mad suddenly, about nothing. I wouldn't walk out of places suddenly, about nothing. I wouldn't snarl at nice people. About what she says is nothing. I wouldn't be "unbearable." Her word, "unbearable." A female word, female as a cat. Well, she's right, too. I am unbearable. "George," he said to the waiter, "I am unbearable, did you know that?" "No, sir, I did not, sir," said the waiter. "I would not call you unbearable, Mr. Kirk." "Well, you don't know, George," he said. "It just happens that I am unbearable. It just happened that way. It's a long story." "Yes, sir," said the waiter.

I could call up the Mortons, he thought. They'll have twos and fours there, too, but they're not so damned happy that they're unbearable. The Mortons are all right. Now look, the Mortons had said to him, if you and Marianne would only stop fighting and arguing and forever analyzing yourselves and forever analyzing everything, you'd be fine. You'd be fine if you got married and just shut up, just shut up and got married. That would be fine. Yes, sir, that would be fine. Everything would work out all right. You just shut up and get married, you just get married and shut up. Everybody knows that. It is practically the simplest thing in the world. . . . Well, it would be, too, if you were twenty-five maybe; it would be if you were twenty-five, and not forty.

"George," he said, when the waiter walked over for his empty glass, "I will be forty-one next November." "But that's not old, sir, and that's a long way off," said George. "No, it isn't," he said. "It's almost here. So is forty-two and forty-three and fifty, and here I am trying to be—do you know what I'm trying to be, George? I'm trying to be happy." "We all want to be happy, sir," said George. "I would like to see you happy, sir." "Oh, you will," he said. "You will, George. There's a simple trick to it. You just shut up and get married. But you see, George, I am an analyzer. I am also a rememberer. I have a pocketful of old used years. You put all those things together and they sit in a lobby getting silly and old." "I'm very sorry, sir," said George.

"And I'll have one more drink, George," he called after the waiter.

He had one more drink. When he looked up at the clock in the lobby it was only 9:30. He went up to his room and, feeling sleepy, he lay down on his bed without turning out the overhead light. When he woke up it was 12:30 by his wristwatch. He got up and washed his face and brushed his teeth and put on a clean shirt and another suit and went back down into the lobby, without looking at the disarranged papers on the tables and on the desk. He went into the dining-room and had some soup and a lamb chop and a glass of milk. There was nobody there he knew. He began to realize that he had to see somebody he knew. He paid his check and went out and got into a cab and gave the driver an address on Fifty-third Street.

There were several people in Dick and Joe's that he knew. There were Dick and Joe, for two—or, rather, for one, because he always thought of them as one; he could never tell them apart. There were Bill Vardon and Mary Wells. Bill Vardon and Mary Wells were a little drunk and gay. He didn't know them very well, but he could sit down with them. . . .

·It was after three o'clock when he left the place and got into a cab. "How are you tonight, Mr. Kirk?" asked the driver. The driver's name was Willie. "I'm fine tonight, Willie," he said. "You want to go on somewheres else?" asked Willie. "Not tonight, Willie," he said. "I'm going home." "Well," said Willie, "I guess you're right there, Mr. Kirk. I guess you're right about that. These places is all right for what they are—you know what I mean—it's O.K. to kick around in 'em for a while and maybe have a few drinks with your friends, but when you come right down to it, home is the best place there is. Now, you take me, I'm hackin' for ten years, mostly up around here—because why? Because all these places know me; you know that, Mr. Kirk. I can get into 'em you might say the same way you do, Mr. Kirk—I have me a couple drinks in Dick and Joe's maybe or in Tony's or anywheres else I want to go into—hell, I've had drinks in 'em with you, Mr. Kirk—like on Christmas night, remember? But I got a home over in Brooklyn and a wife and a couple kids and, boy, I'm tellin' you that's the best place, you know what I mean?"

"You're right, Willie," he said. "You're absolutely right, there."

"You're darn tootin' I am," said Willie. "These joints is all right when a man wants a couple drinks or maybe even get a little tight with his friends, that's O.K. with me——"

"Getting tight with friends is O.K. with me, too," he said to Willie.

"But when a man gets fed up on that kind of stuff, a man wants to go home. Am I right, Mr. Kirk?"

"You're absolutely right, Willie," he said. "A man wants to go home."

"Well, here we are, Mr. Kirk. Home it is."

He got out of the cab and gave the driver a dollar and told him to keep the change and went into the lobby of the hotel. The night clerk gave him his key and then put two fingers into the recesses of the letter box. "Nothing," said the night clerk.

When he got to his room, he lay down on the bed a while and smoked a cigarette. He found himself feeling drowsy and he got up. He began to take his clothes off, feeling drowsily contented, mistily contented. He began to sing, not loudly, because the man in 711 would complain. The man in 711 was a gray-haired man, living alone . . . an analyzer . . . a rememberer . . .

"Make my bed and light the light, for I'll be home late tonight . . ."

A Box to Hide In

I WAITED till the large woman with the awful hat took up her sack of groceries and went out, peering at the tomatoes and lettuce on her way. The clerk asked me what mine was.

"Have you got a box," I asked, "a large box? I want a box to hide in."

"You want a box?" he asked.

"I want a box to hide in," I said.

"Whatta you mean?" he said. "You mean a big box?"

I said I meant a big box, big enough to hold me.

"I haven't got any boxes," he said. "Only cartons that cans come in."

I tried several other groceries and none of them had a box big enough for me to hide in. There was nothing for it but to face life out. I didn't feel strong, and I'd had this overpowering desire to hide in a box for a long time.

"Whatta you mean you want to hide in this box?" one grocer asked me.

"It's a form of escape," I told him, "hiding in a box. It circumscribes your worries and the range of your anguish. You don't see people, either."

"How in the hell do you eat when you're in this box?" asked the grocer. "How in the hell do you get anything to eat?" I said I had never been in a box and didn't know, but that that would take care of itself.

"Well," he said, finally, "I haven't got any boxes, only some pasteboard cartons that cans come in."

It was the same every place. I gave up when it got dark and the groceries closed, and hid in my room again. I turned out the light and lay on the bed. You feel better when it gets dark. I could have hid in a closet, I suppose, but people are always opening doors. Somebody would find you in a closet. They would be startled and you'd have to tell them why you were in the closet. Nobody pays any attention to a big box lying on the floor. You could stay in it for days and nobody'd think to look in it, not even the cleaning-woman.

My cleaning-woman came the next morning and woke me up. I was still feeling bad. I asked her if she knew where I could get a large box.

"How big a box you want?" she asked.

"I want a box big enough for me to get inside of," I said. She looked at me with big, dim eyes. There's something wrong with her glands. She's awful but she has a big heart, which makes it worse. She's unbearable, her husband is sick and her children are sick and she is sick too. I got to thinking how pleasant it would be if I were in a box now, and didn't have to see her. I would be in a box right there in the room and she wouldn't know. I wondered if you have a desire to bark or laugh when someone who doesn't know walks by the box you are in. Maybe she would have a spell with her heart, if I did that, and would die right there. The officers and the elevatorman and Mr. Gramadge would find us. "Funny doggone thing happened at the building last night," the

doorman would say to his wife. "I let in this woman to clean up 10-F and she never come out, see? She's never there more'n an hour, but she never come out, see? So when it got to be time for me to go off duty, why I says to Crennick, who was on the elevator, I says what the hell you suppose has happened to that woman cleans 10-F? He says he didn't know; he says he never seen her after he took her up. So I spoke to Mr. Gramadge about it. 'I'm sorry to bother you, Mr. Gramadge,' I says, 'but there's something funny about that woman cleans 10-F.' So I told him. So he said we better have a look and we all three goes up and knocks on the door

and rings the bell, see, and nobody answers so he said we'd
have to walk in so Crennick opened the door and we walked
in and here was this woman cleans the apartment dead as a
herring on the floor and the gentleman that lives there was in
a box." . . .

The cleaning-woman kept looking at me. It was hard to
realize she wasn't dead. "It's a form of escape," I murmured.
"What say?" she asked, dully.

"You don't know of any large packing boxes, do you?" I
asked.

"No, I don't," she said.

I haven't found one yet, but I still have this overpowering
urge to hide in a box. Maybe it will go away, maybe I'll be all
right. Maybe it will get worse. It's hard to say.

Let Your Mind Alone!

and Other More or Less Inspirational Pieces

For Helen

Contents

PART ONE

Let
Your
Mind
Alone!

Pythagoras and the Ladder

IT WAS in none other than the black, memorable year 1929 that the indefatigable Professor Walter B. Pitkin rose up with the announcement that "for the first time in the career of mankind happiness is coming within the reach of millions of people." Happy living, he confidently asserted, could be attained by at least six or seven people out of every ten, but he figured that not more than one person in a thousand was actually attaining it. However, all the external conditions required for happy living were present, he said, just waiting to be used. The only obstacle was a psychological one. Figuring on a basis of 130,000,000 population in this country and reducing the Professor's estimates to round numbers, we find that in 1929 only 130,000 people were happy, but that between 78,000,000 and 91,000,000 could have been happy, leaving only 52,000,000, at the outside, doomed to discontent. The trouble with all the unhappy ones (except the 52,000,000) was that they didn't Know Themselves, they didn't understand the Science of Happiness, they had no Technique of Thinking. Professor Pitkin wrote a book on the subject; he is, in fact, always writing a book on the subject. So are a number of other people. I have devoted myself to a careful study of as many of these books as a man of my unsteady eyesight and wandering attention could be expected to encompass. And I decided to write a series of articles of my own on the subject, examining what the Success Experts have to say and offering some ideas of my own, the basic one of which is, I think, that man will be better off if he quits monkeying with his mind and just lets it alone. In this, the first of the series, I shall abandon Professor Pitkin to his percentages and his high hopes and consider the author of a best-seller published last summer (an alarming number of these books reach the best-seller list). Let us plunge right into Dr. James L. Mursell's "Streamline Your Mind" and see what he has to contribute to the New Happiness, as Professor Pitkin has called it.

In Chapter VI, which is entitled "Using What You've Got," Dr, Mursell deals with the problem of how to learn and how to make use of what you have learned. He believes, to begin with, that you should learn things by doing them, not by just reading up on them. In this connection he presents the case of a young man who wanted to find out "how to conduct a lady to a table in a restaurant." Although I have been gored by a great many dilemmas in my time, that particular problem doesn't happen to have been one of them. I must have just stumbled onto the way to conduct a lady to a table in a restaurant. I don't remember, as a young man, ever having given the matter much thought, but I know that I frequently worried about whether I would have enough money to pay for the dinner and still tip the waiter. Dr. Mursell does not touch on the difficult problem of how to maintain your poise as you depart from a restaurant table on which you have left no tip. I constantly find these mental authorities avoiding the larger issues in favor of something which seems comparatively trivial. The plight of the Doctor's young man, for instance, is as nothing compared to my own plight one time in a restaurant in Columbus when I looked up to find my cousin Wilmer Thurber standing beside me flecked with buttermilk and making a sound which was

CONDUCTING A LADY TO A TABLE IN A RESTAURANT.

something between the bay of a beagle and the cry of a large bird.

I had been having lunch in the outer of two small rooms which comprised a quiet basement restaurant known as the Hole in the Wall, opposite the State House grounds, a place much frequented by elderly clerks and lady librarians, in spite of its raffish name. Wilmer, it came out, was in the other room; neither of us knew the other was there. The Hole in the Wall was perhaps the calmest restaurant I have ever known; the studious people who came there for lunch usually lunched alone; you rarely heard anybody talk. The aged proprietor of the place, because of some defect, spoke always in whispers, and this added to an effect of almost monasterial quiet. It was upon this quiet that there fell suddenly, that day, the most unearthly sound I have ever heard. My back was to the inner room and I was too disconcerted to look around. But from the astonished eyes of those who sat in front of me facing the doorway to that room I became aware that the Whatever-It-Was had entered our room and was approaching my table. It wasn't until a cold hand was laid on mine that I looked up and beheld Wilmer, who had, it came out, inhaled a draught of buttermilk as one might inhale cigarette smoke, and was choking. Having so fortunately found me, he looked at me with wide, stricken eyes and, still making that extraordinary sound, a low, canine *how-ooo* that rose to a high, birdlike *yeee-eep*, he pointed to the small of his back as who should say "Hit me!" There I was, faced with a restaurant problem which, as I have said, makes that of Dr. Mursell's young man seem very unimportant indeed. What I did finally, after an awful, frozen moment, was to get up and dash from the place, without even paying for my lunch. I sent the whispering old man a check, but I never went back to his restaurant. Many of our mental authorities, most of whom are psychologists of one school or another, will say that my dreadful experience must have implanted in me a fear of restaurants (Restauphobia). It did nothing of the sort; it simply implanted in me a wariness of Wilmer. I never went into a restaurant after that without first making sure that this inveterate buttermilk-drinker was not there.

But let us get back to Dr. Mursell and his young man's peculiar quandary. I suppose this young man must have got to worrying about who went first, the lady or himself. These things, as we know, always work out; if the young man doesn't work them out, the lady will. (If she wants him to go first, she will say, "You go first.") What I am interested in here is not the correct procedure but Dr. Mursell's advice to the young man in question. He writes, "Do not merely learn it in words. Try it over with your sister." In that second sentence he reveals, it seems to me, what these inspirationalists so frequently reveal, a lack of understanding of people; in this case, brothers and sisters. Ninety-nine brothers out of a hundred who were worrying about how to conduct a lady to a table in a restaurant would starve before they would go to their sisters and ask them how the thing is done. They would as lief go to their mothers and have a good, frank talk about sex. But let us, for the sake of the argument, try Dr. Mursell's system.

Sister, who is twenty-one, and who goes around with a number of young men whom her brother frankly regards as pussycats, is sitting by the fire one evening reading André Gide, or *Photoplay*, or something. Brother, who is eighteen, enters. "Where's Mom?" he asks. "How should I know?" she snaps. "Thought you might know that, Stupid. Y'ought to know something," he snaps back. Sister continues to read, but she is obviously annoyed by the presence of her brother; he is chewing gum, making a strange, cracking noise every fifth chew, and this gets on her nerves. "Why don't you spit out that damn gum?" she asks, finally. "Aw, nuts," says her brother, in a falsetto singsong. "Nuts to you, Baby, nuts." There is a long, tense silence; he rustles and re-rustles the evening paper. "Where's Itsy Bitsy Dicky tonight?" he asks, suddenly. "Ditch you for a live gal?" By Itsy Bitsy Dicky, he refers to one Richard Warren, a beau of his sister's, whom he considers a hollyhock. "Why don't you go to hell?" asks his sister, coldly. Brother reads the sports page and begins to whistle "Horses," a song which has annoyed his sister since she was ten and he was seven, and which he is whistling for that reason. "*Stop* that!" she screams, at last. He stops for about five seconds and then bursts out, loudly, "*Cra*-zy over *hor*-ses, *hor*-ses, *hor*-ses, she's a little wi-i-i-ld!" Here we have, I think, a typical meeting between brother and sister. Now, out of it, somehow, we have to arrive at a *tableau vivant* in which the brother asks the sister to show him how to conduct a lady to a table in a restaurant. Let us attempt to work that out. "Oh, say, Sis," the brother begins, after a long pause. "Shut up, you lout!" she says. "No, listen, I want to ask you a favor." He begins walking around the room, blushing. "I've asked Greta Dearing out to dinner tomorrow night and I'm not sure how to get her to the table. I mean whether—I mean I don't know how we both get to the table. Come on out in the hall with me and we'll pretend this room is the restaurant. You show me how to get you over to that table in the corner." The note of falsity is so apparent in this that I need not carry out the embarrassing fiction any longer. Obviously the young man is going to have to read up on the subject or, what is much simpler, just take his girl to the restaurant. This acting-out of things falls down of its own stuffiness.

There is a curious tendency on the part of the How-to-Live men to make things hard. It recurs time and again in the thought-technique books. In this same Chapter VI there is a classic example of it. Dr. Mursell recounts the remarkable experience of a professor and his family who were faced with the necessity of reroofing their country house. They decided, for some obscure reason, to do the work themselves, and they intended to order the materials from Sears, Roebuck. The first thing, of course, was to find out how much roofing material they needed. "Here," writes Dr, Mursell, "they struck a snag." They didn't, he points out, have a ladder, and since the roof was too steep to climb, they were at their wits' end as to how they were going to go about measuring it. You and I have this problem solved already: we would get a ladder. But not, it wonderfully turns out, Dr. Mursell's professor and his family. "For several days," writes Dr. Mursell, "they were completely stumped." Nobody thought of getting a ladder. It is impossible to say how they would have solved their problem had not a guest come finally to visit them. This guest noticed that the angle formed by the two sides of the roof (which were equal in length) was a right angle. Let Dr. Mursell go on, in his ecstatic way, from there. "An isosceles right-angled triangle with the base of known length! Had nobody ever been told that the sum of the squares on the two sides of such a triangle was equal to the square of the hypotenuse? And couldn't anyone do a little arithmetic? How very simple! One could easily figure the measurements for the sides of the roof, and as the length of the house could be found without any climbing, the area could be discovered. The theorem of Pythagoras could be used in place of the ladder."

I think this places Dr. James L. Mursell for you; at any rate it does for me: he is the man who would use the theorem of Pythagoras in place of a ladder. I keep wondering what would have happened if that guest hadn't turned up, or if he had remembered the theorem of Pythagoras the way many people do: the sum of the squares of the two sides of a right-angled triangle is equal to *twice* the sum of the hypotenuse, or some other such variant. Many a person, doing a little arithmetic in this case, would order enough material from Sears, Roebuck to roof seven houses. It seems to me that borrowing a ladder from next door, or buying one from a hardware store, is a much simpler way to go about measuring a roof than waiting for somebody to show up who knows the theorem of Pythagoras. Most people who show up at my house can't remember anything they learned in school except possibly the rule for compound Latin verbs that take the dative. My roof would never be fixed; it would rain in; probably I'd have to sell the house, at a great loss, to somebody who has a ladder. With a ladder of my own, and the old-fashioned technique of thinking, I could get the job done in no time. This seems to me the simplest way to live.

Destructive Forces in Life

THE MENTAL efficiency books go into elaborate detail about how to attain Masterful Adjustment, as one of them calls it, but it seems to me that the problems they set up, and knock down, are in the main unimaginative and pedestrian: the little fusses at the breakfast table, the routine troubles at the office, the familiar anxieties over money and health—the welter of workaday annoyances which all of us meet with and usually conquer without extravagant wear and tear. Let us examine, as a typical instance, a brief case history presented by the learned Mr. David Seabury, author of "What Makes Us Seem So Queer," "Unmasking Our Minds," "Keep Your Wits," "Growing Into Life," and "How to Worry Successfully." I select it at random. "Frank Fulsome," writes Mr. Seabury, "flung down the book with disgust and growled an insult at his wife. That little lady put her hands to her face and fled from the room. She was sure Frank must hate her to speak so cruelly. Had she known it, he was not really speaking to her at all. The occasion merely gave vent to a pent-up desire to 'punch his fool boss in the jaw.'" This is, I believe, a characteristic Seabury situation. Many of the women in his treatises remind you of nobody so much as Ben Bolt's Alice, who "wept with delight when you gave her a smile, and trembled with fear at your frown." The little ladies most of us know would, instead of putting their hands to their faces and fleeing from the room, come right back at Frank Fulsome. Frank would perhaps be lucky if he didn't get a punch in the jaw himself. In any case, the situation would be cleared up in approximately three minutes. This "had she known" business is not as common among wives today as Mr. Seabury seems to think it is. The Latent Content (as the psychologists call it) of a husband's mind is usually as clear to the wife as the Manifest Content, frequently much clearer.

I could cite a dozen major handicaps to Masterful Adjustment which the thought technicians never touch upon, a dozen situations not so easy of analysis and solution as most of theirs. I will, however, content myself with one. Let us consider the case of a man of my acquaintance who had accomplished Discipline of Mind, overcome the Will to Fail, mastered the Technique of Living—had, in a word, practically attained Masterful Adjustment—when he was called on the phone one afternoon about five o'clock by a man named Bert Scursey. The other man, whom I shall call Harry Conner, did not answer the phone, however; his wife answered it. As Scursey told me the story later, he had no intention when he dialled the Conners' apartment at the Hotel Graydon of doing more than talk with Harry. But, for some strange reason, when Louise Conner answered, Bert Scursey found himself pretending to be, and imitating the voice of, a colored woman. This Scursey is by way of being an excellent mimic, and a colored woman is one of the best things he does.

"Hello," said Mrs. Conner. In a plaintive voice, Scursey said, "Is dis heah Miz Commah?" "Yes, this is Mrs. Conner," said Louise. "Who is speaking?" "Dis heah's Edith Rummum," said Scursey. "Ah used wuck fo yo frens was nex doah yo place a Sou Norwuck." Naturally, Mrs. Conner did not follow this, and demanded rather sharply to know

A MENTALLY DISCIPLINED HUSBAND WITH MENTALLY
UNDISCIPLINED WIFE.

who was calling and what she wanted. Scursey, his voice soft
with feigned tears, finally got it over to his friend's wife that
he was one Edith Rummum, a colored maid who had once
worked for some friends of the Conners' in South Norwalk,
where they had lived some years before. "What is it you
want, Edith?" asked Mrs. Conner, who was completely taken
in by the imposter (she could not catch the name of the South
Norwalk friends, but let that go). Scursey—or Edith,
rather—explained in a pitiable, hesitant way that she was
without work or money and that she didn't know what she
was going to do; Rummum, she said, was in the jailhouse
because of a cutting scrape on a roller-coaster. Now, Louise
Conner happened to be a most kind-hearted person, as
Scursey well knew, so she said that she could perhaps find
some laundry work for Edith to do. "Yessum," said Edith.
"Ah laundas." At this point, Harry Conner's voice, raised in
the room behind his wife, came clearly to Scursey, saying,
"Now, for God's sake, Louise, don't go giving our clothes

out to somebody you never saw or heard of in your life."
This interjection of Conner's was in firm keeping with a
theory of logical behavior which he had got out of the Mind
and Personality books. There was no Will to Weakness here,
no Desire to Have His Shirts Ruined, no False Sympathy for
the Colored Woman Who Has Not Organized Her Life.

But Mrs. Conner who often did not listen to Mr. Conner,
in spite of his superior mental discipline, prevailed.* "Where
are you now, Edith?" she asked. This disconcerted Scursey
for a moment, but he finally said, "Ah's jes rounda corna,
Miz Commah." "Well, you come over to the Hotel Graydon,"
said Mrs. Conner. "We're in Apartment 7-A on the seventh
floor." "Yessm," said Edith. Mrs. Conner hung up and so
did Scursey. He was now, he realized, in something of a
predicament. Since he did not possess a streamlined mind, as
Dr. Mursell has called it, and had definitely a Will to
Confuse, he did not perceive that his little joke had gone far
enough. He wanted to go on with it, which is a characteristic
of wool-gatherers, pranksters, wags, wish-fulfillers, and
escapists generally. He enjoyed fantasy as much as reality,
probably even more, which is a sure symptom of Regression,
Digression, and Analogical Redintegration. What he finally
did, therefore, was to call back the Conners and get Mrs.
Conner on the phone again. "Jeez, Miz Commah," he said,
with a hint of panic in his voice, "Ah cain' fine yo
appotoman!" "Where are you, Edith?" she asked. "Lawd,
Ah doan know," said Edith. "Ah's on *some* floah in de Hotel
Graydon." "Well, listen, Edith, you took the elevator, didn't
you?" "Dass whut Ah took," said Edith, uncertainly. "Well,
you go back to the elevator and tell the boy you want off at
the seventh floor. I'll meet you at the elevator." "Yessm,"
said Edith, with even more uncertainty. At this point,
Conner's loud voice, speaking to his wife, was again heard by

* This sometimes happens even when the husband is mentally disciplined and the
wife is not.

Scursey. "Where in the hell is she calling from?" demanded Conner, who had developed Logical Reasoning. "She must have wandered into somebody else's apartment if she is calling you from this building, for God's sake!" Whereupon, having no desire to explain where Edith was calling from, Scursey hung up.

After an instant of thought, or rather Disintegrated Phantasmagoria, Scursey rang the Conners again. He wanted to prevent Louise from going out to the elevator and checking up with the operator. This time, as Scursey had hoped, Harry Conner answered, having told his wife that he would handle this situation. "Hello!" shouted Conner, irritably. "Who is this?" Scursey now abandoned the rôle of Edith and assumed a sharp, fussy, masculine tone. "Mr. Conner," he said, crisply, "this is the office. I am afraid we shall have to ask you to remove this colored person from the building. She is blundering into other people's apartments, using their phones. We cannot have that sort of thing, you know, at the Graydon." The man's words and his tone infuriated Conner. "There are a lot of sort of things I'd like to see you not have at the Graydon!" he shouted. "Well, please come down to the lobby and do something about this situation," said the man, nastily. "You're damned right I'll come down!" howled Conner. He banged down the receiver.

Bert Scursey sat in a chair and gloated over the involved state of affairs which he had created. He decided to go over to the Graydon, which was just up the street from his own apartment, and see what was happening. It promised to have all the confusion which his disorderly mind so deplorably enjoyed. And it did have. He found Conner in a tremendous rage in the lobby, accusing an astonished assistant manager of having insulted him. Several persons in the lobby watched the curious scene. "But, Mr. Conner," said the assistant manager, a Mr. Bent, "I have no idea what you are talking about." "If you listen, you'll find out!" bawled Harry Conner. "In the first place, this colored woman's coming to the hotel was no idea of mine. I've never seen her in my life and I don't want to see her! I want to go to my *grave* without seeing her!" He had forgotten what the Mind and Personality books had taught him: never raise your voice in anger, always stick to the point. Naturally, Mr. Bent could only believe that his guest had gone out of his mind. He decided to humor him. "Where is this—ah—colored woman, Mr. Conner?" he asked, warily. He was somewhat pale and was fiddling with a bit of paper. A dabbler in psychology books himself, he knew that colored women are often Sex Degradation symbols, and he wondered if Conner had not fallen out of love with his wife without realizing it. (This theory, I believe, Mr. Bent has clung to ever since, although the Conners are one of the happiest couples in the country.) "I don't know where she is!" cried Conner. "She's up on some other floor phoning my wife! *You* seemed to know all about it! I had nothing to do with it! I opposed it from the start! But I want no insults from you no matter *who* opposed it!" "Certainly not, certainly not," said Mr. Bent, backing slightly away. He began to wonder what he was going to do with this maniac.

At this juncture Scursey, who had been enjoying the scene at a safe distance, approached Conner and took him by the arm. "What's the matter, old boy?" he asked. "H'lo, Bert," said Conner, sullenly. And then, his eyes narrowing, he began to examine the look on Scursey's face. Scursey is not good at dead-panning; he is only good on the phone. There was a guilty grin on his face. "You——," said Conner, bitterly, remembering Scursey's pranks of mimicry, and he turned on his heel, walked to the elevator, and, when Scursey tried to get in too, shoved him back into the lobby. That was the end of the friendship between the Conners and Bert Scursey. It was more than that. It was the end of Harry Conner's stay at the Graydon. It was, in fact, the end of his stay in New York City. He and Louise live in Oregon now, where Conner accepted a less important position than he had held in New York because the episode of Edith had turned him against Scursey, Mr. Bent, the Graydon, and the whole metropolitan area.

Anybody can handle the Frank Fulsome's of the world, but is there anything to be done about the Bert Scurseys? Can we so streamline our minds that the antics of the Scurseys roll off them like water off a duck's back? I don't think so. I believe the authors of the inspirational books don't think so, either, but are afraid to attack the subject. I imagine they have been hoping nobody would bring it up. Hardly anybody goes through life without encountering his Bert Scursey and having his life—and his mind—accordingly modified. I have known a dozen Bert Scurseys. I have often wondered what happened to some of their victims. There was, for example, the man who rang up a waggish friend of mine by mistake, having got a wrong number. "Is this the Shu-Rite Shoestore?" the caller asked, querulously. "Shu-Rite Shoestore, good morning!" said my friend, brightly. "Well," said the other, "I just called up to say that the shoes I bought there a week ago are shoddy. They're made, by God, of cardboard. I'm going to bring them in and show you. I want satisfaction!" "And you shall have it!" said my friend. "Our shoes are, as you say, shoddy. There have been many complaints, many complaints. Our shoes, I am afraid, simply go to pieces on the foot. We shall, of course, refund your money." I know another man who was always being roused out of bed by people calling a certain railroad which had a similar phone number. "When can I get a train to Buffalo?" a sour-voiced woman demanded one morning about seven o'clock. "Not till two A.M. tomorrow, Madam," said this man. "But that's ridiculous!" cried the woman, "I know," said the man, "and we realize that. Hence we include, in the regular fare, a taxi which will call for you in plenty of time to make the train. Where do you live?" The lady, slightly mollified, told him an address in the Sixties. "We'll have a cab there at one-thirty, Madam," he said. "The driver will handle your baggage."

"Now can I count on that?" she said. "Certainly, Madam," he told her. "One-thirty, sharp."

Just what changes were brought about in that woman's character by that call, I don't know. But the thing might have altered the color and direction of her life, the pattern of her mind, the whole fabric of her nature. Thus we see that a person might build up a streamlined mind, a mind awakened to a new life, a new discipline, only to have the whole works shot to pieces by so minor and unpredictable a thing as a wrong telephone number. On the other hand, the undisciplined mind would never have the fortitude to consider a trip to Buffalo at two in the morning, nor would it have the determination to seek redress from a shoestore which had sold it a faulty pair of shoes. Hence the undisciplined mind runs far less chance of having its purposes thwarted, its plans distorted, its whole scheme and system wrenched out of line. The undisciplined mind, in short, is far better adapted to the confused world in which we live today than the streamlined mind. This is, I am afraid, no place for the streamlined mind.

The Case for the Daydreamer

ALL THE books in my extensive library on training the mind agree that realism, as against fantasy, reverie, daydreaming, and woolgathering, is a highly important thing. "Be a realist," says Dr. James L. Mursell, whose "Streamline Your Mind" I have already discussed. "Take a definite step to turn a dream into a reality," says Mrs. Dorothea Brande, the "Wake-Up-and-Live!" woman. They allow you a certain amount of reverie and daydreaming (no woolgathering), but only when it is purposeful, only when it is going to lead to

CHILD MAKING FLAT STATEMENTS ABOUT A GENTLEMAN'S
PERSONAL APPEARANCE.

realistic action and concrete achievement. In this insistence
on reality I do not see as much profit as these Shapers of
Success do. I have had a great deal of satisfaction and benefit
out of daydreaming which never got me anywhere in their
definition of getting somewhere. I am reminded, as an
example, of an incident which occurred this last summer.

I had been travelling about the country attending dog
shows. I was writing a series of pieces on these shows. Not
being in the habit of carrying press cards, letters of
introduction, or even, in some cases, the key to my car or the
tickets to a show which I am on my way to attend, I had
nothing by which to identify myself. I simply paid my way in,
but at a certain dog show I determined to see if the officials in
charge would give me a pass. I approached a large, heavy-set
man who looked somewhat like Victor McLaglen. His name

was Bustard. Mr. Bustard. "You'll have to see Mr. Bustard,"
a ticket-taker had told me. This Mr. Bustard was apparently
very busy trying to find bench space for old Miss Emily Van
Winkle's Pomeranians, which she had entered at the last
minute, and attending to a number of other matters. He
glanced at me, saw that he outweighed me some sixty
pounds, and decided to make short shrift of whatever it was I
wanted. I explained I was writing an article about the show
and would like a pass to get in. "Why, that's impossible!" he
cried. "That's ridiculous! If I gave you a pass, I'd have to
give a pass to everyone who came up and asked me for a
pass!" I was pretty much overwhelmed. I couldn't, as is usual
in these cases, think of anything to say except "I see." Mr.
Bustard delivered a brief, snarling lecture on the subject of
people who expect to get into dog shows free, unless they are
showing dogs, and ended with "Are you showing dogs?" I
tried to think of something sharp and well-turned. "No, I'm
now showing any dogs," I said, coldly. Mr. Bustard abruptly
turned his back on me and walked away.

As soon as Mr. Bustard disappeared, I began to think of
things I should have said. I thought of a couple of sharp
cracks on his name, the least pointed of which was Buzzard.
Finely edged comebacks leaped to mind. Instead of going
into the dog show—or following Mr. Bustard—I wandered
up and down the streets of the town, improving on my
retorts. I fancied a much more successful encounter with Mr.
Bustard. In this fancied encounter, I, in fact, enraged Mr.
Bustard. He lunged at me, whereupon, side-stepping agilely,
I led with my left and floored him with a beautiful right to
the jaw. "Try that one!" I cried aloud. "Mercy!" murmured
an old lady who was passing me at the moment. I began to
walk more rapidly; my heart took a definite lift. Some
people, in my dream, were bending over Bustard, who was
out cold. "Better take him home and let the other bustards
pick his bones," I said. When I got back to the dog show, I

was in high fettle.

After several months I still feel, when I think of Mr. Bustard, that I got the better of him. In a triumphant daydream, it seems to me, there is felicity and not defeat. You can't just take a humiliation and dismiss it from your mind, for it will crop up in your dreams, but neither can you safely carry a dream into reality in the case of an insensitive man like Mr. Bustard who outweighs you by sixty pounds. The thing to do is to visualize a triumph over the humiliator so vividly and insistently that it becomes, in effect, an actuality. I went on with my daydreams about Mr. Bustard. All that day at the dog show I played tricks on him in my imagination, I outgeneralled him, I made him look silly, I had him on the run. I would imagine myself sitting in a living room. It was late at night. Outside it was raining heavily. The doorbell rang. I went to the door and opened it, and a man was standing there. "I wonder if you would let me use your phone?" he asked. "My car has broken down." It was, of all people, Mr. Bustard. You can imagine my jibes, my sarcasm, my repartee, my shutting the door in his face at the end. After a whole afternoon of this kind of thing, I saw Mr. Bustard on my way out of the show. I actually felt a little sorry about the tossing around I had given him. I gave him an enigmatic, triumphant smile which must have worried him a great deal. He must have wondered what I had been up to, what superior of his I had seen, what I had done to get back at him—who, after all, I was.

Now, let us figure Dr. Mursell in my place. Let us suppose that Dr. Mursell went up to Mr. Bustard and asked him for a pass to the dog show on the ground that he could streamline the dog's intuition. I fancy that Mr. Bustard also outweighs Dr. Mursell by sixty pounds and is in better fighting trim; we men who write treatises on the mind are not likely to be in as good shape as men who run dog shows. Dr. Mursell, then, is rebuffed, as I was. If he tries to get back at Mr. Bustard right there and then, he will find himself saying "I see" or "Well, I didn't know" or, at best, "I just asked you." Even the streamlined mind runs into this Blockage, as the psychologists call it. Dr. Mursell, like myself, will go away and think up better things to say, but, being a realist dedicated to carrying a dream into actuality, he will perforce have to come back and tackle Mr. Bustard again. If Mr. Bustard's patience gives out, or if he is truly stung by some crack of the Doctor's he is likely to begin shoving, or snap his fingers, or say, *"'Raus!,"* or even tweak the Doctor's nose. Dr. Mursell, in that case, would get into no end of trouble. Realists are always getting into trouble. They miss the sweet, easy victories of the day-dreamer.

I do not pretend that the daydream cannot be carried too far. If at this late date, for instance, I should get myself up to look as much like Mr. Bustard as possible and then, gazing into the bathroom mirror, snarl "Bustard. you dog!," that would be carrying the daydream too far. One should never run the risk of identifying oneself with the object of one's scorn. I have no idea what complexes and neuroses might lie that way. The mental experts could tell you—or, if they couldn't, they would anyway.

Now let us turn briefly to the indomitable Mrs. Brande, eight of whose precious words of advice have, the ads for her book tell us, changed the lives of 860,000 people, or maybe it is 86,000,000—Simon & Schuster published her book. (These words are "act as if it were impossible to fail," in case your life hasn't been changed.) Discussing realistic action as against the daydream, she takes up the case of a person, any person, who dreams about going to Italy but is getting nowhere. The procedure she suggests for such a person is threefold: (1) read a current newspaper in Italian, buy some histories, phrase books, and a small grammar; (2) put aside a small coin each day; (3) do something in your spare time to make money— "if it is nothing more than to sit with children while their parents are at parties." (I have a quick picture of the parents reeling from party to party, but that is beside the point.)

I can see the newspaper and the books intensifying the dream, but I can't somehow see them getting anybody to Italy. As for putting a small coin aside each day, everybody who has tried it knows that it does not work out. At the end of three weeks you usually have $2.35 in the pig bank or the cooky jar, a dollar and a half of which you have to use for something besides Italy, such as a C.O.D. package. At that rate, all that you would have in the bank or the jar at the end of six years would be about $87.45. Within the next six years Italy will probably be at war, and even if you were well enough to travel after all that time, you couldn't get into the country. The disappointment of a dream nursed for six years, with a reality in view that did not eventuate, would be enough to embitter a person for life. As for this business of sitting with children while their parents are at parties, anybody who has done it knows that no trip to anywhere, even Utopia, would be worth it. Very few people can sit with children, epecially children other than their own, more than an hour and a half without having their dispositions and even their characters badly mauled about. In fifteen minutes the average child whose parents are at a party can make enough flat statements of fact about one's personal appearance and ask enough pointed questions about one's private life to send one away feeling that there is little, if any, use in going on with anything at all, let alone a trip to Italy.

The long and hard mechanics of reality which these inspirationalists suggest are, it seems to me, far less satisfactory than the soft routine of a dream. The dreamer builds up for himself no such towering and uncertain structure of hope; he has no depleted cooky jar to shake his faith in himself. It is significant that the line "Oh, to be in England now that April's there," which is a definite dream line, is better known than any line the poet wrote about actually being in England. (I guess *that* will give the inspirationalists something to think about.) You can sit up with children if you want to, you can put a dime a day in an empty coffee tin, you can read the Fascist viewpoint in an Italian newspaper, but when it comes to a choice between the dream and the reality of present-day Italy, I personally shall sit in a corner by the fire and read "The Ring and the Book." And in the end it will probaly be me who sends you a postcard from Italy, which you can put between the pages of the small grammar or the phrase book.

A Dozen Disciples

MRS. DOROTHEA Brande, whose theory of how to get to Italy I discussed in the preceding pages, has a chapter in her "Wake Up and Live!" which suggests twelve specific disciplines. The purpose of these disciplines, she says, is to make our minds keener and more flexible. I'll take them up in order and and show why it is no use for Mrs. Brande to try to sharpen and limber up my mind, if these disciplines are all she has to offer. I quote them as they were quoted in a Simon & Schuster advertisement for the book, because the advertisement puts them more succinctly than Mrs. Brande does herself.

"1. Spend one hour a day without speaking except in answer to direct questions."

No hour of the day goes by that I am not in some minor difficulty which could easily become major if I did not shout for help. Just a few hours ago, for example, I found myself in a dilemma that has become rather familiar about my house: I had got tied up in a typewriter ribbon. The whole thing had come unwound from the spool and was wound around me. What started as an unfortunate slip of the hand slowly grew into an enormous involvement. To have gone a whole hour waiting for someone to show up and ask me a question could not conceivably have improved my mind. Two minutes of silence now and then is all right, but that is as far as I will go.

"2. Think one hour a day about one subject exclusively."

Such as what, for example? At forty-two, I have spent a great many hours thinking about all sorts of subjects, and there is not one of them that I want to go back to for a whole solid hour. I can pretty well cover as much of any subject as I want to in fifteen minutes. Sometimes in six. Furthermore, it would be impossible for me, or for Mrs. Brande, or for Simon & Schuster to think for an hour exclusively on one subject. What is known as "psychological association" would be bound to come into the thing. For instance, let us say that I decide to think for a solid hour about General Grant's horse (as good a subject as any at a time when practically all subjects are in an unsettled state). The fact that it is General Grant's horse would remind me of General Grant's beard and that would remind me of Charles Evans Hughes and that would remind me of the NRA. And so it would go on. If I resolutely went back to General Grant's horse again, I would, by association, begin thinking about General Lee's horse, which was a much more famous horse, a horse named Traveller. I doubt if Mrs. Brande even knows the name of General Grant's horse, much less enough about it to keep the mind occupied for sixty minutes. I mean sixty minutes of real constructive thinking that would get her somewhere. Sixty minutes of thinking of any kind is bound to lead to confusion and unhappiness.

"3. Write a letter without using the first person singular."

What for? To whom? About what? All I could possibly think of to write would be a letter to a little boy telling him how to build a rabbit hutch, and I don't know how to build a rabbit hutch very well. I never knew a little boy who couldn't tell me more about building a rabbit hutch than I could tell him. Nobody in my family was ever good at building rabbit hutches, although a lot of us raised rabbits. I have sometimes

AMERICAN MALE TIED UP IN A TYPEWRITER RIBBON.

wondered how we managed it. I remember the time that my
father offered to help me and my two brothers build a rabbit
hutch out of planks and close-meshed chicken wire. Somehow
or other he got inside of the cage after the wire had been put
up around the sides and over the top, and he began to
monkey with the stout door. I don't know exactly what
happened, but he shut the door and it latched securely and he
was locked in with the rabbits. The place was a shambles
before he got out, because nobody was at home at the time
and he couldn't get his hand through the wire to unlatch the
door. He had his derby on in the hutch all during his
captivity and that added to his discomfiture. I remember,
too, that we boys (we were not yet in our teens) didn't at first
know what the word "hutch" meant, but we had got hold of
a pamphlet on the subject, which my brother Herman read
with great care. One sentence in the pamphlet read, "The
rabbits' hutches should be cleaned thoroughly once a week."

It was this admonition which cased my brother one day to get each of the astonished rabbits down in Turn and wash its haunches thoroughly with soap and water.

No, I do not think that anybody can write a letter without using the first person singular. Even if it could be done, I see no reason to do it.

"4. Talk for fifteen minutes without using the first person."

No can do. No going to *try* to do, either. You can't teach an old egoist new persons.

"5. Write a letter in a placid, successful tone, sticking to facts about yourself."

Now we're getting somewhere, except that nothing is more stuffy and conceited-sounding than a "placid, successful tone." The way to write about yourself is to let yourself go. Build it up, exaggerate, make yourself out a person of importance. Fantasy is the food for the mind, not facts. Are we going to wake up and live or are we going to sit around writing factual letters in a placid, successful tone?

"6. Pause before you enter any crowded room and consider your relations with the people in it."

Now, Mrs. Brande, if I did that there would be only about one out of every thirty-two crowded rooms I approached that I would ever enter. I always shut my mind and plunge into a crowded room as if it were a cold bath. That gives me and everybody in the room a clean break, a fresh starting point. There is no good in rehashing a lot of old relations with people. The longer I paused outside a crowded room and thought about my relations with the people in it, the more inclined I would be to go back to the checkroom and get my hat and coat and go home. That's the best place for a person, anyway—home.

"7. Keep a new acquaintance talking, exclusively about himself."

And then tiptoe quietly away. He'll never notice the difference.

"8. Talk exclusively about yourself for fifteen minutes."

And see what happens.

"9. Eliminate the phrases 'I mean' and 'As a matter of fact' from your conversation."

Okie-dokie.

"10. Plan to live two hours a day according to a rigid time schedule."

Well, I usually wake up at nine in the morning and lie there till eleven, if that would do. Of course, I could *plan* to do a lot of different things over a period of two hours, but if I actually started out to accomplish them I would instantly begin to worry about whether I was going to come out on the dot in the end and I wouldn't do any of them right. It would be like waiting for the pistol shot during the last quarter of a close football game. This rule seems to me to be devised simply to make men irritable and jumpy.

"11. Set yourself twelve instructions on pieces of paper, shuffle them, and follow the one you draw. Here are a few samples: 'Go twelve hours without food.' 'Stay up all night and work.' 'Say nothing all day except in answer to questions.'"

In that going twelve hours without food, do you mean I can have drinks? Because if I can have drinks, I can do it easily. As for staying up all night and working, I know all about that: that simply turns night into day and day into night. I once got myself into such a state staying up all night that I was always having orange juice and boiled eggs at twilight and was just ready for lunch after everybody had gone to bed. I had to go to a sanitarium to get turned around. As for saying nothing all day except in answer to questions, what am I to do if a genial colleague comes into my office and says, "I think your mother is one of the nicest people I ever met" or "I was thinking about giving you that twenty dollars you lent me"? Do I just stare at him and walk out of the room? I lose enough friends, and money, the way it is.

"12. Say 'Yes' to every reasonable request made of you in

the course of one day."

All right, start making some. I can't think of a single one offhand. The word "reasonable" has taken a terrible tossing around in my life—both personal and business. If you mean watering the geraniums, I'll do that. If you mean walking around Central Park with you for the fresh air and exercise, you are crazy.

Has anybody got any more sets of specific disciplines? If anybody has, they've got to be pretty easy ones if I am going to wake up and live. It's mighty comfortable dozing here and waiting for the end.

How to Adjust Yourself to Your Work

I FIND that the inspirational books are frequently disposed to touch, with pontifical cheerfulness or owlish mysticism, on the problem of how to get along in the business world, how to adjust yourself to your employer and to your fellow-worker. It seems to me that in this field the trainers of the mind, both lady and gentleman, are at their unhappiest. Let us examine, in this our fourth lesson, what Mrs. Dorothea Brande, who is reputedly changing the lives of almost as many people as the Oxford Group, has to say on the subject. She presents the case of a man (she calls him "you") who is on the executive end of an enterprise and feels he should be on the planning end. "In that case," she writes, "your problem is to bring your talents to the attention of your superior officers with as little crowding and bustling as possible. Learn to write clear, short, definite memoranda and present them to your immediate superior until you are perfectly certain that he will never act upon them. In no other circumstances are you justified in going over his head." Very well, let us start from Mrs. Brande's so-called point of justification in going over your superior's head, and see what happens.

Let us suppose that you have presented your favorite memoranda to your immediate superior, Mr. Sutphen, twice and nothing has happened. You are still not perfectly certain that he will never act upon them. To be sure, he has implied, or perhaps even said in so many words, that he never will, but you think that maybe you have always caught him at the wrong moment. So you get up your memoranda a third time. Mr. Sutphen, glancing at your paper and noting that it is that same old plan for tearing out the west wall, or speeding up the out-of-town truck deliveries, or substituting colored lights for bells, is pretty well convinced that all you do in your working hours is write out memoranda. He figures that you are probably suffering from a mild form of monomania and determines to dispense with your services if you submit any memoranda again. After waiting a week and hearing nothing from Mr. Sutphen, you decide, in accordance with Mrs. Brande's suggestion, to go over his head and take the matter up with Mr. Leffley. In doing so, you will not be stringing along with me. I advise you not to go over Mr. Sutphen's head to Mr. Leffley; I advise you to quit writing memoranda and get to work.

The Mr. Leffleys of this country have enough to do the way it is, or think they have, and they do not like to have you come to them with matters which should be taken up with the Mr. Sutphens. They are paying the Mr. Sutphens to keep you and your memoranda from suddenly bobbing up in front of them. In the first place, if you accost the Mr. Leffleys personally, you become somebody else in the organization whose name and occupation they are supposed to know. Already they know who too many people are. In the second place, the Mr. Leffleys do not like to encounter unexpected memoranda. It gives them a suspicion that there is a looseness somewhere; it destroys their confidence that things are going all right; it shakes their faith in the Mr. Sutphens— and in the Mr. Bairds, the Mr. Crowfuts, and the old Miss Bendleys who are supposed to see that every memorandum has been filed away, or is being acted on. I know of one young man who was always sending to his particular Mr. Leffley, over Mr. Sutphen's head, memoranda done up in limp-leather covers and tied with ribbon, this to show that he was not only clear, short, and definite, but neat. Mr. Leffley did not even glance between the leather covers; he simply told Miss Bendley to turn the thing over to Mr. Sutphen, who had already seen it. The young man was let go and is now a process-server. Keep, I say, your clear, short, and definite memoranda to yourself. If Mr. Sutphen has said no, he means no. If he has taken no action, no action is going to be taken. People who are all the time submitting memoranda are put down as jealous, disgruntled, and vaguely dangerous. Employers do not want them around. Sooner or later Mr. Sutphen, or Mr. Leffley himself, sees to it that a printed slip, clear, short, and definite, is put in their pay envelopes.

My own experience, and the experience of many of my friends, in dealing with superiors has covered a wide range of crucial situations of which these success writers appear to be oblivious and for which they therefore have no recommended course of action (which is probably just as well). I am reminded of the case of Mr. Russell Soames, a friend of mine, who worked for a man whom we shall call Mr. B. J. Winfall. This Winfall, some five or six years ago, in the days when Capone was at large and wholesale shootings were common in Chicago, called Soames into his office and said, "Soames, I'm going out to Chicago on that Weltmer deal and I want you to go along with me." "All right, Mr. Winfall," said Soames. They went to Chicago and had been there only four or five hours when they were calling each other Russell and B. J. and fighting for the check at the bar. On the third day, B. J. called Russell into his bedroom (B. J. had not left his bedroom in thirty-six hours) and said "Russell, before we go back to New York, I want to see a dive, a hideout, a joint. I want to see these gangsters in their haunts. I want to see them in action, by God, if they ever get into action. I think most of it is newspaper talk. Your average gangster is a yellow cur." B. J. poured himself another drink from a bottle on his bedside table and repeated, "A yellow cur." Drink, as you see, made B. J. pugnacious (he had already gone through his amorous phase). Russell Soames tried to argue his chief out of this perilous plan, but failed. When Russell would not contact the right parties to arrange for B. J.'s little expedition, B. J. contacted them himself, and finally got hold of a man who knew a man who could get them into a regular hangout of gorillas and finger men.

Along about midnight of the fourth day in Chicago, B. J. Winfall was ready to set out for the dive. He wore a cap, which covered his bald spot, and he had somehow got hold of a cheap, ill-fitting suit, an ensemble which he was pleased to believe gave him the effect of a hardboiled fellow; as a matter of fact, his nose glasses, his pink jowls, and his paunch betrayed him instantly for what he was, a sedentary businessman. Soames strove to dissuade his boss, even in the taxi on their way to the tough spot, but Winfall pooh-poohed him. "Pooh pooh, Russell," he snarled out of the corner of his mouth, unfamiliarly. "These kind of men are rats." He had brought a flask with him and drank copiously from it. "Rats," he said, "of the first order. The first order, Russell, my boy." Soames kept repeating that he felt B. J. was underrating the dangerousness of the Chicago gangster and begged him to be on his good behavior when they got to the joint, if only for the sake of B. J.'s wife and children and his (Russell's) old mother. He exacted a reluctant promise that B. J. would behave himself, but he was by no means easy in his mind when their taxi finally stopped in front of a low, dark building in a far, dark street. "Leave it to me, Russell, my boy," said B. J. as they got out of the cab. "Leave it to

B.J. ("TWO-GUN") WINFALL, OF NEW YORK CITY.

me." Their driver refused to wait, and Russell, who paid him off, was just in time to restrain his employer from beating on the door of the place with both fists. Russell himself knocked, timidly. A thin Italian with deadly eyes opened the door a few inches, Russell mentioned a name, falteringly, and the man admitted them.

As Russell described it to me later, it was a dingy, smoky place with a rough bar across the back attended by a liver-faced barman with a dirty rag thrown over one shoulder, and only one eye. Leaning on the bar and sitting at tables were a lot of small tough-faced men. They all looked up sullenly when Russell and B. J. walked in. Russell felt that there was a movement of hands in pockets. Smiling amiably, blinking nervously, Russell took his companion's arm, but the latter broke away, strode to the bar, and shouted for whiskey. The bartender fixed his one eye on B. J. with the glowering, steady gaze Jack Dempsey used to give his opponents in the ring. He took his time slamming glasses and a bottle down on the bar. B. J. filled a glass, tossed it off, turned heavily, and faced the roomful of men. "I'm Two-Gun Winfall from New York City!" he shouted. "Anybody *want* anything?"

By the most cringing, obsequious explanations and apologies, Russell Soames managed to get himself and his boss out of the place alive. The secret of accomplishing such a feat as he accomplished that night is not to be found in any of the inspirational books. Not a single one of their impressive bits of advice would get you anywhere. Take Mrs. Brande's now famous italicized exhortation, "*Act as if it were impossible to fail.*" Wasn't B. J. Winfall doing exactly that? And was that any way to act in this particular situation? It was not. It was Russell Soames' craven apologies, his abject humility, his (as he told me later) tearful admission that he and B. J. were just drunken bums with broken hearts, that got them out of there alive. The success writers would never suggest, or even tolerate, any such behavior. If Russell Soames had followed their bright, hard rules of general conduct, he would be in his grave today and B. J. Winfall's wife would be a widow.

If Mrs. Brande is not, as in the case of the memoranda-writer, suggesting a relationship with a superior which I believe we have demonstrated to be dangerous and unworkable (and missing altogether the important problem of how to handle one's employer in his more difficult moments), she is dwelling mystically on the simple and realistic subject of how to deal with one's fellow-workers. Thus, in embroidering the theme that imagination can help you with your fellow-workers, she writes, "When you have seen this, you can work out a code for yourself which will remove many of the irritations and dissatisfactions of your daily work. Have you ever been amused and enlightened by seeing a familiar room from the top of the stepladder; or, in mirrors set at angles to each other, seen yourself as objectively for a second or two as anybody else in the room? It is that effect you should strive for in imagination." Here again I cannot hold with the dear lady. The nature of imagination, as she describes it, would merely terrify the average man. The idea of bringing such a distorted viewpoint of himself into his relation with his fellow-workers would twist his personality laboriously out of shape and, in the end, appall his fellow-workers. Men who catch an unfamiliar view of a room from the top of a stepladder are neither amused nor enlightened; they have a quick, gasping moment of vertigo which turn rapidly into plain terror. No man likes to see a familiar thing at an unfamiliar angle, or in an unfamiliar light, and this goes, above all things, for his own face. The glimpses that men get of themselves in mirrors set at angles to each other upset them for days. Frequently they shave in the dark for weeks thereafter. To ask a man to steadily contemplate this thing he has seen fleetingly in a mirror and to figure it as dealing with his fellow-workers day by day is to ask him to abandon his own character and to step into another, which he both disowns and dislikes. Split personality could easily result, leading to at least fifteen of the thirty-three "varieties of obliquity" which Mr. David Seabury lists in his "How to Worry Successfully," among them Cursory Enumeration, Distortion of Focus, Nervous Hesitation (superinduced by Ambivalence), Pseudo-Practicality, Divergency, Retardation, Emotionalized Compilation, Negative Dramatization, Rigidism, Secondary Adaptation, False Externalization, Non-Validation, Closure, and Circular Brooding.

I don't know why I am reminded at this point of my Aunt Kate Obetz, but I am. She was a woman without any imaginative la-di-da, without any working code save that of direct action, who ran a large dairy farm near Sugar Grove, Ohio, after her husband's death, and ran it successfully. One day something went wrong with the cream separator, and one of her hands came to her and said nobody on the farm could fix it. Should they send to town for a man? "No!" shouted my Aunt Kate. "I'll fix it myself!" Shouldering her way past a number of dairy workers, farm hands and members of her family, she grasped the cream separator and began monkeying with it. In a short time she had reduced it to even more pieces than it had been in when she took hold of it. She couldn't fix it. She was just making things worse. At length, she turned on the onlookers and bawled, "Why doesn't somebody take this goddam thing away from me?" Here was a woman as far out of the tradition of inspiration-alist conduct as she could well be. She admitted failure; she had no code for removing irritations and dissatisfactions; she viewed herself as in a single mirror, directly; she lost her temper; she swore in the presence of subordinates; she confessed complete surrender in the face of a difficult problem; she didn't think of herself as a room seen from the top of a stepladder. And yet her workmen and her family continued to love and respect her. Somebody finally took the cream separator away from her; somehow it was fixed. Her failure did not show up in my aunt's character; she was always the same as ever.

For true guidance and sound advice in the business world we find, I think, that the success books are not the place to look, which is pretty much what I thought we would find all along.

Anodynes for Anxieties

I SHOULD like to begin this lesson with a quotation from Mr. David Seabury's "How to Worry Successfully." When things get really tough for me, I always turn to this selection and read it through twice, the second time backward, and while it doesn't make me feel fine, exactly, it makes me feel better. Here it is:

"If you are indulging in gloomy fears which follow each other round and round until the brain reels, there are two possible procedures:

"First, quit circling. It doesn't matter where you cease whirling, as long as you stop.

"Second, if you cannot find a constant, think of something as different from the fact at which you stopped as you possibly can. Imagine what would happen if you mixed that contrast into your situation. If nothing results to clarify your worry, try another set of opposites and continue the process until you do get a helpful answer. If you persist, you will soon solve any ordinary problem."

I first read this remarkable piece of advice two months ago and I vaguely realized then that in it, somewhere, was a strangely familiar formula, not, to be sure, a formula that would ever help me solve anything, but a formula for something or other. And one day I hit on it. It is the formula by which the Marx brothers construct their dialogue. Let us

take their justly famous scene in which Groucho says to
Chico, "It is my belief that the missing picture is hidden in
the house next door." Here Groucho has ceased whirling, or
circling, and has stopped at a fact, that fact being his belief
that the picture is hidden in the house next door. Now Chico,
in accordance with Mr. Seabury's instructions, thinks of
something as different from that fact as he possibly can. He
says, "There isn't any house next door." Thereupon Groucho
"mixes that contrast into his situation." He says, "Then we'll
build one!" Mr. Seabury says, "If you persist you will soon
solve any ordinary problem." He underestimates the power
of his formula. If you persist, you will soon solve anything at
all, no matter how impossible. That way, of course, lies
madness, but I would be the last person to say that madness
is not a solution.

It will come as no surprise to you, I am sure, that
throughout the Mentality Books with which we have been
concerned there runs a thin, wavy line of this particular kind
of Marxist philosophy. Mr. Seabury's works are heavily
threaded with it, but before we continue with him, let us turn
for a moment to dear Dorothea Brande, whose "Wake Up
and Live!" has changed the lives of God knows how many
people by this time. Writes Mrs. Brande, "One of the most
famous men in America constantly sends himself postcards,
and occasionally notes. He explained the card sending as
being his way of relieving his memory of unnecessary details.
In his pocket he carries a few postals addressed to his office. I
was with him one threatening day when he looked out the
restaurant window, drew a card from his pocket, and wrote
on it. Then he threw it across the table to me with a grin. It
was addressed to himself at his office, and said. 'Put your
raincoat with your hat.' At the office he had other cards
addressed to himself at home."

We have here a muzziness of thought so enormous that it
is difficult to analyze. First of all, however, the ordinary
mind is struck by the obvious fact that the famous American

in question has, to relieve his memory of unnecessary details, burdened that memory with the details of having to have postcards at his office, in his pockets, and at his home all the time. If it isn't harder to remember always to take self-addressed postcards with you wherever you go than to remember to put your raincoat with your hat when the weather looks threatening, then you and I will eat the postcards or even the raincoat. Threatening weather itself is a natural sharp reminder of one's raincoat, but what is there to remind one that one is running out of postcards? And supposing the famous man does run out of postcards, what does he do—hunt up a Western Union and send himself a telegram? You can see how monstrously wrapped up in the coils of his own little memory system this notable American must soon find himself. There is something about this system of buying postcards, addressing them to oneself, writing messages on them, and then mailing them that is not unlike one of those elaborate Rube Goldberg contraptions taking up a whole room and involving bicycles, shotguns, parrots, and little colored boys, all set up for the purpose of eliminating the bother of, let us say, setting an alarm clock. Somehow, I can just see Mrs. Brande's famous man at his desk. On it there are two phones, one in the Bryant exchange, the other in the Vanderbilt exchange. When he wants to remind himself of something frightfully urgent, he picks up the Bryant phone and calls the Vanderbilt number, and when that phone rings, he picks it up and says hello and then carries on a conversation with himself. "Remember tomorrow is wifey's birthday!" he shouts over one phone. "O.K.!" he bawls back into the other. This, it seems to me, is a fair enough extension of the activities of our famous gentleman. There is no doubt, either, but that the two-phone system would make the date stick more sharply in his mind than if he just wrote it down on a memo pad. But to intimate that all this shows a rational disciplining of the mind, a development of the power of the human intellect, an approach to the

Masterful Adjustment of which our Success Writers are so
enamored, is to intimate that when Groucho gets the house
built next door, the missing picture will be found in it.

When it comes to anxieties and worries, Mr. Seabury's
elaborate systems for their relief or solution make the device
of Mrs. Brande's famous American look childishly simple.
Mr. Seabury knows, and apparently approves of, a man
"who assists himself by fancied interviews with wise advisers.
If he is in money difficulties, he has mental conversations
with a banker; when business problems press, he seeks the
aid of a great industrialist and talks his problems over with
this ghostly friend until he comes to a definite conclusion."
Here, unless I am greatly mistaken, we have wish fulfillment,
fantasy, reverie, and woolgathering at their most perilous.
This kind of goings-on with a ghostly banker or industrialist
is an escape mechanism calculated to take a man so far from
reality he might never get back. I tried it out myself one night
just before Christmas when I had got down to $60 in the
bank and hadn't bought half my presents yet. I went to bed
early that night and had Mr. J. P. Morgan call on me. I didn't
have to go to his office; he heard I was in difficulty and called
on me, dropping everything else. He came right into my
bedroom and sat on the edge of the bed. "Well, well, well,"
he said, "what's this I hear about you being down?" "I'm not
so good, J. P.," I said, smiling wanly. "We'll have the roses
back in those cheeks in no time," he said. "I'm not really
sick," I told him. "I just need money." "Well, well, well," he
exclaimed, heartily, "is *that* all we need?" "Yes, sir," I said.
He took out a checkbook. "How'd a hundred thousand
dollars do?" he asked, jovially. "That would be all right," I
said. "Could you give it to me in cash, though—in tens and
twenties?" "Why, certainly, my boy, certainly," said Mr.
Morgan, and he gave me the money in tens and twenties.
"Thank you very much, J. P.," I said. "Not at all, Jim, not at
all!" cried my ghostly friend. "What's going on in there?"
shouted my wife, who was in the next room. It seems that I

had got to talking out loud, first in my own voice and then louder, and with more authority, in Mr. Morgan's. "Nothing, darling," I answered. "Well, cut it out," she said. The depression that settled over me when I realized that I was just where I had been when I started to talk with Mr. Morgan was frightful. I haven't got completely over it yet.

This mental-conversation business is nothing, however, compared to what Mr. Seabury calls "picture-puzzle making in worry." To employ this aid in successful thinking, you have to have fifty or sixty filing cards, or blank cards of some kind or other. To show you how it works, let us follow the case history of one Frank Fordson as Mr. Seabury relates it. It seems that this Fordson, out of work, is walking the streets. "He enters store after store with discouraged, pessimistic proprietors. There are poor show windows and dusty sidewalks. They make Frank morbid. His mind feels heavy. He wishes he could happen on a bright idea." He does, as you shall see. Frank consults a psychologist. This psychologist tells him to take fifty filing cards and write on each of them a fact connected with his being out of work. So he writes on one "out of work" and on another "dusty sidewalks" and on another "poor show windows," etc. You and I would not be able to write down more than fifteen things like that before getting off onto something else, like "I hate Joe Grubig" or "Now is the time for all good men," but Frank can do fifty in his stride, all about how tough things are. This would so depress the ordinary mind that it would go home to bed, but not Frank. Frank puts all of the fifty cards on the floor of the psychologist's office and begins to couple them up at random, finally bringing into accidental juxtaposition the one saying "out of work" and one saying "dull sign." Well, out of this haphazard arrangement of the cards, Frank, Mr. Seabury says, got an idea. He went to the hardware store the next day and offered to shine the store's dull sign if the proprietor would give him a can of polish and let him keep what was left. Then he went around shining

THE FILING-CARD SYSTEM.

other signs, for money, and made $3 that day. Ten days later
he got a job as a window-dresser and, before the year was
out, a "position in advertising."

"Take one of your own anxieties," writes Mr. Seabury.
"Analyze it so as to recall all the factors. Write three score of
these on separate cards. Move the cards about on the floor
into as many different relations as possible. Study each
combination." Mr. Seabury may not know it, but the
possible relations of sixty cards would run into millions. If a
man actually studied each of these combinations, it would at
least keep him off the streets and out of trouble—and also
out of the advertising business, which would be something,
after all. Toy soldiers, however, are more fun.

Now, if this kind of playing with filing cards doesn't strike
your fancy, there is the "Worry Play." Let me quote Mr.
Seabury again. "You should write out a description of your
worry," he says, "divide it into three acts and nine scenes, as
if it were a play, and imagine it on the stage, or in the movies,

with various endings. Look at it impersonally as you would look at a comedy and you might be surprised at the detachment you would gain." I have tried very hard to do this. I try out all these suggestions. They have taken up most of my time and energy for the past six months and got me into such a state that my doctor says I can do only three more of these articles at the outside before I go to a sanitarium. A few years ago I had an old anxiety and I was reminded of it by this "Worry Play" idea. Although this old anxiety has been dead and gone for a long time, it kept popping up in my mind because, of all the worries I ever had, it seemed to lend itself best to the drama. I tried not to think about it, but there it was, and I finally realized I would have to write it out and imagine it on the stage before I could dismiss it from my consciousness and get back to work. Well, it ran almost as long as "Mourning Becomes Electra" and took me a little over three weeks to dramatize. Then, when I thought I was rid of it, I dreamed one night I had sold the movie rights, and so I had to adapt it to the movies (a Mr. Sam Maschino, a movie agent, kept bobbing up in my dreams, hectoring me). This took another two weeks. I could not, however, attain this detachment that Mr. Seabury talks about. Since the old anxiety was my own anxiety, I was the main character in it. Sometimes, for as many as fifteen pages of the play script and the movie continuity, I was the only person on the set. I visualized myself in the main rôle, naturally—having rejected Leslie Howard, John Gielgud, and Lionel Barrymore for one reason or another. I was lousy in the part, too, and that worried me. Hence I advise you not to write out your worries in the form of a play. It is simpler to write them out on sixty pieces of paper and juggle them around. Or talk about them to J. P. Morgan. Or send postcards to yourself about them. There are a number of solutions for anxieties which I believe are better than any of these, however: go out and skate, or take in a basketball game, or call on a girl. Or burn up a lot of books.

The Conscious vs. The Unconscious

IT IS high time that we were getting around to a consideration of the magnum opus of Louis E. Bisch, M.D., Ph.D., formerly Professor of Neuropsychiatry at the New York Polyclinic Medical School and Hospital, and Associate in Educational Psychology at Columbia University, and the author of "Be Glad You're Neurotic." Some of the reassuring chapter titles of his popular treatise are "I'm a Neurotic Myself and Delighted," "You Hate Yourself. No Wonder!," "No, You're Not Going Insane Nor Will Any of Your Fears Come True," "Are Your Glands on Friendly Terms?," and "Of Course Your Sex Life is Far from Satisfactory." Some of you will be satisfied with just these titles and will not go on to the book itself, on the ground that you have a pretty good idea of it already. I should like, however, to have you turn with me to Chapter VII, one of my favorite chapters in all psychomentology, "Your Errors and Compulsions Are Calls for Help."

The point of this chapter, briefly, is that the unconscious mind often opposes what the conscious mind wants to do or say, and frequently trips it up with all kinds of evasions, deceits, gags, and kicks in the pants. Our popular psychiatrists try to make these mysteries clear to the layman by the use of simple, homely language, and I am trying to do the same. Dr. Bisch relates a lot of conflicts and struggles that take place between the Hercules of the Conscious and the Augean Stables of the Unconscious (that is my own colorful, if somewhat labored, metaphor and I don't want to see any of the other boys swiping it). "I myself," writes Dr. Bisch, "forgot the number of a hospital where I was to deliver a lecture when I was about to apologize for my delay. I had talked to that particular hospital perhaps a hundred times before. This was the first time, however, that I was consciously trying to do what unconsciously I did not want to do." If you want unconsciously as well as consciously to call a hospital one hundred times out of one hundred and one, I say your conscious and unconscious are on pretty friendly terms. I say you are doing fine. This little experience of Dr. Bisch's is merely to give you a general idea of the nature of the chapter and to ease you into the discussion gently. There are many more interesting examples of conflict and error, of compulsion and obsession, to come. "A colleague," goes on Dr. Bisch, "told me that when he decided to telephone his wife to say he could not be home for dinner he dialled three wrong numbers before he got his own. 'It's because she always flares up when I'm detained at the office,' he explained." This shows that psychiatrists are just as scared of their wives as anybody else. Of course, I believe that this particular psychiatrist dialled the three wrong numbers on purpose. In the case of all husbands, both neurotic and normal, this is known as sparring for time and has no real psychological significance.

I almost never, I find in going slowly and carefully through Dr. Bisch's chapter, taking case histories in their order, agree with him. He writes, "The appearance of persons whom one dislikes or is jealous of, who have offended in some way or whom one fears, tend to be blotted from the mind." Well, some twelve years ago I knew, disliked, was jealous of, feared, and had been offended by a man whom I shall call Philip Vause. His appearance has not only not been blotted from my mind, it hasn't even tended to be. I can call it up as perfectly as if I were holding a photograph of the man in my hand. In nightmares I still dream of Philip Vause. When, in these dreams, I get on subways, he is the guard; when I fly through the air, the eagle that races with me has his face; when I climb the Eiffel Tower, there he is at the top, his black hair roached back, the mole on the left cheek, the thin-lipped smile, and all. Dr. Bisch goes on to say that "the more disagreeable an incident, the deeper is it finally repressed." To which he adds, "The recollection of the pain attending

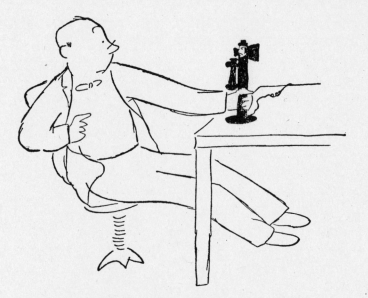

PSYCHIATRIST ABOUT TO PHONE HIS WIFE.

child-birth never lingers long." He has me there.

Dr. Bisch proceeds from that into this: "A man who mislays his hat either dislikes it, wants a new one, experienced unpleasantness when last he wore it, or he does not want to go out. And what you lose you may be sure you do not value, even if it be your wedding ring. Psychologists claim that we lose things because we want to be rid of them or the association they carry, but that we are unwilling to admit the fact to ourselves and actually throw the thing away." This shows you pretty clearly, I think, the point psychologists have reached. I call it mysticism, but I am a polite fellow; you can call it anything you want to. Under any name, it isn't getting us anywhere. Every husband whose tearful wife has lost her wedding ring will now begin to brood, believing (if he strings along with the psychologists instead of with me) that the little darling threw it away, because she is really in love with Philip Vause, and that her tears over her loss are as phony as the plight of a panhandler's family. Let us leave all the sad young couples on the point of separating and go on to Dr. Bisch's analysis of a certain man.

"A certain man," writes Dr. Bisch, "forgot to wind the alarm on several occasions, in consequence of which he was late for work. He also forgot his keys on two occasions and had to wake up his wife in the early hours of the morning. Twice he forgot the furnace at night with the result that there was no heat the next day. In this case the unconscious was trying to tell him that he did not like living in the country although consciously he maintained that he did, for the good of the children." There are, from the standpoint of my own school of psychology, so many fallacies in this piece of analysis that I hardly know where to begin. But let us begin at the beginning, with the failure to wind the alarm clock. Now, a man who does not want to stay home winds the clock so that it will wake him and he can get the hell out and go to the office. There is surely nothing sounder than this. Hence the failure to wind the alarm clock shows that his unconscious was trying to tell him that he did not want to go to the office any more but wanted to stay at his house in the country all the time. The key-forgetting business I simply do not believe. A man who has had to rout out his wife once in the early hours of the morning is not going to forget his key a second time. This is known as Thurber's Empirical Law No. 1. If Dr. Bisch had lived in the country as long and as happily as I have, he would know this simple and unmystical fact: any man can forget to fix the clock and the furnace; especially the furnace, because the clock is usually right where it can be seen, whereas the furnace isn't. Some husbands "forget" to bank the furnace because they have kept hearing funny noises in the cellar all evening and are simply scared to go down there. Hundreds of simple little conscious motives enter into life, Dr. Bisch, hundreds of them.

"A woman," goes on Dr. Bisch, "who wished to consult an attorney about a divorce wrote to him: 'I have been married 22 years.' But the second 2 had evidently been added afterward, indicating that probably she was embarrassed to admit not being able to make a go of it after living with the man so long." How's that again, Doctor? I may be dumb, but I don't exactly catch all that. Couldn't the woman have really been married only 2 years, and couldn't she have added the second 2 indicating that probably she was embarrassed to admit that she was giving up trying to make a go of it after living with the man so *short* a time? Maybe we better just drop this one.

"A woman," continues Dr. Bisch (this is another woman), "who was talking to me about an intended trip to the lakes of northern Italy said: 'I don't wish to visit Lavonia Bay.' She, herself, was surprised, as no such place exists. Inasmuch as the trip was to be a honeymoon, it was 'love, honor and obey' that really was bothering her." I take off my hat to the Doctor's astonishing powers of divination here, because I never would have figured it out. Now that he has given me the key, I get it, of course. "Love, honor, and obey," love-honor-obey, Lavonia Bay. I wonder if he knows the one about the woman who asked the librarian for a copy of "In a Garden." What she really wanted was "Enoch Arden." I like Lavonia Bay better, though, because it is psycho-neurotic, whereas there was nothing the matter with the other poor woman; she just thought that the name of the book was "In a Garden." Dr. Bisch might very likely see something more in this, but the way I've always heard it was that she just thought the name was "In a Garden."

"When a usually efficient secretary," writes Dr. Bisch, "makes errors in typing or shorthand, the excuse of fatigue or indisposition should be taken with a grain of salt. Resentment may have developed toward the employer or the work, or something may unconsciously be bothering her. Some years ago my own secretary often hit the *t* key by mistake. I discovered a young man by the name of Thomas was courting her." That doesn't explain the mistakes of a secretary I had five or six years ago. I had never had a secretary before, and had, indeed, never dictated a letter up to that time. We got some strange results. One of these, in a letter to a man I hoped I would never hear from again, was this sentence: "I feel that the cuneo has, at any rate, garbled the deig." This was not owing to fatigue or indisposition, or to resentment, although there *was* a certain resentment—or even to a young man named Cuneo or Deig. It was simply owing to the fact that my secretary, an Eastern girl, could only understand part of what I, a Middle-Westerner, was saying. In those days, I talked even more than I do now as if I had steel wool in my mouth, and the young lady just did not "get" me. Being afraid to keep asking me what I was trying to say, she simply put down what it sounded like. I signed this particular letter, by the way, just as she wrote it, and I never heard again from the man I sent it to, which is what I had hoped would happen. Psychiatrists would contend that I talked unintelligibly because of that very hope, but this is because they don't know that in Ohio, to give just one example, the word "officials" is pronounced "fishuls," no matter what anybody hopes.

We now go on to the case of a gentleman who deviated from the normal, or uninteresting. "In dressing for a formal dinner," says Dr. Bisch, "a man put on a bright red bow tie. His enthusiasm was self-evident." That is all our psychiatrist says about this one, and I think he is letting it go much too easily; I sense a definite drop here. If I were to say to you that in dressing for a formal dinner last night I put on a bright red bow tie and you were to say merely, "Your enthusiasm was self-evident," I would give you a nasty look and go on to somebody else who would get a laugh out of it, or at least ask what the hell was the idea. For the purpose of analysis in this particular case, I think you would have to know who the man was, anyway. If it was Ernest Boyd, that's one thing; if it was Jack Dempsey, that's another thing; if it was Harpo Marx or Dave Chasen, that's still another thing, or two other things. I think you really have to know who the man was. If the idea was to get a laugh, I don't think it was so very good. As for Dr. Bisch's notion that the man was enthusiastic, I don't see that at all. I just don't see it. Enthusiastic about what?

Our psychiatrist, in this meaty chapter, takes up a great many more cases, many more than I can disagree with in the space at my diposal, but I can't very well leave out the one about the man and the potatoes, because it is one of my favorites. It seems that there kept running through this unfortunate gentleman's mind the words "mashed potatoes, boiled potatoes, mashed potatoes, boiled potatoes"—*that* old line. This went on for days, and the poor fellow, who had a lot of other things he wanted to keep repeating, could only keep repeating that. "Here," says Dr. Bisch, "the difficulty lay in the fact that the man had previously received a reprimand from his employer regarding his easy-going ways with the men who were under him in his department. 'Don't be too soft!' the employer had shouted. 'Be hard!' That very evening his wife served French fried potatoes that were burnt. 'I should be hard with her, too,' he mused. The next day the 'mashed potatoes, boiled potatoes' had been born." Now my own analysis is that the fellow really wanted to kill (mash) his wife and then go out and get fried or boiled. My theory brings in the fried potatoes and Dr. Bisch's doesn't, or not so well, anyway. I might say, in conclusion, that I don't like fellows who muse about getting hard with their wives and then take it out in repeating some silly line over and over. If I were a psychiatrist, I would not bother with them. There are so many really important ailments to attend to.

Sex ex Machina

WITH THE disappearance of the gas mantle and the advent of the short circuit, man's tranquillity began to be threatened by everything he put his hand on. Many people believe that it was a sad day indeed when Bejamin Franklin tied that key to a kite string and flew the kite in a thunderstorm; other people believe that if it hadn't been Franklin, it would have been someone else. As, of course, it was in the case of the harnessing of steam and the invention of the gas engine. At any rate, it has come about that so-called civilized man finds himself today surrounded by the myriad mechanical devices of a technological world. Writers of books on how to control your nerves, how to conquer fear, how to cultivate calm, how to be happy in spite of everything, are of several minds as regards the relation of man and the machine. Some of them are prone to believe that the mind and body, if properly disciplined, can get the upper hand of this mechanized existence. Others merely ignore the situation and go on to the profitable writing of more facile chapters of inspiration. Still others attribute the whole menace of the machine to sex, and so confuse the average reader that he cannot always be certain whether he has been knocked down by an automobile or is merely in love.

Dr. Bisch, the Be-Glad-You're-Neurotic man, has a remarkable chapter which deals, in part, with man, sex, and the machine. He examines the case of three hypothetical men who start across a street on a red light and get in the way of an oncoming automobile. A dodges successfully; B stands still, "accepting the situation with calm and resignation," thus becoming one of my favorite heroes in modern belles-lettres; and C hesitates, wavers, jumps backward and forward, and finally runs head on into the car. To lead you through Dr. Bisch's complete analysis of what was wrong with B and C would occupy your whole day. He mentions

what the McDougallians would say ("Instinct!"), what the
Freudians would retort ("Complexes!"), and what the
behaviorists would shout ("Conditioned reflexes!"). He also
brings in what the physiologists would say—deficient thyroid,
hypoadrenal functioning, and so on. The average sedentary
man of our time who is at all suggestible must emerge from
this chapter believing that his chances of surviving a
combination of instinct, complexes, reflexes, glands, sex, and
present-day traffic conditions are about equal to those of a
one-legged blind man trying to get out of a labyrinth.

Let us single out what Dr. Bisch thinks the Freudians
would say about poor Mr. C, who ran right into the car. He
writes, "'Sex hunger,' the Freudians would declare. 'Always
keyed up and irritable because of it. Undoubtedly suffers
from insomnia and when he does sleep his dream life must be
productive, distorted, and possibly frightening. Automobile
unquestionably has sex significance for him . . . to C the car
is both enticing and menacing at one and the same
time . . . A thorough analysis is indicated. . . . It might take
months. But then, the man needs an analysis as much as
food. He is heading for a complete nervous collapse.'" It is
my studied opinion, not to put too fine a point on it, that Mr.
C is heading for a good mangling, and that if he gets away
with only a nervous collapse, it will be a miracle.

I have not always, I am sorry to say, been able to go the
whole way with the Freudians, or even a very considerable
distance. Even though, as Dr. Bisch says, "One must admit
that the Freudians have had the best of it thus far. At least
they have received the most publicity." It is in matters like
their analysis of men and machines, of Mr. C and the
automobile, that the Freudians and I part company. Of
course, the analysis above is simply Dr. Bisch's idea of what
the Freudians would say, but I think he has got it down
pretty well. Dr. Bisch himself leans toward the Freudian
analysis of Mr. C, for he says in this same chapter, "An
automobile bearing down upon you may be a sex symbol at

that, you know, especially if you dream it." It is my contention, of course, that even if you dream it, it is probably not a sex symbol, but merely an automobile bearing down upon you. And if it bears down upon you in real life, I am sure it is an automobile. I have seen the same behavior that characterized Mr. C displayed by a squirrel (Mr. S) that lives in the grounds of my house in the country. He is a fairly tame squirrel, happily mated and not sex-hungry, if I am any judge, but nevertheless he frequently runs out toward my automobile when I start down the driveway, and then hesitates, wavers, jumps forward and backward, and occasionally would run right into the car except that he is awfully fast on his feet and that I always hurriedly put on the brakes of the 1935 V-8 Sex Symbol that I drive.

I have seen this same behavior in the case of rabbits (notoriously uninfluenced by any sex symbols save those of other rabbits), dogs, pigeons, a doe, a young hawk (which flew at my car), a blue heron that I encountered on a country road in Vermont, and once, near Paul Smiths in the Adirondacks, a fox. They all acted exactly like Mr. C. The hawk, unhappily, was killed. All the others escaped with nothing worse, I suppose, than a complete nervous collapse. Although I cannot claim to have been conversant with the private life and the secret compulsions, the psychoneuroses and the glandular activities of all these animals, it is nevertheless my confident and unswervable belief that there was nothing at all the matter with any one of them. Like Mr. C, they suddenly saw a car swiftly bearing down upon them, got excited, and lost their heads. I do not believe, you see, there was anything the matter with Mr. C, either. But I do believe that, after a thorough analysis lasting months, with a lot of harping on the incident of the automobile, something might very well come to be the matter with him. He might even actually get to suffering from the delusion that he believes automobiles are sex symbols.

It seems to me worthy of note that Dr. Bisch, in reciting the reactions of three persons in the face of an oncoming car, selected three men. What would have happened had they been Mrs. A, Mrs. B, and Mrs. C? You know as well as I do: all three of them would have hesitated, wavered, jumped forward and backward, and finally run head on into the car if

HAPPILY-MATED RABBIT TERRIFIED BY MOTOR-CAR.

some man hadn't grabbed them. (I used to know a motorist who, every time he approached a woman standing on a curb preparing to cross the street, shouted, "Hold it, stupid!") It is not too much to say that, with a car bearing down upon them, ninety-five women out of a hundred would act like Mr. C—or Mr. S, the squirrel, or Mr. F, the fox. But it is certainly too much to say that ninety-five out of every hundred women look upon the automobile as a sex symbol. For one thing,

Dr. Bisch points out that the autombile serves as a sex symbol because of the "mechanical principle involved." But only one woman in a thousand really knows anything about the mechanical principle involved in an automobile. And yet, as I have said, ninety-five out of a hundred would hesitate, waver, and jump, just as Mr. C did. I think we have the Freudians here. If we haven't proved our case with rabbits and a blue heron, we have certainly proved it with women.

To my notion, the effect of the automobile and of other mechanical contrivances on the state of our nerves, minds, and spirits is a problem which the popular psychologists whom I have dealt with know very little about. The sexual explanation of the relationship of man and the machine is not good enough. To arrive at the real explanation, we have to begin very far back, as far back as Franklin and the kite, or at least as far back as a certain man and woman who appear in a book of stories written more than sixty years ago by Max Adeler. One story in this book tells about a housewife who bought a combination ironing board and card table, which some New England genius had thought up in his spare time. The husband, coming home to find the devilish contraption in the parlor, was appalled. "What is that thing?" he demanded. His wife explained that it was a card table, but that if you pressed a button underneath, it would become an ironing board. Whereupon she pushed the button and the table leaped a foot into the air, extended itself, and became an ironing board. The story goes on to tell how the thing finally became so finely sensitized that it would change back and forth if you merely touched it—you didn't have to push the button. The husband stuck it in the attic (after it had leaped up and struck him a couple of times while he was playing euchre), and on windy nights it could be heard flopping and banging around, changing from a card table to an ironing board and back. The story serves as one example of our dread heritage of annoyance, shock, and terror arising out of the nature of mechanical contrivances *per se*. The mechanical principle involved in this damnable invention had, I believe, no relationship to sex whatsoever. There are certain analysts who see sex in anything, even a leaping ironing board, but I think we can ignore these scientists.

No man (to go on) who has wrestled with a self-adjusting card table can ever be quite the man he once was. If he arrives at the state where he hesitates, wavers, and jumps at every mechanical device he enounters, it is not, I submit, because he recognizes the enticements of sex in the device, but only because he recognizes the menace of the machine as such. There might very well be, in every descendant of the man we have been discussing, an inherited desire to jump at, and conquer, mechanical devices before they have a chance to turn into something twice as big and twice as menacing. It is not reasonable to expect that his children and their children will have entirely escaped the stigma of such traumata. I myself will never be the man I once was, nor will my descendants probably ever amount to much, because of a certain experience I had with an automobile.

I had gone out to the barn of my country place, a barn which was used both as a garage and a kennel, to quiet some large black poodles. It was 1 A.M. of a pitch-dark night in winter and the poodles had apparently been terrified by some kind of a prowler, a tramp, a turtle, or perhaps a fiend of some sort. Both my poodles and I myself believed, at the time, in fiends, and still do. Fiends who materialize out of nothing and nowhere, like winged pigweed or Russian thistle. I had quite a time quieting the dogs, because their panic spread to me and mine spread back to them again, in a kind of vicious circle. Finally, a hush as ominous as their uproar fell upon them, but they kept looking over their shoulders, in a kind of apprehensive way. "There's nothing to be afraid of," I told them as firmly as I could, and just at that moment the klaxon

of my car, which was just behind me, began to shriek.
Everybody has heard a klaxon on a car suddenly begin to
sound; I understand it is a short circuit that causes it. But
very few people have heard one scream behind them while
they were quieting six or eight alarmed poodles in the middle
of the night in an old barn. I jump now whenever I hear a
klaxon, even the klaxon on my own car when I push the
button intentionally. The experience has left its mark.
Everybody, from the day of the jumping card table to the day
of the screaming klaxon, has had similar shocks. You can see
the result, entirely unsuperinduced by sex, in the strained
faces and muttering lips of people who pass you on the
streets of great, highly mechanized cities. There goes a man
who picked up one of those trick matchboxes that whir in
your hands; there goes a woman who tried to change a fuse
without turning off the current; and yonder toddles an
ancient who cranked an old Reo with the spark advanced.
Every person carries in his consciousness the old scar, or the
fresh wound, of some harrowing misadventure with a
contraption of some sort. I know people who would not
deposit a nickel and a dime in a cigarette-vending machine
and push the lever even if a diamond necklace came out. I
know dozens who would not climb into an airplane even if it
didn't move off the ground. In none of these people have I
discerned what I would call a neurosis, an "exaggerated"
fear; I have discerned only a natural caution in a world made
up of gadgets that whir and whine and whiz and shriek and
sometimes explode.

I should like to end with the case history of a friend of
mine in Ohio named Harvey Lake. When he was only
nineteen, the steering bar of an old electric runabout broke
off in his hand, causing the machine to carry him through a
fence and into the grounds of the Columbus School for Girls.
He developed a fear of automobiles, trains, and every other
kind of vehicle that was not pulled by a horse. Now, the

psychologists would call this a complex and represent the fear as abnormal, but I see it as a purely reasonable apprehension. If Harvey Lake had, because he was catapulted into the grounds of the Columbus School for Girls, developed a fear of girls, I would call that a complex; but I don't call his normal fear of machines a complex. Harvey Lake never in his life got into a plane (he died in a fall from a porch), but I do not regard that as neurotic, either, but only sensible.

I have, to be sure, encountered men with complexes. There was, for example, Marvin Belt. He had a complex about airplanes that was quite interesting. He was not afraid of machinery, or of high places, or of crashes. He was simply afraid that the pilot of any plane he got into might lose his mind. "I imagine myself high over Montana," he once said to me, "in a huge, perfectly safe tri-motored plane. Several of the passengers are dozing, others are reading, but I am keeping my eyes glued on the door to the cockpit. Suddenly the pilot steps out of it, a wild light in his eyes, and in a falsetto like that of a little girl he says to me, 'Conductor, will you please let me off at One-Hundred-and-Twenty-Fifth-Street?'" "But," I said to Belt, "even if the pilot does go crazy, there is still the co-pilot." "No, there isn't," said Belt. "The pilot has hit the co-pilot over the head with something and killed him." Yes, the psychoanalysts can have Marvin Belt. But they can't have Harvey Lake, or Mr. C, or Mr. S, or Mr. F, or, while I have my strength, me.

Sample Intelligence Test

THE FUZZINESS that creeps into the thought processes of those inspirationalists who seek to clarify the human scene reaches an interesting point in Chapter XIV of "How to Develop Your Personality," by Sadie Myers Shellow, Ph.D. Dr. Shellow was formerly psychologist with the Milwaukee Electric Railway & Light Company. These things happen in a world of endless permutations. I myself was once connected with the Central Ohio Optical Company. I was hired because I had a bicycle, although why an optical company would want a bicycle might appear on the face of it as inexplicable as why a railway-and-light company would want a psychologist. My experience of motormen leads me to believe that they are inarticulate to the point of never saying anything at all, and I doubt if there is a motorman in all Wisconsin who would reveal the story of his early childhood to a psychologist. Dr. Shellow, of course, may have proceeded along some other line, but most psychologists start with your childhood. Or with your sex life. I somehow have never thought of motormen as having sex lives, but this doesn't mean that they don't have them. I feel that this speculation is not getting us anywhere.

Let us return to Dr. Shellow's book. It was first published five years ago, but her publishers have just brought out a dollar edition, which puts the confusion in Chapter XIV within reach of everyone. In 1932, the book went into six printings. The present edition was printed from the original plates, which means that the mistakes which appear in it have gone on and on through the years. The book begins with a prefatory note by Albert Edward Wiggam, a foreword by Morris S. Viteles, and an introduction by Dr. Shellow herself. In Chapter I, first paragraph, Dr. Shellow gives the dictionary definition of "personality" as follows: "The sum total of traits necessary to describe what is to be a person."

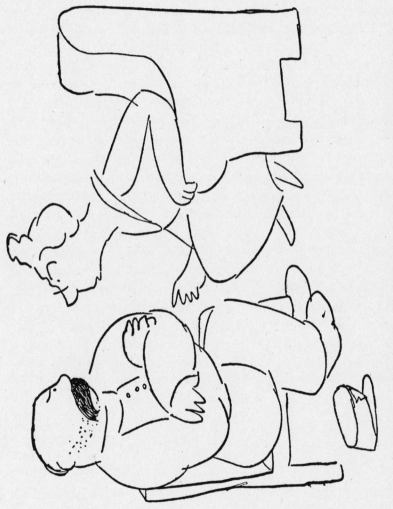

MOTORMAN CONCEALING HIS SEX LIFE FROM A WOMAN PSYCHOLOGIST.

Unless I have gone crazy reading all these books, and I think I have, that sentence defines personality as the sum total of traits necessary to describe an unborn child. If Dr. Shellow's error here is typographical, it looms especially large in a book containing a chapter that tells how to acquire reading skill and gives tests for efficiency in reading. Dr. Shellow tells of a young woman who "was able to take in a whole page at a glance, and through concentrated attention relate in detail what she had read as the words flashed by." If Dr. Shellow used this system in reading the proofs of her book, the system is apparently no good. It certainly *sounds* as if it were no good. I have started out with an admittedly minor confusion—the definition of personality—but let us go on to something so mixed up that it becomes almost magnificent.

Chapter XIV is called "Intelligence Tests," and under the heading "Sample Intelligence Test" twelve problems are posed. There are some pretty fuzzy goings-on in the explanation of No. 11, but it is No. 12 that interests me most; what the Milwaukee motormen made of it I can't imagine. No. 12 is stated as follows: "Cross out the *one* word which makes this sentence absurd and substitute one that is correct: A pound of feathers is lighter than a pound of lead." Let us now proceed to Dr. Shellow's explanation of how to arrive at the solution of this toughy. She writes, "In 12 we get at the critical ability of the mind. Our first impulse is to agree that a pound of feathers is lighter than a pound of lead, since feathers are lighter than lead, but if we look back, we will see that a *pound* of feathers could be no lighter than a *pound* of lead since a pound is always the same. What one word, then, makes the whole sentence absurd? We might cross out the second pound and substitute ounce, in which case we would have: A pound of feathers is heavier than an ounce of lead, and that would be correct. Or we might cross out the word heavier and substitute bulkier, in which case we would have eliminated the absurdity."

We have here what I can only call a paradise of errors. I find, in Dr. Shellow's presentation of the problem and her solution of it, Transference, Wishful Thinking, Unconscious Substitution, Psychological Dissociation, Gordian Knot Cutting, Cursory Enumeration, Distortion of Focus, Abandonment of Specific Gravity, Falsification of Premise, Divergence from Consistency, Overemphasis on Italics, Rhetorical Escapism, and Disregard of the Indefinite Article. Her major error—the conjuring up of the word "heavier" out of nowhere—is enough to gum up any problem beyond repair, but there are other interesting pieces of woolly reasoning in No. 12. Dr. Shellow gets off on the wrong foot in her very presentation of the problem. She begins, "Cross out the *one* word which makes this sentence absurd." That means there is *only* one word which can be changed and restricts the person taking the test to that one word, but Dr. Shellow goes on, in her explanation, to change first one and then another. As a matter of fact, there are five words in the sentence any one of which can be changed to give the sentence meaning. Thus we are all balled up at the start. If Dr. Shellow had written, "Cross out one word which makes this sentence absurd," that would have been all right. I think I know how she got into trouble. I imagine that she originally began, "Cross out one of the words," and found herself face to face with that ancient stumbling block in English composition, whether to say "which *makes* this sentence absurd" or "which *make* this sentence absurd." (I don't like to go into italics, but to straighten Dr. Shellow out you got to go into italics.) I have a notion that Dr. Shellow decided that "make" was right, which of course it is, but that she was dissatisfied with "Cross out one of the words which make this sentence absurd" because here "words" dominates "one." Since she wanted to emphasize "one," she italicized it and then, for good measure, put the definite article "the" in front of it. That would have given her "Cross out the *one* of the words which make this sentence absurd." From there she finally arrived at what she arrived at, and the problem began slowly to close in on her.

I wouldn't dwell on this at such length if Dr. Shellow's

publishers had not set her up as a paragon of lucidity, precision, and logical thought. (Come to think that over, I believe I would dwell on it at the same length even if they hadn't.) Some poor fellows may have got inferiority complexes out of being unable to see through Dr. Shellow's authoritative explanation of No. 12, and I would like to restore their confidence in their own minds. You can't just go batting off any old sort of answer to an intelligence test in this day when every third person who reads these books has a pretty firm idea that his mind is cracking up.

Let us go on to another interesting fuzziness in the Doctor's explanation. Take her immortal sentence: "We might cross out the second pound and substitute ounce," etc. What anybody who followed those instructions would arrive at is: "A pound of feathers is lighter than *a* ounce of lead." Even leaving the matter of weight out of it (which I am reluctant to do, since weight is the main point), you can't substitute "ounce" for "pound" without substituting "an" for "a," thus changing two words. If "an" and "a" are the same word, then things have come to a pretty pass, indeed. If such slip-shoddery were allowed, you could solve the problem with "A pound of feathers is lighter than two pound of lead." My own way out was to change "is" to "ain't," if anybody is interested.

Let us close this excursion into the wonderland of psychology with a paragraph of Dr. Shellow's which immediately follows her explanation of No. 12: "If the reader went through this test quickly before reading the explanation, he may have discovered some things about himself. A more detailed test would be even more revealing. Everyone should at some time or other take a good comprehensive intelligence test and analyze his own defects so that he may know into what errors his reasoning takes him and of what faulty habits of thought he must be aware." I want everybody to file out quietly, now, without any wisecracks.

Miscellaneous Mentation

IN GOING back over the well-thumbed pages of my library of recent books on mental technique, I have come upon a number of provocative passages which I marked with a pencil but, for one reason or another, was unable to fit into any of my preceding chapters. I have decided to take up this group of miscellaneous matters here, treating the various passages in the order in which I come to them. First, then, there is a paragraph from Dr. Louis E. ("Be Glad You're Neurotic") Bisch, on Overcompensation. He writes, "To overcome a handicap and overcompensate is much the same as consciously and deliberately setting out to overcome a superstition. We will say that you are afraid to pass under a ladder. But suppose you defy the superstition and do it anyway? You may feel uneasy for a few hours or a few days. To your surprise, perhaps, nothing dreadful happens to you. This gives you courage. You try the ladder stunt again. Still you find yourself unharmed. After a while you look for ladders; you delight in walking under them; your ego has been pepped up and you defy all the demons that may be!"

Of course, the most obvious comment to be made here is that if you keep looking for and walking under ladders long enough, something *is* going to happen to you, in the very nature of things. Then, since your defiance of "all the demons that may be" proves you still believe in them, you will be right back where you were, afraid to walk under a ladder again. But what interests me most in Dr. Bisch's study of how to "pep up the ego" is its intensification of the very kind of superstition which the person in this case sets out to defy and destroy. To substitute walking under ladders for not walking under ladders is a distinction without a difference. For here we have, in effect, a person who was afraid to walk under ladders, and is now afraid not to. In the first place he avoided ladders because he feared the very fear that that

LADDER PHOBIA.

would put into him. This the psychologists call phobophobia (they really do). But *now* he is afraid of the very fear he had of being afraid and hence is a victim of what I can only call phobophobophobia, and is in even deeper than he was before. Let us leave him in this perfectly frightful mess and turn to our old authority, Mr. David Seabury, and a quite different kind of problem.

"A young woman," writes Mr. Seabury, "remarked recently that she had not continued her literary career because she found her work commonplace. 'And,' she went on, 'I don't want to fill the world with more mediocre writing.' 'What sort of finished product do you expect a girl of twenty-two to produce?' I asked. 'You are judging what you can be in the future by what you are doing in the present. Would you have a little elm tree a year old compare itself with a giant tree and get an inferiority feeling? An elm tree of one year is a measly little thing, but given time it shades a whole house.'" Mr. Seabury does not take into consideration that, given time, a lady writer shades a whole house, too, and that whereas a little elm tree is bound to grow up to be a giant elm tree, a lady writer who at twenty-two is commonplace and mediocre is bound to grow to be a giant of commonplaceness and mediocrity. I think that this young woman is the only young woman writer in the history of the United States who thought that she ought not to go on with her writing because it was mediocre. If ever a psychologist had it in his power to pluck a brand from the burning, Mr. Seabury had it here. But what did he do? He made the young writer of commonplace things believe she would grow to be a veritable elm in the literary world. I hope she didn't listen to him, but I am afraid she probably did. Still, she sounds like a smart girl, and maybe she saw the weakness in Mr. Seabury's "You are judging what you can be in the future by what you are doing in the present." I can think of no sounder judgment to make.

Let us now look at something from Dr. James L.

("Streamline Your Mind") Mursell. In a chapter on "Mastering and Using Language," he brings out that most people do not know how to read. Dr. Mursell would have them get a precise and dogmatic meaning out of everything they read, thus leaving nothing to the fantasy and the imagination. This is particularly unfortunate, it seems to me, when applied to poetry, as Dr. Mursell applies it. He writes, "A large group of persons *seemed* to read the celebrated stanza beginning

> The Assyrian came down like the wolf on the fold
> And his cohorts were gleaming in purple and gold,

and ending

> Where the blue wave rolls nightly on deep Galilee.

"But when a suspicious-minded investigator tested them, quite a number turned out to suppose that the Assyrian's cohorts were an article of wearing apparel and that the last line referred to the astronomical discoveries of Galileo. Is this reading?"

Well, yes. What the second line means is simply that the *cohorts'* articles of wearing apparel were gleaming in purple and gold, so nothing much is distorted except the number of people who came down like the wolf on the fold. The readers who got it wrong had, it seems to me, as deep a poetic feeling (which is the main thing) as those who knew that a cohort was originally one of the ten divisions of a roman legion and had, to begin with, three hundred soldiers, later five hundred to six hundred. Furthermore, those who got it wrong had a fine flaring image of one Assyrian coming down valiantly all alone, instead of with a couple of thousand soldiers to help him, the big coward. As for "Where the blue wave rolls nightly on deep Galilee," the reading into this of some vague association with the far, lonely figure of Galileo lends it a misty poetic enchantment which, to my way of thinking, the

line can very well put up with. Dr. Mursell should be glad
that some of the readers didn't think "the blue wave" meant
the Yale football team. And even if they had, it would be all
right with me. There is no person whose spirit hasn't at one
time or another been enriched by some cherished tranfiguring
of meanings. Everybody is familiar with the youngster who
thought the first line of the Lord's Prayer was "Our Father,
who art in heaven, Halloween be thy Name." There must
have been for him, in that reading, a thrill, a delight, and an
exaltation that the exact sense of the line could not possibly
have created. I once knew of a high-school teacher in a small
town in Ohio who for years had read to his classes a line that
actually went "She was playing coquette in the garden below"
as if it were "She was playing croquet in the garden below."
When, one day, a bright young scholar raised his hand and
pointed out the mistake, the teacher said, grimly, "I have
read that line my way for seventeen years and I intend to go
on reading it my way." I am all for this point of view. I
remember that, as a boy of eight, I thought "Post No Bills"
meant that the walls on which it appeared belonged to one
Post No Bill, a man of the same heroic proportions as
Buffalo Bill. Some suspicious-minded investigator cleared
this up for me, and a part of the glamour of life was gone.

We will now look at a couple of items from the very latest
big-selling inspirational volume, no less a volume than Mr.
Dale Carnegie's "How to Win Friends and Influence
People." Writes Mr. Cargenie, "The New York Telephone
Company conducts a school to train its operators to say
'Number please' in a tone that means 'Good morning, I am
happy to be of service to you.' Let's remember that when we
answer the telephone tomorrow." Now it seems to me that if
this is something we have deliberately to remember, some
thing we have to be told about, then obviously the operators
aren't getting their message over. And I don't think they are.
What I have always detected in the voices of telephone
operators is a note of peremptory willingness. Their tone

always conveys to me "What number do you want? And don't mumble!" If it is true, however, that the operator's tone really means "Good morning, I am happy to be of service to you," then it is up to the subscriber to say, unless he is a curmudgeon, "Thank you. How are you this morning?" If Mr. Carnegie doesn't know what the operator would say to that, I can tell him. She would say, "I am sorry, sir, but we are not allowed to give out that information." And the subscriber and the operator would be right back where they are supposed to be, on a crisp, business-like basis, with no genuine "good morning" and no real happiness in it at all.

I also want to examine one of Mr. Carnegie's rules for behavior in a restaurant. He writes, "You don't have to wait until you are Ambassador to France or chairman of the Clambake Committee of the Elk's Club before you use this philosophy of appreciation. You can work magic with it every day. If, for example, the waitress brings us mashed potatoes when we ordered French fried, let's say 'I'm sorry to trouble you, but I prefer French fried.' She'll reply. 'No trouble at all,' and will be glad to do it because you have shown respect for her." Now, it is my belief that if we said to the waitress, "I'm sorry to trouble you, but I prefer French fried," she would say, "Well, make up ya mind." The thing to say to her is simply, "I asked for French fried potatoes, not mashed potatoes." To which, of course, she might reply, under her breath, "Well, take the marbles outa ya mouth when ya talkin'." There is no way to make a waitress really glad to do anything. Service is all a matter of business with her, as it is with the phone operators, and Mr. Carnegie might as well face the fact. Anyway, I do not see any "philosophy of appreciation" in saying to a waitress, "I'm sorry to trouble you, but I prefer French fried." Philosophy and appreciation are both capable of higher flights than that. "How are you, Beautiful?" is a higher form of appreciation than what Mr. Carnegie recommends, and it is not very high.

But at least it isn't stuffy, and "I'm sorry to trouble you, but I prefer French fried" is; waitresses hate men who hand them that line.

For a final example of mistaken observation of life and analysis of people, I must turn again to the prolific Mr. Seabury. He writes that once, at a dinner, he sat opposite "a tall, lanky man with restless fingers" who was telling the lady on his right about his two dogs and their four puppies. "It was obvious," says Mr. Seabury, "that he had identified himself with the mother dog and was accustomed to spend a good deal of his time in conversation with her about the welfare of her young." Having been a dog man myself for a great many years, I feel that I am on sounder ground there than Mr. Seabury. I know that no dog man ever identifies himself with the mother dog. There is a type of dog man who sometimes wistfully identifies himself with the father dog, or would like to, at any rate, because of the comparative freedom, lack of responsibility, and general carefree attitude that marks the family life of all father dogs. But no dog man, as I have said, ever identifies himself with the mother dog. He may, to be sure, spend a good deal of his time in conversation with her, but this conversation is never about the welfare of her young. Every dog man knows that there is nothing he can say to any mother dog about the welfare of her young that will make the slightest impression on her. This is partly because she does not know enough English to carry on a conversation that would get very far, and partly because, even if she did, she would not let any suggestions or commands, coaxings or wheedlings, influence her in the least.

Every dog man, when his mother dog has had her first pups, has spent a long time fixing up a warm bed in a nice, airy corner for the mother dog to have her pups in, only to discover that she prefers to have them under the barn, in a hollow log, or in the dark and inaccessible reaches of a storeroom amidst a lot of overshoes, ice skates, crokinole boards, and ball bats. Every dog man has, at the risk of his temper and his limbs, grimly and resolutely dug the mother dog and her pups out from among the litter of debris that she prefers, stepping on the ball bats, kneeling on the ice skates, and put her firmly into the bassinet he has prepared for her, only to have her carry her pups back to the nest among the overshoes and the crokinole boards during the night. In the end, every dog man has let the mother dog have her way, having discovered that there is nothing he can do, much less say, that will win her over to his viewpoint in the matter. She refuses to identify herself with him and he becomes too smart to try to identify himself with her. It would wear him to a frazzle in a week.

PART TWO

Other More or Less Inspirational Pieces

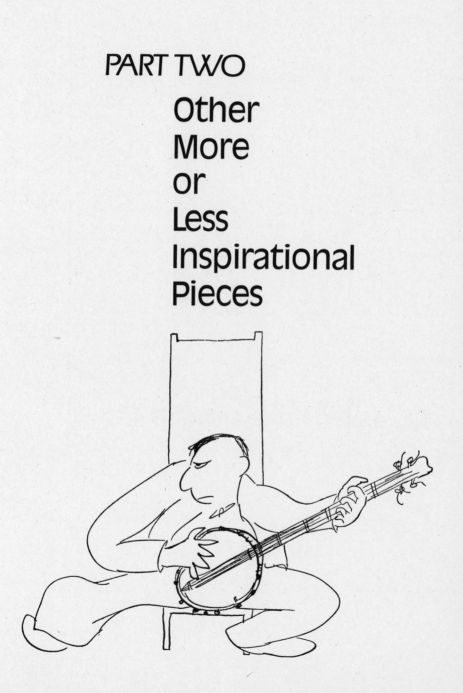

The Breaking Up of the Winships

THE TROUBLE that broke up the Gordon Winships seemed to me, at first, as minor a problem as frost on a windowpane. Another day, a touch of sun, and it would be gone. I was inclined to laugh it off, and, indeed, as a friend of both Gordon and Marcia, I spent a great deal of time with each of them, separately, trying to get them to laugh it off, too—with him at his club, where he sat drinking Scotch and smoking too much, and with her in their apartment, that seemed so large and lonely without Gordon and his restless moving around and his quick laughter. But it was no good; they were both adamant. Their separation has lasted now more than six months. I doubt very much that they will ever go back together again.

It all started one night at Leonardo's, after dinner, over their Bénédictine. It all started innocently enough, amiably even, with laughter from both of them, laughter that froze finally as the clock ran on and their words came out sharp and flat and stinging. They had been to see "Camille." Gordon hadn't liked it very much. Marcia had been crazy about it because she is crazy about Greta Garbo. She belongs to that considerable army of Garbo admirers whose enchantment borders almost on fanaticism and sometimes even touches the edges of frenzy. I think that, before everything happened, Gordon admired Garbo, too, but the depth of his wife's conviction that here was the greatest figure ever seen in our generation on sea or land, on screen or stage, exasperated him that night. Gordon hates (or used to) exaggeration, and he respects (or once did) detachment. It was his feeling that detachment is a necessary thread in the fabric of a woman's charm. He didn't like to see his wife get herself "into a sweat" over anything and, that night at Leonardo's, he unfortunately used that expression and made that accusation.

Marcia responded, as I get it, by saying, a little loudly (they had gone on to Scotch and soda), that a man who had no abandon of feeling and no passion for anything was not altogether a man, and that his so-called love of detachment simply covered up a lack of critical appreciation and understanding of the arts in general. Her sentences were becoming long and wavy, her words formal. Gordon suddenly began to pooh-pooh her; he kept saying "Pooh!" (an annoying mannerism of his, I have always thought). He wouldn't answer her arguments or even listen to them. That, of course, infuriated her. "Oh, pooh to you, too!" she finally more or less shouted. He snapped at her, "Quiet, for God's sake! You're yelling like a prizefight manager!" Enraged at that, she had recourse to her eyes as weapons and looked steadily at him for a while with the expression of one who is viewing a small and horrible animal, such as a horned toad. They then sat in moody and brooding silence for a long time, without moving a muscle, at the end of which, getting a hold on herself, Marcia asked him, quietly enough, just exactly what actor on the screen or on the stage, living or dead, he considered greater than Garbo. Gordon thought a moment and then said, as quietly as she had put the question, "Donald Duck." I don't believe that he meant it at the time, or even thought that he meant it. However that may have been, she looked at him scornfully and said that that speech

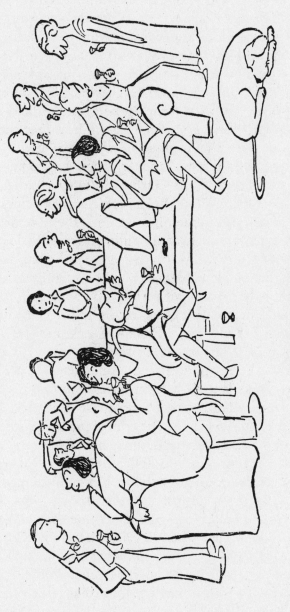

COCKTAIL PARTY, 1937.

just about perfectly represented the shallowness of his intellect and the small range of his imagination. Gordon asked her not to make a spectacle of herself—she had raised her voice slightly—and went on to say that her failure to see the genius of Donald Duck proved conclusively to him that she was a woman without humor. That, he said, he had always suspected; now, he said, he knew it. She had a great desire to hit him, but instead she sat back and looked at him with her special Mona Lisa smile, a smile rather more of contempt than, as in the original, of mystery. Gordon hated that smile, so he said that Donald Duck happened to be exactly ten times as great as Garbo would ever be and that anybody with a brain in his head would admit it instantly. Thus the Winships went on and on, their resentment swelling, their sense of values blurring, until it ended up with her taking a taxi home alone (leaving her vanity bag and one glove behind her in the restaurant) and with him making the rounds of the late places and rolling up to his club around dawn. There, as he got out, he asked his taxi-driver which he liked better, Greta Garbo or Donald Duck, and the driver said he liked Greta Garbo best. Gordon said to him, bitterly, "Pooh to you, too, my good friend!" and went to bed.

The next day, as is usual with married couples, they were both contrite, but behind their contrition lay sleeping the ugly words each had used and the cold glances and the bitter gestures. She phoned him, because she was worried. She didn't want to be, but she was. When he hadn't come home, she was convinced he had gone to his club, but visions of him lying in a gutter or under a table, somehow horribly mangled, haunted her, and so at eight o'clock she called him up. Her heart lightened when he said, "Hullo," gruffly: he was alive, thank God! His heart may have lightened a little, too, but not very much, because he felt terrible. He felt terrible and he felt that it was her fault that he felt terrible. She said that she was sorry and that they had both been very silly, and he growled something about he was glad she realized *she'd* been silly, anyway. That attitude put a slight edge on the rest of her words. She asked him shortly if he was coming home. He said sure he was coming home; it was his home, wasn't it? She told him to go back to bed and not be such an old bear, and hung up.

The next incident occurred at the Clarkes' party a few days later. The Winships had arrived in fairly good spirits to find themselves in a buzzing group of cocktail-drinkers that more or less revolved around the tall and languid figure of the guest of honor, an eminent lady novelist. Gordon late in the evening won her attention and drew her apart for one drink together and, feeling a little high and happy at that time, as is the way with husbands, mentioned lightly enough (he wanted to get it out of his subconscious), the argument that he and his wife had had about the relative merits of Garbo and Duck. The tall lady, lowering her cigarette-holder, said, in the spirit of his own gaiety, that he could count her in on his side. Unforntuately, Marcia Winship, standing some ten feet away, talking to a man with a beard, caught not the spirit but only a few of the words of the conversation, and jumped to the conclusion that her husband was deliberately reopening the old wound, for the purpose of humiliating her in public. I think that in another moment Gordon might have brought her over, and put his arm around her, and admitted his "defeat"—he was feeling pretty fine. But when he caught her eye, she gazed through him, freezingly, and his heart went down. And then his anger rose.

Their fight, naturally enough, blazed out again in the taxi they took to go home from the party. Marcia wildly attacked the woman novelist (Marcia had had quite a few cocktails), defended Garbo, excoriated Gordon, and laid into Donald Duck. Gordon tried for a while to explain exactly what had happened, and then he met her resentment with a resentment that mounted even higher, the resentment of the misunderstood husband. In the midst of it all she slapped him. He looked at her for a second under lowered eyelids and then said, coldly, if a bit fuzzily, "This is the end, but I want you to go to your grave knowing that Donald Duck is *twenty times* the artist Garbo will ever be, the longest day you, or she, ever live, if you *do*—and I can't understand, with so little to live for, why you should!" Then he asked the driver to stop the car, and he got out, in wavering dignity. "Caricature! Cartoon!" she screamed after him. "You and Donald Duck both, you—" The driver drove on.

The last time I saw Gordon—he moved his things to the club the next day, forgetting the trousers to his evening clothes and his razor—he had convinced himself that the point at issue between him and Marcia was one of extreme importance involving both his honor and his integrity. He said that now it could never be wiped out and forgotten. He said that he sincerely believed Donald Duck was as great a creation as any animal in all the works of Lewis Carroll, probably even greater, perhaps much greater. He was drinking and there was a wild light in his eye. I reminded him of his old love of detachment, and he said to the hell with detachment. I laughed at him, but he wouldn't laugh. "If," he said, grimly, "Marcia persists in her silly belief that the Swede is great and that Donald Duck is merely a caricature, I cannot conscientiously live with her again. I believe that he is great, that the man who created him is a genius, probably our only genius. I believe, further, that Greta Garbo is just another actress. As God is my judge, I believe that! What does she expect me to do, go whining back to her and pretend that I think Garbo is wonderful and that Donald Duck is simply a cartoon? Never!" He gulped down some Scotch straight. "Never!" I could not ridicule him out of his obsession. I left him and went over to see Marcia.

I found Marcia pale, but calm, and as firm in her stand as Gordon was in his. She insisted that he had deliberately tried to humiliate her before that gawky so-called novelist, whose clothes were the dowdiest she had ever seen and whose affectations obviously covered up a complete lack of individuality and intelligence. I tried to convince her that she was wrong about Gordon's attitude at the Clarkes' party, but she said she knew him like a book. Let him get a divorce and marry that creature if he wanted to. They can sit around all day, she said, and all night, too, for all I care, and talk about their precious Donald Duck, the damn comic strip! I told Marcia that she shouldn't allow herself to get so worked up about a trivial and nonsensical matter. She said it was not silly and nonsensical to her. It might have been once, yes, but it wasn't now. It had made her see Gordon clearly for what he was, a cheap, egotistical, resentful cad who would descend to ridiculing his wife in front of a scrawny, horrible stranger who could not write and never would be able to write. Furthermore, her belief in Garbo's greatness was a thing she could not deny and would not deny, simply for the sake of living under the same roof with Gordon Winship. The whole thing was part and parcel of her integrity as a woman and as an—as an, well, as a woman. She could go to work again; he would find out.

There was nothing more that I could say or do. I went home. That night, however, I found that I had not really dismissed the whole ridiculous affair, as I hoped I had, for I dreamed about it. I had tried to ignore the thing, but it had tunnelled deeply into my subconscious. I dreamed that I was out hunting with the Winships and that, as we crossed a snowy field, Marcia spotted a rabbit and, taking quick aim, fired and brought it down. We all ran across the snow toward the rabbit, but I reached it first. It was quite dead, but that was not what struck horror into me as I picked it up. What struck horror into me was that it was a white rabbit and was wearing a vest and carrying a watch. I woke up with a start. I don't know whether that dream means that I am on Gordon's side or on Marcia's. I don't want to analyze it. I am trying to forget the whole miserable business.

My Memories of D. H. Lawrence

IF YOU wander around in bookstores you will have come upon several books about D. H. Lawrence: Mr. John Middleton Murry's autobiography, Frieda Lawrence's memoirs, Keith Winter's *roman à clef* called "Impassioned Pygmies," etc. These are all comparatively recent; a complete bibliography going back to the time of Lawrence's death would run into hundreds of items, maybe thousands. The writing man is pretty much out of it if he hasn't written something about how hard it was to understand, to talk to, and to get along generally with D. H. Lawrence; and I do not propose to be out of it. I had my difficult moments on account of the Master, and I intend to tell about them—if Mr. Murry will quit talking for a moment and let me talk.

I first met D. H. Lawrence on a train platform in Italy twelve years ago. He was pacing up and down. There was no mistaking the reddish, scraggly beard, the dark, beetling eyebrows, the intense, restless eyes. He had the manner of a man who was waiting for something; in this case, I think it was the train. I had always wanted to meet the great artist and here was my golden opportunity. I finally screwed my courage up to the accosting point and I walked over and accosted him. "D. H. Lawrence?" I said. He frowned, stopped, pulled a watch out of his vest pocket, and held it up to me so that I could see the dial. "No speak Eyetalian," he said. "Look for yourself." Then he walked away. It had been about 10:12 or 10:13 A.M. by his watch (I had 10:09 myself, but I may have been slow). Since we both got on the train that pulled into the station a few minutes later, I contrived to get into the same compartment with him and to sit down next to him. I found him quite easy to talk to. He seemed surprised that I spoke English—on the platform he had taken me for an Italian who wanted to know what time it was. It turned out after a few minutes of rather puzzling conversa-

DR. KARNS.

tion that his name was George R. Hopkins and that he had
never heard of D. H. Lawrence. Hopkins was a resident of
Fitchburg, Massachusetts, where he had a paper factory. He
wished to God he was back in the United States. He was a
strong Coolidge man, thought every French person was
depraved, and hadn't been able to find a decent cup of coffee
in all Europe. He had a married daughter, and two sons in
Penn State, and had been having trouble with a molar in his
lower jaw ever since he arrived at Le Havre, some three
weeks before. He wouldn't let anybody monkey with it, he
said, except a certain Dr. Karns in Fitchburg. Karns was an
Elk and a bird-dog fancier in addition to being the best
dentist in the United States.

This encounter did not discourage me. I determined to
meet D. H. Lawrence before I came back to America, and
eventually I sat down and wrote him a note, asking him for
the opportunity of meeting him (I had found out where he

was living at the time—in Florence, I believe, though I may be wrong). I explained that I was a great admirer of his—I addressed him simply as Dear Master—and that I had some ideas about sex which I thought might interest him. Lawrence never received the letter, it transpired later, because I had unfortunately put it in the wrong envelope. He got instead a rather sharp note which I had written the same evening to a psychoanalyst in New York who had offered to analyze me at half his usual price. This analyst had come across some sketches I had made and had apparently jumped to the conclusion that it would be interesting to try to get at what was behind them. I had addressed this man in my note simply as "sir" and I told him that if he wanted to analyze somebody he had better begin with himself, since it was my opinion there was something the matter with him. As for me, I said, there was nothing the matter with me. This, of course, was the letter that Lawrence got, owing to the shifting of envelopes, and I was later to understand why I never heard from Lawrence and also why I kept hearing from the analyst all the time. I hung around Europe for several months waiting for a letter from Lawrence, and finally came home, in a low state of mind.

I eventually met, or rather talked with, D. H. Lawrence about six months after I got back to New York. He telephoned me one evening at my apartment. "Hello" I said into the transmitter. "Hello," a voice said. "Is this Mr. Thurber?" "Yes," I said. "Well, this is D. H. Lawrence," said the voice. I was taken back; for a moment I couldn't say a word, I was so surprised and excited. "Well, well," I said, finally, "I didn't know you were on this side." "This is the right side to be on, isn't it?" he asked, in a rather strained voice (I felt that he was excited, too). "Yes, it is," I said. "Well," said Lawrence, "they turned me over on my right side because my left side hurts me so." Thereupon he began to sing "Frankie and Johnny." He turned out to be a waggish friend of mine who had heard my stories about trying to get in touch with D. H. Lawrence, and was having me on.

I never did get to meet D. H. Lawrence, but this I rarely admit. Whenever I am at a cocktail party of literary people and the subject of Lawrence comes up, I tell my own little anecdote about the Master: how he admired Coolidge, how he had trouble with his teeth, how he liked to sing "Frankie and Johnny." These anecdotes are gaining considerable currency and I have no doubt that they will begin to creep into autobiographies of the man in a short time. Meanwhile I have become what you could almost call allergic to famous writers. I suppose this is the natural outgrowth of my curious and somewhat disturbing relationship with D. H. Lawrence. I cannot truthfully say that any part of that relationship was satisfactory, and therefore I am trying to forget D. H. Lawrence, which makes me about the only writer in the world who is. It is a distinction of a sort.

The Case Against Women

A BRIGHT-EYED woman, whose sparkle was rather more of eagerness than of intelligence, approached me at a party one afternoon and said, "Why do you hate women, Mr. Thurberg?" I quickly adjusted my fixed grin and denied that I hated women; I said I did not hate women at all. But the question remained with me, and I discovered when I went to bed that night that I had been subconsciously listing a number of reasons I do hate women. It might be interesting—at least it will help pass the time—to set down these reasons, just as they came up out of my subconscious.

In the first place, I hate women because they always know

where things are. At first blush, you might think that a perverse and merely churlish reason for hating women, but it is not. Naturally, every man enjoys having a woman around the house who knows where his shirt studs and his briefcase are, and things like that, but he detests having a woman around who knows where *everything* is, even things that are of no importance at all, such as, say, the snapshots her husband took three years ago at Elbow Beach. The husband has never known where these snapshots were since the day they were developed and printed; he hopes, in a vague way, if he thinks about them at all, that after three years they have been thrown out. But his wife knows where they are, and so do his mother, his grandmother, his great-grandmother, his daughter, and the maid. They could put their fingers on them in a moment, with that quiet air of superior knowledge which makes a man feel that he is out of touch with all the things that count in life.

A man's interest in old snapshots, unless they are snapshots of himself in action with a gun, a fishing rod, or a tennis racquet, languishes in about two hours. A woman's interest in old shapshots, particularly of groups of people, never languishes; it is always there, as the years roll on, as strong and vivid as it was right at the start. She remembers the snapshots when people come to call, and just as the husband, having mixed drinks for everybody, sits down to sip his own, she will say, "George, I wish you would go and get those snapshots we took at Elbow Beach and show them to the Murphys." The husband, as I have said, doesn't know where the snapshots are; all he knows is that Harry Murphy doesn't want to see them; Harry Murphy wants to talk, just as he himself wants to talk. But Grace Murphy says that she wants to see the pictures; she is crazy to see the pictures; for one thing, the wife, who has brought the subject up, wants Mrs. Murphy to see the photo of a certain costume that the wife wore at Elbow Beach in 1933. The husband finally puts down his drink and snarls, "Well, where are they, then?" The wife, depending on her mood, gives him either the look she reserves for spoiled children or the one she reserves for drunken workmen, and tells him he knows perfectly well where they are. It turns out, after a lot of give and take, the slightly bitter edge of which is covered by forced laughs, that the snapshots are in the upper right-hand drawer of a certain desk, and the husband goes out of the room to get them. He comes back in three minutes with the news that the snapshots are not in the upper right-hand drawer of the certain desk. Without stirring from her chair, the wife favors her husband with a faint smile (the one that annoys him most of all her smiles) and reiterates that the snapshots *are* in the upper right-hand drawer of the desk. He simply didn't look, that's all. The husband knows that he looked; he knows that he prodded and dug and excavated in that drawer and that the snapshots simply are not there. The wife tells him to go look again and he will find them. The husband goes back and looks again—the guests can hear him growling and cursing and rattling papers. Then he shouts out from the next room. "They are *not* in this *drawer*, just as I told you, Ruth!" The wife quietly excuses herself and leaves the guests and goes into the room where her husband stands, hot, miserable, and defiant—and with a certain nameless fear in his heart. He has pulled the desk drawer out so far that it is about to fall on the floor, and he points at the disarray of the drawer with bitter triumph (still mixed with that nameless fear). "Look for yourself!" he snarls. The wife does not look. She says with quiet coldness, "What is that you have in your hand?" What he has in his hand turns out to be an insurance policy and an old bankbook—and the snapshots. The wife gets off the old line about what it would have done if it had been a snake, and the husband is upset for the rest of the evening; in some cases he cannot keep anything on his stomach for twenty-four hours.

Another reason I hate women (and I am speaking, I believe, for the American male generally) is that in almost every case where there is a sign reading "Please have exact change ready," a woman never has anything smaller than a ten-dollar bill. She gives ten-dollar bills to bus conductors and change men in subways and other such persons who deal in nickels and dimes and quarters. Recently, in Bermuda, I saw a woman hand the conductor on the little railway there a bill of such huge denomination that I was utterly unfamiliar with it. I was sitting too far away to see exactly what it was, but I had the feeling that it was a five-hundred-dollar bill. The conductor merely ignored it and stood there waiting—the fare was just one shilling. Eventually, scrabbling around in her handbag, the woman found a shilling. All the men on the train who witnessed the transaction tightened up inside; that's what a woman with a ten-dollar bill or a twenty or a five-hundred does to a man in such situations—she tightens him up inside. The episode gives him the feeling that some monstrous triviality is threatening the whole structure of civilization. It is difficult to analyze this feeling, but there it is.

Another spectacle that depresses the male and makes him fear women, and therefore hate them, is that of a woman looking another woman up and down, to see what she is wearing. The cold, flat look that comes into a woman's eyes when she does this, the swift coarsening of her countenance, and the immediate evaporation from it of all humane quality make the male shudder.He is likely to go to his stateroom or his den or his private office and lock himself in for hours. I know one man who surprised that look in his wife's eyes and never afterward would let her come near him. If she started toward him, he would dodge behind a table or a sofa, as if he were engaging in some unholy game of tag. That look, I believe, is one reason men disappear, and turn up in Tahiti or the Arctic or the United States Navy.

I (to quit hiding behind the generalization of "the male") hate women because they almost never get anything exactly right. They say, "I have been faithful to thee, Cynara, after

THE COLD, FLAT LOOK.

my fashion" instead of "in my fashion." They will bet you
that Alfred Smith's middle name is Aloysius, instead of
Emanuel. They will tell you to take the 2:57 train, on a day
that the 2:57 does not run, or, if it does run, does not stop at
the station where you are supposed to get off. Many men,
separated from a woman by this particular form of impre-
cision, have never showed up in her life again. Nothing so
embitters a man as to end up in Bridgeport when he was
supposed to get off at Westport.

I hate women because they have brought into the currency
of our language such expressions as "all righty" and "yes
indeedy" and hundreds of others. I hate women because they
throw baseballs (or plates or vases) with the wrong foot
advanced. I marvel that more of them have not broken their
backs. I marvel that women, who coordinate so well in
languorous motion, look uglier and sillier than a goose-
stepper when they attempt any form of violent activity.

I had a lot of other notes jotted down about why I hate women, but I seem to have lost them all, except one. That one is to the effect that I hate women because, while they never lose old snapshots or anything of that sort, they invariably lose one glove. I believe that I have never gone anywhere with any woman in my whole life who did not lose one glove. I have searched for single gloves under tables in crowded restaurants and under the feet of people in darkened movie theatres. I have spent some part of every day or night hunting for a woman's glove. If there were no other reason in the world for hating women, that one would be enough. In fact, you can leave all the others out.

No Standing Room Only

THE THEATRE page of the "World-Telegram" carried this little note one evening: "Saturday afternoon was something of an event at the Broadhurst, for 'Victoria Regina' had just rounded out fifty-two weeks on Broadway and Helen Hayes, the sentimentalist, wanted to do something to celebrate the occasion. So she called Harry Essex, the company manager, backstage and suggested that only fifty-two standees be admitted into the matinee. By curtain rise only that number of vertical playgoers were allowed into the playhouse; those turned away got no explanation from the box office."

Robert Browning says somewhere in his poems that Providence often seems to "let twenty pass and stone the twenty-first." Miss Hayes goes Providence thirty-two better and thus is about two and a half times as lenient. She didn't have the fifty-third man stoned, either, or otherwise roughly handled, but he must have been just about as bewildered and sore as if he had been. To celebrate the anniversary of a popular play by refusing to let certain people in to see it sets a new precedent for celebrations, particularly sentimental celebrations. I somehow have the idea that Harry Essex, the company manager, didn't really understand what Miss Hayes said. I think she probably suggested that the first fifty-two persons who asked for standing room be let in free. That's more along the old, established lines of celebration and sentiment, and sounds more like Miss Hayes, somehow. I don't know whether it sounds like Mr. Essex or not, but I imagine it doesn't. I never heard of a company manager who would let fifty-two people in free; on the other hand, I never heard of one who would keep people out when they wanted to pay to get in. Of course, it may be that the box-office man got mixed up on his instructions, but that doesn't sound like a box-office man. I don't suppose we will ever get to the bottom of it all, but I can't help wondering what happened when the fifty-third person showed up and wanted to pay to get into the show. Let us try to reconstruct his conversation with the box-office man:

MR. FIFTY-THREE: I want a ticket, please.

BOX-OFFICE MAN: Standing room only.

MR. FIFTY-THREE: All right, give me standing room.

BOX-OFFICE MAN: But—uh—I just remembered—there is standing room but I can't sell you any.

MR. FIFTY-THREE: What did you say?

BOX-OFFICE MAN: I say there is standing room but I can't sell you any.

MR. FIFTY-THREE: I don't get it. It sounds as if you kept saying there is standing room but you can't sell me any.

BOX-OFFICE MAN: That's what I said.

MR. FIFTY-THREE: Well, say it again. Some other way.

BOX-OFFICE MAN: All I have is no standing room. No standing room only.

MR. FIFTY-THREE: Huh?

BOX-OFFICE MAN: Look—if you come back *next* Saturday, or even tonight, I could let you in even if it were more

crowded in there than it is now, but I can't tell you why.

MR. FIFTY-THREE: I want to get in now. I'd rather stand when there are fewer standees.

BOX-OFFICE MAN: I can't let you in.

MR. FIFTY-THREE: Why can't you?

BOX-OFFICE MAN: I just can't, that's all.

MR. FIFTY-THREE: What's the matter with me?

BOX-OFFICE MAN: Nothing's the matter with you.

MR. FIFTY-THREE: Well, something must be the matter with somebody.

BOX-OFFICE MAN: No, nothing's the matter, exactly.

MR. FIFTY-THREE: Well, *approximately*, what's the matter?

BOX-OFFICE MAN: I can't sell you a ticket to stand.

MR. FIFTY-THREE: You sold the man right ahead of me standing room, because I saw you.

BOX-OFFICE MAN: If he'd been behind you, *you* could have got in, but *he* couldn't.

MR. FIFTY-THREE: Are you Charles MacArthur?

BOX-OFFICE MAN: No.

MR. FIFTY-THREE: Why? Why? Why?

BOX-OFFICE MAN: Because I'm not.

MR. FIFTY-THREE: No, no, I mean why can't I *get in*?

BOX-OFFICE MAN: I can't tell you. I can't give any explanation.

MR. FIFTY-THREE: Do you *know* why I can't get in?

BOX-OFFICE MAN: I don't want to talk about it.

By this time, Mrs. Fifty-four and Mrs. Fifty-five, and a lot of other women on up to Mrs. Seventy-two, are pushing, and they finally dislodge Mr. Fifty-three and demand standing room. The box-office man has to get rid of them, which is harder than getting rid of Mr. Fifty-three, lots harder. Just how many bewildered people were turned away in all on this sentimental occasion, I don't know, but I'm glad I wasn't the box-office man.

The American Airlines, now, has the good old-fashioned

idea of celebrating a sentimental occasion. They recently decided to give a prize to the millionth person who chanced to show up and ask for passage on one of their planes. Up showed the lucky Mr. Theodore Colcord Baker. He was given a free trip to Europe on the Hindenburg and a thousand dollars in cash. It would take a hundred thousand dollars to get me to ride on the Hindenburg or any other Zeppelin, but that is beside the point. The point is that when Mr. Baker showed up he wasn't told that American Airlines wouldn't let him ride on one of their planes. The sentiment of that would have been lost on Mr. Baker, even if it had been explained to him. It would have been lost on Miss Hayes and Mr. Essex, too, particularly if they were in a hurry to fly somewhere. Of course, if Mr. Fifty-three had been in a hurry to see "Victoria Regina" he probably wouldn't have waited a year, but the sentiment in both cases is the same. I'm not trying to compare a plane ride to a matinée, I'm trying to compare Helen Hayes to American Airlines; even so, I would be the last to say that Miss Hayes should have given anyone a thousand dollars. I just think she should have let Mr. Fifty-three in.

I've brooded about this affair for quite a few days and nights now, and out of it I have hit on a kind of revenge for Mr. Fifty-three, if he still is as mad as I think he is. My plan would be hard to work but it would be a lot of fun. In "Victoria Regina," as you know, Prince Albert dies, rather early in the play. Now my idea is to have Mr. Fifty-three, if he has any spunk at all, don the uniform of a court announcer some Saturday afternoon, put on makeup, slip backstage when nobody is looking, and, in the scene after Albert's death, walk boldly onstage and, with a gesture toward the door, say, loudly, "The Royal Consort, Prince Albert!" They would either have to ring the curtain down or else Mr. Vincent Price, who plays Prince Albert, would have to walk on again, as fit as a fiddle but with nothing to say, except maybe that he was feeling a lot better than he had been. That would put Miss Hayes in a very sentimental spot. But perhaps I have brooded about the whole business too long. I guess I have.

Nine Needles

ONE OF the more spectacular minor happenings of the past few years which I am sorry that I missed took place in the Columbus, Ohio, home of some friends of a friend of mine. It seems that a Mr. Albatross, while looking for something in his medicine cabinet one morning, discovered a bottle of a kind of patent medicine which his wife had been taking for a stomach ailment. Now, Mr. Albatross is one of those apprehensive men who are afraid of patent medicines and of almost everything else. Some weeks before, he had encountered a paragraph in a Consumers' Research bulletin which announced that this particular medicine was bad for you. He had thereupon ordered his wife to throw out what was left of her supply of the stuff and never buy any more. She had promised, and here now was another bottle of the perilous liquid. Mr. Albatross, a man given to quick rages, shouted the conclusion of the story at my friend: "I threw the bottle out the bathroom window and the medicine chest after it!" It seems to me that must have been a spectacle worth going a long way to see.

I am sure that many a husband has wanted to wrench the family medicine cabinet off the wall and throw it out the window, if only because the average medicine cabinet is so filled with mysterious bottles and unidentifiable objects of all kinds that it is a source of constant bewilderment and exasperation to the American male. Surely the British medicine cabinet and the French medicine cabinet and all the other medicine cabinets must be simpler and better ordered than ours. It may be that the American habit of saving everything and never throwing anything away, even empty bottles, causes the domestic medicine cabinet to become as cluttered in its small way as the American attic becomes cluttered in its major way. I have encountered few medicine cabinets in this country which were not pack-jammed with something between a hundred and fifty and two hundred different items, from dental floss to boracic acid, from razor blades to sodium perborate, from adhesive tape to coconut oil. Even the neatest wife will put off clearing out the medicine cabinet on the ground that she has something else to do that is more important at the moment, or more diverting. It was in the apartment of such a wife and her husband that I became enormously involved with a medicine cabinet one morning not long ago.

I had spent the weekend with this couple—they live on East Tenth Street near Fifth Avenue—such a weekend as left me reluctant to rise up on Monday morning with bright and shining face and go to work. They got up and went to work, but I didn't. I didn't get up until about two-thirty in the afternoon. I had my face all lathered for shaving and the washbowl was full of hot water when suddenly I cut myself with the razor. I cut my ear. Very few men cut their ears with razors, but I do, possibly because I was taught the old Spencerian free-wrist movement by my writing teacher in the grammar grades. The ear bleeds rather profusely when cut with a razor and is difficult to get at. More angry than hurt, I jerked open the door of the medicine cabinet to see if I could find a styptic pencil and out fell, from the top shelf, a little black paper packet containing nine needles. It seems that this wife kept a little paper packet containing nine needles on the top shelf of the medicine cabinet. The packet fell into the soapy water of the washbowl, where the paper rapidly disintegrated, leaving nine needles at large in the bowl. I was,

"AND THE MEDICINE CHEST AFTER IT!"

naturally enough, not in the best condition, either physical or mental, to recover nine needles from a washbowl. No gentleman who has lather on his face and whose ear is bleeding is in the best condition for anything, even something involving the handling of nine large blunt objects.

It did not seem wise to me to pull the plug out of the washbowl and let the needles go down the drain. I had visions of clogging up the plumbing system of the house, and also a vague fear of causing short circuits somehow or other (I know very little about electricity and I don't want to have it explained to me). Finally, I groped very gently around the bowl and eventually had four of the needles in the palm of one hand and three in the palm of the other—two I couldn't find. If I had thought quickly and clearly, I wouldn't have done that. A lathered man whose ear is bleeding and who has four wet needles in one hand and three in the other may be said to have reached the lowest known point of human efficiency. There is nothing he can do but stand there. I tried transferring the needles in my left hand to the palm of my right hand, but I couldn't get them off my left hand. Wet needles cling to you. In the end, I wiped the needles off onto a bathtowel which was hanging on a rod above the bathtub. It was the only towel that I could find. I had to dry my hands afterward on the bathmat. Then I tried to find the needles in the towel. Hunting for seven needles in a bathtowel is the most tedious occupation I have ever engaged in. I could find only five of them. With the two that had been left in the bowl, that meant there were four needles in all missing—two in the washbowl and two others lurking in the towel or lying in the bathtub under the towel. Frightful thoughts came to me of what might happen to anyone who used that towel or washed his face in the bowl or got into the tub, if I didn't find the missing needles. Well, I didn't find them. I sat down on the edge of the tub to think, and I decided finally that the only thing to do was wrap up the towel in a newspaper and take it away with me. I also decided to leave a note for my friends explaining as clearly as I could that I was afraid there were two needles in the bathtub and two needles in the washbowl, and that they better be careful.

I looked everywhere in the apartment, but I could not find a pencil, or a pen, or a typewriter. I could find pieces of paper, but nothing with which to write on them. I don't know what gave me the idea—a movie I had seen, perhaps, or a story I had read—but I suddenly thought of writing a message with a lipstick. The wife might have an extra lipstick lying around and, if so, I concluded it would be in the medicine cabinet. I went back to the medicine cabinet and began poking around in it for a lipstick. I saw what I thought looked like the metal tip of one, and I got two fingers around it and began to pull gently—it was under a lot of things. Every object in the medicine cabinet began to slide. Bottles broke in the washbowl and on the floor; red, brown, and white liquids spurted; nail files, scissors, razor blades, and miscellaneous objects sang and clattered and tinkled. I was covered with perfume, peroxide, and cold cream.

It took me half an hour to get the debris all together in the middle of the bathroom floor. I made no attempt to put anything back in the medicine cabinet. I knew it would take a steadier hand than mine and a less shattered spirit. Before I went away (only partly shaved) and abandoned the shambles, I left a note saying that I was afraid there were needles in the bathtub and the washbowl and that I had taken their towel and that I would call up and tell them everything—I wrote it in iodine with the end of a toothbrush. I have not yet called up, I am sorry to say. I have neither found the courage nor thought up the words to explain what happened. I suppose my friends believe that I deliberately smashed up their bathroom and stole their towel. I don't know for sure, because they have not yet called me up, either.

A Couple of Hamburgers

IT HAD been raining for a long time, a slow, cold rain falling out of iron-colored clouds. They had been driving since morning and they still had a hundred and thirty miles to go. It was about three o'clock in the afternoon. "I'm getting hungry," she said. He took his eyes off the wet, winding road for a fraction of a second and said, "We'll stop at a dog-wagon." She shifted her position irritably. "I wish you wouldn't call them *dog*-wagons," she said. He pressed the klaxon button and went around a slow car. "That's what they are," he said. "Dog-wagons." She waited a few seconds. "*Decent* people call them *diners*," she told him, and added, "Even if you call them diners, I don't like them." He speeded up a hill. "They have better stuff than most restaurants," he said. "Anyway, I want to get home before dark and it takes too long in a restaurant. We can stay our stomachs with a couple hamburgers." She lighted a cigarette and he asked her to light one for him. She lighted one deliberately and handed it to him. "I wish you wouldn't say 'stay our stomachs,'" she said. "You know I hate that. It's like 'sticking to your ribs.' You say that all the time." He grinned. "Good old American expressions, both of them," he said. "Like sow belly. Old pioneer term, sow belly." She sniffed. "My ancestors were pioneers, too. You don't have to be vulgar just because you were a pioneer." "Your ancestors never got as far west as mine did," he said. "The real pioneers travelled on their sow belly and got somewhere." He laughed loudly at that. She looked out at the wet trees and signs and telephone poles going by. They drove on for several miles without a word; he kept chortling every now and then.

"What's that funny sound?" she asked, suddenly. It invariably made him angry when she heard a funny sound. "What funny sound?" he demanded. "You're always hearing funny sounds." She laughed briefly. "That's what you said when the bearing burned out," she reminded him. "You'd never have noticed it if it hadn't been for me." "I noticed it, all right," he said. "Yes," she said. "When it was too late." She enjoyed bringing up the subject of the burned-out bearing whenever he got to chortling. "It was too late when *you* noticed it, as far as that goes," he said. Then, after a pause, "Well, what does it sound like *this* time? All engines make a noise running, you know." "I know all about that,"

she answered. "It sounds like—it sounds like a lot of safety pins being jiggled around in a tumbler." He snorted. "That's your imagination. Nothing gets the matter with a car that sounds like a lot of safety pins. I happen to know that." She tossed away her cigarette. "Oh, sure," she said. "You always happen to know everything." They drove on in silence.

"I want to stop somewhere and get something to *eat*!" she said loudly. "All right, all right!" he said. "I been watching for a dog-wagon, haven't I? There hasn't been any. I can't make you a dog-wagon." The wind blew rain in on her and she put up the window on her side all the way. "I won't stop at just any old diner," she said. "I won't stop unless it's a cute one." He looked around at her. "Unless it's a *what* one?" he shouted. "You know what I mean," she said. "I mean a decent, clean one where they don't slosh things at you. I hate to have a lot of milky coffee sloshed at me." "All right," he said. "We'll find a cute one, then. You pick it out. I wouldn't know. I might find one that was cunning but not cute." That struck him as funny and he began to chortle again. "Oh, shut up," she said.

Five miles farther along they came to a place called Sam's Diner. "Here's one," he said, slowing down. She looked it over. "I don't want to stop there," she said. "I don't like the ones that have nicknames." He brought the car to a stop at one side of the road. "Just what's the matter with the ones that have nicknames?" he asked with edgy, mock interest. "They're always Greek ones," she told him. "They're always Greek ones," he repeated after her. He set his teeth firmly together and started up again. After a time "Good old Sam, the Greek," he said, in a singsong. "Good old Connecticut Sam Beardsley, the Greek." "You didn't see his name," she snapped. "Winthrop, then," he said. "Old Samuel Cabot Winthrop, the Greek dog-wagon man." He was getting hungry.

On the outskirts of the next town she said, as he slowed down, "It looks like a factory kind of town." He knew that she meant she wouldn't stop there. He drove on through the place. She lighted a cigarette as they pulled out into the open again. He slowed down and lighted a cigarette for himself. "Factory kind of town than *I* am!" he snarled. It was ten miles before they came to another town. "Torrington," he growled. "Happen to know there's a dog-wagon here because I stopped in it once with Bob Combs. Damn cute place, too, if you ask me." "I'm not asking you anything," she said, coldly. "You think you're *so* funny. I think I know the one you mean," she said, after a moment. "It's right in the town and it sits at an angle from the road. They're never so good, for some reason." He glared at her and almost ran up against the curb. "What the hell do you mean 'sits at an angle from the road'?" he cried. He was very hungry now. "Well, it isn't silly," she said, calmly. "I've noticed the ones that sit at an angle. They're cheaper, because they fitted them into funny little pieces of ground. The big ones parallel to the road are the best." He drove right through Torrington, his lips compressed. "Angle from the *road*, for God's sake!" he snarled, finally. She was looking out her window.

On the outskirts of the next town there was a diner called The Elite Diner. "This looks—" she began. "I see it, I see it!" he said. "It doesn't happen to look any cuter to me than any goddam—" she cut him off. "Don't be such a sorehead, for Lord's sake," she said. He pulled up and stopped beside the diner, and turned on her. "Listen," he said, grittingly, "I'm going to put down a couple of hamburgers in this place even if there isn't one single inch of chintz or cretonne in the whole—" "Oh, be still," she said. "You're just hungry and mean like a child. Eat your old hamburgers, what do I care?" Inside the place they sat down on stools and the counterman walked over to them, wiping up the counter top with a cloth as he did so. "What'll it be, folks?" he said. "Bad day, ain't it? Except for ducks." "I'll have a couple of—" began the husband, but his wife cut in. "I just want a pack of cigarettes," she said. He turned around slowly on his stool and stared at her as she put a dime and a nickel in the cigarette machine and ejected a package of Lucky Strikes. He turned to the counterman again. "I want a couple of hamburgers," he said. "With mustard and lots of onion. *Lots* of onion!" She hated onions. "I'll wait for you in the car," she said. He didn't answer and she went out.

He finished his hamburgers and his coffee slowly. It was terrible coffee. Then he went out to the car and got in and drove off, slowly humming "Who's Afraid of the Big Bad

Wolf?" After a mile or so, "Well," he said, "what was the matter with the Elite Diner, milady?" "Didn't you *see* that cloth the man was wiping the counter with?" she demanded. "Ugh!" She shuddered. "I didn't happen to want to eat any of the counter," he said. He laughed at that comeback. "You didn't even notice it," she said. "You never notice anything. It was filthy." "I noticed they had some damn fine coffee in there," he said. "It was swell." He knew she loved good coffee. He began to hum his tune again; then he whistled it; then he began to sing it. She did not show her annoyance, but she knew that he knew she was annoyed. "Will you be kind enough to tell me what time it is?" she asked. "Big *bad* wolf, big *bad* wolf—five minutes o' five—tum-dee-*doo*-dee-dum-m-m." She settled back in her seat and took a cigarette from her case and tapped it on the case. "I'll wait till we get home," she said. "If you'll be kind enough to speed up a little." He drove on at the same speed. After a time he gave up the "Big Bad Wolf" and there was deep silence for two miles. Then suddenly he began to sing, very loudly, *H*-A-double-R-*I*-G-A-*N spells Harrr*-i-gan—" She gritted her teeth. She hated that worse than any of his songs except "Barney Google." He would go on to "Barney Google" pretty soon, she knew. Suddenly she leaned slightly forward. The straight line of her lips began to curve up ever so slightly. She heard the safety pins in the tumbler again. Only now they were louder, more insistent, ominous. He was singing too loud to hear them. "Is a *name* that *shame* has never been con-*nec*-ted with—*Harrr*-i-gan, that's *me!*" She relaxed against the back of the seat, content to wait.

The Case of the Laughing Butler

A LADY who signed herself "Hostess" wrote recently to Elinor Ames, who clears up matters of etiquette for the distraught readers of the *Daily News,* "How many cocktails should a hostess serve before a meal? Sometimes I feel so embarrassed because the dinner is ready but the guests go right on drinking in the living room and I can't find a tactful way to urge them out to dinner. I have no maid so must announce dinner myself." To which Miss Ames replied, "Never serve more than two cocktails before dinner, for the guest who has several cocktails and an assortment of canapés and hors-dœuvre will suffer a loss of appetite. Why not try a laughing imitation of a butler? Stand at the door and say, in clear tones, 'Dinner is served.' If your manner is pleasant but pointed—and there are no more cocktails—your guests will follow you into the dining room."

Here we have stated, by Hostess, one of the problems of American home life today, and one which you and I—and, in her heart of hearts, Miss Ames herself—know cannot be solved by imitating a butler. One might as well try to dispose of some such problem as "What shall one do about sex?" by imitating a butler. To give a brief history of cocktails-before-dinner, every school child knows, of course, that the trouble began when liquor was substituted for tea as a late-afternoon and early-evening beverage. The old-fashioned tea party was easy to handle; your Aunt Clara or your little niece could handle it, and have the whole house in apple-pie order again by half past six. Nobody ever drank more than one or two cups of tea (three at the outside), and even if he did it had no other effect than to make him slightly stupid. There was never any disposition on the part of tea drinkers to go on and on with the thing; nobody ever crept into the guest room and lay down; nobody shouted. I do not pretend that such things occur at all parties where cocktails are served; what I mean to say is that they never occurred at tea parties. The tea party could be decorous to the point of stuffiness, it had all the drawbacks of the stone-sober, but it was eminently manageable. Then came, as we all know, gin, and with it the problem with which Hostess finds herself confronted.

The weakness of Miss Ames' attempt to cope with the cocktail problem, the proof of her uncertainty and lack of confidence in her own plan, lies in that curious suggestion of hers, "Why not try a laughing imitation of a butler?" If she had had any faith in her ability to help Hostess out, she would not have answered a hard question by asking another question. Well, let me answer that question for Hostess, who must be pretty bewildered. In the first place, if a hostess stands at the door and laughs, nobody is going to get the idea that she is imitating a butler, for the simple reason that butlers do not laugh. You have to give an unsmiling and dignified imitation of a butler or the whole thing falls flat. Furthermore, it is extremely difficult for a woman in a dinner gown to imitate a butler. I doubt if any woman except Beatrice Lillie could get away with it, and she probably has a butler. (Miss Ames' implication that the presence of an actual butler would solve the cocktail problem we need not bother with here further than to say it wouldn't.) Moreover, a roomful of guests who have had only two cocktails are not going to be amused by, or cater to, anybody doing imitations of any kind whatsoever. To enjoy imitations, or even pay attention to imitations, people must have about five cocktails, at which point they will, of course, begin giving imitations themselves—the gentleman with mustaches doing Hitler and Charlie Chaplin. Gentlemen—or ladies—imitating Chaplin are likely to be a nuisance in a crowded room, particularly if they try going around a corner on one foot. Getting people who are doing imitations out to the dining room would be next to impossible.

But let us, for the sake of the argument, consider Miss Ames' specific case, that of a hostess who, having served two

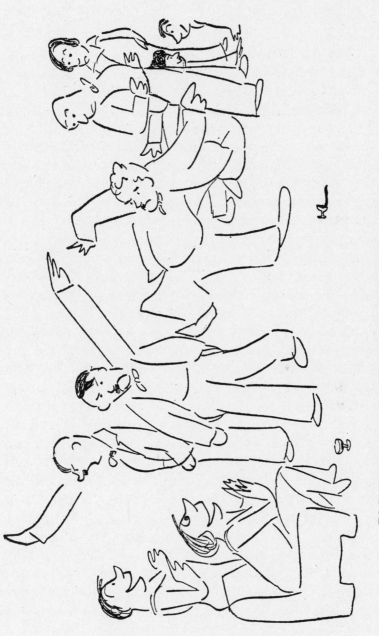

TO ENJOY IMITATIONS PEOPLE MUST HAVE ABOUT FIVE COCKTAILS.

cocktails and determining not to serve any more, stands at
the door and gives a laughing imitation of a butler. Nothing,
beyond a few strained little laughs, is going to happen. The
hostess is simply going to stand there, her idiotic laughter
dying, while a roomful of people, each holding his empty
glass rigidly before him, regard their hostess with cold grins.
There is only one thing for Hostess to do at this point, and I
shall express it by paraphrasing one of Miss Ames' own
sentences, as follows: "If your manner is pleasant but
pointed—and there are no more cocktails—you are going to
have to make some more cocktails." This has become the
accepted thing, and there is nothing to do but accept it.
Dinner can always wait for one more round, or if it can't, it is
going to, anyway.

There is really only one way for a hostess to speed her
guests to the dinner table after two cocktails, but it is a
remedy that is worse than the malady. I refer to the serving of
purple or blue cocktails or cocktails of any color not
ordinarily encountered in liquor glasses. Strangely colored
cocktails, made up of liquid odds and ends, can be, and often
are, served by women like Hostess. As Marjorie Hillis says in
"Live Alone and Like It," "Worse even than the woman who
puts marshmallows into a salad is the one who goes in for
fancy cocktails." (Miss Hillis knows quite a lot about serving
drinks, but she has a one-cocktail delusion about Old-
Fashioneds. She writes, "Old-Fashioneds come into the
economy class after a fashion, because of the fact that you
make them singly, and *usually people don't expect two.*" I
believe it can safely be said that nothing in the world
depresses a guest so much as only one Old-Fashioned.) The
serving of fancy cocktails, then—to get back to the fancy
cocktails—is one way out for Hostess. It will be an even
better way out if she serves with them canapés made of
anchovy paste mixed with marmalade, or something of the
sort, and gives each gentleman a dainty little cocktail napkin
to worry about. This will get the guests out to dinner all right

but it will also get them out of the house right after dinner, probably never to return. There don't have to be any marshmallows in the salad. Thus we see that there is no perfect, or even near-perfect, solution to Hostess's problem in this country.

In France our problem does not come up because the French look on cocktails before dinner as an invention of the devil (*une invention du diable*). No proper French person would ever let himself in for any such quandary as confronts Hostess; first, because it is repugnant to the French to dull the palate with gin and rye, thus spoiling the taste for food, and, second, because it costs too much (*c'est trop cher*). Many Americans have no real taste for food, or, if they have, they are so worried or nervous by late afternoon that they don't care. Thus it has come about that a great number of Americans, instead of giving up cocktails before dinner, are largely giving up dinner after cocktails. A professor out in Ohio has announced that because of this Americans are rapidly becoming a one-meal race, having the time and inclination only for a cup of coffee and a piece of toast in the morning. The professor's conclusion seems to be that when the barbarians come down from the North they will find a people so badly nourished that they will be a pushover.

I happen to be an old-fashioned host who does not believe in the abandonment of dinner after cocktails. This is probably because I rarely have a chance to have more than one cocktail at my own dinner parties, owing to the fact that I usually have to go out for ice, and hence have just worked up an appetite when dinner is announced, or by the time it should be announced. Dinner guests have a way of showing up at my house quite early, bringing anywhere from one to six people with them. Sometimes it is somebody's father who just wanted to stop in and see me before he took his train; sometimes it is four or five friends of one of my guests, with whom he has been having a quick one at Joe's or somewhere, and who thought they would just drop in and say hello;

sometimes it is that bald man with the nose glasses and that middle-aged woman in the brown dress who so often show up at people's houses at five-thirty or six o'clock. In these cases the ice, of course, runs out and I have to go out and get some more (the ice-cube system is not, I believe, here to stay, unless it gets a great deal better). Thus I usually find myself over in Bleecker or Sullivan Street at seven o'clock of the evening I am giving a dinner party, trying to explain to some Italian that I have to have ice. Of course, I usually try to phone for the ice first, but that never works, as you know if you have tried it. You can get Tony Angelli or Tony Dibello on the phone, all right, but you can't make him understand that you want ice. You say, "Hello—Angelli's?," and a thick, low voice says, "Hodda wodda poosh?" "Could you deliver some ice right away to such-and-such a number?" you ask, above the racket of the cocktail drinkers. "You gudda poosh what?" says the voice. You never really get beyond that, whatever it is, so you have to go out for the ice. It is useless to send a servant. No servant has ever been known to find an Italian ice-dealer.

On one occasion I waited for half an hour in the steamy kitchen of a house in Sullivan Street until the Italian ice-man, who had disappeared after a brief and excited talk with me, came back with some white wine. He had thought I wanted white wine. It was very late when I got back with the ice that time and everybody had a good laugh at me, to be sure, coming in with the ice. When I go out for the ice now, I usually snatch a couple of sandwiches at a delicatessen. It isn't much, but it is something. My own experience is simply one example of why it is impossible to solve the cocktails-before-dinner problem as glibly and briefly as Miss Ames tries to solve it. I don't like to think of Hostess standing there at the door, laughingly imitating a butler, hoping everybody will clap hands and file gaily out to dinner. Life isn't that simple.

Bateman Comes Home

(Written After Reading Several Recent Novels about the Deep South and Confusing them a Little—as the Novelists Themselves Do—with "Tobacco Road" and "God's Little Acre")

OLD NATE Birge sat on the rusted wreck of an ancient sewing machine in front of Hell Fire, which was what his shack was known as among the neighbors and to the police. He was chewing on a splinter of wood and watching the moon come up lazily out of the old cemetery in which nine of his daughters were lying, only two of whom were dead. He began to mutter to himself. "Bateman be comin' back any time now wid a thousan' dollas fo' his ol' pappy," said Birge. "Bateman ain' goin' let his ol' pappy starve nohow." A high, cracked voice spoke inside the house, in a toneless singsong. "Bateman see you in hell afore he do anything 'bout it," said the voice. "Who dat?" cried Birge, standing up. "Who dat sayin' callumy 'bout Bateman? Good gahd amighty!" He sat down quickly again. His feet hurt him, since he had gangrene in one of them and Bless-Yo-Soul, the cow, had stepped on the other one that morning in Hell Hole, the pasture behind Hell Fire. A woman came to the door with a skillet in her hand. Elviry Birge was thin and emaciated and dressed in a tattered old velvet evening gown. "You oughtn' speak thataway 'bout Bateman at thisatime," said Birge. "Bateman's a good boy. He go 'way in 1904 to make his pappy a thousan' dollas." "Thuh hell wuth thut," said Elviry, even more tonelessly than usual. "Bateman ain' goin' brang we-all no thousan' dollas. Bateman got heself a place fo' dat thousan' dollas." She shambled back into the house. "Elviry's gone crazy," muttered Birge to himself.

A large woman with a heavy face walked into the littered

yard, followed by a young man dressed in a tight blue suit. The woman carried two suitcases; the young man was smoking a cigarette and running a pocket comb through his hair. "Who dat?" demanded Birge, peering into the dark. "It's me, yore Sister Sairy," said the large woman. "An' tuckered as a truck horse." The young man threw his cigarette on the ground and spat at its burning end. "Mom shot a policeman in Chicago," he said, sulkily, "an' we hadda beat it." "Whut you shoot a policeman fo', Sairy?" demanded Birge, who had not seen his sister for twenty years. "Gahdam it, you cain' go 'round doin' that!" "That'll be one o' Ramsay's jokes," said Sairy. "Ramsay's a hand for jokes, he is. Seems like that's all he *is* a hand for." "Ah, shut yore trap before I slap it shut," said Ramsay. He had never been in the deep South before and he didn't like it. "When do we eat?" he asked. "Ev'body goin' 'round shootin' police-men," muttered Birge, hobbling about the yard. "Seem lak ev'body shootin' policemen 'cept Bateman. Bateman, he's a good boy." Elviry came to the door again, still carrying the skillet; as they had had no food since Coolidge's first term, she used it merely as a weapon. "Whut's ut?" she asked, frowning into the dark. The moon, grown tired, had sunk back into the cemetery again. "Come ahn out, cackle-puss, an' find out," said Ramsay. "Look heah, boy!" cried Birge. "I want me more rev'rence outa you, gahdam it!" "Hello, Elviry," said Sairy, sitting on one of her suitcases. "We come to visit you. Ain't you glad?" Elviry didn't move from the doorway.

"We-all thought you-all was in *She*cago," said Elviry, in her toneless voice. "We-all was in all Chicago," said Ramsay, "but we-all is here all, now all." He spat. "Dam ef he ain' right, too," said Birge, chuckling. "Lawdy gahd! You bring me a thousan' dollas, boy?" he asked, suddenly. "I ain't brought nobody no thousand dollers," growled Ramsay. "Whine you make yerself a thousand dollers, you old buzzard!" "Don' lem call me buzzard, Elviry!" shouted

Birge. "Cain' you hit him wid somethin'? Hit him wid dat skillet!" Elviry made for Ramsay with her skillet, but he wrested it away from her and struck her over the head with it. The impact made a low, dull sound, like *sponk*. Elviry fell unconscious, and Ramsay sat down on her, listlessly. "Hell va place ya got here," he said.

At this juncture a young blonde girl, thin and emaciated but beautiful in the light of the moon (which had come up again), ran into the yard. "Wheah you bin, gal?" demanded Birge. "Faith is crazy," he said to the others, "an' they ain' nobody knows why, 'cause I give her a good Christian upbringin' ef evah a man did. Look heah, gal, yo' Aunt Sairy heah fo' a visit, gahdam it, an' nobody home to welcome her. All my daughters 'cept Prudence bin gone fo' two weeks now. Prudence, she bin gone fo' two yeahs." Faith sat down on the stoop. "Clay an' me bin settin' fire to the auditorium," she said. Birge began whittling at a stick. "Clay's her third husban'," he said. "'Pears lak she should pay some 'tention to her fifth husban', or leastwise her fo'th, but she don'. I don' understan' wimmin. Seem lak ev'body settin' fire to somethin' ev'time I turn my back. Wonder any buildin's standin' in the whole gahdam United States. You see anythin' o' Bateman, gal?" "I ain' seen anythin' o' anybody," said Faith. "Now that is a bald-face lie by a daughter I brought up in the feah o' hell fire," said Birge. "Look heah, gal, you cain' set fire to no buildin' 'thout you see somebody. Gahd's love give that truth to this world. Speak to yo' Aunt Sairy, gal. She jest kill hesef a *po*liceman in *She*cago." "Did you kill a policeman, Aunt Sairy?" Faith asked her. Sairy didn't answer her, but she spoke to Ramsay. "You sit on this suitcase an' let me sit on Elviry a while," she said. "Do as yo' Motha tells you boy," said Birge. "Ah, shut up!" said Ramsay, smoking.

Ben Turnip, a half-witted neighbor boy with double pneumonia, came into the yard, wearing only overalls. "Ah seed you-all was a-settin'," he said, bursting into high,

BATEMAN COMES HOME.

toneless laughter. "Heah's Bateman! Heah's Bateman!" cried Birge, hobbling with many a painful gahdam over to the newcomer. "You bring me a thousan' dollas, Bateman?" Elviry came to, pushed Ramsay off her, and got up. "That ain' Bateman, you ol' buzzard," she said, scornfully. "That's only Ben Turnip an' him turned in the haid, too, lak his Motha afore him." "Go 'long, woman," said Birge. "I reckon I know moan son. You bring yo' ol' pappy a thousan' dollas, Bateman?" "Ah seed you-all was a-settin'," said Ben Turnip. Suddenly he became very excited, his voice rising to a high singsong. "He-settin', I-settin', you-settin', we-settin'," he screamed. "Deed-a-bye, deed-a-bye, deed-a-bye, die!" "Bateman done gone crazy," mumbled Birge. He went back and sat down on the sewing machine. "Seem lak ev'body gone crazy. Now, that's a pity," he said, sadly. "Nuts," said Ramsay.

"S'pose you-all did see me a-settin'," said Ben Turnip, belligerently. "Whut uv ut? Cain' Ah set?" "Sho, sho, set yosef, Bateman," said Birge. "I'll whang ovah his haid wid Elviry's skillet fust pusson say anything 'bout you settin'. Set yosef." Ben sat down on the ground and began digging with a stick. "I done brong you a thousan' dollas," said Ben. Birge leaped from his seat. "Glory gahd to Hallerlugie!" he shouted. "You heah de man, Elviry? Bateman done . . ."

If you keep on long enough it turns into a novel.

Footnotes on a Course of Study

I HARDLY know where to begin in trying to summarize for you a pamphlet called "The Technique of Good Manners," by one Mary Perin Barker, which has fallen into my hands. I might begin, I suppose, by saying that it was first got up to be used, and was used, as a course of study at Newark College of Engineering, but that would only start you asking questions, and all I know is that Newark College of Engineering is a college. Mrs. Barker's little book was devised to instruct the men students there how to act from the time they got up until the time they went to bed. These students used to meet with the author for two-hour discussion periods; whether they still do or not I don't know; at any rate, the brochure has now been put into general circulation, with an introductory note by Dr. Dexter S. Kimball, Dean of the College of Engineering of Cornell University. Mrs. Barker teaches proper behavior in the classroom, the ballroom, the laboratory, and the office. She tells you how to answer the phone (you should never grab it up and shout "Yeah?"), how to take a girl to a dance, how to greet one's office mates (you say "Hello there," with a smile, and "mean it"), and so on.

Being a woman, Mrs. Barker goes into italics in surprising places now and then. For instance, she writes, early in this course of study, that a man should have "a razor, a *good* hairbrush, a toothbrush and a pants presser." Well, that's a woman for you, putting the quality of a hairbrush above the quality of a razor. Somehow, I can just see the razor she has in mind, and the hairbrush too, as far as that goes. I don't want any part of either one of them. I don't care whether I'm well groomed or not. I don't want to be groomed, anyway; never have. I just want to get up and dress and be let alone. This makes me a boor, I know, and Mrs. Barker, being a cultivated lady (she believes that men should shave under their arms and points out that "for years they have done so at the foreign beach resorts"), Mrs. Barker hates a boor, but we all might as well know where we stand to begin with. It just happens that I do practically nothing the way Mrs. Barker says it should be done. For one thing, I usually argue with people when my clothes are rumpled and my hair is in my eyes. Mrs. B. intimates that you get much farther if you are well dressed. She writes, "One friend of mine says that she never starts an argument unless she is well dressed." I know women like that, too, and they're just as well dressed at the end as they were when they started. And yet nothing so upsets the ill-groomed man as to have a woman come out of an argument with him just as well groomed as when she went in, and talking in the same cool tones, with the same faint smile on her lips. I know them.

To go on to other items in Mrs. Barker's code of behavior for men, she says that it is entirely out of place to use handkerchiefs to "clean shoes, to dust furniture, or to wipe automobile grease or laboratory acid from the hands." I don't know about the automobile grease or the laboratory acid, and I don't care about the furniture-dusting, but I do know that for cleaning shoes there is nothing so handy or so efficient as a handkerchief. The handkerchief a man uses on his shoes he can always tuck away quickly in his pocket

FOR CLEANING SHOES THERE IS NOTHING SO HANDY AS A HANDKERCHIEF.

where his wife can't see it; on the way to the office he can toss it into a trash receptacle. If he uses a towel, on the other hand, his wife is bound to find it, confront him with it, and say, "What have you been doing with this, may I ask— dipping sheep?" That is likely to ruin the man's day.

As to table manners, I concede most of Mrs. Barker's points, but I cannot go the whole way with her about introductions. She contends that in introducing people a clue to their interests is often a kindness. Thus: "Mr. Smith, may I introduce Mr. Jones? Mr. Jones has just returned from South America, where he has been inspecting a mine." I leave out, reluctantly, any discussion of the probability that Mr. Jones' statement about inspecting a mine was just a cock-and-bull story he told his wife when he packed up to go to South America. (I still think it was a cock-and-bull story, though.) Let us suppose that I am the Mr. Smith who has just been introduced to this Mr. Jones. Well, I would be more embarrassed by the introduction than helped. I know absolutely nothing about mines and almost as little about South America. Naturally, after Mrs. Barker's introduction, Mr. Jones would expect me to say something to him about his mine. I can see him standing there, waiting. And I know just how the talk would go for the first few minutes. "Well," I would say, and stop. Then: "How is the mine?" Mr. Jones would raise his eyebrows slightly and say, stiffly, "I beg your pardon?" I would then (sparring for time) wipe my shoes with a handkerchief, look up, find his eyes still on me, and say, "I mean—is the mine all right?" Mr. Jones would be certain to read into this some veiled aspersion on his mine (particularly if it was a woman, and not a mine, that he had down there), and in a short while we would be enemies for life. That would be all right with me, too, because I have enough friends the way it is, but I am thinking of the young Newark engineers who haven't any friends.

I kept trying to remember, in reading Barker on Behavior, that it was originally written for these young Newark engineers and not for me. But even so, I am not sure that it was fitting or fair for her to tell them that "the girl who is a total loss in a ballroom may have a good many attractive girl friends to whom she would gladly introduce you, and furthermore, she may be a real person whom you would like to know outside the ballroom." Now, I don't set myself up as the greatest authority in the world on this subject, but I have known a great many total losses in my day, and I can say in all fairness and calmness that not one of them ever brought up a lot of attractive girl friends whom she was glad to introduce me to. I don't believe that any total loss in the country has a lot of attractive girl friends or, if she has, that she would be eager to introduce you to them. Moreover, I never knew a total loss who proved to be a real person whom I liked very much to know outside the ballroom. I'll admit that I never saw any of these losses outside the first ballroom in which I met them, but a man of the world does not have to go through every experience to know what it is like. Furthermore, I have compared notes with other men of the world. They all say the same thing.

Mrs. Barker takes up a lot of other topics which I should like to go into, but I have neither the time nor the tolerance for all of them. I do, however, feel impelled to discuss her rule No. 1 under "A Few Rules to be Remembered in Your Association with Women." This rule is: "Ladies always go first except going upstairs, or in a possibly dangerous place. The gentleman goes ahead to help her into a boat, up a slippery incline, or up a ladder." That may be a good rule for the stronger and more agile young engineers, but it is hardly a rule which may be applied, as Mrs. Barker applies it here, to all gentlemen, including the sedentary and the nearsighted. In my own case, I can think of no woman friend of mine who would dream of letting me step into a canoe and then try to hand her into it. Most of my women friends would be perfectly willing—and eager—to get into the canoe first, rules or no rules, and then help me in—with the aid of their husbands, a couple of ropes, and a board. My difficulties with watercraft began some fifteen years ago at Green Lake, New York, when in stepping into a canoe I accidentally trod on a sleeping Boston terrier that I didn't know was in the canoe. I had a firm hold on a young woman's hand at the time, since I was about to assist her into the canoe (I was a stickler for rules in my youth). What followed was a deplorable and improbable fiasco, but it followed. The woman I was assisting at the time and the women she has talked to about the happenings of that day—in other words, all my other women friends—would rather stay behind and burn up than follow me up a ladder. And as for a slippery incline, nobody who saw me try to recover a woman's English sheep-dog puppy for her one icy day two years ago in Sixth Avenue at Fourteenth Street—the dog had slipped its leash—would want to follow me up a slippery incline. That goes for the dog, too.

Remembrance of Things Past

I READ the other day about some chickens that got drunk on mash; out in Iowa, I believe it was. I was reminded of the last chickens that I got drunk. They belonged to a French woman who owned a farm in Normandy, near Granville, where I stayed from early spring until late autumn, ten years ago. The drunken chickens make as good a point of beginning as any for my recollections of Madame Goriaut, who owned the farm. I feel that I owe her some small memoir.

I recall the little farmhouse clearly. I saw it first in a slanting rain, as I walked past sheep meadows in which poppies were blooming. A garrulous, tall old man with a blowing white beard walked with me to the farm. He dealt in clocks and watches and real estate, and it was in his dim, ticking shop in the village of Cassis that I had heard of Madame Goriaut's and the room on the second floor which she rented out when she could. I think he went along to be sure that he would get his commission for directing me there.

The room was long and high and musty, with a big, soft bed, and windows that looked out on the courtyard of the place. It was like a courtyard, anyway, in form and in feeling. It should have held old wagon wheels and busy men in leather aprons, but the activity I remember was that of several black-and-white kittens stalking each other in a circular bed of red geraniums, which, of course, is not like a courtyard, but nevertheless I remember the space in front of the house as being like a courtyard. A courtyard, let us say, with black-and-white kittens stalking each other in a circular bed of red geraniums.

The kittens were wild and unapproachable. Perhaps the fear of man had been struck into their hearts by Madame Goriaut. She was a formidable woman, almost, in a way, *épouvantable* (*épouvantable* was her favorite word—everything was *épouvantable:* the miserable straw crop, the storms off the Channel, the state of the nation, America's delay in getting into the war). Madame was large and shapeless and possessed of an unforgettable toothiness. Her smile, under her considerable mustache, was quick and savage and frightening, like a flash of lightning lighting up a ruined woods. Whether she was tremendously amused (as by the fidgetings of a hanging rabbit—they hang rabbits for the table in Normandy) or tremendously angry (as over the breaking of a crock by her sulky little daughter) you could not determine by her expression. She raised her upper lip and showed her teeth and bellowed, in anger as well as in gaiety. You could identify her moods only by her roaring words, which reverberated around the house like the reports of shotguns. There was no midpoint in her spirit: she was either greatly pleased, usually about nothing much, or greatly displeased, by very little more.

Like many French people in the provinces, Madame Goriaut believed that all Americans were rich. She would ask me if I had not paid a thousand francs for my shoes. My spectacle rims were of solid gold, to be sure. I carried—was it not so?—a thousand dollars in my pockets for tobacco and odds and ends. I would turn my pockets inside out to show her this was not true. At these times she frightened me. It was not too fantastic to conceive of Madame Goriaut creeping

into one's room at night with a kitchen knife and a basket, come to pluck one's thousand dollars and one's life as she might pluck spinach. I was always slightly alarmed by her. She had but little English—"I love you," "kiss me," "thousand dollars," "no," and "yes." I don't know where she learned these words, but she enjoyed repeating them, in that order, and with heavy delight, like a child who has learned a poem. Sometimes she gave me the shudders saying, apropos of nothing at all, "I love you, kiss me, thousand dollars, no, yes."

Madame Goriaut was a widow. Her husband had been a great professor, she told me. He had died a few years before, leaving her the farm, no money, and two five-act plays in blank verse. She showed the plays to me the first day I was there. They were written in ink in a fine hand. I picked them up and put them down with an imitation of awed pleasure. I wondered what her husband could have been like, the great professor. I found out a little now and then. Once I asked her if she had a photograph of him and she said no, because he had believed that in the transference of one's image to a film or plate there departed a certain measure of one's substance. Did I believe this was true? I said I did indeed. I was afraid to refute any of the convictions of the great professor when Madame put them to me with her leer and her fierce, sudden laugh. Of these convictions the only other I remember is that M. Goriaut believed he would come back after death as a *hirondelle*, or swallow. There were a lot of swallows around the farmhouse and the barns, and Madame Goriaut asked me if I thought that one of them was her husband. I asked her, in turn, if any of the swallows had ever made her a sign. She bellowed with laughter. I couldn't tell much about that laugh. I couldn't tell what she had thought of her husband alive, or what she believed of him dead.

I got the chickens drunk one Sunday morning by throwing them pieces of bread soaked in Calvados, strong, new Calvados. Madame had invaded my room one Saturday night after dinner to ask me again why America had got into the war so late. She was bitter on that subject. While she talked she noticed that I had a bottle of Bénédictine on my desk. She said that Bénédictine was not the thing; I must have Calvados, the grand *eau de vie* of the region; she would give me a bottle of it. She went downstairs and brought it up to me, a large bottle. *"Voilà!"* she roared, planking it down on the table. I thanked her. Later she charged me seven francs for it on my weekly bill. I couldn't drink the stuff, it was so green and violent, so I fed it to the chickens. They got very drunk and fell down and got up and fell down again. Madame did not know what was the matter, and she raged around the village about a new disease that had come to kill the chickens and to impoverish her. The chickens were all right by Monday morning—that is, physically. Mentally, I suppose, it was their worst day.

Once I went with Madame Goriaut and her daughter, who was about seven but was peaked and whiny and looked twelve, to a village fair in Cassis. The little girl led the family donkey by his halter. It turned out when we got there that they were going to offer the donkey for sale; it seems that they offered him for sale every year at the fair. Madame hung a little sign around his neck saying that he was for sale; she had carried the sign to the fair wrapped in a newspaper. Nobody bought the donkey, but one man stepped up and asked how old he was. The little girl replied, "Twelve years!" Madame Goriaut flew into one of her rages and cuffed the child to the ground with the back of her hand. "But he has only eight years, Monsieur!" she bellowed at the man, who was moving away. She followed him, bellowing, but he evaded her and she returned, still bellowing. She told me later that the donkey was twenty-four years old. Her daughter, she said, would make some man a miserable wife one day.

After the fair we went to a three-table *terrasse* on a narrow sidewalk in front of a tawdry café in the village and she ordered Calvados. There was, I noticed, a small insect in my glass when it was set in front of me. I called to the waiter, but he had gone back into the café and didn't hear me. Madame asked what was the matter, and I showed her the insect in the bottom of the glass. She shrugged, said, *"Ah, là!,"* and exchanged glasses with me. She drank the insect placidly. When I paid for the drinks, I brought out a new five-franc note. The little girl's eyes widened and she grabbed for it. *"Quel joli billet de cinq francs!"* she squealed. Her mother slapped her down again, shouting that the *joli billet* belonged to Monsieur, who was a wealthy gentleman unused to *épouvantables* children. The little girl cried sullenly. *"Par exemple!"* cried Madame, with her toothy leer. "But you may make her a small present when you leave us." We had another drink against the black day when I should leave them.

The day I left a man came for me and my bags in a two-wheeled cart. It was getting on toward November and Normandy had grown chill. A cold rain was falling. I piled my bags in the back of the cart and was about to shake hands with Madame when the little girl squealed that I had not given her the present I had promised her. I took a five-franc note from my billfold and handed it to her. She grabbed it and ran, screaming in delight, a delight that turned to terror as Madame, bellowing her loudest, set off in pursuit. They disappeared around a corner of the house, and I could hear them screaming and bellowing in the orchard behind the house. I climbed into the cart and told the man to drive on. He said it was always like that with the young ones nowadays, they wanted everything for themselves. I was gone long before Madame came back, as I suppose she did, to say goodbye. I couldn't have faced her. I sometimes wonder about the little girl. She must be seventeen by now, and is probably already making some man a miserable wife.

Something About Polk

HURRYING TOWARD Shiloh through the pages of Mr. W. E. Woodward's "Meet General Grant," a book published nine years ago, which I only recently came upon—in the library of a summer hotel—I ran into a provocative marginal note, indignantly written with pencil, on page 73. In the middle of that page occurs this sentence by Mr. Woodward: "James K. Polk, an insignificant Tennessee politician, who was almost unknown to the American people, was nominated by the Democrats . . ." The pencilled note in the margin opposite this said sharply, "Governor of Tennessee. Twice Speaker of the House of Representatives. The Jackson leader in the fight against the U. S. Bank. Almost unknown?"

I left General Grant and Mr. Woodward to shift for themselves, and gave myself up to quiet contemplation of this astonishing note. Here was the bold imprint of a person who, eighty or more years after Polk's death, could actually give three facts about the man. I was moved to wonder and a kind of admiration for this last of the Polk men, rising up so unexpectedly out of that margin, shaking a white, tense fist, defending his hero. For of all our array of Presidents, there was none less memorable than James K. Polk. If ten patriots, picked at random, were asked to list the names of all the Presidents, it is likely that most of them would leave out the name of the eleventh. Even if they remembered his name, surely none of them could put down a fact about him. He was a man of no arresting achievement. The achievements that our mysterious marginal apologist puts down are certainly not the kind of achievements that make a man well known. Who knows the name of the present Governor of Tennessee? How many people know the name of the Speaker of the House? (Did I hear somebody say Joe Cannon?)

There are a number of other Presidents whom the average patriot, in making a list, might leave out, but in his day each of these others was notable for something unusual, no matter how minor. Pierce was thrown from his horse in the Mexican War, wearing the uniform of a brigadier general; he was the youngest man to be elected to the Presidency up to that time. Andrew Johnson's wife taught him to write; he was said to have been cockeyed one day when, as Vice-President, he addressed the Senate; he was the only President who was ever impeached. Buchanan was the only bachelor President. Tyler served eggnogs and mint juleps in the White House. The first Harrison died in office. And so it goes, the enlivening story of all the Presidents except Polk. It is unquestionably true that he was almost unknown to the American people when he was elected. They never got to know him well; after his term was over, he retired to his home and died there three months later.

The trouble with Polk was that he never did anything to catch the people's eye; he never gave them anything to remember him by; nothing happened to him. He never cut down a cherry tree, he didn't tell funny stories, he was not impeached, he was not shot, he didn't drink heavily, he didn't gamble, he wasn't involved in scandal. He was a war President, to be sure, but his activities in the White House during the Mexican War were overshadowed by the activities in the field of an old buzzard named Zachary Taylor, whose soldiers called him "Old Rough and Ready." Polk never had a nickname; it is likely that he was James to his friends, not Jim. His closest friend—his Farley, his Harry Daugherty—was a man you have never heard of. His name was Gideon J. Pillow.

James K. Polk seemed destined to be overshadowed by other men. He was once even overshadowed by a mythical man, and many who have forgotten the name of Polk will remember the name of the mythical man. In 1844 the Whigs circulated the story that Polk had once taken a gang of Negroes to the South to be sold, each one branded "J.K.P." When asked where they had got this infamous story, the Whigs said they had read it in an authoritative travel book written by one Baron Von Roorback. There was no such man, but the word "roorback," meaning a last-minute political trick, has gone into the American language. And the real man the mythical man wrote about has been forgotten. I encountered the Roorback story in Carl Sandburg's "Abraham Lincoln: The Prairie Years," in which I also found an anecdote about Mrs. Polk, but none about Mr. Polk. Thus he was even overshadowed by his wife. It seems that at a reception following Polk's inaugural, someone said to Mrs. Polk, "Madam, you have a very genteel assemblage tonight." to which Mrs. Polk replied, "Sir, I have never seen it otherwise." It wasn't very much, to be sure, but it was something; it has lived a hundred years. The President himself that night does not appear to have opened his trap.

One begins to feel sorry for poor Mr. Polk and the oblivion that has fallen upon him. Here is a President of the United States unremembered for any deed, unremembered even for any anecdote. I am for the formation of a Society for the Invention of Amusing Anecdotes about James K. Polk. I am willing to suggest a few myself to get the thing started. In fifty or a hundred years these anecdotes will begin to appear in histories and biographies. The forgotten President deserves a break; after all, he was a splendid gentleman. Let us see what we can do for James K. Polk, whom Abraham Lincoln once called a "bewildered, confounded, miserably perplexed man."

We might begin with that crack of Lincoln's. Old Gideon Pillow, let us say, came to Polk one day and told him that Abe Lincoln had said he was "bewildered, confounded, and miserably perplexed." "You tell Lincoln," said Polk, "that I've never been so bewildered I couldn't tell the back of a shovel from a piece of writing paper." A little cruel, to be sure, but then Lincoln had asked for it; at least we are showing that our man had spirit. He also had a nice whimsey. A Democrat office-seeker once stormed into his office (we will say) and confronted the President. "First they tell me to see Gideon Pillow and then they tell me to see you," said the man. "I don't know *where* to go." "Ah," said the President, "shunted from Pillow to Polk." Not one of the great puns, perhaps, but it shows our man was human and quick on the uptake. Personally, I think everybody is going to like this next anecdote, about Polk and General Zachary Taylor (that's what we need, anecdotes of the Lincoln-Grant variety). It seems that an indignant Whig came to Polk one day and told him that General Taylor was drinking too much. "He has to," said Polk. "If he didn't see twice as many of those cowardly Mexicans as there really are, he wouldn't have the heart to fight them." The Whig visitor was outraged. "Do you mean to say that you recommend drinking?" he demanded. "Not for myself, if that's what you mean," said Polk. "You see, what *I* have to look at is Whigs."

These are all that I can think of myself, and I am afraid that none of them is going to hurl our hero into immortality, but at least they are a start in the right direction. Let somebody else try it. There's no great rush.

Aisle Seats in the Mind

I FOLLOW as closely as anyone, probably more closely than most people, the pronouncements on life, death, and the future of the movies as given out from time to time by Miss Mary Pickford. Some friends of mine think that it has even become a kind of obsession with me. I wouldn't go so far as to say that, but I do admit that many times when I would ordinarily sit back and drink my brandy and smoke a cigar and become a little drowsy mentally and a little sodden intellectually, something that Mary Pickford has just said engages my inner attention so that instead of dozing off, I am kept as bright-eyed and alert as a hunted deer. Often I wake up at night, too, and lie there thinking about life, and death, and the future of the movies. Miss Pickford's latest arresting observation came in an interview with a *World-Telegram* correspondent out in Beverly Hills. Said Miss Pickford, in part, "Any type of salaciousness is as distasteful to Mr. Lasky as it is to me. There will be no salaciousness at all in our films.

Not one little bit! We will consider only those stories which will insure wholesome, healthy, yet vital entertainment. *Be a guardian, not an usher, at the portal of your thought.*"

Miss Pickford has a way which I can only call intriguing, much as I hate the word, of throwing out little rounded maxims, warnings, and morals at the ends of her paragraphs. I had a great-aunt who did the same thing, and in my teens she fascinated and frightened me; perhaps that is why Miss Pickford's exhortations so engross me, and keep me from the dicing tables, the dens of vice, and the more salacious movies, poems, and novels. Miss Pickford's newest precept has occupied a great many of my waking hours since I read it, and quite a few of my sleeping ones. In the first place, it has brought me sharply up against the realization that I am not a guardian at the portal of my thought and that, what is more, being now forty-two years of age, I probably never will be. What I am like at the portal of my thought is one of those six-foot-six ushers who used to stand around the lobby of the Hippodrome during performances of "Jumbo." (They were not really ushers, but doormen, I think, but let us consider them as ushers for the sake of the argument.) What I want to convey is that I am *all* usher, as far as the portal of my thought goes, terribly usher. But I am unlike the "Jumbo" ushers or any other ushers in that I show any and all thoughts to their seats whether they have tickets or not. They can be under-age and without their parents, or they can be completely cockeyed, or they can show up without a stitch on; I let them in and show them to the best seats in my mind (the ones in the royal arena and the gold boxes).

I don't want you to think that all I do is let in *salacious* thoughts. Salacious thoughts can get in along with any others, including those that are under-age and those that are cockeyed, but my mental audience is largely made up of thoughts that are, I am sorry to say, idiotic. For days a thought has been running around in the aisles of my mind, singing and shouting, a thought that, if I were a guardian, I would certainly have barred at the portal or thrown out instantly as soon as it got in. This thought is one without reason or motivation, but it keeps singing, over and over, to a certain part of the tune of "For He's a Jolly Good Fellow," these words:

> A message for Captain Bligh,
> And a greeting to Franchot Tone.

I hope it doesn't slip by the guardian at your own portal of thought, but, whether it does or not, it is sung to that part of the aforementioned tune the words of which go "Which nobody can deny, which nobody can deny." And it is pretty easy, if you are the usher type, to let it into your mind, where it is likely to get all your other thoughts to singing the same thing, just as Donald Duck did to the orchestra in "The Band Concert." Where it came from I don't know. Thoughts like that can spot the usher type of mind a mile away, and they

A TRIO OF THOUGHTS.

seek it out as tramps seek out the backdoors of generous farm wives.

Just last Sunday another vagrant thought came up to the portal of my mind, or, rather, was shown up to the portal of my mind, and I led it instantly to a seat down front, where much to my relief, it has been shouting even more loudly than the Captain Bligh-Franchot Tone thought and is, in fact, about to cause that thought to leave the theatre. This new thought was introduced at my portal by my colored maid, Margaret, who, in seeking to describe a certain part of the electric refrigerator which she said was giving trouble, called it "doom-shaped." Since Margaret pronounced that wonderful word, everything in my mind and everything in the outside world has taken on the shape of doom. If I were a true guardian of the portal of my thought, I would have refused that expression admittance, because it is too provocative, too edgy, and too dark, for comfort, but then I would have missed the unique and remarkable experience that I had last Sunday, when, just as night was falling, I walked down a doom-shaped street under a doom-shaped sky and up a doom-shaped staircase to my doom-shaped apartment. Like Miss Pickford, I am all for the wholesome, the healthy, and the vital, but sometimes I think one's mind can become, if one is the guardian type, too wholesome, healthy, and vital to be much fun. Any mind, I say boldly here and now, which would not let a doom-shaped thought come in and take a seat is not a mind that I want around.

As in all my discourses about Miss Pickford and her philosophy, I am afraid I have drifted ever so slightly from the main point, which, in this case, I suppose, is the question of keeping salacious thoughts out of the mind, and not doom-shaped ones, or Franchot Tone. Miss Pickford, however, is to blame for my inability to stick to the exact point, because of her way of following up some specific thought, such as the unanimity of her and Mr. Lasky's feelings about salaciousness, with an extremely challenging and all-encompassing injunction, such as that everybody should be a guardian at the portal of his thought, and not an usher.

I have brooded for a long time about the origin of Miss Pickford's injunction. I am not saying that she did not think it up herself. It's hers and she's welcome to it, as far as I am concerned (I'd rather have "doom-shaped" for my own). But I somehow feel that she was quoting someone and that the only reason she didn't add "as the poet has it" or "as the fella said" is that she naturally supposes that everybody would know who wrote the line. I don't happen to know; I don't happen ever to have heard it before. It may be that it is a product of one of the immortal minds, but somehow I doubt that. To me it sounds like Eddie Guest or the late Ella Wheeler Wilcox. It may have been tossed off, of course, in a bad moment, by John Cowper Powys, or Gene Tunney, or Senator Victor Donahey of Ohio, but I am inclined to think not. If you should happen to know, for certain, that it is the work of Shakespeare or Milton, there is no use in your calling me up about it, or sending a telegram. By the time I could hear from you, I would have got it out of my mind, and only "doom-shaped" would be there, sitting in a darkened theatre. I would like that, so please let us alone.

Suli Suli

I ALWAYS try to answer Abercrombie & Fitch's questions (in their advertisements) the way they obviously want them answered, but usually, if I am to be honest with them and with myself, I must answer them in a way that would not please Abercrombie & Fitch. While that company and I have always nodded and smiled pleasantly enough when we met, we have never really been on intimate terms, mainly because we have so little in common. For one thing, I am inclined to be nervous and impatient, whereas Abercrombie & Fitch are at all times composed and tranquil. In the case of a man and a woman this disparity in temperament sometimes works out all right, but with Abercrombie & Fitch and me it is different: neither one of us is willing to submerge any part of his personality in the other, or compromise in matters of precedent, habit, or tradition. Yet in spite of all the natural barriers between Abercrombie & Fitch and myself, we are drawn to each other by a curious kind of fascination, or perhaps it is only me who is drawn to them. Not long ago I dropped in at their store to browse around among all the glittering objects, when suddenly I was faced by a tall and courteous but firm clerk who asked me if there was anything he could do for me. I said instantly, "I want to buy a javelin."

Now, it is true that I have always wanted to buy a javelin, because I have always wanted to see how far I could throw one, but two things had, up to the day I am telling about, kept me from going ahead with the thing. First, I had been afraid that I would not be able to throw a javelin as far as Babe Didrikson used to throw one, and I knew that the discovery that a woman could throw anything farther than I could throw it would have a depressing effect on me and might show up in my work and in my relationships with women. Second, I did not know how Abercrombie & Fitch, of whom I have ever been slightly in awe, would take my wanting to buy a javelin. They are, to be sure, a very courteous firm, but they have a way of looking at you sometimes as if you had left your spoon in your coffee cup. However, all my fears and uncertainties were beside the point, because here I was, finally asking Abercrombie & Fitch for a javelin.

"A *javelin*?" asked Abercrombie & Fitch (I shall call the

clerk that), and I knew instantly from his inflection that he did not think I should have a javelin and, furthermore, I knew that I was not going to get one. Somehow or other it was not the thing for a tall, thin man in a blue suit to come in and ask for a javelin. I was, naturally, embarrassed. "I— uh—yes, I had thought some of purchasing a javelin," I said. "It's for a rather—a sort of special use, in a way, I mean, what I want, of course, is *two* javelins; that is, a *pair* of javelins, so that I could cross them, like oars, you know, or guns, above a mantelpiece. I have oars and guns, of course, but I—I—" Beyond this I could not go with a story that was becoming more and more difficult for me and, I daresay, stranger and stranger to Abercrombie & Fitch. A kind of feverish high note was in my voice, a note that always betrays me when I am lying. "I am very sorry," said Abercrombie & Fitch, his eyebrows raised slightly, "but we have no javelins in stock." He paused; then, "I could order one for you." He knew, you see, that I really only wanted one; my story about wanting two had not fooled him for a minute. I think he also suspected that I wanted to find out whether I could throw the thing as far as Babe Didrikson. Abercrombie & Fitch can read me like a book; I don't know just why. I told the clerk to let it go, not to bother, and to cover my confusion I bought a set of lawn bowls, although I have no lawn that I could possibly use for bowls. I believe the clerk knew that, too.

But I am straying from the point I began with, about Abercrombie & Fitch's questions, the ones I can almost never answer the way they would like to have them answered. Take the one recently printed in an advertisement in the *New Yorker*. Under a picture of a man fishing in a stream were these words: "Can't you picture youself in the middle of the stream with the certain knowledge that a wise old trout is hiding under a ledge and defying you to tempt him with your skillfully cast fly?" My answer, of course, is "No." Especially if I am to be equipped the way the gentleman in the illustration is equipped: with rod, reel, line, net, hip boots, felt hat, and pipe. They might just as well add a banjo and a parachute to my equipment, along with a grandfather's clock, for with anything at all to handle in the middle of a rushing brook I would drown faster than you could say "J. Robins." The wise old trout would have the laugh of his life, especially when I begin to cast. I tried casting in a stream only twice, and the first time I caught a tree and the second time I barely missed landing one of a group of picnickers. Therefore, I cannot agree with Abercrombie & Fitch's ad when it says further: "Words are poor to express the delight of just handling a beautiful rod with a sweet-singing reel and a line that seems alive as it answers the flick of your wrist." It seems alive all right, but it answers different men in different ways; with me, it is surly to the point of impudence. No, I am afraid I am not going to send for one of the fly-fishing catalogues the company advertised or drop in and look at their "complete trout outfits." Abercrombie & Fitch would know, just glancing at me, that I would be at the mercy of the complete trout outfit, and of the trout, too—if they were brave enough to come at me when I went down in a tangle of rod, reel, line, net, boots, pipe, and hat.

I am sorry to have to say this to Abercrombie & Fitch, but fishing of any kind is something I don't like to picture myself doing. Oh, I've tried fishing of various kinds, but I never seemed to get the hang of any of them. I still remember a gay fishing party I went on with a lot of strong men and beautiful girls, when I was still fairly strong myself. It was a fine day and it was a pleasant creek and the fish were biting. Everybody except me was pulling in perch and pickerel, or whatever they were—all fish look exactly alike to me. I kept pulling out of the water an aged and irritable turtle. No matter where I moved along the bank or where I dropped my line, I would hook the turtle. Nobody else got him, but I got him variously, by the leg, the back of his shell, and his belly, but never securely; he wouldn't swallow the hook, he just monkeyed with it. He would always drop back into the water as I was about to haul him in. I didn't really want him, but I wanted to get him out of the way. It furnished a great deal of amusement for everybody, except me and the turtle. Another time I went fishing on Lake Skaneateles with a group of people, including a lovely young woman named Sylvia. On this occasion I actually did hook a fish, even before anybody else had a bite, and I brought it into the rowboat with a great plop. Then, not having had any experience with a caught fish, I didn't know what to do with it. I had had some vague idea that a fish died quietly and with dignity as soon as it was

flopped into a boat, but that, of course, was an erroneous idea. It leaped about strenuously. I got pretty far away from it and stared at it. The young lady named Sylvia finally grabbed it expertly and slapped it into insensibility against the sides and bottom of the boat. I think it was perhaps then that I decided to go in for javelin-throwing and began to live with the dream of being able to throw a javelin farther than Babe Didrikson. A man never completely gets over the chagrin and shock of having a woman handle for him the fish he has caught.

As for deep-sea fishing, you and I—and Abercrombie & Fitch—know that an old turtle-catcher is not going to be able to cope with a big-game fish that fights you for ten or twelve hours and drags you from Miami to Jacksonville. Every time I read an article about deep-sea fishing I realize more thoroughly than ever that, as far as I am concerned, all the sailfish and tuna and tarpon are as safe as if they were in bank vaults. In a recent piece in *Esquire*, Mr. Hemingway tells about a man who hooked an eighty-pound fish which, before the man could pull it in, was grabbed up far below the surface by some unknown monster of the deep, who took a bite at it and let it go. When the original quarry was brought up, it was seen that the other fish had "squeezed it and held it so that every bit of the insides of the fish had been crushed out while the huge fish moved off with the eighty-pound fish in its mouth." "What size of a fish would that be?" Mr. Hemingway asks. He needn't look at me. I do not stick in boats very well, particularly if they are being jerked around by a fish that has another fish in its mouth, and I never expect to get near enough to their habitat to make even a wild guess as to their size.

Then there was an article I came on in, of all magazines, the *East African Annual*, for 1934-35, called "Sea Fishing Off the Coast of Kenya," by Mr. Hugh Copley. In Africa, you can get big, strong black natives (Suli Suli they are called, I think) to go out in a boat with you, but I am afraid they would only hamper and confuse me. Mr. Copley lists the names of the big fish you can pursue along the Kenya coast, giving first the English name, then the technical name, and then the native, or Swahili, name. The list begins this way: "1. The sailfish (Istiophorus gladius), Suli Suli. 2. Herschel's spearfish (Makaira herscheli), Suli Suli." The predicaments that an American, and I mean me, might get into deep-sea fishing with a native that called everything Suli Suli are infinite. I don't even like to think about it. Nor would I ever be able to look after my tackle the way Mr. Copley says it should be looked after, because I would never get anything else done except that, day in and day out. He writes, "Lines must be dried every evening. Reels taken apart and greased. When the fishing trip is over soak all the lines for a night in fresh water and they dry thoroughly for a whole day. All hooks, wire traces, must be greased; gaffs cleaned with emery paper and then greased. The rod should be examined for broken whippings; these replaced and the rod given three coats of best coach varnish." I have a pretty vivid picture of what I would look like after all that greasing and regreasing. And then, of course, the whole thing falls down for me when it comes to the three coats that have to be put on the rod. I might go into Abercrombie & Fitch and ask for a javelin, as indeed I did, but I would never think of going up to one of their clerks and saying, "I should like to buy a bottle of coach varnish." I have no idea what would happen, but the episode would be, I am sure, most unfortunate.

An Outline of Scientists

HAVING BEEN laid up by a bumblebee for a couple of weeks, I ran through the few old novels there were in the cottage I had rented in Bermuda and finally was reduced to reading "The Outline of Science, a Plain Story Simply Told," in four volumes. These books were published by Putnam's fifteen years ago and were edited by J. Arthur Thomson, Regius Professor of Natural History at the University of Aberdeen. The volumes contained hundreds of articles written by various scientists and over eight hundred illustrations, forty of which, the editor bragged on the flyleaf, were in color. A plain story simply told with a lot of illustrations, many of them in color, seemed just about the right mental fare for a man who had been laid up by a bee. Human nature being what it is, I suppose the morbid reader is more interested in how I happened to be laid up by a bee than in what I found in my scientific research, so I will dismiss that unfortunate matter in a few words. The bee stung me in the foot and I got an infection (staphylococcus, for short). It was the first time in my life that anything smaller than a turtle had ever got the best of me, and naturally I don't like to dwell on it. I prefer to go on to my studies in "The Outline of Science," if everybody is satisfied.

I happened to pick up Volume IV first and was presently in the midst of a plain and simple explanation of the Einstein theory, a theory about which in my time I have done as much talking as the next man, although I admit now that I never understood it very clearly. I understood it even less clearly after I had tackled a little problem about a man running a hundred-yard dash and an aviator in a plane above him. Everything, from the roundness of the earth to the immortality of the soul, has been demonstrated by the figures of men in action, but here was a new proposition. It seems that if the aviator were travelling as fast as light, the stop watch held by the track judge would not, from the aviator's viewpoint, move at all. (You've got to make believe that the aviator could see the watch, which is going to be just as hard for you as it was for me.) You might think that this phenomenon of the unmoving watch hand would enable the runner to make a hundred yards in nothing flat, but, if so, you are living in a fool's paradise. To an aviator going as fast as light, the hundred-yard track would shrink to nothing at all. If the aviator were going *twice* as fast as light, the report of the track judge's gun would wake up the track judge, who would still be in bed in his pajamas, not yet having got up to go to the track meet. This last is my own private extension of the general theory, but it seems to me as sound as the rest of it.

I finally gave up the stop watch and the airplane, and went deeper into the chapter till I came to the author's summary of

a scientific romance called "Lumen," by the celebrated
French astronomer, M. Flammarion (in my youth, the
Hearst Sunday feature sections leaned heavily on M.
Flammarion's discoveries). The great man's lurid little
romance deals, it seems, with a man who died in 1864 and
whose soul flew with the speed of thought to one of the stars
in the constellation Capella. This star was so far from the
earth that it took light rays seventy-two years to get there,
hence the old man's soul kept catching up with light rays

from old historical events and passing them. Thus the man's
soul was able to see the battle of Waterloo, fought backward.
First the man's soul—oh, let's call him Mr. Lumen—first Mr.
Lumen saw a lot of dead soldiers and then he saw them get
up and start fighting. "Two hundred thousand corpses, come
to life, marched off the field in perfect order," wrote M.
Flammarion. Perfect order, I should think, only backward.

   I kept going over and over this section of the chapter on
the Einstein theory. I even tried reading it backward, twice as

fast as light, to see if I could capture Napoleon at Waterloo while he was still home in bed. If you are interested in the profound mathematical theory of the distinguished German scientist, you may care to glance at a diagram I drew for my own guidance, as follows:

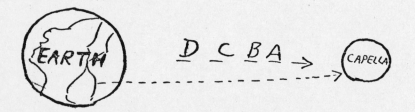

Now, A represents Napoleon entering the field at Waterloo and B represents his defeat there. The dotted line is, of course, Mr. Lumen, going hell-for-leather. C and D you need pay no particular attention to; the first represents the birth of Mr. George L. Snively, an obscure American engineer, in 1819, and the second the founding of the New England Glass Company, in 1826. I put them in to give the thing roundness and verisimilitude and to suggest that Mr. Lumen passed a lot of other events besides Waterloo.

In spite of my diagram and my careful reading and rereading of the chapter on the Einstein theory, I left it in the end with a feeling that my old grip on it, as weak as it may have been, was stronger than my new grip on it, and simpler, since it had not been mixed up with aviators, stop watches, Mr. Lumen, and Napoleon. The discouraging conviction crept over me that science was too much for me, that these brooding scientists, with their bewildering problems, many of which work backward, live on an intellectual level which I, who think of a hundred-yard dash as a hundred-dash, could never attain to. It was with relief that I drifted on to Chapter

XXXVI, "The Story of Domesticated Animals." There wouldn't be anything in that going as fast as light or faster, and it was the kind of thing that a man who has been put to bed by a bee should read for the alleviation of his humiliation. I picked out the section on dogs, and very shortly I came to this: "There are few dogs which do not inspire affection; many crave it. But there are some which seem to repel us, like the bloodhound. True, man has made him what he is. Terrible to look at and terrible to encounter, man has raised him up to hunt down his fellowman." Accompanying the article was a picture of a dignified and mournful-looking bloodhound, about as terrible to look at as Abraham Lincoln, about as terrible to encounter as Jimmy Durante.

Poor, frightened little scientist! I wondered who he was, this man whom Mr. J. Arthur Thomson, Regius Professor of Natural History at the University of Aberdeen, had selected to inform the world about dogs. Some of the chapters were signed, but this one wasn't, and neither was the one on the Einstein theory (you were given to understand that they had all been written by eminent scientists, however). I had the strange feeling that both of these articles had been written by the same man. I had the strange feeling that *all* scientists are the same man. Could it be possible that I had isolated here, as under a microscope, the true nature of the scientist? It pleased me to think so; it still pleases me to think so. I have never liked or trusted scientists very much, and I think now that I know why: they are afraid of bloodhounds. They must, therefore, be afraid of frogs, jack rabbits, and the larger pussy-cats. This must be the reason that most of them withdraw from the world and devote themselves to the study of the inanimate and the impalpable. Out of my analysis of those few sentences on the bloodhound, one of the gentlest of all breeds of dogs, I have arrived at what I call Thurber's Law, which is that scientists don't really know anything about anything. I doubt everything they have ever discovered. I don't think light has a speed of 7,000,000 miles per second at all (or whatever the legendary speed is). Scientists just think light is going that fast, because they are afraid of it. It's so terrible to look at. I have always suspected that light just plodded along, and now I am positive of it.

I can understand how that big baby dropped the subject of bloodhounds with those few shuddering sentences, but I propose to scare him and his fellow-scientists a little more about the huge and feral creatures. Bloodhounds are sometimes put on the trail of old lost ladies or little children who have wandered away from home. When a bloodhound finds an old lady or a little child, he instantly swallows the old lady or the little child whole, clothes and all. This is probably what happened to Charlie Ross, Judge Crater, Agnes Tufverson, and a man named Colonel Appel, who disappeared at the battle of Shiloh. God only knows how many thousands of people bloodhounds have swallowed, but it is probably twice as many as the Saint Bernards have swallowed. As everybody knows, the Saint Bernards, when they find travellers fainting in the snow, finish them off. Monks have notoriously little to eat and it stands to reason they couldn't feed a lot of big, full-grown Saint Bernards; hence they sick them on the lost travellers, who would never get anywhere, anyway. The brandy in the little kegs the dogs wear around their necks is used by the Saint Bernards in drunken orgies that follow the killings.

I guess that's all I have to say to the scientists right now, except *boo!*

Highball Flags

IT IS a matter of common knowledge among smart sea-going gentlemen (if you keep your eyes open, you will have read about it) that the ubiquitous yachtsman can now purchase a cocktail flag for his pleasure craft. To quote an item I recently read on the subject, the flag has "a red glass on a white field" and it means "We're serving drinks." When it is flown upside down, it means, "Who has a drink?" I know very little about the ways of yachtsmen but I have always thought of them as rather reserved, aristocratic gentlemen, not given to garrulity in flags, or to announcing private parties with flags, or to public—or rather high-seas—cadging of drinks with flags. Apparently I was wrong. The ancient practice of sailing a ship, once the prerogative of strong, silent men of retiring disposition, appears about to go the way the canoe went when the ukulele came along. The advent of the cocktail flag, with its strange device, seems likely to lead to a deplorable debasing of the dignity of yachts and yachting—and yachtsmen. Surely anybody will have to be allowed aboard who can climb aboard—that is, when the flag is flown right side up; and certainly all sorts of common and vulgar boats are going to come alongside, roaring and singing (and possibly carrying nothing but gin and ginger ale), when the flag is flown upside down. It is too late now to do anything about this except to suggest some further flag signals; as long as yachts are going in for open drinking and carousing, they may as well do the thing up right. No yachting party which has gone so far as to fly the cocktail flag upside down is going to be satisfied with that. There are a lot of other things the people on board will want to say, after they have run out of drinks and are bawling for more, and an array of signals for these other things might just as well be arranged now. I have a few suggestions to make along this line; yachtsmen can take them or they can leave them alone. What I propose is a series of highball flags, to be run up after the cocktail flag has been struck.

Flag No. 1: The head of a woman, blue, on a white field. This means "My wife is the finest little girl in all the world."

Flag No. 2: Steel-colored fist on a crimson field. This means "I can lick any other yachtsman within sight of this flag." If flown upside down, this means the same thing plus

"HONEY, HONEY, BLESS YOUR HEART."

"with one hand tied behind me."

Flag No. 3: Six gray fists rampant on a dark-blue field. This means "Let's all go over and beat hell out of the Monarch of Bermuda" (or whatever other large, peaceful ship is lying nearest the yacht and the other yachts it is talking to).

Flag No. 4: White zigzag lightning flash on black field. This means "Let's have one more quick one and then we'll get the hell out of here."

Flag No. 5: Large scarlet question mark on white field. This means "Has anybody got a tenor on board?"

Flag No. 6: Red eye and pendent pear-shaped silver tear on black field. This means "You're bes' frien' ev' had." If hung upside down, it means "You're fines' ship ev' seen."

Flag No. 7: White stocking on scarlet field. This means "We want women!"

Flag No. 8: Black zigzag lightning flash on white field. This means the same as No. 4.

Flag No. 9: Four male heads, white eyes, red, open mouths, on smoky-gray field. This means, if right side up, "Let's sing 'Honey, Honey, Bless Your Heart'"; if upside down, "Let's sing 'I had a Dream, Dear.'" There should be one hundred other similar flags for the one hundred other songs men sing when in their cups, and also, a black flag with a white thumb centered; when hung with the thumb pointing up, this means "O. K., you pitch it"; when hung with the thumb pointing down, it means "No, not 'Sweet Adeline'!"

Flag No. 111: Horizontal white line on sable field. This means "I got to lie down."

Flag No. 112: A large plain yellow flag. This means "I said I got to lie *down*!"

If you have any other ideas, don't send them to me, for my yellow flag is flying, upside down (which means "Gone to bed"); send them to Abercrombie & Fitch. They are selling the cocktail flags, or anyway they have them in stock.

Mrs. Phelps

WHEN I went to Columbus, Ohio, on a visit recently, I called one afternoon on Mrs. Jessie Norton, an old friend of my

mother's. Mrs. Norton is in her seventies, but she is in bright possession of all her faculties (except that she does not see very well without her spectacles and is forever mislaying them). She always has a story to tell me over the teacups. She reads my fortune in the tea leaves, too, before I go, and for twenty years has told me that a slim, blonde woman is going to come into my life and that I should beware of the sea. Strange things happen to Mrs. Norton. She is psychic. My mother once told me that Mrs. Norton had been psychic since she was seven years old. Voices speak to her in the night, cryptically, persons long dead appear to her in dreams, and even her waking hours are sometimes filled with a mystic confusion.

Mrs. Norton's story this time dealt with a singular experience she had had only a few months before. It seems that she had gone to bed late on a blowy night, the kind of night on which the wind moans in the wires, and telephone bells ring without benefit of human agency, and there are inexplicable sounds at doors and windows. She had felt, as she got into bed, that something was going to happen. Mrs. Norton has never in her life had the feeling that something was going to happen that something hasn't happened. Once it was the Columbus flood, another time it was the shooting of McKinley, still another time the disappearance forever of her aged cat, Flounce.

On the occasion I am telling about, Mrs. Norton, who lives alone in a vast old graystone apartment building known as Hampton Court, was awakened three hours after midnight by a knocking on her back door. Her back door leads out into a treeless and rather dreary courtyard, as do all the other back doors in the building. It is really four buildings joined together and running around a whole block, with the courtyard in the center. Mrs. Norton looked out her bedroom window and saw two women standing at her door below—there was a faint light striking down from somewhere. She was for a moment convinced that they were not live women, but this conviction was dispelled when one of them called up to her. Mrs. Norton then recognized the voice of a Mrs. Stokes, a portly, jolly, gray-haired woman, also a resident of Hampton Court, which is inhabited largely by old ladies who are alone in the world. "Something terrible has happened," said Mrs. Stokes. The other woman did not say anything and did not look up. Mrs. Norton had the impression that she was weeping. She told them to wait a moment, pulled a wrapper around herself, and went down and let them in.

It came out that the father of the other woman, a Mrs. Phelps, who had just recently moved into Hampton Court, had dropped dead a few minutes before in her apartment. He had come to visit her that day and now he was dead. Mrs. Phelps, a mild little old woman with white hair, sobbed quietly. It seemed that she had run instantly to Mrs. Stokes, her nearest neighbor in the building, and Mrs. Stokes had suggested that they get Mrs. Norton before going to the old man, because Mrs. Norton was psychic and therefore just the person to turn to in the event of a sudden death before dawn. Mrs. Phelps said that she had heard her father fall in his bedroom and, rushing in, had found that he was dead. She was sure that he was dead—there was no need to call a doctor; but would Mrs. Norton telephone for an—an undertaker?

Mrs. Norton, not yet fully awake, suggested that it might be a good idea to make the ladies some tea. Tea was a quieting thing and the brewing of it would give Mrs. Norton a while to think. So Mrs. Norton made the tea and the three ladies each drank a cup of it, slowly, talking of other things than the tragedy. Mrs. Phelps seemed to feel much better. Mrs. Norton then wanted to know if there was any particular undertaker that Mrs. Phelps would like to call in and Mrs. Phelps named one, whom I shall call Bellinger. So Mrs. Norton phoned Bellinger's, and a sleepy voice answered and said a man would be right over to Mrs. Phelps' apartment. At this Mrs. Phelps said, "I think I would like to go back to father alone for a moment. Would you ladies be kind enough to come over in a little while?" Mrs. Norton said they would be over as soon as she got dressed, and Mrs. Phelps left. "She seems very sweet," said Mrs. Stokes. "It's the first time I've really talked to her. It's very sad. And at this time of the night, too." Mrs. Norton said that it was a terrible thing, but that, of course, it was to be expected, since Mrs. Phelps' father must have been a very old man, for Mrs. Phelps looked to be sixty-five at least.

When Mrs. Norton was dressed, the two ladies went out into the bleak courtyard and made their way slowly across it and knocked at the back door of Mrs. Phelps' apartment. There was no answer. They knocked more loudly, taking turns, and then together, and there was still no answer. They could see a light inside, but they heard no sound. Bewildered and alarmed (for Mrs. Phelps had not seemed deaf), the two ladies went through Mrs. Stokes' apartment, which was right next door, and around to Mrs. Phelps' front door and rang the bell. It rang loudly and they rang it many times, but no one came to the door. There was a light on in the hall. They could not hear anyone moving inside.

It was at this juncture that Bellinger's man arrived, a small, grumpy man whose overcoat was too large for him. He took over the ringing of the bell and rang it many times, insistently, but without success. Then, grumbling to himself, he turned the doorknob and the door opened and the three walked into the hallway. Mrs. Norton called and then Mrs. Stokes called and then Bellinger's man shouted, but there was no other sound. The ladies looked at Bellinger's man in frank twittery fright. He said he would take a look around. They heard him going from room to room, opening and closing doors, first downstairs and then upstairs, now and then calling out "Madam!" He came back downstairs into the hallway where the ladies were and said there was nobody in the place, dead or alive. He was angry. After all, he had been roused out of his sleep. He said he believed the whole thing was a practical joke, and a damned bad practical joke, if you asked him. The ladies assured him it was not a joke, but he said "Bah" and walked to the door. There he turned and faced them with his hand on the knob and announced that in thirty-three years with Bellinger this was the first and only time he had ever been called out on a case in which there was no corpse, the first and only time. Then he strode out the door, jumped into his car, and drove off. The ladies hurried out of the apartment after him.

They went back to Mrs. Norton's apartment and made some more tea and talked in excited whispers about the curious happenings of the night. Mrs. Stokes said she did not know Mrs. Phelps very well but that she seemed to be a pleasant and kindly neighbor. Mrs. Norton said that she had known her only to nod to but that she had seemed very nice. Mrs. Stokes wondered whether they should call the police, but Mrs. Norton said that the police would be of no earthly use on what was obviously a psychic case. The ladies would go to bed and get some sleep and go over to Mrs. Phelps' apartment when it was daylight. Mrs. Stokes said she didn't feel like going back to her apartment—she would have to pass Mrs. Phelps' apartment on the way—so Mrs. Norton said she could sleep in her extra bed.

The two women, worn out by their experience, fell asleep shortly and did not wake up until almost ten o'clock. They hurriedly got up and dressed and went over to Mrs. Phelps' back door, on which Mrs. Norton knocked. The door opened and Mrs. Phelps stood there, smiling. She was fully dressed and did not look grief-stricken or tired. "Well!" she said. "This *is* nice! Do come in!" They went in. Mrs. Phelps led them into the living-room, a neat and well-ordered room, and asked them to take chairs. They sat down, each on the edge of her chair, and waited. Mrs. Phelps talked pleasantly of this and that. Did they ever see anything grow like her giant begonia in the window? She had grown it from a slip that a Mrs. Bricker had given her. Had they heard that the Chalmers child was down with the measles? The other ladies murmured responses now and then and finally rose and said that they must be going. Mrs. Phelps asked them to run in any time; it had been so sweet of them to call. They went out into the courtyard and walked all the way to Mrs. Norton's door without a word, and there they stopped and stared at each other.

That, aggravatingly enough, is where Mrs. Norton's story ended—except for the bit of information that Mrs. Stokes, frightened of Mrs. Phelps, had moved away from Hampton Court a week after the night of alarm. Mrs. Norton does not believe in probing into the psychic. One must take, gratefully, such glimpses of the psychic as are presented to one, and seek no further. She had no theories as to what happened to Mrs. Phelps after Mrs. Phelps "went back to her father." The disappearance fitted snugly into the whole pattern of the night and she let it go at that. Mrs. Norton and Mrs. Phelps have become quite good friends now, and Mrs. Phelps frequently drops in for tea. They have had no further adventures. Mrs. Phelps has not mentioned her father since that night. All that Mrs. Norton really knows about her is that she was born in Bellefontaine, Ohio, and sometimes wishes that she were back there. I took the story for what it was, fuzzy edges and all: an almost perfect example of what goes on in the life that moves slowly about the lonely figure of Mrs. Jessie Norton, reading the precarious future in her tea leaves, listening to the whisperings and knockings of the ominous present at her door. Before I left her she read my fortune in the teacup I had drunk from. It seems that a slight, blonde woman is going to come into my life and that I should beware of the sea.

Guns and Game Calls

I WANDERED into Stoeger's famouse gun house in Fifth Avenue the other morning to see if they could repair my derringer. The way I came to have a derringer is rather odd and quite unlike me, really. I had been up in Winsted, Connecticut, and on the way back I stopped my car in front of a little shop in the town. In the window, on a table, lay the derringer. It was a very old derringer. As you may know, a derringer is a small knob-handled, short-barreled pistol with which ladies and gentlemen used to shoot at one another in the old days. The one I came upon had been found, the man in the shop told me, on Canaan Mountain by a Sunday wanderer a few weeks before. It had lain there in the rains and snows of many years, dropped perhaps by a tired soldier or a fallen duellist. It bore the number 247 in the iron of its barrel, showing that it was one of the very earliest derringers.

The man said it was in firing condition and, sure enough, it cocked with a smart click and the hammer fell with a smart click when I pulled the trigger. I bought it for five dollars and brought it to New York, where for more than a week I carried it about with me wherever I went, clicking it at people. Finally I wore the trigger spring out and it wouldn't work any more, so when I was passing Stoeger's the other day, I thought I would go in and ask whether they could repair it.

I know very little about guns, the old derringer being the first gun I have ever owned. Therefore I was a bit awed and uneasy to find myself standing at a counter in Stoeger's facing a muscular, keen-eyed salesman who, I discerned at a glance, knew all about guns. In a hasty look around, as he asked me crisply what he could do for me, I noticed that there did not appear to be, in the whole store, any old guns such as you find on mountains. Everything was modern, shiningly new, elaborately chased and engraved, and apparently expensive (I found out later that a new Luger costs $100, in case you were thinking of giving anyone a new Luger). Well, there I was, facing this muscular, keen-eyed salesman who knew all about guns, from King micormetered autolocking peep-sights (price $4.50) to the Paragon 236E de luxe special over-and-under shotgun (price $1,150). (I'll tell later how I happen to know the names and prices of those things.)

"It's—ah—it's about a derringer," I said finally, in a low and confidential tone. The man led me promptly, without a word, to a long glass showcase and brought out of it a derringer, a brand-new Remington double-barrelled, two-shot, rim-fire derringer. I looked it over frowningly, felt its weight, sighted along the barrel, and put it back on the counter. I was in a considerable predicament because I didn't want to buy a new derringer and I had led the salesman to believe that I did. I was too timid, of course, to bring up now the subject of my old, rusty, single-barrelled, one-shot, powder-and-ball, flint-fired, mountain-found derringer. The moment for that had gone by. I finally got out of the predicament when he brought up the question of a pistol permit. I haven't got one, of course, and that let me out. I was about to creep away when I noticed a pile of Stoeger's "Catalog and Handbook" on the counter. They cost fifty cents each and I bought one—it seemed the least that I could do.

Every man, I think now, should own a gun catalog and handbook. I spent the whole evening going through mine,

AMERICAN DERRINGER.

from Enfield rifles to Webley automatics, and I know enough names and facts and figures and calibers to impress, if not the average member of what Stoeger's calls "the shooting fraternity," at least the average Desdemona one is likely to encounter in the metropolitan area. I know just off-hand, for instance, that you can buy a Harrington & Richardson vest-pocket revolver that weighs only eight ounces and has a barrel only 1⅛ inches long, just the thing for a lady to slip into her evening bag when she goes up to see her escort's etchings after the opera. I know a lot of other things, too, but I am saving them all for dinner-table small talk. All, that is, except what I know about English and American game calls. That knowledge I am willing to share with people because it is too complicated for dinnner-table small talk and because I am generous enough to let people in on what may solve some of their Christmas-list problems. Not everybody is going to give a set of English and American game calls this season, and whoever does is likely to be thought of among his friends as a sophisticated and ingenious fellow.

Stoeger's then, has stocked sets of fifteen different game calls, twelve English and three American. They are of various shapes and sizes, and look like everything from a patrolman's whistle to something that has been accidentally wrenched off a camshaft (the pheasant and screech-owl call, for example). If you own the whole set of fifteen game galls, you can call all the following creatures: pheasant, screech owl, quail, black-bird, stoat, stag, heath hen (don't waste your breath on this one), moor hen, water hen, grouse, rabbit, fox, partridge, lapwing, hawk, buzzard owl, duck, teal, widgeon, snips, redshank, sandpiper, goose, turkey, lark, woodcock, and oystercatcher.

Not everyone, of course, is going to be able to call all of these birds and beasts offhand, the way he might shoot dice. To manipulate a game call expertly requires, I could see by the catalog, not only skill and practice but, I suspect, a natural inborn gift, or frenzy. Take the English snipe call, for example. This is an instrument that looks like a combination biscuit-cutter and fountain pen, and it is, I gather, as difficult to play upon as a saxophone. On it you can call not only the snipe but the redshank, sandpiper, and oystercatcher (an oystercatcher is a water bird that catches oysters). Says the catalog: "Redshank: render a series of plaintive, whistling notes by placing the tongue against mouthpiece of whistle and giving five short, sharp blasts, terminating suddenly. Sandpiper: note is similar to redshank only longer and more trilling, interspersed by low, mournful notes." None of us, I think, is going to be proficient enough on the snipe call to get a redshank and then a sandpiper in quick succession, and I, for one, am not even going to try to summon an oyster-catcher, much as I would like to see one, because to do that, the catalog says, you must give "a strong, sharp note, made by removing the tongue and quickly replacing it," a little feat that died with Houdini.

On the stag call, which looks like a darning egg, one must produce "a long blow, increasing and then dying down (similar to a cow's 'low')." Stay away, I should advise, from that one. It is extremely difficult to get within earshot of

EUROPEAN OYSTERCATCHER.

a stag, and the stag-caller is bound to be in constant danger of finding himself entirely surrounded by cows, or, what is worse, bulls. The English rabbit call (the only American calls are the turkey, duck, and the American snipe) leaves me somewhat confused because it apparently does not attract rabbits at all, but foxes. "With a little practice," says the catalog, "a lifelike imitation of a rabbit can be obtained which acts as an excellent fox decoy." The sound made is a high-pitched squeal, which is not, I suppose, the way one rabbit attracts another rabbit. Most of the foxhunters I know are lusty, florid fellows who hunt foxes in the great tradition of "View hallo!" and "There goes the —— now!" I can't somehow picture any foxhunter I have ever seen standing in a woodsy dell and squealing like a rabbit. And this call, mind you, is an English call! Maybe they are softening up over there.

Passing over the stoat and the widgeon, which I am pleased to regard merely as a bit of mild Stoeger spoofing, I pause, in concluding my survey, to warn you against the lark call. I happen to know the case history of one man who used a lark call. He was a Frenchman who lived near Nice, and the brief and unhappy account of his lark hunt got into the candid pages of the invaluable *Éclaireur de Nice et du Sud-Est* some ten years ago when I was sojourning on the Riviera. It seems that this gentleman climbed a tree and, having cunningly concealed himself in the foliage, began blowing on his lark call—"short, sharp in and out breaths, varying with buzzing sound in mouth at same time," says the catalog (try that on your lark call). Well, this man was so good that he was suddenly riddled with shotgun slugs from the weapon of another hunter, who had been royally taken in by the remarkable imitation. The thing to do with your English and American game-call set is simply to put it away somewhere in your den and think of it as an interesting collection, like so many old derringers. Nobody wants to get shot for a lark, or gored by an unsympathetic and disillusioned bull.

The Hiding Generation

ONE AFTERNOON almost two years ago, at a cocktail party (at least, this is the way I have been telling the story), an eager middle-aged woman said to me, "Do you belong to the Lost Generation, Mr. T?" and I retorted, coldly and quick as a flash, "No, Madam, I belong to the Hiding Generation."

As a matter of fact, no woman ever asked me such a question at a cocktail party or anywhere else. I thought up the little dialogue one night when I couldn't sleep. At the time, my retort seemed pretty sharp and satirical to me, and I hoped that some day somebody *would* ask me if I belonged to the Lost Generation, so that I could say no, I belonged to the Hiding Generation. But nobody ever has. My retort, however, began working in the back of my mind. I decided that since I was apparently never going to get a chance to use it as repartee, I ought to do something else with it, if only to get it out of the back of my mind. About ten months ago I got around to the idea of writing a book called "The Hiding Generation," which would be the story of my own intellectual conflicts, emotional disturbances, spiritual adventures, and journalistic experiences, something in the manner of Malcolm Cowley's "Exile's Return" or Vincent Sheean's "Personal History." The notion seemed to me a remarkably good one, and I was quite excited by it. I bought a new typewriter ribbon and a ream of fresh copy paper; I sharpened a dozen pencils; I got a pipe and tobacco. Then I sat down at the typewriter, lighted my pipe, and wrote on a sheet of paper "The Hiding Generation, by James Thurber." That was as far as I got, because I discovered that I could not think of anything else to say. I mean anything at all.

Thus passed the first five or six hours of my work on the book. In the late afternoon some people dropped in for cocktails, and I didn't get around to the book again for two more days. Then I found that I still didn't have anything to say. I wondered if I had already said everything I had to say, but I decided, in looking over what I had said in the past, that I really hadn't ever said anything. This was an extremely depressing thought, and for a while I considered going into some other line of work. But I am not fitted for any other line of work, by inclination, experience, or aptitude. There was consequently nothing left for me but to go back to work on

"The Hiding Generation." I decided to "write it in my mind," in the manner of Arnold Bennett (who did practically all of "The Old Wives' Tale" in his head), and this I devoted myself to for about seven months. At length I sat down at the typewriter once more, and there I was again, tapping my fingers on the table, lighting and relighting my pipe, getting up every now and then for a drink of water. I figured finally that maybe I had better make an outline of the book;

SOME PEOPLE DROPPED IN FOR COCKTAILS.

probably all the writers I had in mind—and there was a pretty big list of them now, including Walter Duranty and Negley Farson—had made an outline of what they were going to say, using Roman numerals for the main divisions and small letters "a" and "b," etc., for the subdivisions. So I set down some Roman numerals and small letters on a sheet of paper. First I wrote "I. Early Youth." I could think of no subdivisions to go under that, so I put down "II. Young Manhood." All I could think of to go under that was "a.

Studs Lonigan." Obviously that wouldn't do, so I tore up the sheet of paper and put the whole thing by for another week.

During that week I was tortured by the realization that I couldn't think of anything important that had happened to me up to the time I was thirty-three and began raising Scotch terriers. The conviction that nothing important had happened to me until I was thirty-three, that I had apparently had no intellectual conflicts or emotional disturbances, or anything, reduced me to such a state of dejection that I decided to go to Bridgeport for a few days and stay all alone in a hotel room. The motivation behind this decision is still a little vague in my mind, but I think it grew out of a feeling that I wasn't worthy of going away to Florida or Bermuda or Nassau or any other nice place. I had Bridgeport "coming to me," in a sense, as retribution for my blank youth and my blank young manhood. In the end, of course, I did not go to Bridgeport. I took a new sheet of paper and began another outline.

This time I started out with "I. University Life. a. Intellectual Conflicts." No other workable subdivisions occurred to me. The only Emotional Disturbance that came to my mind was unworthy of being incorporated in the book, for it had to do with the moment, during the Phi Psi May Dance of 1917, when I knocked a fruit salad onto the floor. The incident was as bald as that, and somehow I couldn't correlate it with anything. To start out with such an episode and then just leave it hanging in the air would not give the reader anything to get his teeth into. Therefore I concentrated on "Intellectual Conflicts," but I could not seem to call up any which had torn my mind asunder during my college days. Yet there *must* have been some. I made a lot of little squares and circles with the pencil for half an hour, and finally I remembered one intellectual conflict—if you could call it that. It was really only an argument I had had with a classmate at Ohio State University named Arthur Spencer, about "Tess of the D'Urbervilles." I had taken the view that the hero of the book was not justified in running away to South America and abandoning Tess simply because she had been indiscreet in her youth. Spencer, on the other hand, contended the man was fully justified, and that he (Spencer) would have run away to South America and left Tess, or any other woman, under the circumstances—that is, if he had had the money. As a matter of fact, Spencer settled down in East Liverpool, Ohio, where he is partner in his father's hardware store, and married a very nice girl named Sarah Gammadinger, who had been a Kappa at Ohio State.

I came to the conclusion finally that I would have to leave my university life out of the book, along with my early youth and young manhood. Therefore, my next Roman numeral, which would normally have been IV, automatically became I. I placed after it the words "Paris: A New World. a. Thoughts at Sea." It happened that upon leaving the university, in 1918, I went to Paris as a clerk, Grade B, in the American Embassy. In those days I didn't call it clerk, Grade B, I called it attaché, but it seemed to me that the honest and forceful thing to do was to tell the truth. The book would have more power and persuasion if I told the truth— providing I could remember the truth. There was a lot I couldn't remember, I found out in trying to. For instance, I had put down "Thoughts at Sea" after "a" because I couldn't recall anything significant that had happened to me during the five months I spent in Washington, D. C., before sailing for France. (Furthermore, it didn't seem logical to put a subdivision called "Washington Days" under a general heading called "Paris: A New World.") Something, of course, must have happened to me in Washington, something provocative or instructive, something that added to my stature, but all that comes back to me is a series of paltry little memories. I remember there was a waitress in the Post Café, at the corner of Thirteenth and E Streets, whose last name was Rabbit. I've forgotten her first name and even what she looked like, but her last name was Rabbit. A Mrs. Rabbit. Then there was the flu epidemic, during which I gargled glycothymoline three times a day. All the rest has gone from me.

I found I could remember quite a lot about my days at sea on my way to Paris: A New World. In the first place, I had bought a box of San Felice cigars to take with me on the transport, but I was seasick all the way over and the cigars were smoked by a man named Ed Corcoran, who travelled with me. He was not sick a day. I believe he said he had never been sick a day in his life. Even some of the sailors were sick, but not Corcoran. No, sir. He was constantly in and out of our stateroom, singing, joking, smoking my cigars. The other thing I remembered about the voyage was that my trunk and suitcase failed to get on the ship; they were put by mistake on some other ship—the Minnetonka, perhaps, or the Charles O. Sprague, a coastwise fruit steamer. In any case, I didn't recover them until May, 1920, in Paris, and the Hershey bars my mother had packed here and there in both the trunk and the suitcase had melted and were all over everything. All my suits were brown, even the gray one. But I am anticipating myself. All this belongs under "Paris: A New World. b. Paris."

I was just twenty-five when I first saw Paris, and I was still a little sick. Unfortunately, when I try to remember my first impressions of Paris and the things that happened to me, I get them mixed up with my second trip to Paris, which was seven years later, when I was feeling much better and really got around more. On that first trip to Paris I was, naturally enough, without any clothes, except what I had on, and I had to outfit myself at once, which I did at the Galeries Lafayette. I paid $4.75 in American money for a pair of B.V.D.s. I remember that, all right. Nothing else comes back to me very clearly; everything comes back to me all jumbled up. I tried about five times to write down a comprehensive outline of my experiences in Paris: A New World, but the thing remained sketchy and trivial. If there was any development in my character or change in my outlook on life during that

phase, I forget just where it came in and why. So I cut out the
Paris interlude.

I find, in looking over my accumulation of outlines, that
my last attempt to get the volume started began with the
heading "I. New York Again: An Old World." This was
confusing, because it could have meaning and pertinence
only if it followed the chapter outlined as "Paris: A New
World," and that had all been eliminated along with my
Early Youth, Young Manhood, and University Days. Moreover, while my life back in New York must have done a
great deal to change my character, viewpoint, objectives, and
political ideals, I forget just exactly how this happened. I am
the kind of man who should keep notes about such things. If
I do not keep notes, I simply cannot remember a thing. Oh, I
remember odds and ends, as you have seen, but they
certainly would not tie up into anything like a moving
chronicle of a man's life, running to a hundred and fifty
thousand words. If they ran to twenty-five hundred words, I
would be going good. Now, it's a funny thing: catch me in a
drawing-room, over the coffee and liqueurs, particularly the
Scotch-and-sodas, and I could hold you, or at least keep
talking to you, for five or six hours about my life, but
somebody would have to take down what I said and organize
it into a book. When I sit down to *write* the story of my life,
all I can think of is Mrs. Rabbit, and the Hershey bars, and
the B.V.D.'s that came within two bits of costing five bucks.
That is, of course, until I get up to the time when I was
thirty-three and began raising Scotch terriers. I can put down
all of that, completely and movingly, without even making
an outline. Naturally, as complete and as moving as it might
be, it would scarcely make a biography like, say, Negley
Farson's, and it certainly would not sustain so pretentious a
title as "The Hiding Generation." I would have to publish it
as a pamphlet entitled "The Care and Training of Scotch
Terriers." I am very much afraid that that is what my long
arduous struggle to write the story of my life is going to come

down to, if it is going to come down to anything.

Well, all of us cannot write long autobiographies. But *almost* all of us can.

Wild Bird Hickok and His Friends

IN ONE of the many interesting essays that make up his book called "Abinger Harvest," Mr. E. M. Forster, discussing what he sees when he is reluctantly dragged to the movies in London, has set down a sentence that fascinates me. It is: "American women shoot the hippopotamus with eyebrows made of platinum." I have given that remarkable sentence a great deal of study, but I still do not know whether Mr. Forster means that American women have platinum eyebrows or that the hippopotamus has platinum eyebrows or that American women shoot platinum eyebrows into the hippopotamus. At any rate, it faintly stirred in my mind a dim train of elusive memories which were brightened up suddenly and brought into sharp focus for me when, one night, I went to see "The Plainsman," a hard-riding, fast-shooting movie dealing with warfare in the Far West back in the bloody seventies. I knew then what Mr. Forster's curious and tantalizing sentence reminded me of. It was like nothing in the world so much as certain sentences which appeared in a group of French paperback dime (or, rather, twenty-five centime) novels that I collected a dozen years ago in France. "The Plainsman" brought up these old pulp thrillers in all clarity for me because, like that movie, they dealt mainly with the stupendous activities of Buffalo Bill and Wild Bill Hickok; but in them were a unique fantasy, a special inventiveness, and an imaginative abandon beside which the

movie treatment of the two heroes pales, as the saying goes,
into nothing. In moving from one apartment to another
some years ago, I somehow lost my priceless collection of
contes héroïques du Far-Ouest, but happily I find that a great
many of the deathless adventures of the French Buffalo Bill
and Wild Bill Hickok remain in my memory. I hope that I
shall recall them, for anodyne, when with eyes too dim to
read, I pluck finally at the counterpane.

In the first place, it should perhaps be said that in the
eighteen-nineties the American dime-novel hero who appears
to have been most popular with the French youth—and
adult—given to such literature was Nick Carter. You will
find somewhere in one of John L. Stoddard's published
lectures—there used to be a set in almost every Ohio
bookcase—an anecdote about how an American tourist, set
upon by *apaches* in a dark *rue* in the nineties, caused them to
scatter in terror merely by shouting, *"Je suis Nick Carter!"*
But at the turn of the century, or shortly thereafter, Buffalo
Bill became the favorite. Whether he still is or not, I don't
know—perhaps Al Capone or John Dillinger has taken his
place. Twelve years ago, however, he was going great guns—
or perhaps I should say great dynamite, for one of the things
I most clearly remember about the Buffalo Bill of the French
authors was that he always carried with him sticks of
dynamite which, when he was in a particularly tough spot—
that is, surrounded by more than two thousand Indians—he
hurled into their midst, destroying them by the hundred.
Many of the most inspired paperbacks that I picked up in my
quest were used ones I found in those little stalls along the
Seine. It was there, for instance, that I came acorss one of my
favorites, "Les Aventures du Wild Bill dans le Far-Ouest."

Wild Bill Hickok was, in this wonderful and beautiful tale,
an even more prodigious manipulator of the six-gun than he
seems to have been in real life, which, as you must know, is
saying a great deal. He frequently mowed down a hundred or
two hundred Indians in a few minutes with his redoubtable

pistol. The French author of this masterpiece for some mysterious but delightful reason referred to Hickok sometimes as Wild Bill and sometimes as Wild Bird. *"Bonjour, Wild Bill!"* his friend Buffalo Bill often said to him when they met, only to shout a moment later, *"Regardez, Wild Bird! Les Peaux-Rouges!"* The two heroes spent a great deal of their time, as in "The Plainsman," helping each other out of dreadful situations. Once, for example, while hunting Seminoles in Florida, Buffalo Bill fell into a tiger trap that had been set for him by the Indians—he stepped onto what turned out to be sticks covered with grass, and plunged to the bottom of a deep pit. At this point our author wrote, *"'Mercy me!' s'écria Buffalo Bill."* The great scout was rescued, of course, by none other than Wild Bill, or Bird, who, emerging from the forest to see his old comrade in distress, could only exclaim *"My word!"*

It was, I believe, in another volume that one of the most interesting characters in all French fiction of the Far West appeared, a certain Major Preston, alias Preeton, alias Preslon (the paperbacks rarely spelled anyone's name twice in succession the same way). This hero, we were told when he was introduced, "had distinguished himself in the Civil War by capturing Pittsburgh," a feat which makes Lee's invasion of Pennsylvania seem mere child's play. Major Preeton (I always preferred that alias) had come out West to fight the Indians with cannon, since he believed it absurd that nobody had thought to blow them off the face of the earth with cannon before. How he made out with his artillery against the forest skulkers I have forgotten, but I have an indelible memory of a certain close escape that Buffalo Bill had in this same book. It seems that, through an oversight, he had set out on a scouting trip without his dynamite—he also carried, by the way, cheroots and a flashlight—and hence, when he stumbled upon a huge band of redskins, he had to ride as fast as he could for the nearest fort. He made it just in time. "Buffalo Bill," ran the story, "clattered across the drawbridge

"VOUS VOUS PROMENEZ TRÈS TARD CE SOIR, MON VIEUX!"

and into the fort just ahead of the Indians, who, unable to stop in time, plunged into the moat and were drowned." It may have been in this same tale that Buffalo Bill was once so hard pressed that he had to send for Wild Bird to help him out. Usually, when one was in trouble, the other showed up by a kind of instinct, but this time Wild Bird was nowhere to be found. It was a long time, in fact, before his whereabouts were discovered. You will never guess where he was. He was "taking the baths at Atlantic City under orders of his physician." But he came riding across the country in one day to Buffalo Bill's side, and all was well. Major Preeton, it sticks in my mind, got bored with the service in the Western hotels and went "back to Philadelphia" (Philadelphia appears to have been the capital city of the United States at this time). The Indians in all these tales—and this is probably what gave Major Preeton his great idea—were seldom seen as individuals or in pairs or small groups, but prowled about in well-ordered columns of squads. I recall, however, one drawing (the paperbacks were copiously illustrated) which showed two *Peaux-Rouges* leaping upon and capturing a scout who had wandered too far from his drawbridge one night. The picture represented one of the Indians as smilingly taunting his captive, and the caption read, *"Vous vous promenez très tard ce soir, mon vieux!"* This remained my favorite line until I saw one night in Paris an old W. S. Hart movie called "Le Roi du Far-Ouest," in which Hart, insulted by a drunken ruffian, turned upon him and said, in his grim, laconic way, *"Et puis, après?"*

I first became interested in the French tales of the Far West when, one winter in Nice, a French youngster of fifteen, who, it turned out, devoted all his spending money to them, asked me if I had ever seen a "wishtonwish." This meant nothing to me, and I asked him where he had heard about the wishtonwish. He showed me a Far West paperback he was reading. There was a passage in it which recounted an adventure of Buffalo Bill and Wild Bill during the course of which Buffalo Bill signalled to Wild Bird "in the voice of the wishtonwish." Said the author in a parenthesis which at that time gave me as much trouble as Mr. Forster's sentence about the platinum eyebrows does now, "The wishtonwish was seldom heard west of Philadelphia." It was some time— indeed, it was not until I got back to America—that I traced the wishtonwish to its lair, and in so doing discovered the influence of James Fenimore Cooper on all these French writers of Far West tales. Cooper, in his novels, frequently mentioned the wishtonwish, which was a Caddoan Indian name for the prairie dog. Cooper erroneously applied it to the whippoorwill. An animal called the "ouapiti" also figured occasionally in the French stories, and this turned out to be the wapiti, or American elk, also mentioned in Cooper's tales. The French writer's parenthetical note on the habitat of the wishtonwish only added to the delightful confusion and inaccuracy which threaded these wondrous stories.

There were, in my lost and lamented collection, a hundred other fine things, which I have forgotten, but there is one that will forever remain with me. It occurred in a book in which, as I remember it, Billy the Kid, alias Billy the Boy, was the central figure. At any rate, two strangers had turned up in a small Western town and their actions had aroused the suspicions of a group of respectable citizens, who forthwith called on the sheriff to complain about the newcomers. The sheriff listened gravely for a while, got up and buckled on his gun belt, and said, *"Alors, je vais demander ses cartes d'identité!"* There are few things, in any literature, that have ever given me a greater thrill than coming across that line.

Doc Marlowe

I WAS too young to be other than awed and puzzled by Doc Marlowe when I knew him. I was only sixteen when he died. He was sixty-seven. There was that vast difference in our ages and there was a vaster difference in our backgrounds. Doc Marlowe was a medicine-show man. He had been a lot of other things, too: a circus man, the proprietor of a concession at Coney Island, a saloon-keeper; but in his fifties he had traveled around with a tent-show troupe made up of a Mexican named Chickalilli, who threw knives, and a man called Professor Jones, who played the banjo. Doc Marlowe would come out after the entertainment and harangue the crowd and sell bottles of medicine for all kinds of ailments. I found out all this about him gradually, toward the last, and after he died. When I first knew him, he represented the Wild West to me, and there was nobody I admired so much.

I met Doc Marlow at old Mrs. Willoughby's rooming house. She had been a nurse in our family, and I used to go and visit her over week-ends sometimes, for I was very fond

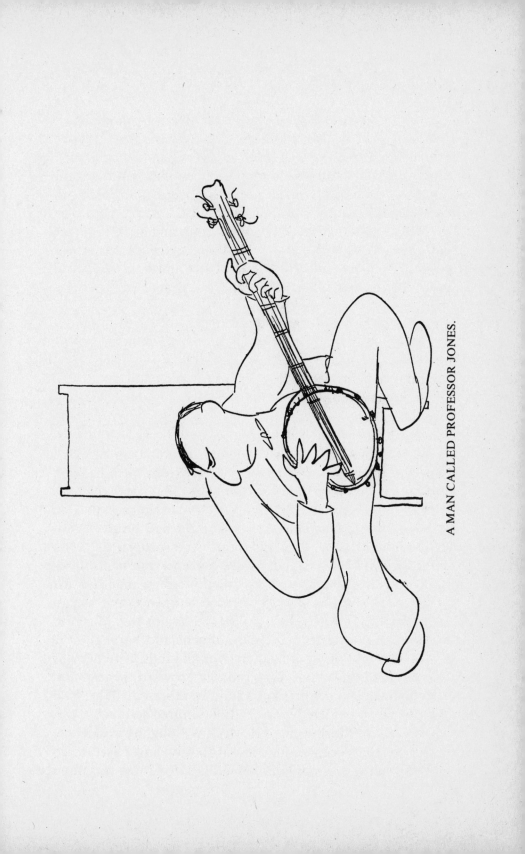

A MAN CALLED PROFESSOR JONES.

of her. I was about eleven years old then. Doc Marlowe wore scarred leather leggings, a bright-colored bead vest that he said he got from the Indians, and a ten-gallon hat with kitchen matches stuck in the band, all the way around. He was about six feet four inches tall, with big shoulders, and a long, drooping mustache. He let his hair grow long, like General Custer's. He had a wonderful collection of Indian relics and six-shooters, and he used to tell me stories of his adventures in the Far West. His favorite expressions were "Hay, boy!" and "Hay, boy-gie!," which he used the way some people now use "Hot dog!" or "Doggone!" He told me once that he had killed an Indian chief named Yellow Hand in a tomahawk duel on horseback. I thought he was the greatest man I had ever seen. It wasn't until he died and his son came on from New Jersey for the funeral that I found out he had never been in the Far West in his life. He had been born in Brooklyn.

Doc Marlowe had given up the road when I knew him, but he still dealt in what he called "medicines." His stock in trade was a liniment that he had called Snake Oil when he travelled around. He changed the name to Blackhawk Liniment when he settled in Columbus. Doc didn't always sell enough of it to pay for his bed and board, and old Mrs. Willoughby would sometimes have to "trust" him for weeks at a time. She didn't mind, because his liniment had taken a bad kink out of her right limb that had bothered her for thirty years. I used to see people whom Doc massaged with Blackhawk Liniment move arms and legs that they hadn't been able to move before he "treated" them. His patients were day laborers, wives of streetcar conductors, and people like that. Sometimes they would shout and weep after Doc had massaged them, and several got up and walked around who hadn't been able to walk before. One man hadn't turned his head to either side for seven years before Doc soused him with Blackhawk. In half an hour he could move his head as easily as I could move mine. "Glory be to God!" he shouted. "It's the secret qualities in the ointment, my friend," Doc Marlowe told him, suavely. He always called the liniment ointment.

News of his miracles got around by word of mouth among the poorer classes of town—he was not able to reach the better people (the "tony folks," he called them)—but there was never a big enough sale to give Doc a steady income. For one thing, people thought there was more magic in Doc's touch than in his liniment, and, for another, the ingredients of Blackhawk cost so much that his profits were not very great. I know, because I used to go to the wholesale chemical company once in a while for him and buy his supplies. Everything that went into the liniment was standard and expensive (and well-known, not secret). A man at the company told me he didn't see how Doc could make much money on it at thirty-five cents a bottle. But even when he was very low in funds Doc never cut out any of the ingredients or substituted cheaper ones. Mrs. Willoughby had suggested it to him once, she told me, when she was helping him "put up a batch," and he had got mad. "He puts a heap of store by that liniment being right up to the mark," she said.

Doc added to his small earnings, I discovered, by money he made gambling. He used to win quite a few dollars on Saturday nights at Freck's saloon, playing poker with the marketmen and the railroaders who dropped in there. It wasn't for several years that I found out Doc cheated. I had never heard about marked cards until he told me about them and showed me his. It was one rainy afternoon, after he had played seven-up with Mrs. Willoughby and old Mr. Peiffer, another roomer of hers. They had played for small stakes (Doc wouldn't play cards unless there was some money up, and Mrs. Willoughby wouldn't play if very much was up). Only twenty or thirty cents had changed hands in the end. Doc had won it all. I remember my astonishment and indignation when it dawned on me that Doc had used the marked cards in playing the old lady and the old man. "You

didn't cheat *them*, did you?" I asked him. "Jimmy, my boy,"
he told me, "the man that calls the turn wins the money." His
eyes twinkled and he seemed to enjoy my anger. I was
outraged, but I was helpless. I knew I could never tell Mrs.
Willoughby about how Doc had cheated her at seven-up. I
liked her, but I liked him, too. Once he had given me a whole
dollar to buy fireworks with on the Fourth of July.

I remember once, when I was staying at Mrs. Willoughby's,
Doc Marlowe was roused out of bed in the middle of the
night by a poor woman who was frantic because her little girl
was sick. This woman had had the sciatica driven out of her
by his liniment, she reminded Doc. He placed her then. She
had never been able to pay him a cent for his liniment or his
"treatments," and he had given her a great many. He got up
and dressed, and went over to her house. The child had colic,
I suppose. Doc couldn't have had any idea what was the
matter, but he sopped on liniment; he sopped on a whole
bottle. When he came back home, two hours later, he said he
had "relieved the distress." The little girl had gone to sleep
and was all right the next day, whether on account of Doc
Marlowe or in spite of him I don't know. "I want to thank
you, Doctor," said the mother, tremulously, when she called
on him that afternoon. He gave her another bottle of
liniment, and he didn't charge her for it or for his
"professional call." He used to massage, and give liniment
to, a lot of sufferers who were too poor to pay. Mrs.
Willoughby told him once that he was too generous and too
easily taken in. Doc laughed—and winked at me, with the
twinkle in his eye that he had had when he told me how he
had cheated the old lady at cards.

Once I went for a walk with him out Town Street on a
Saturday afternoon. It was a warm day, and after a while I
said I wanted a soda. Well, he said, he didn't care if he took
something himself. We went into a drugstore, and I ordered a
chocolate soda and he had a lemon phosphate. When we had
finished, he said, "Jimmy, my son, I'll match you to see who

pays for the drinks." He handed me a quarter and he told me to toss the quarter and he would call the turn. He called heads and won. I paid for the drinks. It left me with a dime.

I was fifteen when Doc got out his pamphlets, as he called them. He had eased the misery of the wife of a small-time printer and the grateful man had given him a special price on two thousand advertising pamphlets. There was very little in them about Blackhawk Liniment. They were mostly about Doc himself and his "Life in the Far West." He had gone out to Franklin Park one day with a photographer—another of his numerous friends—and there the photographer took dozens of pictures of Doc, a lariat in one hand, a six-shooter in the other. I had gone along. When the pamphlets came out, there were the pictures of Doc, peering around trees, crouching behind bushes, whirling the lariat, aiming the gun. "Dr. H. M. Marlowe Hunting Indians" was one of the captions. "Dr. H. M. Marlowe after Hoss-Thieves" was another one. He was very proud of the pamphlets and always had a sheaf with him. He would pass them out to people on the street.

Two years before he died Doc got hold of an ancient, wheezy Cadillac somewhere. He aimed to start traveling around again, he said, but he never did, because the old automobile was so worn out it wouldn't hold up for more than a mile or so. It was about this time that a man named Hardman and his wife came to stay at Mrs. Willoughby's. They were farm people from around Lancaster who had sold their place. They got to like Doc because he was so jolly, they said, and they enjoyed his stories. He treated Mrs. Hardman for an old complaint in the small of her back and wouldn't take any money for it. They thought he was a fine gentleman. Then there came a day when they announced that they were going to St. Louis, where they had a son. They talked some of settling in St. Louis. Doc Marlowe told them they ought to buy a nice auto cheap and drive out, instead of going by train—it wouldn't cost much and they could see the country,

give themselves a treat. Now, he knew where they could pick
up just such a car.

Of course, he finally sold them the decrepit Cadillac—it
had been stored away somewhere in the back of a garage
whose owner kept it there for nothing because Doc had
relieved his mother of a distress in the groins, as Doc
explained it. I don't know just how the garage man doctored
up the car, but he did. It actually chugged along pretty
steadily when Doc took the Hardmans out for a trial spin.
He told them he hated to part with it, but he finally let them
have it for a hundred dollars. I knew, of course, and so did
Doc, that it couldn't last many miles.

Doc got a letter from the Hardmans in St. Louis ten days
later. They had had to abandon the old junk pile in West
Jefferson, some fifteen miles out of Columbus. Doc read the
letter aloud to me, peering over his glasses, his eyes
twinkling, every now and then punctuating the lines with
"Hay, boy!" and "Hay, boy-gie!" "I just want you to know,
Dr. Marlowe," he read, "what I think of low-life swindlers
like you [Hay, boy!] and that it will be a long day before I put
my trust in a two-faced lyer and imposture again [Hay, boy-
gie!]. The garrage man in W. Jefferson told us your old
rattle-trap had been doctored up just to fool us. It was a low
down dirty trick as no swine would play on a white man
[Hay, boy!]." Far from being disturbed by the letter, Doc
Marlowe was plainly amused. He took off his glasses, after
he finished it and laughed, his hand to his brow and his eyes
closed. I was pretty mad, because I had liked the Hardmans,
and because they had liked him. Doc Marlowe put the letter
carefully back into its envelope and tucked it away in his
inside coat pocket, as if it were something precious. Then he
picked up a pack of cards and began to lay out a solitaire
hand. "Want to set in a little seven-up game, Jimmy?" he
asked me. I was furious. "Not with a cheater like you!" I
shouted, and stamped out of the room, slamming the door. I
could hear him chuckling to himself behind me.

The last time I saw Doc Marlowe was just a few days before he died. I didn't know anything about death, but I knew he was dying when I saw him. His voice was very faint and his face was drawn; they told me he had a lot of pain. When I got ready to leave the room, he asked me to bring him a tin box that was on his bureau. I got it and handed it to him. He poked around in it for a while with unsteady fingers and finally found what he wanted. He handed it to me. It was a quarter, or rather it looked like a quarter, but it had heads on both sides. "Never let the other fella call the turn, Jimmy, my boy," said Doc, with a shadow of his old twinkle and the echo of his old chuckle. I still have the two-headed quarter. For a long time I didn't like to think about it, or about Doc Marlowe, but I do now.

Food Fun for the Menfolk

FIVE OR six weeks ago, someone who signed himself simply A Friend sent me a page torn from the Sunday magazine section of the *Herald Tribune*. "I thought this might interest you," he wrote. Unfortunately, he failed to mark the particular item he had in mind. On one side of the page was an article called "New Thoughts about Awnings," which, naturally, didn't interest me at all. I turned the page over and came to this announcement: "Why shouldn't you be among the prize winners in our reader-recipe contest for dishes made with plain or prepared gelatin?" The answer to that was so simple as to be silly, so I went on to another column and a recipe for "Plum Surprise." That couldn't have been what A Friend wanted me to see, for the least of my interests in this world, the least of anybody's interests, is Plum Surprise.

Gradually, by this process of elimination, I came to an article called "Shower Parties, Up-to-Date!" (the exclamation point is the author's). This was without doubt what A Friend wished to bring to my attention. I read the article with mingled feelings of dismay and downright dread and then threw it away. But it haunted me for weeks. I realized finally that "Shower Parties, Up-to-Date!" presented one of those menaces which it is far better to face squarely than to try to ignore, so I dug it up again and you and I are now going to face it together. If we all stand as one, we can put a stop to the ominous innovation in shower parties which the author of the article, Miss Elizabeth Harriman, so gaily suggests.

It is Miss Elizabeth Harriman's contention that *it is high time to invite the bridegroom and his men friends to shower parties for the bride!* (The italics and the exclamation point are mine.) "Nowadays," she says, flatly, "the groom insists on being included in the party." Without descending to invective, mud-slinging, or the lie direct, I can only say that you and I and Miss Harriman have never met a groom and, what is more, are never going to meet a groom who insists on being included in a shower party given for his bride. A groom would as soon wear a veil and carry a bouquet of lilies of the valley and baby's-breath as attend a shower party. Particularly the kind of shower party which Miss Harriman, with fiendish glee, goes on to invent right out of her own head. Let her start it off for you herself: "After supper— which should be simple—comes the 'shower,' and here's where we surprise the bride—and the groom—by not giving them a complete set of kitchen equipment. With a mischievous twinkle in our eye, we deposit in front of the happy couple a bushel basket, saying 'The grocer left this a little early for your new home, but you'd better open it now.'" I will take up the story of what is supposed to happen next myself, with a glint of cold horror in my eye.

It seems that the bushel basket is covered with a large piece of brown paper marked with the date of the forthcoming wedding. The very thought of a prospective bridegroom standing in a group of giggling women, with mischievous twinkles in their eyes, and looking at a bushel basket covered with brown paper bearing the date of his wedding is enough to convince anybody that Miss Harriman has got the wrong group of people together. But let us see what happens further (both according to Miss Harriman and according to me). In the basket, she says, are six brown-paper bags. The groom is made to pick up one of these, marked "What the Groom Gets." No groom in the United States would open a bag of that description—he is going through enough the way things are—but let us suppose that he does. Do you know what falls out of it, amid screams of laughter? A peach falls out of it. The bride now picks up a second brown-paper bag, labelled "What the Bride Gets." If you can't picture the look on the face of the groom at this point, I can. Well, out of this bag comes a box of salt marked "Genuine Old Salt." It seems that Miss Harriman has made the groom in this particular case "an ardent fisherman"—hence, Genuine Old Salt. Of course, that wouldn't work in the case of a groom who was not an ardent fisherman. All the guests would just stand there, with their mischievous twinkles turning to puzzled stares. If the groom is *not* an ardent fisherman, Miss Harriman suggests that the bride's bag contain "a ginger-bread man cutter." You can hear the pleased roars of the groom and his men friends. "By George," they cry, "this is more fun than a barrel of monkeys!" Everybody is so interested that nobody wonders whether drinks are going to be served, or anything of that sort. There are four brown-paper bags yet to be opened, you see.

The bride now opens the first of these bags, marked simply "The Bride." From this emerge, amid the ecstatic squeals of the ladies, an old potato, a new potato, a borrowed rolling pin, and a blue plum. All the men stare blankly at this array and one of them begins to wonder where they keep the liquor in this house; but the girls explain about the contents of the bag. "Don't you see, Joe? It's 'something old and something new, something borrowed and something blue.'" "What's the potatoes for?" says Joe, gloomily (he is the man who was wondering where they keep the liquor). "I don't get it." "Well, Bert gets it," says the woman who has been explaining to Joe. Bert is a man whose guts Joe hates. "Let him have it," says Joe. This is one of his worst evenings, and there are still three brown-paper bags to be opened. The groom is now holding one of these, on which is printed "The Groom Is In the Kitchen Closet." There is a Bronx cheer from somewhere (probably from Harry Innis) and the groom grins redly; he wishes he were back in college. You and I know that the groom would simply put this bag back in the basket muttering something about it must be getting late, but Miss Harriman says he would open it. All right, he opens it. And pulls out a toy broom. At this point the groom's embarrassment and Joe's gloom are deeper than ever. "What's the idea?" Joe growls. "Stupid!" cries one of the ladies, gaily. "Don't you know 'Here comes the groom, stiff as a groom— stiff as a broom,' I mean?" "No," says Joe. He now moves directly on the pantry to see what there is in the way of drinks around the place. What he finds, in the icebox, is a Mason jar filled with cranberry juice. Joe instantly begins to look for his hat and overcoat, but the hostess captures him. There is more fun to come, she tells him—it is still *frightfully* early, only about eight-thirty.

The hostess leads Joe back to the bushel basket and pulls a fifth bag out of it, which she asks him to open; it is labelled "What the Guests Have." "What's the idea?" Joe grumbles, holding the bag as if it were a doily or a diaper. "Open it, silly!" squeal the excited girls, several of whom, however, are now squealing a little less excitedly than they have been. Joe finally opens the bag and pulls out a box of rice and a box of thyme marked "Good Thyme." "Thyme," mutters Joe, blankly, pronouncing the "h." He hands the boxes to the groom, who distractedly puts them back in the brown bag

THE HOSTESS HANDS EACH GUEST, INCLUDING JOE, A PIECE OF
CARDBOARD.

and puts the brown bag back in the bushel basket. One of the
women hastily takes the bag out and opens it again, putting
the rice and the thyme on the table. A slight chill falls over
the party, on account of the groom's distraction and Joe's
sullenness. There is a bad pause, not helped any by Harry
Innis's wide yawn, but the hostess quickly hands the sixth
and last brown bag to the bride, who extracts from it "a
small jar of honey and a moon-shaped cooky-cutter." Joe
takes the cooky-cutter from the bride; he is mildly interested
for the first time. "What's this thing belong on?" he asks.
Somebody takes it away from him. The groom glances at his
wristwatch. It is not yet nine o'clock. "Isn't this fun, dear?"
asks his bride. "Yeh, sure. Swell." The bride realizes, with a
quick intuition, that she is losing her hold on the groom. If
she is a smart bride, she will be taken suddenly ill at this
point and the groom will have to see her home (and Joe will
have a chance to cry out with great concern, "Is there any
whiskey in the house?"). But let us suppose that the bride is
too dumb to realize why she is losing her hold on the groom.

The party in this case goes right on. Miss Harriman has a lot more plans for it; she again has a mischievous twinkle in her eye.

The hostess—I shall just call her Miss Harriman—now hands each guest, including Joe, a piece of cardboard ruled off into twenty-five numbered squares (you can look up the article yourself). Each of the squares is large enough for a word to be written in it. Several of the men who have pencils swear they haven't, but Miss Harriman manages to dig up twenty-two pencils and two fountain pens from somewhere. Harry Innis puts his piece of cardboard on the arm of a davenport, stands up, and says, "Whatta you say we all run up to Tim's for a highball?" At this, Joe instantly puts on his overcoat, but one of the women makes him take it off, whispering harshly that he will break Miss Harriman's heart if he doesn't stay. "Aw," says Joe, and slumps into a chair. Mrs. Innis is quietly giving Harry a piece of her mind in a corner.

Miss Harriman now appears before everybody with an *enormous* piece of cardboard, also ruled off into twenty-five squares. Each square contains a dab of some kitchen staple or other: a dab of salt, a dab of pepper, a dab of sugar, a dab of flour, a dab of cayenne, a dab of sage, a dab of cinnamon, a dab of coffee, a dab of tea, a dab of dry mustard, a dab of grated cheese, a dab of baking powder, a dab of cocoa, and dabs of twelve other things. "The bride has her groceries all mixed up!" Miss Harriman sings out brightly. "You must all help her straighten them out! Everybody may look at the things on my cardboard and feel them, too, but nobody must dare taste! Then you write down in the corresponding squares on your own cardboard what you think the different things are!" Most of the men are now standing in a corner talking about the new Buick. One of them has folded his cardboard double and then folded that double and is absently tearing it into strips. Only Bert and two other men stick in the staples game; they identify the salt, sugar, pepper, coffee, and tea, and let it go at that. Ten of the twelve women present get all the answers right. The prize is a can of pepper and, not knowing whom to give it to, Miss Harriman just puts it on a table and claps her hands for attention. She announces that there is another food game to come. "Geezuss," says Joe.

Let Miss Harriman describe the next game in her own words. "In a large pan we gather together as many different vegetables and fruits as we can find—a bunch of carrots, a few beets, a turnip or two, potatoes white and sweet, parsley, lettuce, beans, oranges, grapefruit, pineapple, cherries, bananas—oh, anything. On a tray are placed string, tooth-picks, paper towelling, waxed paper, pins, knives, scissors, melon-ball scoops, and any other kitchen implements. This game calls for partners, and as this is a food shower, we try to think of all the foods that seem to go together—Salt and Pepper; Liver and Bacon; Corned Beef and Cabbage; Cream and Sugar, etc. Half the ingredients are written on one color paper, the other on another color, and the guests match them for partners."

If, like Joe (who has drawn Liver and, for partner, a Miss Bacon whom he has been avoiding all evening), you haven't got the idea yet, let me explain. The guests are supposed to manufacture the effigies of brides out of all these materials. Whoever makes the funniest or most original bride wins. (There are a lot of gags at this point, the men guffawing over in their corner. Bill Pierson tells the one about the social worker and the colored woman.) Of this bride-making game Miss Harriman writes: "Loud guffaws and wild dashes to the supply table will result." (She is right about the loud guffaws.) "Imaginations will run riot and hidden talents will come to the fore." But meanwhile, under cover of the loud guffaws and the wild dashes, Joe, Harry Innis, and the groom have slipped out of the house and gone on up to Tim's. When the bride discovers that the groom has disappeared she is distraught, for she thinks she has lost him for good, and I would not be surprised if she has.

An appropriate prize for this contest is, according to Miss Harriman, "a bridal bouquet of scallions and radishes with streamers of waxed paper, presented as someone plays 'Here Comes the Bride.'" You can imagine how Joe would have loved that if he had stayed. But he and Harry Innis and the groom are on their fifth highball up at Tim's. "And so our kitchen shower ends," writes Miss Harriman, happily, "with demands for another wedding as an excuse for more food fun." You have to admire the woman for whatever it is she has.

Goodbye, Mr. O. Charles Meyer!

I AM leaving in a few days the apartment I have lived in for almost a year, on the corner of Eighth Street and Fifth Avenue. Its living-room windows and my bedroom window look out over Eighth Street to the west. Eighth Street is so far below that I cannot make out its signs. The top of a building hides the Jefferson Market clock. All the roofs I see are the same roof; they are indistinguishable, one from another. There is only one thing I shall remember: a sign high up on a building in Eighth Street near Sixth Avenue which says in letters four feet tall, "O. Charles Meyer." Mr. Meyer is in the upholstering business. The sign tells you all about it. I see O. Charles Meyer the first thing every morning when I wake up, and during the day whenever I look out the window, and I go to bed knowing that he is out there, as sturdy and staunch as the little toy soldier. In the months that have gone by, O. Charles Meyer has taken on the semblance of a friend to me. His name is as familiar as the name of any friend I have.

I do not, of course, know O. Charles Meyer in the flesh, but I have a certainty of what he is like, a large, heavy man, elderly and kindly, with the peering eyes of a person who has spent his life puttering with the upholstery of chairs and sofas. In the old chairs and sofas that have been brought to him for reupholstering he has found scissors and penknives and necklaces and unopened letters and hundreds of thousands of dollars in bills which little old ladies have hidden away. If this is not true, I don't want to be told so. O. Charles Meyer is, after all, my own creation. "My O. Charles," I could say of Mr. Meyer as Willa Cather said "My Antonia" of a certain Miss Shimerda. I figure him as having a number of sons: O. Freddy, O. Samuel, O. George, O. Charles, Jr., and—if it is not too much to ask—O. Henry. I think there may have been three daughters, O. Grace, O. Patience, and O. Charity, but they all married upholsterers in beaver hats and went away, many years ago. I do not want to know what the O. stands for.

I have a sentimental feeling about O. Charles Meyer and I shall hate to leave him, but I am going to have to because my lease is running out and some new tenants will be moving in. I have no other person to turn to of O. Charles Meyer's peculiar stature as an intimate. It will take me a long time to get used to not seeing him in the morning and all day long. One gets sentimentally attached to curious things in this city of steel and cement. In Connecticut, where I used to have a farm, I could look out the window of the room I worked in and see an apple tree, an ancient russet apple tree. I got to know each bend and twist of its branches. It was a friendly and familiar tree, but, like all ancient apple trees, it began to lose its branches; a branch fell off in every storm, so that the appearance of the old tree was always changing. O. Charles Meyer, on the other hand, has always remained the same. O. Charles Meyer is immutable. Eighth Street changes under him in its restless way, people move in and out of the apartments round about, but O. Charles Meyer goes on forever. In such permanence one finds a sense of peace and assurance.

If I ever have to have any upholstering work done, I would want to take it to O. Charles Meyer, but I would be afraid to. I would be afraid that some crisp clerk in the establishment might say to me, "O. Charles Meyer? Why, there is no O. Charles Meyer any longer. Would you like to talk to Mr. Hinkley? Or Mr. Bence?" Something would go out of my life that would make me miserable, if that happened. I would feel that I couldn't trust anything or anybody any more, if O. Charles Meyer let me down. And yet something constantly nags at me—I like to think it's curiosity and not distrust— something nags at me to call up O. Charles on the phone and do something about him. I feel that there is a certain roundness lacking in my association with him. I feel that whereas he has meant a lot to me, I have meant nothing at all

TURNING UP WITH A GREEN PLUSH CHAIR OF HIS OWN TO SIT IN.

to him. I hate to leave my apartment without making a gesture of some kind on his behalf. It has occurred to me to ask him to a cocktail party (I see him turning up with a green plush chair of his own to sit in). I have thought of phrasing my note to him something like this:

"Mr. O. Charles Meyer,

"Eighth Street,

"Dear Mr. Meyer: Will you come to a cocktail party at my apartment tomorrow from 5 to 7? If there is no such person as you, please do not reply." There is a chance here, of course, that Mr. Meyer—or Mr. Hinkley, or Mr. Bence— might turn my note over to the police. It would be a nasty bit of evidence in case any suit should ever be filed against me to commit me to an institution. I can hear a lawyer making the most of it. "If it please the Court, I should like to submit in evidence, as State's Exhibit A, this note I hold in my hand. This is a note written by the defendant to one O. Charles

Meyer, an upholsterer, inviting Mr. Meyer to a cocktail party. The defendant had never met this man Meyer in his life, as the note proves, and furthermore did not even know whether there *was* such a man. What is more, the note shows that the defendant did not even want to find *out* whether there was such a man. Now, the State contends quite simply . . ."

I suppose, everything considered, that I better drop my relationship with O. Charles Meyer right where it is. The chances are, however, that I will drop around the day before I leave, just to say goodbye and to tell him how much I will miss him, in which case will probably be committed before the summer is out. I'll try not to call on him. I'll try to let it go at this. Goodbye, Mr. O. Charles Meyer! Don't upholster any electric chairs!

What Are the Leftists Saying?

FOR A long time I have had the idea that it would be interesting to attempt to explain to an average worker what the leftist, or socially conscious, literary critics are trying to say. Since these critics are essentially concerned with the improvement of the worker's status, it seems fitting and proper that the worker should be educated in the meaning of their pronouncements. The critics themselves believe, of course, in the education of the worker, but they are divided into two schools about it: those who believe the worker should be taught beforehand why there must be a revolution, and those who believe that he should be taught afterward why there was one. This is but one of many two-school systems which divide the leftist intellectuals and keep them so busy in controversy that the worker is pretty much left out of things. It is my plan to escort a worker to a hypothetical, but typical, gathering of leftist literary critics and interpret for him, insofar as I can, what is being said there. The worker is likely to be so confused at first, and so neglected, that he will want to slip out and go to Minsky's; but it is important that he stay, and I hope that he has already taken a chair and removed his hat. I shall sit beside him and try to clarify what is going on.

Nothing, I must explain while we are waiting for the gentlemen to gather, is going to be easy. This is partly because it is a primary tenet of leftist criticism to avoid what is known as Oversimplification. This is a word our worker is going to encounter frequently at the gathering of critics and it is important that he understand what it means. Let me get at it by quoting a sentence from a recent review in *The Nation* by a socially conscious critic: "In so far as men assert and counter-assert, you can draw an assertion from the comparison of their assertions." As it stands, that is not oversimplified, because no one can point to any exact or absolute meaning it has. Now I will oversimplify it. A says, "Babe Ruth is dead" (assertion). B says "Babe Ruth is alive" (counter-assertion). C says, "You guys seem to disagree" (assertion drawn from comparison of assertions). Here I have brought the critic's sentence down to a definite meaning by providing a concrete instance. Leftist criticism does not believe in that, contending that all thought is in a state of motion, and that in every thought there exists simultaneously "being," "non-being," and "becoming," and that in the end every thought disappears by being absorbed into its opposite. I am afraid that I am oversimplifying again.

Let us get back to our meeting. About sixteen leftist literary critics have now gathered in the room. Several are talking and the others are not so much listening as waiting for an opening. Let us cock an ear toward Mr. Hubert

Camberwell. Mr. Camberwell is saying, "Sinclair Lewis
had dramatized the process of disintegration, as well as his
own dilemma, in the outlines of his novels, in the progress
of his characters, and sometimes, and most painfully, in
the lapses of taste and precision that periodically weaken
the structure of his prose." This is a typical leftist critic's
sentence. It has a facile, portentous swing, it damns a
prominent author to hell, and it covers a tremendous
amount of ground. It also has an air of authority, and
because of this the other critics will attack it. Up speaks
a Mr. Scholzweig: "But you cannot, with lapses of any
kind, *dramatize* a process, you can only *annotate* it."
This is a minor criticism, at best, but it is the only one Mr.
Scholzweig can think of, because he agrees in general with
what has been said about Sinclair Lewis (whose books he has
never been able to read). At this point Donald Crowley
announces that as yet nobody has *defined* anything; that is,
nobody has defined "lapses," "dramatize," "process," or
"annotate." While a small, excited man in shell-rim glasses is
asking him how he would define the word "definition" in a
world of flux, let us listen to Mr. Herman Bernheim. Mr.
Bernheim is muttering something about Camberwell's
"methodology" and his failure to "implement" his argument.
Now, "methodology," as the leftist intellectuals use it, means
any given wrong method of approach to a subject. "To
implement" means (1) to have at the tip of one's tongue
everything that has been written by any leftist since Marx, for
the purpose of denying it, and (2) to possess and make use of
historical references that begin like this: "Because of the
more solidly articulated structure of French society, the
deep-seated sentiments and prejudices of the northern
French, and the greater geographical and political accessi-
bility of France to the propaganda of the counter-Reforma-
tion," etc., etc.

The critics have by this time got pretty far away from
Camberwell's analysis of Sinclair Lewis, but this is the

customary procedure when leftists begin refuting one another's statements, and is one phase of what is known as "dialectic." Dialectic, in this instance, means the process of discriminating one's own truth from the other person's error. This leads to "factionalism," another word our worker must be familiar with. Factionalism is that process of disputation by means of which the main point at issue is lost sight of. Now, the main point at issue here—namely, the analysis of Sinclair Lewis—becomes even more blurred by the fact that a critic named Kyle Forsythe, who has just come into the room, gets the erroneous notion that everybody is discussing Upton Sinclair. He begins, although it is not at all relevant, to talk about "escapism." Escapism means the activities of anyone who is not a leftist critic or writer. The discussion, to our worker, will now appear to get so far out of hand that we must bring him a Scotch-and-soda if we are to hold his interest much longer. He will probably want to know whether one leftist intellectual ever agrees with another, and, under cover of the loud talking, I shall explain the one form of agreement which these critics have. I call it the "that he— but when" form of agreement. Let us say that one leftist critic writes in a liberal weekly as follows: "I like poetry, but I don't like Tennyson." Another leftist critic will write often in the same issue and immediately following the first one's article: "That he likes poetry, we must concede Mr. Blank, but when he says that Tennyson is a great poet, we can only conclude that he does not like poetry at all." This is, of course, greatly oversimplified.

Midnight eventually arrives at our party and everybody begins "unmasking" everybody else's "ideology." To explain what unmasking an ideology means, I must give an example. Suppose that I were to say to one of the critics at this party, "My country, 'tis of thee, sweet land of liberty." He would unmask my ideology—that is expose the background of my illusion—by pointing out that I am the son of wealthy bourgeois parents who employed an English butler. This is not true, but my ideology would be unmasked, anyway. It is interesting to note that it takes only one leftist critic to expose anybody's ideology, and that every leftist critic unmasks ideologies in his own special way. In this sense, Marxist criticism is very similar to psychoanalysis. Ideology-unmasking is a great deal like dream interpretation and leads to just as many mystic results.

A general midnight unmasking of ideologies at a gathering of leftist literary critics is pretty exciting, and I hope that a second Scotch-and-soda will persuade our worker to stay. If he does, he will find out that when your ideology is unmasked, you can't do anything with it, because it has no "social currency." In other words, anything that you say or do will have no more validity than Confederate money.

The party now breaks up, without ill feeling, because the critics have all had such a good time at the unmasking. A leftist critic gets as much fun out of disputation, denial, and disparagement as a spaniel puppy gets out of a steak bone. Each one will leave, confident that he has put each of the others in his place and that they realize it. This is known as the "united front." On our way out, however, I must explain to the worker the meaning of an extremely important term in Marxist criticism; namely, "Dialectical Materialism." Dialectical Materialism, then, is based on two fundamental laws of dialectics: the law of the permeation of opposites, or polar unity, and the law of the negation of the negation, or development through opposites. This second proposition is the basic law of all processes of thought. I will first state the law itself and then support it with examples . . . Hey, worker! Wait for baby!

How to Write an Autobiography

THE COMMUNIST intellectuals know a lot more than I do, and while I am the first, or among the first, anyway, to admit it, I am also the first to explain why. For one thing, they keep all the letters they get from intellectual friends and use them in their writings; and, for another thing, they keep carbon copies of all the letters they write. Everybody gets off a few pretty good cracks, comments, and the like in his letters, but almost everybody forgets them after he sends them off. I suspect there is a type of author (both Communist and bourgeois) who, dashing off, in a letter, a sentence or a paragraph, or even a phrase, he thinks is pretty good, copies it down before he mails the letter. But the Communist intellectuals, as I say, keep carbon copies of the whole works. This seems to me unfair, for some reason; maybe I don't mean unfair, maybe I mean something else, but if I do, I mean something I don't like.

Take "An American Testament," published not long ago. It was written by one of America's brightest Communist intellectuals, Mr. Joseph Freeman. It runs, I have estimated, to 330,000 words. I can't go back through the book and find all the letters Mr. Freeman quotes, and I doubt if he could, but I can find some of them. On page 191, for instance, there is a paragraph beginning: "'For me personally'—Irwin [Edman] wrote me from Dresden in the fall of 1920—'the world these last few weeks has been almost romantically perfect. I have been moving, to quote your own phrase, through rich experiences, though not swiftly; not swiftly because the experiences have been too rich to hurry through.'" The letter, or the part of it that is quoted, runs to about three hundred words. It is followed by a thousand-word letter Mr. Freeman wrote to Mr. Edman in answer to his, and at the end of that Mr. Freeman writes: "To this long disquisition, Irwin replied from Venice three days later"—

and there follow five hundred words of that. Then comes part of a long letter from Irwin in Rome. This is followed by a letter from Louis Smith, and that is followed by Mr. Freeman's answer, and *that* is followed by a letter from "Mac's sister-in-law Lillian," and then comes Mr. Freeman's answer to her, and then a long letter he wrote to Professor James Harvey Robinson, to which Professor Robinson did not reply (if he had, I know darn well the letter would have been printed, together with Mr. Freeman's answer to it). All these letters were written seventeen years ago, but there they are.

Now, whether or not these letters are interesting or important is beside the point I want to make, but I suppose it is only fair to give some idea of what they are like. Take the opening sentence of Mr. Freeman's thousand-word letter to Mr. Edman. He wrote: "It was my idealistic, religious, artistic bias which made me blind to pragmatism." That is the topic sentence of a letter which somehow does not sound like a letter to a friend at all. It sounds more like an essay written to save in a file and someday print in a book. You get the inescapable feeling that the original was sent to a friend in order to get a well-written essay in return, which also could be used in the book. That, of course, is one way to get a book together, and the fact that it is not my way is not so much because I don't like the studied and disingenuous tone of the whole thing as because I could never keep a carbon copy or a letter for fifteen or twenty years, the way Mr. Freeman can. If I keep a letter two weeks, I am doing fine. Then, too, my friends never write me long letters dealing with profound subjects. Their letters are usually hurried and to the point, and they sometimes deal with matters which I wouldn't want to have exposed in a book even after I was dead.

Mr. Irwin Edman and some of Mr. Freeman's other correspondents are well-known writers, and whereas I have got a few letters from well-known writers in my time, none of them would be usable in a book even if I could find them. Some of them are both illegible and illiterate, as if they had been written at a bar. Few of them say anything, really, that anybody would want to read, and none of them sounds as if it had been rewritten several times, the way Mr. Freeman's letters to his friends, and theirs to him, sound. Communist

intellectuals are the most facile and articulate of all writers, and words come out of most of them like water from a faucet, so I can't say for sure the letters were rewritten; I just say they sound rewritten. (Rewriting a letter to a girl is all right, under certain circumstances, but that's as far as I will go.)

I happen to remember a letter one well-known writer sent to me some years ago, because it contained only one sentence. It read: "Will you please for God's sake come back with my shoes?" That's all; just that one sentence. And I wouldn't have got that if he had been able to get me on the phone. It seems that this author and myself and a couple of lecturers from Hollywood went to the author's apartment one night. Around five o'clock in the morning, the argument on idealism, religion, art, and pragmatism having rather worn me out, I took off my shoes and lay down on the author's bed. When I got up, I put on his shoes by mistake—not the ones he had on, of course, although I could have done that, but another pair, apparently his favorites. I noticed on my way home that I couldn't walk very well—my feet hurt—but I put it down to the argument. The next morning, however, I had a terrible time getting the shoes on. They were two sizes too small for me, but since I thought they were my own, I could only believe that my feet had swelled. I started to walk up Fifth Avenue, with the gait of a man who is stalking a bird across wet cement. It was pretty painful, and I finally had to take a cab. I suffered all day, but the next morning the author's letter came in asking me to bring back his shoes, and you can imagine my relief, both physical and mental. I had been on the point of going to a doctor. None of this really belongs in a book.

Such letters as I get from persons other than friends of mine are usually written with pen and ink, and often on blue or purple paper. These are almost impossible to make out, and I couldn't use them in a book even if I wanted to. I have one at hand now, for instance, which came just a day or two ago and hasn't been lost yet. I'll quote the first few lines the way I make them out (the letter is written in black India ink on aquamarine paper):

DEAR MR. THUMBER:

    For agree blest you've been out of my perine parasites. The obline being in case you're interested, a girl whose name escapes me, but merits swell pecul, and I know you'd know who she is.

That's all I can get out of that. It appears to be signed Keriumiy Luud Roosool, or Kaasaat. Nothing, of course, could be done with it. Even when I can decipher all but a word or two of my correspondence (I never get *every* word), nothing much can be done with it. For instance, I got a postcard last January from a famous man in Washington, and although I practically mastered it, I don't see how I could ever work it into a book. I will quote it verbatim:

WASHINGTON, D. C.
JAN. 8, 1937
MR. JAMES THURBER—On reading some back numbers of N. Yorker came across article, "An Outline of Science." It is plain you know a thing or two about science, but—heh! heh! heh! heh!—[illegible word]. Especially speed of light & those terrible bloodhounds.
Yours Truly, ALBERT GAMBLE,
Hobo Scientist
(Originator of famous Fireball-Waterball Theory of Swimming Continents.)

I'm afraid I'm not going to be able to use any letters or other communications in my own 300,000-word testament, unless I make up some—and I didn't make up Mr. Gamble's—or sneak a few out of Mr. Freeman's book. He'd probably never miss them.

After the Steppe Cat, What?

THERE ARE many signs which indicate that our civilization is on the wane, and these are to be seen not only in the economic, political, and military phenomena of our dying day, which are portentously analyzed in every periodical one picks up, but also in a tiny phenomenon here, a small paragraph there. Poets have a quick eye to detect these minute portents of the approaching end. The clairvoyant Stephen Vincent Benét was probably just one step ahead of actuality when he wrote of observing a termite which held in its tiny jaws a glittering crumb of steel. Morris Bishop, another seer who views tomorrow clearly, has written of the

THE AARDVARK.

time when in the mothproof closet will dwell the moth.

It is all very interesting to indulge in polysyllabic discussions of dialectical materialism and dialectical idealism, of democracy and the totalitarian state, of Marxist hope and capitalist illusion, but I am more interested in wondering whether the fleck of dust that got in my eye yesterday may not have been all that was left of a planet like ours which burned out a million years ago, ten hundred billion miles away. Perhaps I was struck with that wonder because once in Carthage, two thousand years ago, the gleam of a Roman shield got in my eye or a speck of that sand which was to conquer the very conquerors of one of the oldest and strongest civilizations known to man. A bit of steel glittering here, a moth fluttering there, a handful of dust in the air: these are the signs of doom.

Perhaps some manifestations of the sort always accompany any politico-social collapse. Then again, who is there to say for sure that political and social collapse doesn't merely accompany such manifestations? Which reached Rome first, the Visigoth or the wolf? It is a momentous question, calling for a great amount of research, and I am sorry I haven't got space to pursue it. I have space for only a few random notes on this general theme, which may haply lead some scientist—or some poet—to a more exhaustive treatment of the subject.

Let us look, first, at a paragraph in the *New York Times*, not long ago, by its Berlin correspondent, Mr. Otto D. Tolischus.

> This winter's extraordinary character is already arousing concern for this year's crops; and in addition, certain districts, especially Silesia, complain of a veritable plague of rats and mice. German agricultural quarters are now engaged in a hot public debate regarding charges that the many draining, land reclamation, and river regulation projects the National Socialist regime has undertaken are so interfering with the country's water economy as to turn Germany gradually into a steppe. There are assertions by experts that certain unmistakable steppe animals and plants are already beginning to make themselves at home in Germany.

Here we see how the Nazi land-reclamation engineers are beginning to make Germany into a steppe, exactly as the United States' land-*wasting* pioneers began to make this country into a Sahara. There would appear to be no way out, in a time of world decay, no matter what you do. It proceeds by curious, inexorable laws of its own, this ending of a jaded civilization, that a new way of life may begin. Nature helps along the destruction by sending her rodents in hordes to gnaw at the very foundations of man's existence. Thus rats and mice appear in Silesia—and don't get one hundredth the attention that LaGuardia got when he gnawed only at German pride. And yet these rodents are a hundred times more important, for they will outlast LaGuardia—and German pride, too—as the mollusks from which Tyrian dye was made have outlived Tyre and the Tyrians.

The desert into which America is turning is perhaps more

THE BANDICOOT.

familiar than the steppe into which Germany is changing. A steppe is a large tract of arid land characterized by xerophilous vegetation—that is, plant life that can stand the absence or scarcity of moisture. It is a primitive sort of land, flat and treeless, suitable for open warfare, fit for man and his activities in the last stages of a civilization. Among the "unmistakable steppe animals" that will eventually trot into Berlin is the steppe cat, a small wildcat. It has grayish-white fur, useful as camouflage in the open spaces, but it is interesting to note that it also has blackish transverse bands, a coloration obviously developed by nature to serve as camouflage when it finally reaches the cities, where it can creep unnoticed between car tracks and behind picket fences.

Walter Lippman recently insisted in the *Atlantic Monthly* that "Communism and fascism are not only much alike as systems of government; they are alike in the inwardness of their purpose." To which I feel impelled to add that the systems and purposes of man are all one to the steppe cat. And to the termite, the rat, the mouse, the grasshopper, the locust, the caterpillar, the weevil, the wombat, the rabbit, the aardvark, the bandicoot, the Scotch terrier, the cockroach,

THE WOMBAT.

the coddling moth, and the Colorado potato beetle, to name just a few of the thousands of insects and animals that will go to town with the steppe cat when the Great Invasion begins.

In the olden days, of which Omar sang, it was the lion and the lizard that moved sleepily into the courtyard of the palace; they had no system and no purpose, so that man, rising again from the ashes of his ruined civilization, could easily oust them. The next and greatest invasion of the lower species will find, I think, all the living things, with a kind of planned economy, moving in on man, who has too long been keeping a hostile and fearful eye on his fellow man, to the exclusion of any interest in the steppe cat and the steppe cat's million allies. Pick up any large dictionary and turn the pages—you'll have to turn only one or two—till you come to the picture of a pest of some sort. In the majority of cases you will find under its name these descriptive phrases: "now widely distributed" and "often causing great damage." There is a bug that works at the foundation of houses; there is one that destroys each kind of tree; there is one that gets into tea and spices; there is one that specializes in the ruining of tobacco; there is even one, common to the Congo, that seeks to inhabit the human eye.

Working quietly through the ages, the insects and the rodents, at once specialists and collectivists, have prepared themselves, I believe, to take over the world. I see no reason to believe that they will not make a better job of it than man. One July day in 1863, a handful of troopers rode idly into a town called Gettysburg, in Pennsylvania. The inhabitants glanced at them and went about their business. There could be no war in that little town; the troopers would ride away. Two or three steppe cats are observed in Germany, and the fact is recorded briefly on page 8 of the *New York Times.*

Not long ago Dr. Earnest A. Hooton, Havard professor of anthropology and President of the American Association of Physical Anthropologists, announced in a lecture that man is deteriorating—in behavior, in physique, and in intelligence. This was not news to those of us who have our ears to the steppe. I think it also quite probable that it was not news to the steppe cat. In the course of his talk Dr. Hooton pointed out that man has not added any new domestic animals to his collection since the time when animals were first put to use. He might have extended this observation to include the prophecy that one day the animals may begin, in their own way, to domesticate man, who, as Dr. Hooton said, is becoming ludicrous in body, ineffective in culture, and moronic in intelligence. In short, a set-up for animals, which are becoming less ludicrous, more cunning, and smarter every year.

Dr. Hooton also said that man is "not yet successful in his fight against micro-organisms, to any great extent." To which he might have added that, while man is peering into microscopes at micro-organisms, the steppe cat has slipped into Germany. It was not so long ago that the praying mantis came in a horde to look over New York City. You could find them reconnoitering high up on the Empire State Building. They peered into bedrooms and kitchens from window sills.

THE STEPPE CAT.

They were all over the place. Then they quietly went away. The papers and the public treated it as a curious but unimportant phenomenon, that visit. I regard it as an extremely significant occurrence. Scouting planes in advance of the infantry, the tanks, and the bombers.

Where Cathage once stood in her glory and pride there rises a cluster of modern villas, forming a suburb of the modern city of Tunis. Thus has the greatness of a sovereign power diminished. To what new kind of metropolis may Tunis someday become a suburb? Look through your field glasses at the nearest steppe land—look close to the ground.

There—see that grayish-white blur, with the blackish transverse bands?

Women Go On Forever

THE OUTLOOK for the continuance of the life of man on this earth, in the style to which he has been accustomed, is, as everybody must surely know, not very bright. Socially, economically, physically and intellectually, Man is slowly going, I am reliably informed, to hell. His world is blowing over; his day is done. I have the word of a hundred scientists and psychologists for this sorry fact. You have but to pick up the nearest book or magazine—or the one right next to it—to read the disconcerting news.

There have been prophecies of doom, such as Oswald Spengler's; there have been diagnoses of the malady, such as Dr. Carrel's; there have been programs for its correction, such as Karl Marx's; there have been sociological formulas for its clarification, such as Pareto's; there have even been whole new cosmogonies proposed, such as H. G. Wells'. Each expert, in his fashion, has analyzed the decline of Mankind and most of them have prescribed remedies for the patient. But none of them, I believe, has detected the fact that although Man, as he is now traveling, is headed for extinction, Woman is not going with him. It is, I think, high time to abandon the loose generic term "Man," for it is no longer logically inclusive or scientifically exact. There is Man and there is Woman, and Woman is going her own way.

Scientists, statisticians, actuaries, all those men who place numbers above hunches, figures above feelings, facts above possibilities, the normal above the phenomenal, will tell you that the life span of the average man is, and will remain, approximately the same as the life span of the average woman. This is because, with their eyes on the average, they fail to discern the significant. The significant is never, to begin with, larger than a man's hand, and sometimes it is no larger than a hole in a dike—or a three-line item in the New York *Times*.

It was on January 14, 1937, that I clipped this bit of significance from the pages of that newspaper: "La Salle, Ont.—Cheerful, remarkably agile, Mrs. Felice Meloche celebrated her 104th birthday here yesterday. Mrs. Meloche sang for her guests the French song 'Alouette' without a quaver in her voice."

Since that day I have kept track of news items dealing with persons who have lived to be 100 years old or older, and the record is provocative. It contains the names of six men. Four of them were written about because they had died. The oldest of the six was 103. The record contains the names of 37 women. Twenty-four of the items, or about two-thirds, reported how the ladies celebrated their birthdays—by singing, dancing, riding in airplanes, playing kettle-drums, running foot races, chinning themselves or entertaining their great-great-grandchildren. Let us look at the record for one week, the last week in March—a record that is confined, because of the short scope of my news sources, to greater New York and the region roundabout:

On March 25, Mrs. Amorette E. Fraser of Brooklyn celebrated her 101st birthday by taking a vigorous walk, riding in a taxi, standing for two hours to greet dozens of visitors, and denouncing the Roosevelt Administration. On March 28, Mrs. Emily S. Andrews, of Plainfield, New Jersey, celebrated her 101st birthday by entertaining 100 guests at tea—an event which she took in her stride. On March 29, the Burlington County Almshouse in New Jersey was destroyed by fire and among those saved was "Uncle Joe" Willow, aged 103. As reporters gathered around and were about to interview this remarkable ancient, who should emerge casually from the flames, fit as a fiddle and chipper as a lark, but "Aunt Mary" Asay, aged 114? When Joe Willow was ten years old and in the fourth grade, Mary Asay was 21—and probably married and running a big household. "The fire," said the story in the New York *Herald Tribune*, "was discovered by a 132-year-old nurse"—no, I'm wrong there. It was discovered by a nurse in the 132-year-old east wing of the building. But anyway, here was Mary Asay, born when James Monroe was President, one of the numerous outstanding proofs of my theory that women are tending to become immortal, that the day will come when they will never die. They are flourishing on all sides of us, singing and dancing and denouncing the Administration, these deathless ladies, some of whom have outlived their husbands by periods ranging from 50 to 100 years.

The increasingly tenacious hold on life of the female of the human species begins, my researches show, at birth. I recently asked an eminent obstetrician whether, if a baby he was about to deliver were in foetal distress, he would prefer it to be a boy or a girl. Prefacing his hesitant answer with the cautious announcement that there are no scientific data to go by, he said he would prefer it to be a girl. Does any obstetrician, I asked him, believe for a moment that five *males* would have survived up there in Callander, Ontario, on that historic night? To which, since, again lacking data, he declined to reply, I replied for him; no. The birth of five females and their survival against incredible odds assumes the clear nature of a portent that only the Scientist is too blind to see. Man's day is indeed done; the epoch of Woman is upon us.

I should like in conclusion to call attention to figures I and II which accompany this treatise and which you probably thought I had forgotten. They are, you will observe, absolutely identical faces, save that one (Fig. I) is male and the other (Fig. II) is female.

Yet is easy to discern in the male physiognomy the symptoms of that extinction which threatens his sex: an air of uncertainty, an expression of futility, a general absence of "hold," which are inescapable.

There is about the female, on the other hand, a hint of survival, a threat of perpetuation, a general "Here I am and here I always will be," which are equally unmistakable. The male is obviously not looking at anything; he is lost in the moody contemplation of an existence which is slipping away

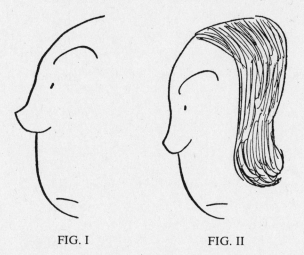

FIG. I   FIG. II

from him; already its outlines are far and vague. The female unquestionably has her eyes on an objective; you can feel the solid, sharp edges of her purpose.

It was, unless I've got my notes mixed up, our old friend Professor Ernest A. Hooton of Harvard who, in the course of a recent lecture on the physical and mental decline of Mankind, observed that "when women reach a certain age they seem to become immortal." I think that he and I have got hold of something. Just what good it will do us, being males, I do not know.

The Wood Duck

MR. KREPP, our vegetable man, had told us we might find some cider out the New Milford road a way—we would come to a sign saying "Morris Plains Farm" and that would be the place. So we got into the car and drove down the concrete New Milford road, which is black in the center with the dropped oil of a million cars. It's a main-trunk highway; you can go fifty miles an hour on it except where warning signs limit you to forty or, near towns, thirty-five, but nobody ever pays any attention to these signs. Even then, in November, dozens of cars flashed past us with a high, ominous whine, their tires roaring rubberly on the concrete. We found Morris Plains Farm without any trouble. There was a big white house to the left of the highway; only a few yards off the road a small barn had been made into a roadside stand, with a dirt driveway curving up to the front of it. A spare, red-cheeked man stood in the midst of baskets and barrels of red apples and glass jugs of red cider. He was waiting on a man and a woman. I turned into the driveway—and put the brakes on hard. I had seen, just in time, a duck.

It was a small, trim duck, and even I, who know nothing about wild fowl, knew that this was no barnyard duck, this was a wild duck. He was all alone. There was no other bird of any kind around, not even a chicken. He was immensely solitary. With none of the awkward waddling of a domestic duck, he kept walking busily around in the driveway, now and then billing up water from a dirty puddle in the middle of the drive. His obvious contentment, his apparently perfect adjustment to his surroundings, struck me as something of a marvel. I got out of the car and spoke about it to a man who had driven up behind me in a rattly sedan. He wore a leather jacket and high, hard boots, and I figured he would know what kind of duck this was. He did. "That's a wood duck," he said. "It dropped in here about two weeks ago, Len says, and's been here ever since."

The proprietor of the stand, in whose direction my informant had nodded as he spoke, helped his customers load a basket of apples into their car and walked over to us. The duck stepped, with a little flutter of its wings, into the dirty puddle, took a small, unconcerned swim, and got out again, ruffling its feathers. "It's rather an odd place for a wood duck, isn't it?" asked my wife. Len grinned and nodded; we all watched the duck. "He's a banded duck," said Len. "There's a band on his leg. The state game commission sends out a lot of 'em. This'n lighted here two weeks ago—it was on a Saturday—and he's been around ever since." "It's funny he wouldn't be frightened away, with all the cars going by and all the people driving in," I said. Len chuckled. "He seems to like it here," he said. The duck wandered over to some sparse grass at the edge of the road, aimlessly, but with an air of settled satisfaction. "He's tame as anything," said Len. "I guess they get tame when them fellows band 'em." The man in the leather jacket said, "'Course they haven't let you shoot wood duck for a long while and that might make 'em tame, too." "Still," said my wife (we forgot about the cider for the moment), "it's strange he would stay here, right on the road almost." "Sometimes," said Len, reflectively, "he goes round back o' the barn. But mostly he's here in the drive." "But don't they," she asked, "let them loose in the woods after they're banded? I mean, aren't they supposed to stock up the forests?" "I guess they're supposed to," said Len, chuckling again. "But 'pears this'n didn't want to."

An old Ford truck lurched into the driveway and two men in the seat hailed the proprietor. They were hunters, big, warmly dressed, heavily shod men. In the back of the truck was a large bird dog. He was an old pointer and he wore an expression of remote disdain for the world of roadside commerce. He took no notice of the duck. The two hunters said something to Len about cider, and I was just about to chime in with my order when the accident happened. A car went by the stand at fifty miles an hour, leaving something scurrying in its wake. It was the duck, turning over and over on the concrete. He turned over and over swiftly, but lifelessly, like a thrown feather duster, and then he lay still. "My God," I cried, "they've killed your duck, Len!" The accident gave me a quick feeling of anguished intimacy with the bereaved man. "Oh, now," he wailed. "Now, that's awful!" None of us for a moment moved. Then the two hunters walked toward the road, slowly, self-consciously, a little embarrassed in the face of this quick incongruous ending of a wild fowl's life in the middle of a concrete highway. The pointer stood up, looked after the hunters, raised his ears briefly, and then lay down again.

It was the man in the leather jacket finally who walked out to the duck and tried to pick it up. As he did so, the duck stood up. He looked about him like a person who has been abruptly wakened and doesn't know where he is. He didn't ruffle his feathers. "Oh, he isn't quite *dead!*" said my wife. I knew how she felt. We were going to have to see the duck die; somebody would have to kill him, finish him off. Len stood beside us. My wife took hold of his arm. The man in the leather jacket knelt down, stretched out a hand, and the duck moved slightly away. Just then, out from behind the barn, limped a setter dog, a lean white setter dog with black spots. His right back leg was useless and he kept it off the ground. He stopped when he saw the duck in the road and gave it a point, putting his head out, lifting his left front leg, maintaining a wavering, marvellous balance on two legs. He was like a drunken man drawing a bead with a gun. This new menace, this anticlimax, was too much. I think I yelled.

What happened next happened as fast as the automobile accident. The setter made his run, a limping, wobbly run, and he was in between the men and the bird before they saw him. The duck flew, got somehow off the ground a foot or two, and tumbled into the grass of the field across the road, the dog after him. It seemed crazy, but the duck could fly— a little, anyway. "Here, here," said Len, weakly. The hunters shouted, I shouted, my wife screamed, "He'll kill him! He'll *kill* him!" The duck flew a few yards again, the dog at his tail. The dog's third plunge brought his nose almost to the duck's tail, and then one of the hunters tackled the animal and pulled him down and knelt in the grass, holding him. We all breathed easier. My wife let go Len's arm.

Len started across the road after the duck, who was fluttering slowly, waveringly, but with a definite purpose, toward a wood that fringed the far side of the field. The bird

was dazed, but a sure, atavistic urge was guiding him; he was going home. One of the hunters joined Len in his pursuit. The other came back across the road, dragging the indignant setter; the man in the leather jacket walked beside them. We all watched Len and his companion reach the edge of the wood and stand there, looking; they had followed the duck through the grass slowly, so as not to alarm him; he had been alarmed enough. "He'll never come back," said my wife. Len and the hunter finally turned and came back through the grass. The duck had got away from them. We walked out to meet them at the edge of the concrete. Cars began to whiz by in both directions. I realized, with wonder, that all the time the duck, and the hunters, and the setter were milling around in the road, no one has passed. It was as if traffic had been held up so that our little drama could go on. "He couldn't o' been much hurt," said Len. "Likely just grazed and pulled along in the wind of the car. Them fellows don't look out for anything. It's a sin." My wife had a question for him. "Does your dog always chase the duck?" she asked. "Oh, that ain't my dog," said Len. "He just comes around." The hunter who had been holding the setter now let him go, and he slunk away. The pointer, I noticed, lay with his eyes closed. "But doesn't the duck mind the dog?" persisted my wife. "Oh, he minds him," said Len. "But the dog's never really hurt him none yet. There's always somebody around."

We drove away with a great deal to talk about (I almost forgot the cider). I explained the irony, I think I explained the profound symbolism, of a wild duck's becoming attached to a roadside stand. My wife strove simply to understand the duck's viewpoint. She didn't get anywhere. I knew even then, in the back of my mind, what would happen. We decided, after a cocktail, to drive back to the place and find out if the duck had returned. My wife hoped it wouldn't be there, on account of the life it led in the driveway; I hoped it wouldn't because I felt that would be, somehow, too pat an ending. Night was falling when we started off again for Morris Plains Farm. It was a five-mile drive and I had to put my bright lights on before we got there. The barn door was closed for the night. We didn't see the duck anywhere. The only thing to do was to go up to the house and inquire. I knocked on the door and a young man opened it. "Is—is the proprietor here?" I asked. He said no, he had gone to Waterbury. "We wanted to know," my wife said, "whether the duck came back." "What?" he asked, a little startled, I thought. Then, "Oh, the duck. I saw him around the driveway when my father drove off." He stared at us, waiting. I thanked him and started back to the car. My wife lingered, explaining, for a moment. "He thinks we're crazy," she said, when she got into the car. We drove on a little distance. "Well," I said, "he's back." "I'm glad he is, in a way," said my wife. "I hated to think of him all alone out there in the woods."

The Admiral on the Wheel

WHEN THE colored maid stepped on my glasses the other morning, it was the first time they had been broken since the late Thomas A. Edison's seventy-ninth birthday. I remember that day well, because I was working for a newspaper then and I had been assigned to go over to West Orange that morning and interview Mr. Edison. I got up early and, in reaching for my glasses under the bed (where I always put them), I found that one of my more sober and reflective Scotch terriers was quietly chewing them. Both tortoiseshell temples (the pieces that go over your ears) had been eaten and Jeannie was toying with the lenses in a sort of jaded way. It was in going over to Jersey that day, without my glasses, that I realized that the disadvantages of defective vision (bad eyesight) are at least partially compensated for by its peculiar advantages. Up to that time I had been in the habit of going to bed when my glasses were broken and lying there until they were fixed again. I had believed I could not go very far without them, not more than a block, anyway, on account of the danger of bumping into things, getting a headache, losing my way. None of those things happened, but a lot of others did. I saw the Cuban flag flying over a national bank, I saw a gay old lady with a gray parasol walk right through the side of a truck, I saw a cat roll across a street in a small striped barrel, I saw bridges rise lazily into the air, like balloons.

I suppose you have to have just the right proportion of sight to encounter such phenomena: I seem to remember that oculists have told me I have only two-fifths vision without what one of them referred to as "artificial compensation" (glasses). With three-fifths vision or better, I suppose the Cuban flag would have been an American flag, the gay old lady a garbage man with a garbage can on his back, the cat a piece of butcher's paper blowing in the wind, the floating bridges smoke from tugs, hanging in the air. With perfect vision, one is extricably trapped in the workaday world, a prisoner of reality, as lost in the commonplace America of 1937 as Alexander Selkirk was lost on his lonely island. For the hawk-eyed person life has none of those soft edges which for me blur into fantasy; for such a person an electric welder is merely an electric welder, not a radiant fool setting off a sky-rocket by day. The kingdom of the partly blind is a little like Oz, a little like Wonderland, a little like Poictesme. Anything you can think of, and a lot you never would think of, can happen there.

For three days after the maid, in cleaning the apartment, stepped on my glasses—I had not put them far enough under the bed—I worked at home and did not go uptown to have them fixed. It was in this period that I made the acquaintance of a remarkable Chesapeake spaniel. I looked out my window and after a moment spotted him, a noble, silent dog lying on a ledge above the entrance to a brownstone house in lower Fifth Avenue. He lay there, proud and austere, for three days and nights, sleepless, never eating, the perfect watchdog. No ordinary dog could have got up on the high ledge above the doorway, to begin with; no ordinary people would have owned such an animal. The ordinary people were the people who walked by the house and did not see the dog. Oh, I got my glasses fixed finally and I know that now the dog has gone, but I haven't looked to see what prosaic object occupies the spot where he so staunchly stood guard over one of the last of the old New York houses on Fifth Avenue; perhaps an unpainted flowerbox or a cleaning cloth dropped from an upper window by a careless menial. The moment of disenchantment would be too hard; I never look out that particular window any more.

Sometimes at night, even with my glasses on, I see strange and unbelievable sights, mainly when I am riding in an automobile which somebody else is driving (I never drive myself at night out of fear that I might turn up at the portals of some mystical monastery and never return). Only last summer I was riding with someone along a country road when suddenly I cried at him to look out. He slowed down and asked me sharply what was the matter. There is no worse experience than to have someone shout at you to look out for something you don't see. What this driver didn't see and I did see (two-fifths vision works a kind of magic in the night) was a little old admiral in full-dress uniform riding a bicycle at right angles to the car I was in.

He might have been. starlight behind a tree. or a billboard advertising Moxie; I don't know—we were quickly past the place he rode out of; but I would recognize him if I saw him again. His beard was blowing in the breeze and his hat was

set at a rakish angle, like Admiral Beatty's. He was having a swell time. The gentleman who was driving the car has been, since that night, a trifle stiff and distant with me. I suppose you can hardly blame him.

To go back to my daylight experiences with the naked eye, it was me, in case you have heard the story, who once killed fifteen white chickens with small stones. The poor beggars never had a chance. This happened many years ago when I was living at Jay, New York. I had a vegetable garden some seventy feet behind the house, and the lady of the house had asked me to keep an eye on it in my spare moments and to chase away any chickens from neighboring farms that came pecking around. One morning, getting up from my typewriter, I wandered out behind the house and saw that a flock of white chickens had invaded the garden. I had, to be sure, misplaced my glasses for the moment, but I could still see well enough to let the chickens have it with ammunition from a pile of stones that I kept handy for the purpose. Before I could be stopped, I had riddled all the tomato plants in the garden, over the tops of which the lady of the house had, the twilight before, placed newspapers and paper bags to ward off the effects of frost. It was one of the darker experiences of my dimmer hours.

Some day, I suppose, when the clouds are heavy and the rain is coming down and the pressure of realities is too great, I shall deliberately take my glasses off and go wandering out into the streets. I daresay I may never be heard of again (I have always believed it was Ambrose Bierce's vision and not his whim that caused him to wander into oblivion). I imagine I'll have a remarkable time, wherever I end up.